T0365209

CYCLES A MEMOIR

CYCLES A MEMOIR

The 7-Year Cycles of Self-Evaluation

Ilanga

 iUniverse®

CYCLES A MEMOIR
THE 7-YEAR CYCLES OF SELF-EVALUATION

iUniverse books may be ordered through booksellers or by contacting:

iUniverse
1663 Liberty Drive
Bloomington, IN 47403
www.iuniverse.com
844-349-9409

ISBN: 978-1-5320-9014-1 (sc)
ISBN: 978-1-5320-9016-5 (hc)
ISBN: 978-1-5320-9015-8 (e)

Library of Congress Control Number: 2021921534

Print information available on the last page.

iUniverse rev. date: 12/23/2021

I am dedicating this book to my intelligent, young Nephews and Nieces, their children, friends and peers the world over. They are the powerful forces behind *my* Purpose and I hope to be able to assist the "smart" youth of today in exploring their lives and aid them in the process of finding *their* Purpose.

They can all think different, be different and dream their dreams; but my hope is that they will learn to be smart about it.

I also dedicate my life to you…I am sure.

CONTENTS

PREFACE

The Life for me has been an unusual one, I must say, and I echo the many colleagues, friends and family members who have said to me, "Your life is extraordinary, interesting, fascinating…you should write a book!" Others have said, "You live in a world of fantasy and make some of us believe that we do too! You make it look easy!" I have to admit that I agree wholeheartedly. I have had days, even years when I realized that I have always been unusual and that "my reality" is not the same as most people's reality. It is not usual for most people to live their whole lives consistently with *positivity, wonder* and *surprise* among the everyday struggles and survival we all experience; but for me that is how it's always been.

Fortunately, I was born a brown baby; if I wasn't, then maybe those incidents I write about here that occurred by circumstance or coincidence would not be of value or truth. And maybe I - being the alternative thinker I have always been - somehow hurled myself into this world to a family that I surveyed and found to be the perfect family to teach me the things I needed to live **The Life**. The lessons I learned from this remarkable family were studies in *Determination, How to Be,* and *Love*.

Presently, I am 78 years of age and living in the **12th Cycle** of my life. At this point I am just trying to be a simple writer with a message for those of you who are much younger; who have your dreams and fantasies but still need to learn how to make them "materialize" and most importantly to know and believe that they are owned by **YOU**; the fabulous Dream-maker. After all, this is **YOUR Dream!** I was in my twenties when I discovered that if I

ix

evaluated myself at the end of every seven-year cycle, I could analyze: **Where I've been, Where I am Presently** and **Where I want to go**, and by using this technique, I could have some sense of control over my own life!

This book is about Self-Help and should be read now at a crucial time in your life; but probably won't be because of the deterrents and distractions that cause most people to lose focus on who and what matter most. So, if you don't read it now, that's okay too; but place it on your bookshelf because you will read it later... during your inquiring years of desperation! Around the age of 35, suddenly we feel like "oldies" and some of us become adults; but some of don't and we need to ask ourselves why that is. This question can only be answered honestly by both those who have become adults and those who haven't reached that level of maturity yet. **The Seven Year Cycles of Self-Evaluation** and its process provide a knowledge that you can only find within yourselves. My words are written for the intelligent, ageless reader who wants to *Know* and *Live* and *Believe* that "There is More." Certainly, there is "Much More."

INTRODUCTION

"Education is a Witness to Success."

I have written the honest words in this book, and I attest to this statement, being an undeniable witness to my success. Therefore; the *choice* that I made, once I had fully realized this civil opportunity to share, serve, and offer my personal experiences, was knowing that "To Educate is my Responsibility." How I arrived at that *Knowing* was by earning it, through social and theological studies, career travel, observation of people, my particular environment, and most importantly, the learnings from my teachers of all ages. I have grouped the Life experiences according to age and a specific time period of seven years. Therefore, one *Cycle* is every seven years.

The valuable lessons learned from these groups of teachers will be capsulized here, with just a brief "takeaway" quote of each cycle.

1st Cycle: (1 to 7 years of age) *To Explore* is what one must do; always! Teachers of this age are Masters at this!

2nd Cycle: (8 to 14) *To Create is a wonderful thing!*

3rd Cycle: (15-21) *To Have Fun, To Laugh a Lot, To Always Remember!*

4th Cycle: (22 to 28) *Everything must change!*

5th Cycle: (29 to 35) *To be Determined!* or maybe even *Fail at Personal Success* (not at the efforts and success of career achievement; but when the teachers *push* h*ard* not to fail!)

6th Cycle: (36 to 42) *Single or Coupled* become aware that the time has come to educate their children with the real nourishment they need: *Education.* These masterful teachers of all ages have provided me with the knowledge to *Find Myself,* to discover *Who I Am,* and how to find the elusive *how-to manual for Living The Life as YOU Want to Be!*

Certainly, the *Cycles* continue on to the "7th, 8th, 9th, etc., but my concern and intent here in these writings, is to focus on the *fabulous young people* whom I have met in *The Life,* between the ages of fifteen to forty two (some of whom are also teachers) and they, somehow by their own nature, have dazzled me with their *Persona, Intelligence,* and *Thirst,* for self-identity and the knowledge to succeed *far beyond* the limits they have set for themselves or proposed by "Conventional thought." This is a specific age group that I need to share *something else* with from my heart and *Soul* which is also referred to as the *Spirit* of one, which is embodied in the person YOU are.

Spirit is the essence of your physical energy, thought, and purpose; therefore, I am writing this book from *the spirit within me.*

Those of you who are reading these words and are between the ages of fifteen and twenty-eight, will be asking or have asked, "Hey; What the hell is going on?" within my family, my friends, the country, the world, and Me! Your next question should be, "Is it Me or is it Them" that's screwing up my life? Presently, we are closing the year 2018, so let's be *real.* Not only within you but yes, there's a lot going on in this country and the world!

The younger ones in this group, the **3rdCycle** are still having *Fun* and the **4thCycle** group are going through the dynamic *Changes* of *self-identity,* "What am I doing… I gotta get off my ass and do what?" The following **5thCycle** is the real "face-to- face" question "Am I making the right *Choice?*" And the **6thCycle** is the "Cruise cycle" for those who have accomplished and achieved their goals. But if they are coupled or with a child or children, their whole story is about *US*. Personal indulgences, liberty, and time are no longer available and are put on "the back burner" for later cooking! Whereas, those who are single have the liberty and time and are still able to make their personal *Choices*. "Be Strong, Be Determined, and Dare to be Brave!" are my words to those who need to *Challenge* themselves. It is YOU who decides that.

THE 7-YEAR CYCLES OF SELF-EVALUATION

A non-fiction semi-biographical narrative of a man in quest of Self-Realization and the process to attain its truth.

The Ilanga Cycles		Born July 22nd 1940
1940... 1946–1st	1947... 1954–2nd	1955... 1961–3rd
1962... 1968–4th	1969... 1975–5th	1975... 1982–6th
1983... 1989–7th	1990... 1996–8th	1997... 2003–9th
2003...2010–10th	2011...2017–11th	2018...2024–12th

The 7-Year Cycles of Life:

1st Cycle: 1 to 7 (years of age) 2nd Cycle: 8 to 14 (years of age) 3rd Cycle: 15 to 21 4th Cycle: 22 to 28 5th Cycle: 29 to 35 6th Cycle: 36 to 42 7th Cycle: 43 to 49 8th Cycle: 50 to 56 9th Cycle: 57 to 63 10th Cycle: 64 to 70 11th Cycle: 71 to 77 12th Cycle: 78 to 84 .... To be continued, for some.

Throughout our journey through *The Life,* from the year of our birth and every 7 years thereafter, the 7 Year Cycles of Life begin. They represent a defined block of conscious time for us to measure our personal potential and evolvement from: *Where we've been, Where we are today, and Where we aim to be,* at the end of each Cycle. One can only begin to consciously self-evaluate at the wonderful age of fifteen, which is the swing into the **3rd Cycle (15-21 years of age)** the most important of all. The reason being that this is the first

Cycle of conscious *Identity, Choices, and Exploration.* These three directives remain and are bonded to the child's destiny throughout every Cycle thereafter. Once a child of this age is introduced to this method of *Self-Evaluation,* it eventually funnels into the realm of *Self-Realization* at the threshold of the 3rdCycle. This introduction can simply *happen* by just discussing with the child, *Life* as he or she would understand it at their age of wisdom. Within a calm and settled environment, there will always come an opportunity or, *a moment of love,* to inspire a child. Begin an interactive dialogue of their past years of fun and growing, bringing to the surface their thoughts of the past. What Relatives, friends, and people can they remember who left an impression? And what about their first serious scolding and how it felt, and the thereafter *naughty* childlike sequences that include the consequences of all their actions. This is the opportunity for a child to learn how to reflect and begin to understand for the first time, the meaning of their life. The 1st and 2nd Cycles are the platform in which we base the components of our measurement. This dialogue with a child or children will give you the opportunity to interject this method of informing them of their 1st and 2nd Cycles, and that there is *a New Cycle* of the next seven years that is to come. Inspire them to believe that this is going to be an exciting and different learning experience of *Awareness* as to one's personal self, friends, associates, school and work, and that this is a positive direction that can be charted, followed, and is applicable to the principle of self-development if YOU make it happen! Children at this age in *The Life* begin to slowly learn the word *Commitment,* it's rules and definition.

Throughout this learning process in their young, awkward lives, we are teaching them to commit to "this and that" but not often enough do we share with them the precious knowledge and values of *Self-Commitment;* and therefore it is later in their young life they discover that it's demand is a necessary tool to achieve and sustain a successful and vigilant personal life. With this method, even adults of any age are able to begin to transform and direct their lives into a more focused and positive direction from the moment they become aware of the 7-Year Cycles of Self-Evaluation. Simply count every seven years from the date of birth. Within each Cycle, from it's beginning to end and with a *Conscious Mind,* focus on that particular period of time: Where you were, your surroundings, your ambitions, and all of the attributes that developed and shaped your persona of the person you were *then.* Toward the end and the beginning of each Cycle you will find that during these transitional periods, personal difficulties of *Choice* ensue regarding Direction, Relationships and Beliefs. For some of us, these can be periods of confusion and doubt! Suddenly, we find ourselves caught and tangled in a stressful emotional whirlwind of turmoil that needs to be finalized by a definite *Choice.* The pressure of severe anxiety perpetrated by coming to a final decision of *Choice* has caused many of us to make a *Bad One,* a bad choice that needs to be corrected and consciously worked on.

Unfortunately, it is only during the following **4ᵗʰ Cycle (21-28 years of age)** that this correction of a bad choice can be attempted; and if it is not corrected then, thereafter *the Choice* remains as a negative energy and thought throughout this Cycle, struggling to be balanced by and within other choices that are positive and going in a determined direction. It is due to the ignorance of the 7 Cycles that we all have made an unwise choice or two in determining the shape, direction, and existence of our lives. But through various support systems, some of us were, and are able to challenge, work through and let go of a bad *Choice* and move forward within this realm of balance. It is a natural human occurrence that every Cycle becomes a turning point of direction during our physical existence, a Life Change, and another chapter of YOUR story (so to speak) and it is up to YOU alone, to be conscious and aware that this Life Change is happening! One must adhere to this directive with a charted outline and a positive plan, and with the clarified thought of: "Where is my life is going" and "what am I doing with it" *Now*. Throughout the life that we live there are many questions we ask ourselves, but not often *enough of* ourselves. It is by this evaluation process of commitment to ourselves, exploration, and honesty with ourselves that many of our answers can be found.

CHAPTER ONE

My 1st Cycle (1 to 7 years of age), has left me with a few strong impressions and clouded memories that I believe are deeply embedded with a profound message of importance to my existence here in *The Life* because they are still indelible within my consciousness today. I became aware of this consistent dwell on the thoughts of these elusive memories that would come and go quickly during some period of my 3rd Cycle (15 to 21 years of age); but I was too young and immature to accept the *belief* that these past memories were also a thread to my future.

It was not until the onset of my 4th Cycle (22-28 years of age) that I began to believe that these non-tangible memories did have substance and significance to my everyday life, and questions of *acceptance* surfaced for me to answer. I am sure that the life experiences I was having then and during the previous Cycle helped me to shape the decision of my honest acceptance. It was not until later that the blockage of clouded memory dissipated or became removed somehow, and I began to have more frequent clear memorable "flashes" of my birth, infancy, surrounding peoples, and significant childhood events that had occurred in the 1st and 2nd Cycles of my life. These interesting and mysterious flashes soon became a part of my search and exploration of the intriguing memories that I often questioned: "Why do we have them?" and "What do they mean?" The answers to those two questions did not become clear to me until I was halfway into my 4th Cycle of The Life.

Being born into a large family of nine, and being the youngest of six boys and one year older than our only Sister, I had many reliable

1

sources to go to for the unanswered questions of my youth. Always attentively listening to the family stories, I was reminded of what I was like then as a person (a loner) my varied interests, my playmates, friends, family members, and my selective unusual environmental surroundings. I must have been an inquisitive child during my first two Cycles, because I can recall being told throughout my younger years, "You ask too many questions!" It could be that because of my inquisitive nature, very often I would connect a story or an overheard adult conversation with one of the flashes, memories, impressions, or visions, that I would have. By questioning myself and the validity of this fusion, I began to understand and confirm what was necessary for me to know, which is that: "There is another dimension of existence that I must try to understand, to become a part of and make real."

Born in a rural Cape Cod Massachusetts shack, the memory of my birth or primal stage of infancy is vague and mysterious to me; but it is there in my mind and has been since I was about ten years of age, an indelible memory of myself lying on my back (maybe on my mother's lap or bed) looking upwards into the blurry big faces of three adults surrounded in bright light peering over me! I see nothing else. My youthful thoughts of this memory were infused with the questions of "Who were these three adults, and why were they there?" Today, these old questions are still unanswered, and the desire for them to be answered lies somewhere quietly floating within the pool of understanding that "What will be will be" in this delusive existence we call *The Life*.

My father, a serious man, hard-working laborer of plumbing and gas fitting, and the sole provider of seven young children, was a busy man and less tolerant than my mother to answer such silly or foolish questions such as: "Do people dream when they're awake?" or "Why do kids have mothers and fathers?" I discovered soon enough that I was barking up the wrong tree with my father and gravitated towards my mother or often my oldest brother who were always there to provide me with answers they knew that I could take away and be satisfied. *Jibberish talk* is what she would say whenever I opened my mouth to expound upon a wild random thought beginning with the word "Why?" She would abruptly interrupt me and jokingly say, "Oh, here we go with your jibberish again!" I think she used the word *Jibberish* to untangle and understand the many words that were to come pouring from my mouth. I guess I must have been called a very "curious" child. Towards the end of my first Cycle I became aware that the word *Curiosity* was a big thing! It meant: "Finding out things that you don't know about." So, for me, that word *Curiosity* had all the answers to all the questions, and for a child of that age it had tempting and alluring elements of the unknown, of daring, of adventure, fun, exploration, and a fascinating word meaning a weird thing called *Freedom.*

I closed my 1st Cycle (1-7 years of age) with a huge "family drama" not long after we had moved from our small Cape Cod village to Boston. It all began on a hot Summer day, along with my sister, one year younger than I. I can remember well, sharing my disconcerted thoughts with her of how our fun had changed; and now, here we were living in a confined apartment building with long upward stairs to climb, a fenced-in backyard, with no sandy or dusty paths to walk! And now, we would have funny looking big roads called "Streets" that we were told never to enter by my parents and big brothers. I was determined to convince my little Sister that we should overstep our front of the house area and boring play yard boundaries and go to "That bunch of trees way down the street!" This was a flourishing growth of green about 300 yards beyond our apartment building that often caught my eye and always attracted my curious attention. On this day, I pleaded and convinced her of our boredom and funless days and that "We must go now!" A triumphant smile beamed across my face when I heard her frightened tiny voice meekly whisper "O.K.!" Well, that was enough for me, and as reluctant as she was, we held hands and began on our adventurous stroll to the enticing bunch of trees. After a few steps, I began to feel in the tiny hand I was holding, the intense tremor of fear vibrating in her little body as we took each cautious step, passing a few houses and gardens as we approached our final destination. Feeling her fear was a lesser concern, I believed that once we arrived there, her angst and worry would dissipate at the wonder our eyes were about to see. The excitement generated by this adventure finally becoming *Real* to me and actually happening was my concern, and therefore all fear of any due consequences was banished in my mind.

As we slowly approached the flourishing growth of green, I could see that it was not what I thought it to be! It was not the edge of the woods like our home in Cape Cod! It was actually one very large Elm tree in full growth and bloom that had sprouted on a house lot. Fortunately, it was on the opposite side of the street, which of course we wouldn't dare to cross! "Wow!" We just stood there awed and in amazement that it wasn't what I had thought it to be: a bunch of trees or the woods, but instead "It was just one big tree!" We were fascinated with its size and huge umbrella branches that were thick and long, hovering high above our heads and reaching out to our side of the street! And we were cool beneath its canopy of shade, out of the hot Sun that had by now had risen to its noontime position overhead. We suddenly realized that our four little feet were standing on a sidewalk corner of a narrow dusty unpaved roadway that led to what appeared to be a big wide dusty path like the ones at our real former home faraway, but this one is really much bigger, I thought. "This is not a street," I said to her, "Look way down there, where we can't see!" The palm of her little hand was cupped above her eyebrows, and for better viewing she leaned her little body forward, in fear of taking one small step. It was the unknowing of what was way down there that prompted me to take steps forward without saying a word. I tightened the grip on my little sister's hand with a squeeze, a gestured signal, and a soft whisper to "Not say a word to anyone about this!" A necessary whisper because her soul was honest, and she would always tell my mother the stories of our day at play, giggle, and continue on "blabbing-away" about our fun; and in childish delight, expound proudly in her innocence, what she enjoyed most of whatever we did that day. Keeping her "mum" on this adventure and not "Spilling the beans" would be a difficult task for me to oversee every day. I quickly lowered my body to a squat so our eyes met. "Hey, if we don't say anything, we're not fibbing!" I said to her. "But if we tell anybody, then maybe we're gonna fib about something!" Her eyes blinked a few times revealing that she agreed with my words and she grudgingly nodded her head meaning yes and whispered "o.k." allowing us to proceed onward to "Somewhere." Slowly, with caution, holding hands and inching our small footsteps forward to get closer to what we couldn't see, kept us moving. I am sure that any fears of our wander that we had at that moment were dissipated by the awe of what our eyes were seeing; until they got clouded in a gust of blowing dust caused by an automobile slowly making passage to the main street where the big Elm tree lived. After a quick eye rub, we found ourselves pressed against a high chicken wire fence facing "A real house, like we use to live in, down the Cape," I reminisced out loud, comparing it to our city home, a tenement with many stairs to climb up to our apartment on the 2nd floor. We eyed each other quizzically and agreed that we were no longer in the City; but how we got "here" puzzled us greatly because we weren't driven in a car. "I think we walked home to the Cape," I said to my sister; and without looking at me her eyes filled with beautiful wonder, and she quietly murmured a long sustained "Yea..!" Resting next to the old country-style house was an abandoned rusty looking wheeled barrow. "That's just like ours," I said to her excitedly! But I only hear another sustained and enthralled, "Yea!"

We peered through the high wired fence, eyes wide open, feeling fearless and caught in the rapture of our freedom; but disappointment eclipsed our joyful vision with the realization that that we were on the outside looking in on a garden of colorful wild flowers; some so close to the fence, that we could touch them. And beyond the tall flowers, we saw an old white Nanny Goat. "Look, she's just like ours," I said, as her ears perked up, waiting and listening to the new sound of our voices. "Where's the Nanny?" my sister asked without glancing at me. I replied, "Over there, near that chicken shack!" "Where?" she whined, "I don't see." "Look!" I abruptly interrupted. "See, where all those chickens are running around here and there playing and having fun? Look there!" Today, if I were to describe in one word what we were experiencing and seeing, peering through that wired fence, I would use the word *awestruck*. It took a short while for us to release our little clutched fingers from the fence and begin to remove ourselves from there to somewhere else; but then a new sound that we had never heard in the city turned us around to face a horse-driven, flat-bed four-wheeled wagon. The sound of horse's hoofs beat on the earth and stirred up small puffs of dust from the narrow, unpaved roadway. An old man was sitting in the high seat of the wagon with bridal reins in his hands, yelling out loudly words we didn't know or understand. It was not until years later that we were told that he was saying something about "rags" that he was begging for from the families that lived in the neighborhood. We were totally captivated by the sound and sight of this wooden wagon, and we felt more comfortable and safer feeling that we were close to our house in Cape Cod. Reluctant to display my anxiety and fear of the unknown to her, and to admit the "Bad Choice" we had made of leaving the front of the house, I somehow mustered up enough confidence within myself to say quietly, "Our house must be way down over that hill! Yea, I think I see it! Let's go!" The faraway place that we couldn't see got closer in our sight as our little steps got slower and into a final creep that led us to a bunch of greenery where we could hide ourselves. Suddenly realizing where we had actually stopped, crouched low and frightened, I was shocked! "I don't see our house!" my sister's voice softly squealed. I covered her mouth very quickly with my free hand and leaned my face to hers; "Oooh, you know what?" my voice quivered, "This is that alleyway that the guys (referring to our older brothers) talk about all the time, when Ma and Daddy ask them where they've been, and they always say this place, *Horrigan's Alley*! We better get out of here!" My frightened voice echoed in her ear as I leaped up and made a quick dash to go. My trembling fingers and hand were clamped onto my sister's tiny wrist, pulling her by one arm to safety as my swift speed had us racing back down the dusty road. Two or three times I could hear her voice wildly screaming at me, "Wait!" And each time that I turned my head to look back at her, she was clouded in the dust being kicked up from our feet. We kept racing all the way to the main street and the sidewalk corner where the big tree grew. Arriving safely with our hearts pounding hard and gasping for a lifesaving breath or two, we were unable to even look up in each other's faces or to speak! Breathless, panting and wheezing, we braced ourselves securely with our feet planted to the sidewalk, knees bent and our little bodies hunched over forward, gripping our knees with our hands.

The second part of this narrative continues and begins with the agreed promise to one another to "Never, never, speak of this to anyone, for the rest of our lives!" And holding to that bond, we never did, until this moment now, that I speak of it.

Not long after our adventure happened, we did learn that the dusty alley was a roadway into "That far-away place we couldn't see," which was a small hidden cul-de-sac, embedded with large looming trees that separated a row of single and two-family homes.

A row of trees split the cul-de-sac space through its center. On one side was a row of single-family town houses, on the other side, backyard gardens of the homes that faced the main street where we lived (the same street that my sister and I had just walked). A year or so later, we discovered that we had only walked around one city-block, and "The Hill" in the distance where I thought our house would be, was a declining roadway entrance to the backyard and parking spaces for the residents who lived beyond the cul-de-sac. It was soon after our adventure that we both learned that the wide dusty path and hidden, shady cul-de-sac was actually named

Champney Place and that *Horrigan's Alley* was just another alley in the local area where the guys played and did teenage things.

The mutual agreement was the very first secret we shared and maybe that needed to be fortified by *Trust*, a word we'd never heard, and something we'd never known; so to say to her, "Trust me,.. everything is gonna be o.k." was just not in my vocabulary! I must have spoken some choice words to calm her anxiety and stop her repetitive "whine" of "Uh, oh, we're gonna get a beating just like the big guys!"

Over and over she would whine this lament and then stop for a short while. And then after a surge of rambling thoughts flooded her little mind with fear, she would begin again. This time she said, "I wanna go home!" Of course, this was my biggest fear, to return home. I knew this, and it haunted me as well! Hearing her whine of our foreseeable doom over and over must have annoyed me or disturbed me enough to reach far into my mind for some relief from her haunting refrain. Maybe reaching elsewhere into my frightened mind meant that I wanted to actually be moving from where we were to "Someplace Else," but certainly not to home!

Composing myself to not show my fear, and to calm her from her incessant whining, I said, "Come-on, let's walk over there, a little more up the street where the Sun is shining. We can talk better in the Sun, it's too shady here!" We always enjoyed talking together and playing in the light of the Sun in our confined backyard, shadow dancing with our black shadows trying to catch each other's fast movements in constant motion. She and I never did like the day's eventual darkness to come because that was a definite signal that bedtime followed soon thereafter. So, maybe it was our little conversation in the warm light of the Sun that invoked the choice

9

words I spoke that in some way dissipated our fears of the alley and the dreadful thought of what would happen to us when we got home. Whatever words that were spoken in confidence must have established a trust between us that made us both have a feeling of safety and assurance to continue our travel to "Elsewhere". It was then that we began our steps forward, leaving behind the big tree and the dusty sidewalk corner and our impending fears, and *Trusted* that all was going to be fine if we didn't think about it, talk about it; and if we didn't go back home; and we didn't!

How we ambled our way through, crossing a few of the tar-paved, wide main streets and secretive alleyways in the Roxbury neighborhood, I don't know. Huge tenement dwellings and store fronts lined both sides of the main street as far as our squinting eyes could see! Our small feet slowly walked forward as our little heads were shifting left, right, up and down, and our eyes were wide with excitement, catching all the images that appeared at every turn. We paused and gasped in awe, as buildings and adults towered high above our heads like never before! "These pictures are alive and real," I thought. We had only seen pictures like this in our preschool story books or in the newspapers, "But never in real life!" Captivated by these new images, we totally forgot about ducking our little bodies in shaded doorways to hide ourselves from *the guys* whom we knew by this time of day were in search of their lost little brother and sister. Oblivious to hiding, camouflage, or secrecy, we simply adapted to our newly found freedom, and bravely walked our way.

My thoughts today of this childhood adventure and the profound impressions that were mired within me soon surfaced after I had entered my 4th Cycle at twenty-two years of age, in 1962. This *new character* emboldened with the thirst for adventure, freedom and all the answers to "Why?" was like a new version of myself sitting in the saddle on a flying horse, bravely taking hold of the reins and galloping untamed through *The Life* and its vast wilderness of wonder. I had easily made the choice to *fly*.

And now back to that obscure word, *Freedom, a* reality that I had tasted, touched felt and experienced for a moment in my 1st Cycle, but had never realized the true definition and experience until I was already into my 3rdCycle (20 years of age). This was when I first traveled from copious Boston to Baltimore, Maryland and had my first encounter with America's racial disease.

My experience was a typically American culture occurrence that was rampant during the 1950's; "The "Lunch Counter" rejection policy that forbade a black man or woman to sit at a lunch counter and be served a meal! This was a prevalent epidemic of injustice happening every day in the southern part of the United States and which eventually provoked the 1960's Civil Rights Act, created to abolish this policy of discrimination.

"Where y'all from?" asked the plump white man behind the lunch counter. "Boston," I naively answered. He paused for a moment, and then said firmly with conviction, "Oh...well, "Y'all cain't sit here and eat, ya know!" I was surprised, baffled and confused by the words that came out of his mouth because it made no sense to me at all, and my immediate response was to question, "Why not, how come? There's seats over there where we can sit!" The burly man took a couple of steps towards me from his position behind the counter, leaned forward and faced me, piercing me with deep blue eyes that appeared to be on fire. "I know y'all coming from where y'all coming from, just cain't understand it a'tall, But, y'all cain't stay here and eat! So it's best for y'all to go on outta-here 'fore some trouble a starting!"

he said, and turning away from me, took a step back and fixed his eyes on something beneath the counter. I was about to respond to his aggression, when one of my older brothers grabbed my arm, pulling me away and leading the group of us out the screened door and onto the street. We passed a few store fronts before we stopped and gathered in a serious conversation about the gun beneath the counter, the South and to never return. Later that afternoon, our band, *The G-Clefs* (a very popular Doo-Wop and R.&B., vocal group) had an appearance on the "Buddy Dean" television show in front of an audience of white teenagers who gasped and were struck with surprise when the stage curtain opened and they saw *The G-Clefs* with their five black faces! Our hit recording at the time, "I Understand Just How You Feel" had the sound and texture of a popular white vocal group, (not the cool sounds of Doo-Wop or Rhythm & Blues). After their initial shock, the audience accepted their surprise for the two minutes of our onstage performance. My personal performance was muddled and impacted from the hateful confrontation earlier that day, and my thoughts were not on the song, but in sorrow for these teenagers. I could feel their deep disappointment...but I knew they could never feel mine.

From that day on, I insisted on learning more about the many realms of freedom and precisely what it *meant* for me. Shortly thereafter, I was introduced to civil activism and how to live "Free" by any means necessary. It was during this Cycle when I realized, that "Happiness cannot exist for me without the freedom 'To Be' everything and all that I am!" This was the foundation of my everyday thought then...and is today as well.

Back to the childhood adventure that my sister and I were wandering-through on that memorable day. We walked along the concrete sidewalks that lined the streets of Roxbury, long into the hot sunny mid-afternoon. A neighborhood candy store, modestly placed on a street corner caught our eyes and beckoned us to come inside. When I opened the screen door for my sister to enter, our eyes opened wide with delight at what we saw: Long wooden shelves stocked and fully lined with large, transparent glass jars filled to the brim with delicious candies of all colors and shapes! Brown, thick chocolate bars and chunks begging to be touched, laid neatly on a countertop with other edible sweets easy enough to pick up with two little fingers. The entire floor space was a clutter of boxes, big aluminum tubs filled with various candies, and two large wooden barrels that floated sour and dill pickles that rolled and turned in their fermented juice. A happy-faced, brown-skinned man wearing a long white apron approached us from some dark, hidden area of the candy store. I remember nothing of any type of business transaction (and surely we had no money) but I do remember us both digging into a small brown bag of tasty candies as we left the candy store, nibbling and chewing as we continued our slow pace to *Somewhere* or *Something Else*.

I have a vivid recall of a refreshing moment when our tired and hot sweaty bodies were walking towards a water fountain that we could see from a distance. As we arrived, it bubble up and spouted a flow of cool water that I quickly plowed my face into. I slurped it up and then lifted my little sister for her fair share of the refreshing delight. "Ummmmh," I heard and felt a sustained, vibrating humming sound move through her little body. Lowering her from the fountain, she planted her feet to the pavement, and exclaimed "Aaaaaah!" Totally satisfied, we sat near the bubbling fountain on a small rock nestled among some silky green grass. Sitting comfortably on the rock with our feet off the ground and legs stretched out, our two little backs were resting against an old black wrought iron fence, with thick long jail like bars shooting upward and capped with spear-like arrow-head points, at the height of about 5-feet. But what captured our attention most was a huge iron gateway that signaled to walkers a welcoming entrance into "Somewhere"! We watched, as people passed through the gate embellished with ornate ironwork designs. "Where are these big people coming and going from?" I asked thoughtfully as we chewed and nibbled on candy from our brown bag. "What ya think is in there?" "I dunno," she said, shrugging her tiny shoulders up and down without glancing at me. The cheeks of her face were bulging full of candy as she slowly climbed down from the rock to stand and peer through the wrought ironed fence. "I see only flowers," she said. "Bunches, bunches and bunches!" That was enough for me to close the brown bag I held in one hand, leap off the rock, and bravely say "Oh! Let's go see how many!"

I jumped up so fast that I almost forgot to grab her little hand for the quick dash! As we passed through the welcoming gateway, discussing who was going to count all the red flowers and who was going to count all the yellow ones, we suddenly entered an absolute "Paradise" of unusual beauty. Our eyes opened wide to an open space, landscaped and pristinely manicured as far as we could see. Coming to a complete stop with our jaws dropped, we both kept repeating two words. My loudly spoken word was "Wow!" and then her agreeable word would follow quietly "Yeah." Grasping her hand again, we began to move forward on a narrow concrete path, our nostrils filling with the many fragrances caught on the soft wind, being sent to us from a patch of colorful, tall flowers like we had never seen before! The flowers we knew grew free and naturally wild in the fields of Cape Cod and in the gardens of the homes we had just passed. But here, in this hidden paradise of pristine, almost surreal beauty, was something we had never seen before. This indelible cartoon-like fantasy image has stayed in my mind for many years and is still there to this day.

"This is where the big people come to cool off when they're hot, I think," I said to my sister. For many, it was truly an oasis from the day's heat. It was a large area blanketed with beautiful green grass, a million big trees and endless colorful flowers. It was the neighborhood's public park; bustling with singing birds and butterflies and lots of people, sitting alone or in twos or threes, perched on scattered wooden benches, quietly talking to each other and sometimes laughing. At that moment, our little bodies began to tremble as we saw a group of soldiers in brown uniforms approaching. We quickly hid behind a patch of tall flowers, crouched low in our floral hideout, bodies tightly pressed together. I felt her tremble with fright. "Oooh, there's Daddy!" she said, with her little voice of whine and whisper. (Our Father was a military man during that time.) "It can't be," I said in a big brother's knowing tone of voice. "He's working! and, Daddy's a colored soldier, Those are white soldiers! Shhh, duck your head!" We shut our eyes tight and listened to their heavy, hard soled boots pass by, talking and laughing. Relief came to us only after we released ourselves from our tight huddle of body sweat and realized that we were safe from the soldiers who would "Surely tell our father, if they saw us!" So, we comfortably remained there awhile, nibbling and sucking on our sweet candies beneath the towering tall flowers of our secret hideout; a peaceful and delicious moment of time when the *tranquility, freedom,* and the feeling of

Oneness with everything surrounding us, letting us believe that there was after all, "Something-Else" that is always there for us to be a part of. And yes, there are those of us who do absorb this moment of our own, and feel the *Oneness* within themselves and all things; but it is not often valued and cherished enough by so many of us; and sometimes, not even recognizing this deserved moment of totally being the *natural person* we are created or designed to be; in harmony and balance with oneself and all living things and the Universe.

I advise the young people of today who are living their 3rd and 4th Cycles (15 to 28 years of age) to soulfully try his or her best "To not be afraid to live *The Life*" in becoming the actual person **YOU** are! "Hell No! There should be no fear in that!" Nor should there be fear in any challenge or obstacles that are here every day, all day for our personal selves to undertake! These two Cycles of *time* need to be fearless and demanding of choice for **YOU** first, and then your family and other loved ones. If not; "Self-Identity is lost"! We are here on this planet earth to be whomever **We** are, and it is our individual, personal and divine choice to decide **Who that is.** The honest fact is, one must analyze who he or she is *today* in order to know the many possibilities of who he or she will be *tomorrow*! A thoughtful moment of self-analysis, truth, and recognizing **Who and what you are** can be a peaceful moment, and one to strive for in a young life. This process can produce a wonderful human being… if one wants to become this person.

Before we cautiously emerged from our secret floral hide-out, my sister and I were in the midst of discussing the dreadful idea of returning home, when suddenly within our confined, shady peaceful canopy of tall flowers, a flying bumble bee entered and began buzzing actively around us in a fast zig-zag pattern, buzz'n and zoom'n here and there swiftly to protect itself from our four fast swinging arms! We muffled our high-pitched squealing voices, until we were finally able to untangle our entwined bodies and flee from our churned up bed of brown earth. "Oh, wow, look, you're all dirty!" I said, as we stood and faced each other's dirty face and clothes. She looked up at me with her beautiful smiling brown eyes, "So; You too!" she said, with a tone of equality in her voice.

Recalling, this childhood adventure comes to me very easily because it has never been forgotten. I can still picture clearly, our little feet following the winding, cemented footpath that led us to another huge iron structure. This one was circular and ornately decorated with prominent images of ladies pouring fast rushing water from buckets they were holding in their arms; and like a waterfall, it gushed out of the buckets splashing down into a large reservoir basin of stone, edged with a high wall where people were sitting; apparently designed to be the people's monument. I can still see those happy children laughing and playing and getting wet in the splashes of water gushing out of the mouth of a fish statue that they joyfully clung to and played with. The small, circular basin that topped the fountain had long, flowing streams of water gracefully falling down and flowing into the reservoir basin below. My sister and I also got wet and played there for awhile. As we began to walk away, we carried the loud sounds of rushing water and happy children's laughter with us. We were suddenly surprised to hear musical sounds and voices raised in song. Grasping her hand tighter and pulling on her arm, I hurriedly said, "Oh, come on, let's go see!" "No!" I could hear her whine, "I wanna go home! I'm scared. We're gonna get a good "Spanning!" Oh no, not again, I thought; and not wanting her to begin her continuous whine, along with the tears and fears, I was stumped with my selfish problem of what to do now? As Luck would have it, our winding cement path led us around a large green bush of sprouting plants and as the music became louder to our ears, we turned to see a young boy playing music on his guitar and singing songs. A small crowd of people sat listening as we did; but we were crouched and hiding inside the large green plant. The young boy gently strummed and picked the strings of his guitar, playing the sounds of country & western music, and we listened and quietly whispered about our older brother who also played guitar, both agreeing that he was better than this boy!

From the time we entered our "Paradise" known in the neighborhood as Madison Park, it was calm and peaceful. On the other side of the wrought iron fence, the city sounds of motor cars, trucks, trolleys, and horse driven wagons, were happening all at once in a world and a space all their own. Here in Paradise, the air was fresh, clean and cool, and uninterrupted by the usual neighborhood sounds and visuals of apartment dwellings and backyard clothes lines (long white ropes, connected to windows and houses and hung with the day's wash of wet or dried clothes pinned tightly on the lines by small wooden clothes pins). Clean clothes, white sheets, rugs and bedding, all hung flapping about and being dried by the sunshine and the wind. The Automatic Home Dryer did not appear in our neighborhood until the late 1950's, and the old folks were reluctant to embrace this big white box called an electrical appliance that spun your wet clothes dry with hot air, vibrated and bounced up and down on the floor, roaring with sounds of a whirling motor! "It just don't seem right!" they would say. "It ain't healthy!"

In the park, the music filled the air and the peoples' ears with melodies and lyrics that they knew, and their voices harmoniously joined with the young boy's leading vocal. My sister and I were mesmerized and caught up in this musical rapture, forgetting the most important thought that we needed to hide, and soon found ourselves sitting bravely in front of our large green plant, exposed and free, to become a part of the crowd and their joy. Moment by moment, I could feel myself slowly being carried away in the swirl and rapture of time, the music, the people, and the strange familiarity of my surroundings that suddenly (and inexplicably) had caused my mind to separate from my body and *opened* itself to knowing all and believing all of what my eyes were seeing.

"Ow, stop!" my sister said, "You're hurting my hand!" Unknowingly, I had grasped her hand and was squeezing it tightly throughout my "visionary" moment. I could hear in my ears, definitive words of honesty quietly pouring from my mouth.

"Karen," I said, "I think I've been here before!" Her small angelic face beamed brightly at me and her eyes opened wide, looking like sparkling brown diamonds! "Me too," she said, smiling happily, and then quickly turning her face to the music in freedom, just swinging and swaying her little body and dancing with her mind.

Of the many childhood adventures and stories that every child must experience in their life, there will always be a haunting, special one that remains most memorable throughout The Life. For me, it is this adventurous childhood story of my sister's and my first experience of self-realization that unfolded to us during our 1st-Cycle (1 to 7 years of age).

Consciously thinking, analyzing, and evaluating that experience throughout the years, and along with the unanswered questions and facts of not knowing why this occurred, and why I recalled it did not prevent me from seeking the meaning and the truth of that unusual and weird day at play! Understanding it today as being a premonition then of what was to come (possibly), prepared me for the awareness and the ongoing development of the innate *Intuition* within me, voicing itself and urging me to: believe in what I feel and what I see, rely on it, act on it, and move forward! Fortunately, I am able to rely on my intuition as a guide leading me in the direction that I want to go. I believe the absolute *Trust* of such a blessing and its grounded root stems from this early childhood experience and unknowingly supported the trust that I had in myself to believe that *Something Else* and a *Surprise* is always there for you, if there is no fear of taking a step and reaching for it!

"To abolish Fear is to open the door to Trust," and it is a way to exercise and develop the innate intuition already there within us, just waiting for a seed of trust to be planted.

My sister and I were awakened from our musical rapture by the crowd's applause and their standing ovation for the young guitarist and a signal to us that all of this joy had come to an end. A void of emptiness and expectation shrouded the moment as we sat there waiting to be surprised again, waiting for something else to happen. Nothing did. The roots of the large, green landscaped plant that we were sitting in front of were embedded in the earth's soil, rich dark brown, freshly laid, and clean enough to be eaten. "Stop eating that dirt!" I said to her; "Look at your face!" I had noticed her reaching one hand behind her back, grabbing a handful, sneaking her hand from around her back and shoving it in her mouth. "I'm hungry!" she said, mumbling with a mouth full of dirt. I did not feel or think hunger until she said it. "Well, don't eat anymore, cause ya know you'll get sick, like before!" We both loved the taste and crunch of clean dirt in our mouths and were always chewing on the clean, dark earth where we use to live, in our Cape Cod village. She had gotten very sick once from an over-eat of delicious dirt shortly before we moved to Boston; I had to remind her of that! "Remember what Ma told me?" I said. "If you see her eating dirt, stop her! And you stop too, with that foolishness!" My mother used the word *Foolishness* with purpose to let you know that "you'd better stop and think of what you're doing or saying, or you're going to have a problem with me!" I did stop, not long after that intentional discipline was directly delivered. "Yea, let's go home and eat!" I said to her dirty face, as I quickly jumped up and bent over forward to brush dirt and grass from my short pants and t-shirt; and she doing the same to her earth-soiled sundress, blotched with candy colored stains and sweet syrup drippings that were once sticky and now hardened, dried, and stuck to the sheer, thin fabric. Her dirty little face that once beamed so brightly, instantly transformed into a mask of fear like I've never seen before, just as I was about to say "Oh, Ma is gonna"…when I suddenly felt heavy hands grabbing tightly on my arm! Two of our older brothers who had been on the search for us throughout the afternoon had finally found their wandering little brother and sister, *lost in paradise* and their wonderful world of wonder, that the city officials and neighbors called, Madison Park. That horrific moment of instant-panic fright, gloom and doom, exploded and happened all at once when the tight grip on my arm instantly stopped the flow of blood through that arm, causing a numbness from my elbow down to my finger tips! What do I remember of that? I don't, nothing more! I guess "The lights went-out" from that moment-on. Since, I have never recalled the trip back home, or the words that were spoken between the four of us (and I am sure there were many); nor do I have any recollection of the consequences received for selfishly choosing that day *to* be mine and for the innocent but clever manipulation forced upon my sister. Family stories of our adventure and dramatic rescue that day were told in later years, revealing that I was severely scolded and "captured" in the house for several days; playing school, doing chores and cutting out paper dolls with my sister while squatting on the linoleum-covered floor of our living room in the family's modest apartment on number 2 Madison Street.

CHAPTER TWO

My 2nd Cycle (8 to 14 years of age) began and continued with the Dogma of The Church. My mother's honest and sincere passion for the Roman Catholic religion became infectious to my sister and I. We would go as a trio, seriously marching to church every Sunday and on special early evenings of the week to commemorate the selected and special Holy Saints to whom she was devoted! Always on the night before the following feast day honoring a Saint, our bedtime story would be of that Saint and we would have a book of pictures, images, and big words to struggle with while carefully listening to her tell her story of the Saint. She wouldn't be reading from the book but only saying what she envisioned in her mind and what she believed about that Saint. She would lovingly speak of St. Francis Of Assisi and St. Martin De Porres whom I think were her two favorites, along with the Blessed Virgin Mary. On Christine's dedicated nights (after an early dinner and a well-run household along with her seven children calm and without foolishness) her joy was to turn on a radio program hosted by Bishop, Fulton J. Sheen and/or Cardinal, Richard J. Cushing of Boston, and listen and pray the Rosary on bended knees.

She was a non-fanatical devotee, moderate in her worship of Catholicism and never imposing her beliefs on anyone else. She had the wisdom to balance her life with a smile and an honest presence that displayed all that she believed in and that she was a woman of God. I am not too sure that my father believed in God or was ever thoroughly convinced of The God idea. He didn't attend church services or belong to any religion, nor did I ever hear him speak of or mention the name of God unless he used the colloquialism "Goddamn" in humor or general conversation; but I never did hear him use the word in a blasphemous manner. A proud, obstinate, and self-owned man with dignity who possessed confidence and a deep loving warmth that most likely contributed to this unique marriage of a mutual oneness, understanding, respect and love.

"A woman with wisdom will always choose the right man." "A wise man proudly yields, to the honorable measure of Acceptance." My mother knew well, that his physical and mental strengths were as powerful and equal to the softness of his heart. Today, neither he nor my mother would have any opposition to or struggle with the idea of Gay Marriage because they both understood *completely* that "Marriage is between two honest people."

Religion was the norm in our house, and my vulnerability of being religious and reverent was targeted and became an obsession to me. The baseball field didn't interest me except to watch my brothers and their friends playing; and I had to be there only because they had the responsibility that day to keep an eye on me. For me, it was more fun to be at home, playing with the thoughts and the fantasy of religion and its inspiring force within me. And then the time came when all of that force and religious *energy* eventually oozed out of every pore on my little body and collectively came together all at once in an explosion of creative energy that compelled me to construct in a small corner of our living room, an altar of praise and worship, modeled after those in any Roman Catholic Church. I put up a large Crucifix, centered high up on the wall so you would raise your eyes as you knelt on a small bench and prayed, and an actual Tabernacle enclosing a copper chalice. I displayed statues of Saints and the Virgin Mary, a Holy water basin, so you could bless yourself with the sign of The Cross and genuflect on bended knee before passing by the Crucifix. This was an Altar of praise and worship solely constructed for me to play with! I became respected by every member of the family; including my father. Playing church or playing school were two of my favorite in-house activities on rainy summer days or the cold and snowy days of winter.

At St. Richard's Church, I became an eager and enthusiastic Altar Boy after my *First Communion* rites of sacrament; and at the age of 11-years, I unexpectedly became a Godfather. At the time of the Baptism Rite, I fully understood the role of a Godfather, the sacred sacrament, the Christening procedures of holding and handling an infant child and the altar boy duties that were performed, because I had already served many of the Baptismal Masses by this time. Therefore, on that precious day, holding this infant pink baby cradled in one arm, my right hand holding a flickering flame bouncing and leaping off the tip of a long white candle was a day so memorable, vividly-clear, and trusted, that it lives within the Soul and Mind of this aged man today whom I call...ME.

The Pastor, Father Patrick Noonan was administering the sacrament in words of Latin and English, and I, listening and absorbing every word he spoke, was shocked when he abruptly stopped! An adult conversation about 5 minutes long was happening above my head. The conversation finally ended among the five confused but calm adults: The parents of the child, the Godfather to be, my Mother, the Godmother to be and Father Noonan. Father looked down at me with a lingering pause, and then slowly squatting down to my eye level to meet mine with his Irish deep-blue eyes, bluntly said, "Would you like to be the Godfather to this child of God?" I had tilted my head down and into the infant's face with her little eyes shut tight, still in disbelief that I was holding a child of God in my arms. I was to be her Sanctified Godfather, to love and care for her all of her life. I had only one question for God: "Is this forever and ever?" The candle in my right hand trembled and wobbled, and the flickering flame of fire danced and leaped even higher. Father Noonan's trust-filled and penetrating eyes convinced me to give my head a very quick nod of "Yes." I stood speechless as warm salty tears ran down my face and I felt a kind of joy I had never felt before!

I did become the Godfather, and my mother became the Godmother to baby "Pamela" who peacefully slept through her botched Baptism ceremony; botched due to a divorce that the intended Godfather had undergone, disqualifying him from being the Godfather. It was a church law upheld at that time and applied at the very last moment with haste. Later that afternoon at home my mother explained to me the "How" and "Why" of what had happened to suddenly allow us to become the Godparents to this wonderful child of God, who happens to be my 2nd generation cousin. These two memorable incidents of religious actions: the creation of an Altar, and the Baptismal Rite, I find to be significant to the destined and personal journey I am on to self-realization, simply for the purpose of understanding more of who I am and for seeking answers to the questions of how and why I have taken this shape or guise To Be. "Is it of my choice? And why are there intuition and forces that compel me to think of a 'higher achievement' to attain other than that of a perfect human being?" And what resources do I have within myself and my surroundings to work with as tools, to strive for and maintain a healthy physical, mental, and spiritual balance in my every day existence here on this planet Earth? I believe these questions deserve answers. Each one of us are traveling through *The Life* on a personal journey destined for "Something" or "Somewhere" for reasons and choices of their own; and yet, there are those of us who are born and live every day unconscious and oblivious, simply existing in the ignorance of that realization, and thinking that the present day is enough to handle. For them, their personal journey is maybe limited, and saddled with a "backpack full of ignorance".

My words are for the ageless, but primarily are intended for those of you today who are young in years now, and moving through or simply existing, in the 3rd, 4th and 5th Cycles (15 to 35 years of age) and struggling with the sometimes complex and painful personal issues of "Self-Identity," "Self-Confidence," "Choice," and "Direction." Please hear me *clearly*. **YOU** will Know, once you've arrived at the end of your 5th Cycle (35 years of age), that **YOU** have missed your opportunity and potential challenge to reach and attain "Your Choice" and your inspiration, to excel in your *highest achievements* should you not adhere to at least some of this "Jibberish" that I am writing! It will be *almost* too late then! That part of the game that The Life has played on you is now over. There is no second chance to win; but certainly, by being *aware* of this *almost* missed opportunity, and now knowing exactly why and how that opportunity was missed, try your best to act and **YOU** can score points to add to the second choice of your nature. *Bravo!* to those of you who don't need a second chance because of the personal foundation of discipline and choice already established in your previous Cycle and *Bravo!* to those who take action now! Because when that specific opportunity is missed, a new challenge arises!. The 5th-Cycle (36-42 years of age), begins with a new idea of *Self* and continues on cultivating the second *Choice, Career,* or *Dream!*

Hopefully it is clear, that Your 3rd-Cycle is the cycle of "Prep" for the 4th Cycle which is your "Prime Time"! Be alert to this, be conscious of this, and do not allow the most dynamic and most important period of your life to slip away quickly and easily, by doing what **YOU** know you should not be doing, especially in your 4th-Cycle! Your 3rd Cycle is there for you to establish and cultivate the **YOU** of your first choice, career, or dream. The 4th Cycle is to apply yourself to that commitment; but if you don't, there is a third game to play in the 5th Cycle but with more challenge, effort and age to be considered and "Realized."

My 2nd Cycle was not only filled with the joy of playing with religion, but also, being outdoors playing in the sun or in the winter's cold, with a gang of kids my age and older who lived on our street or nearby. Daily all day and often into early evening the street games would be continuous and actively going on: Kick the Can, Hide and Seek, 1-2-3 Red-Light, Body and Ball-Tag, as well as roller-skates, pieced-together bicycles, self-made, hand-crafted go-carts and foot-scooters! Rigorous backyard boxing matches between the neighborhood teens who battled each other for fame would attract street shoppers and eager spectators on a Saturday afternoon.

I was near the end of my 3rd Cycle, when I began to understand the importance of *The Life*, how I should live it, and the subjective reasons why. I managed to satisfy the yearning and thirst of this esoteric information with many library visits, interesting people, and travel. The limited answers and the many unanswered questions, I somehow understood and accepted for their worth, and that is when *The Life* began to unfold for me, when I was confronted with the realization that there are no answers…yet.

——— CHAPTER THREE ———

It is because of this original theory of self-evaluation, its method and its process, which allows me now in this day and at my age, to affirm that my personal experiences and the astute consciousness of my 1st and 2nd Cycles (as well as the learning process of the other Cycles that followed) have consequently led me to believe that *Happiness* is not discovered, nor is it gifted; it is *earned.* If you are "in the pursuit of happiness," then one day soon, look in the mirror!* Be face to face with **YOU**! Analyze, scrutinize, and have a discourse with the image that **YOU** see. Be as objective and egoless as you can possibly be and think about that. Relax, and breathe slowly. Take some time to really understand yourself.

If what you see reflected contains the understanding of *humility, sacrifice, love, honesty, humor, the arts, humanity,* and above all, *children,* then you are able to earn your happiness; because these are the essential elements needed to pursuit the *reality* of happiness and its personal self-achievement.

And I will remind you that "Wisdom has no age!" So, don't wait to be aged to believe that you are wise! I advise you to be aware of your wisdom during your 3rd and 4th Cycles; Learn to discern exactly who you are, and why.

Mirror-Exercises and Technique: Pages:

Commit to yourself, to discipline and learn this practice by simply being conscious and *aware* as you are having *fun* and going-through your *changes* remember that you must: *Be Young, Be Free,* but *Be Wise* because **YOU** ARE!

It was during my 3rd and 4th Cycles that a fantastic and brilliant professional musical career flourished for me. And certainly, a sense of *happiness* came along with the undeniable choice of becoming a performing artist; along with all its excitement and glamour, travel, and hard work. Prior to this, and after deciding (at about the age of 14) not to become a Jesuit Priest or The Pope, the arts of music, dance, theater, and writing, had always been of interest to me. So, consequently and thereafter, the performing arts and the pursuit of happiness were what I wanted my world to be about every day. And it was.

I was already into the very exciting 3rd Cycle of *The Life* when my professional music career was flourishing, successful and in full swing. And, being a member of the infamous 1950's/60's Doo-Wop vocal group called The G-Clefs, I was a fortunate teenager! The group consisted of myself, three of my older brothers, and our neighborhood friend who lived next door to our apartment house on Madison Street. So, by this time in our relationship and career, he had become "the other brother." The legendary, Original G-Clefs retired from the performing stage in 2012, after a brilliant musical career of 58 years together, living and celebrating their gift of music. We were four biological brothers; and all four, dedicated singers in the St. Richard's Boys Choir during our younger years. The "other brother" was of different faith and unable to become a member; but he would sometimes come to choir rehearsals just to sing, and Father Noonan didn't mind at all. When the group formed in 1955, it was my mother who suggested the group's name be The G-Clefs and I am certain that she prayed daily, and was assured by her faith, that "Her Gifted Boys" would not come to harm in the vulnerable show business world that they loved and were blessed with. And I must say of her faith and unusual power, that she did make us feel and believe that we were gifted, blessed and protected.

Amidst all of this wonderful fame and glory and fan clubs, girls, parties, great performances and hard work; a seething yearning, a need, an intuition stirred quietly within my Soul that was craving, begging and asking *for more.*

Whenever The G-Clefs were not touring nationally - basically living in two cities, Boston and New York City - and being busy with recordings and the preferred local gigs between the two cities; a less rigid time schedule allowed me a slice of freedom from the professional aspect of my work to explore the other potentials that I might have and didn't know about. And maybe these other sides of me just could be the new foods that my hungry Soul was asking for. I was young, but I was also 3rd and 4th Cycle "Wise"! The time, the opportunity, and the need to explore **ME** was there, and it was to my advantage to Snatch it up! A slice of freedom to feed my hungry Soul.

Whenever possible, the G-Clef's wardrobe of tuxedos, shiny shoes and high-waisted cummerbunds, were abandoned by me in rebellion of non-conformity and my exhilarating Bohemian lifestyle of all day dreaming, lighting candles, drinking glasses of wine and reading the poetry of Emerson, Baldwin, Langston Hughes, and the profound words of so many others. The "Bohemian Fantasy" that loomed over me, was to live in Paris, France, become a performing artist, wearing a tilted beret, and have honest conversations with friends gathered in a smoke-filled dark and shadowy dungeon Café! And naturally, being there, smoking and sipping on glasses of the deep red wine we'd pour from the bottles lined up for us and placed at arm's reach on the red & white checkered table cloth, complete with a burning candle dripping it's wax through the long hours after midnight 'till the first light of dawn. I imagined myself dressed as an artist would be, sitting in a Parisian café, wrapped in a lengthy scarf or draped in an ethnic, woven Poncho, modestly dressed and usually wearing the color black. On the table, sits a sketchpad for doodles and quick notes and a book at my elbow to supposedly signify that I was an intellectual, biting the tip of a long cigarette holder, sending slinky streams of white sensual smoke up into the air. I also very much liked the feeling of warmth and truth I got from being huddled together with dear friends from all nations and all creeds, feeling the *Oneness* in conversation, thought, and civility. This happened often in Harvard Square; but in my mind I visualized it happening in Paris, France! And then of course, there's the morning's grand finale of hot French Roast coffee and warm croissants, for those of us with unfinished conversations yet to unfold and the need to enjoy sitting outdoors together (at a different café) to greet the new day, the morning sun and to give gratitude for all that is! My bohemian fantasy actually did come to be realized many years later in Paris, France!

As it is so with every young woman and man of this age and in their own time of self-realization, the conquest to succeed and the desire to establish "something" of self-achievement was so for me as well! These two Cycles were a whirlpool of emotions, love, dreams, personal dramatic conflicts, and as well, the upheaval of American social unrest.

As a young black man during the 1960's, my actions and emotional involvement with political and social activism became a key issue with me, as it was with many African-American artists at that time who felt that it was fair game for us to use the performing stage as a platform for our protest songs, voices, dances, and messages against the Vietnam War, "Jim Crow" segregation, the injustice of civil rights, and all of the social diseases that plagued the streets of America. The red white and blue flag had become historically stained with American blood and social fears.

But for some of us artists who were Black, White, Hispanic and Native-American, this engagement with the social protest movement didn't go well with the moguls and management within the music industry; causing cancellations of already booked engagements, along with the artist's refusal to work a gig at a venue where they knew the racial climate there was dangerous to them; or as artists that had to play by the rules of the social-game: "To remain in the dressing room, and to only show your black or brown face on stage, in front of the spotlight, at showtime!" *Deplorable, Unacceptable,* and *Almost Unforgivable* was the brazen "Shout-Out" then all over the country and in every city, by "We The People"! My visible onstage protests consisted of not wearing shoes with a tuxedo, or maybe sporting a headband or a scarf brandishing the vibrant colors of red, black and green, the obvious colors of the radical Black Movement. But my onstage antics of protest were totally ignored by audiences sipping on cocktails or stuffed-olive Martinis! Songs of civil protest that I would deliberately sing by Bob Dylan, Joan Baez, Stevie Wonder, or Boston's own Jackie Washington (Jack Landron), were totally unheard, uncalled-for, and very quickly "fell on deaf ears"!

It was quite astonishing for me to notice that what was happening onstage was alive and full of feeling, and simultaneously what was happening in the audience, was not *alive* at all! The fashionably-dressed and starched audience, there to be noticed and admired, were simply having a cocktail-chat, totally oblivious to the fact of their absurdity! They mostly all resembled the cut-out paper dolls my sister and I played with as children! All with pasted-on smiles, the same pink plastic faces and cardboard clothes! All just standing there looking dead and without life's energy; untouched and unmoved by the music. Whereas, to the more progressive, enlightened and enthusiastic audiences such as college and university students at theater concerts, and of course the dedicated night club "Groupies," my onstage antics of protest were always recognized and received with a refreshing, mindful, and joyful exuberance full of understanding and commonality!

"Why I was not Free to *Express*, *Learn*, and *Be* troubled me! This all-consuming and cancerous thought infused my mind each day with daydreaming whenever time allowed; and gradually it started to interfere with my onstage performances. Fortunately, or coincidently, my personal thoughts and actions during that time coincided with those of the music industry. A new phase of recognition was happening in the updated catalogue of the history of American music. Now, Folk, Soul, and R&B were finally being recognized! The vocal expressions and the rhythms that were happening all over the country and in the hearts of the people, were finally added to the catalogue's music list of Jazz, Country, and Classical, etc. The romance of Doo-Wop, the stomp of Rock & Roll, and Pop Music, cautiously took a back seat to what was actually "Cooking" in the hot boiler-pot of American music at that time. It was a troubling time for many artists, until this new phase of policies, conditions and expressions of American music allowed The G-Clefs to perform and record their own original music and other genres of their choice. And this new musical phase consequently allowed me to perform freely and to be more selective in the songs where I would be singing the lead vocal. The eminent culmination of this new phase happening in the music industry and also for The G-Clefs was positive; and it was the right time for this remarkable change through-out the whole country!

My preference of songs to sing onstage or on recordings was not of romance, but of protest. Often, before or after a G-Clef performance, a slight sense of remorse and a hint of selfishness would toy with my mind and I would take refuge in the dressing room, escaping from the entertainer's social requirement of networking with fans and the usual "Meet and Greets" in nightclubs, theaters and concerts halls. The G-Clefs were friendly and personable, therefore our dressing room was like a magnet attracting other artists who performed in the shows; but the stories, laughter and the artists' intimate dressing room talk didn't interfere with or interrupt my purpose of being there. I took refuge not to be alone, but to read books, think, and simply to study *The Life, People,* and the plastic transparent bubble that I seemed to be captured in and was clearly seeing through. The scenes of familiarity that I could see on the *Outside* evoked a desire and a passion within me to be *There* and not *Inside* of this conventional bubble of withering interest. The dressing room became my study hall, my classroom, and a place to dream.

"Is it me, or is it Us inside this plastic bubble?" became an important question for me to answer. I already knew, believed and had experienced the fearlessness, the feeling, and the *Self-owned expression* of *Freedom* that came to me from the joy, excitement, and incentive, of my 1st Cycle's wonderful "Childhood Adventure!" And also, the intrinsic values of *Self* that my parents established within our family home got me to the question of "Is it me, or is it them?"

A man or woman who is not free and honest within themselves, or with their partner, their family, or within their home or surrounding environment, know it! They know they're missing something! They see, feel and hear the inborn call of freedom everyday of their lives; and intuitively they can sense the oppressive limitations and desires that one who is "Caged" can feel, elude to, and exist in, often with remorse, living each day with the "Someday" mode of thinking, trying to find their own "Freedom". But they are sadly destined and fixed with the permanent possibility of never knowing **WHO** they really are, waiting for a "Someday" that will never come without the action required to seize it!

I have a dear friend who is presently enjoying the onset of her 7th Cycle (43 to 49 years of age). We had met in 1992; she was about seventeen years old and I was fifty-two. Her mother was a dancer in my dance company during the 1970's. My friend, who has been "happily" married for many years is beloved by her husband and three children, now all in their twenties, single and away from home. The children are exploring *The Life*, themselves, their environment, their careers and relationships, and whatever else is out there for them except for one, the youngest, who is twenty-two years old. He is still searching for "Something" on his telephone, in video games, or on Netflix. She's hoping soon that he will outgrow his middle school passion and stumble onto "Something Else."

My dear friend's husband, apparently was a wise young man during his 4th and 5th Cycles, charting his career and family planning, because today he is fine. His wife is still loved, his children are healthy goal striving young adults who love him deeply, and his family's future is well secured emotionally and financially; all due to his personal achievement and career success. His golfing has improved greatly; and his basement *Man Cave* is loaded with his toys, his thoughts, and his way! "This isolation is called *Kingdom*, if you know what I mean," she said, loaded with shooting darts of sarcasm.

My dear friend is an intelligent woman living her 7th Cycle with recognizable beauty, motherly love and a warm smile filled with a living spirit to go forward. She is a professional career woman who aspired to her dreams of Interior Design. Her vicarious encouragement for her daughter "Cali" to also become a dancer was futile; she was a dance student too awkward to dance, but still loved it! Also, Cali's playful obsession was to drape herself with rolls of willowy fabrics before they were cut and designed for costumes. She would unroll a long length of fabric, wrap herself in it and then dance; skipping and leaping frantically across the floor of the studio; dramatically stepping and stumbling. She would say that the fabric made her feel lively and free, like a "Real" dancer!

In time, Cali and I got to know each other well and our bond of friendship became mutual. She loved "good" music, all types flavors and colors, with or without a beat; and she loved to sing! She would write songs and lyrics that would often amaze me; showing her hidden and very mature talent and her extraordinary comprehension of music, unusual for one of her age. I was always fascinated by her cleverness and how she would somehow weave that knowledge into a conversation with a melodic twist, always with a remarkable sound of wisdom flowing into my music and word-loving ears!

Together, we laughed with honesty; basically, at ourselves! We both knew intuitively, and understood that we were *weird, silly and ageless!* She, was in her 3[rd]Cycle at that time, and I, unfolding my 5th; but we only discussed age whenever I thought that she was going a bit too far for her age! She had the capacity to fill her mind with many future weeds that would be left to untangle, if one did not remind her of the consequences. We kept our words true to one another and throughout our years of loving friendship we've been very close friends.

The last few doubtful years of my friend's marriage to her husband were a big surprise to him. "I had to tell him that I was lesbian, Ilanga," she said to me in a telephone conversation we had a few years ago. At this time, our east coast and west coast residencies were only separated by a telephone cable; but our presence together always collided without any distance between us, connected by her words of honesty, pride and self-survival. "When I was telling him, I felt like a beautiful song without words, Ilanga!", she began to say; "But, the lyrics to my song never surfaced until later!" The seconds of silence that followed were hers alone, and I listened carefully until she said, "I wanted to sing loud, Ilanga! You know me but, "How can a song be sung if the words aren't there? It's like, how can a dance be a dance without a body?" (she paused, very frustrated) "What am I saying?...I know you know what I mean! The lyrics...they just weren't there!"

My dear friend's voice of honesty anchored there and into the limbo of silence I immediately sliced through with a ramble of questions; "So, how did you tell him? I mean, after over 20 years together, what did you say? How did he take this?" I asked. "Oh, not so well" she said; "But, he did like how I presented it to him!"

Her laughter ended with a thought I could hear in the back of her mind; "Well, one day, I decided to costume myself and dress like Ellen Degeneres! I whipped up a plate of delicious hors d'oeuvres and danced away like Ellen into the Man Cave!" She laughed hard again. "Oh Ilanga, I don't know what made me do it this way, but I did, and it had to be done, then!" she said. I listened with no obvious expectations of what the outcome of this story would be, knowing her as I do, and she continued, "He and the kids were all there in the Man Cave. It was a Sunday afternoon; you know, a family day together of lunch and sports on television. It was the only few hours in the week that we were allowed in his Man Cave, so, earlier in the day, I had already set and prepared the Karaoke machine; and with remote in hand, I busted through the door of the Man Cave, singing my own ambiguous written lyrics with what I thought had a message of my anxiety with "something going on inside of me, but I don't know what, along with the chorus of Cindy Lauper's "Girls Just Wanna Have Fun!" She burst out laughing again, and with a tone of satisfaction in her voice she added, "Oh, Ilanga, he loved it! And of course, he had no idea of the intended message, but the girls did!" His comment was brief after the kid's applause; and it was something-like, "Oh, Mom's giving us half time entertainment even before half-time! That's great dear, Thanks!" He turned himself around quickly in haste looking for what had shut off his game on his television and easily said, "Hey, pass me the remote you left over there!"

Hearing these words from my dear friend, provoked me to feel her always vibrant energy of positivity and optimism about any issue, controlled and assured by her confidence; a wise and dynamic woman, strong with her disciplines and attitudes from Dance, and always sure of her direction. "Did you feel then, or maybe do you feel now, any sense of selfishness?" I asked her bluntly, and waited patiently for an answer. "I thought about all of that," she said; "but you know, I came to the final conclusion of that about a year or two before I told him!" "Hold on," I said to her; because I had to think for a second or two about what a nonsense question I had asked!

This woman had always been a giver ever since I'd known her. "I don't know you to be a selfish person," I said; trying to make up for the other question. "Oh my God, Ilanga, I love you. You really know me," she said appreciatively, with thought, voicing her words with an almost child-like quality. She sighed in her brief pause, and continued, lifting her voice to proclaim her well-earned freedom. She confided, "Ilanga, remember a while back when the girls were teenagers, and you and I had a long conversation about teenage craziness, and you were talking about that *Seven-Year Cycle* thing?" I responded with a chuckle, "Oh yea...the girls were just a bit into their 3rd Cycle and they were pulling you through it with them!" That pushed our laughter-button for a few moments. "Oh, I know," she said after her laugh; oh, it was awful! Well, I can't say awful, no; because some good did come out of that for me, eventually. And I don't remember if I told you; but at that time, my oldest, Cali was putting the old man and I through her gay thing! Did I tell you that?" "No!" I replied, "I never got that part of the saga; but maybe that's when we lost contact for awhile when I was working abroad." "Ah...yes, maybe," she said. "Well, the *good* that came-out of that "saga", and the clear recall of that incredible cycle conversation is, I am certain, the melody that helped me to write my own lyrics to Cindy Lauper's song! And I know that you can completely understand, feel me, and know, exactly what I'm saying; and, only God knows how much I love you for this, and for our times together. And (she paused for a thought) since Cali's *thing* and also, the many months of emotional anguish - just scrutinizing myself, evaluating and realizing what I've given of myself to my family for twenty-two years - this in itself was an awakening to my unselfishness and also gave insight into the huge question of *selfishness* itself! And Ilanga,

I had to ask myself, what about ME?! But the answer or message I got in all of this came to me in a weird way, from Cali's endearing declaration. We were all gathered at dinner one night at home when she announced to us that she was gay! We were having dessert, and she had finished hers. She busied her napkin at her mouth and began saying, "And now, my dear sister, and you my dear brother, Mom and Dad, to "top-off" that delicious dessert, I have sweeter words to tell you guys!" Ilanga, Cali's eyes were *loving* and her face was *glowing*! And then, in such a delicate way she said, "I am your Gay Daughter, Mom and Dad; and I am your Gay Sister, my dear Brother and Sister!" And she sat there and watched us, just smiling the most beautiful smile I've ever seen on her face before! Ilanga, that day I felt so damn proud of her! She was soulfully honest, to herself and to her family! She clarified for us, every thought and reason of her gayness, her liberty, and how it empowers her daily, with strength and self-esteem, and the drive to keep going forward and to do the best things that she is capable of doing! And, she said, "No matter what anybody thinks or says, she still loves everybody, even if they don't love her!" Oh, Ilanga, that was me! Absolute, and without a doubt! Believe me! As Cali was declaring all of this to us, I was sitting-there hearing ME! There she was, my twenty-three year old daughter with my voice, voicing me, and with my *Spirit*; and there I was, face to face with myself, hearing and seeing ME! I guess it was much like your cycles mirror thing!" she said, and paused, "Oh Ilanga, it was weird! If I didn't know better, I'd call this shit uncanny! It really blew my mind!"

I could hear remnants of words in my dear friend's voice repeating "Really, Really!" and I interrupted her possible third attempt. "Wow!.. Oh, I'm sure it-did!" I said; "But wait! With all of what you've just said; now, let's be real! You know that I like to hear two sides of every story, and if there's a third side, I'll listen to that-one too!" We both laughed at that and I continued saying; "Now, you know that I'm curious to know what HE said, and how HE responded to this madness; and also, what impact was he "Slammed" with and left with now, in these times?" You know what I mean; suddenly living with the fact that he has two lesbian women living in "HIS" house!" She howled with laughter! Then finally pulling herself together; she said, "Oh, please! You know what? As we were all sitting there listening to Cali, and he next to me, *The man of the house* nudges me in the ribs and whispers, "All that shit she's saying... does that mean that she's 'Coming Out' or something like that?" "Oh God, He sounded just like the Archie Bunker character in the TV show *All In The Family*! I just looked at him and quickly flashed a *shut your mouth* stare, daring him to say another word! Cali's words were profound with the fact that she now felt wholesome and complete, and I was watching her be an amazing ME! She helped me realize that it was only a part of myself that I was living and being loved for; and I thought, am I to be dying for this, also? And am I taking this dormant and un-loved dark side of me to my grave?! I decided that, listening to Cali, and loving the three others sitting next to me, the *incomplete-me* and not the *whole-me* was just something that I was not going to live with anymore! I guess I got tired of saying *Someday*. That's the only way I can explain it!" she said.

My dear friend's 7th Cycle is now being lived with a freedom and self-reliance that she'd never known or exercised before! Her relationship with her daughter Cali is as *One*. They work together, and are dedicated "Sisters on a mission!" Her son is now in college and her younger daughter is now married. The last I heard, was that "The Man" remains in the solitude of his cave with acceptance and love for his beloved family; but cannot help but disagree with "that kind" of family love! As for my friend, her "Someday" mode of thought disappeared when her latent challenge *To Be* was acted upon and realized. She loved her family enough to pursue her own happiness; and her choice was made with Liberty and Love.

CHAPTER FOUR

Television: The designated instrument or tool used to foster social manipulation, our way of thinking and the American way of life. A deliberate way of sending a "Message" of seeding the thoughts of how to think about anything at all or about yourself! Television informs us what to think about. "And, *it will think for you* if you allow it to." We lie relaxed on the couch for hours, with our reliable remote-control device at arm's reach, residing in our comfort zones. This curious square box, originally a furniture piece called a *console* with a screen on the front and tubes on the back and inside, became a household item in the homes of the American people. It was during the mid-1950's when Television first arrived in our neighborhood.

I somehow dodged the tempting influence of television via the everyday realities of my personal interests in family, study, friends, and my intense work in the music industry performing with my brothers, The G-Clefs. With our continued success and popularity throughout the 1960's, I certainly enjoyed, appreciated and was grateful for all that had come to me; but I was still haunted with the fact that this was not *real* happiness for me. I kept thinking, "There must be more to it, there must be *Something Else;* there always is. Everything changes; even the social unrest is changing the landscape of the country!"

It was during the onset of my 4th Cycle (22-23 years of age) when intuitively, I felt the need to act on "Something" that had to be "Changed" or is "Changing" and to be alert! It was at this time that I began and made my first attempt to practice the self-evaluation process that I have undergone throughout the years;

but the overwhelming question to myself then, was *How*? It was at this time that I knew this significant question had to be answered: How do I challenge myself, the "Norm" and why not? This was the ambiguous answer and the task that I committed to at the onset of my 4th cycle. An identity crisis loomed over me and the *Who* and the *What* I had become confused me greatly. I felt caged and trapped by external conditions that caused me anxiety and mental conflict with every thought; underlined with a faith to overcome. I was not sure which direction to take, nor was I able to clearly identify with myself satisfactorily and completely. It was in the midst of this Cycle that I realized and instinctively felt that a concrete sense of self-identity had to be established right away to fulfill my commitment to *challenge myself*, especially in regard to "The Norm" and the "Conformity" that I highly resented. By this time, my Bohemian fantasy of living in Paris had been put on the back burner to slowly simmer.

I had taken a diversion from anything that was of dire national interest, and subsequently, becoming a Black-American "Hippie" seemed to fit my agenda of *freedom*, along with my social, political, and non-conformist values. I was a famous G-Clef when in New York, and when in Boston, a *free* and joyful Harvard Square hippie! We held group singing "Hootenannies" and late-night through mid-morning "hang-outs" that would happen in the square, immediately after hearing the voices and seeing the faces of Joan Baez, Ritchie Havens, Jackie Washington (Jack Landron), Bob Dylan, Ian & Sylvia, and many more of the folk singing giants of the mid-sixties musical period that performed until the 1:a.m. closing time at Club 47; a dark and smoky Coffee House hidden away on a small shadowy Cambridge street. The ideology of "Hippie-ness" was of freedom, action, and universal love; and this was enough to satisfy and calm my young and whirl-wind mind.

On the New York side of things, all was in my favor. After our committed New York City and Las Vegas engagements, The G-Clefs were scheduled for a European cities' tour that was to be followed by a six-month engagement at an exclusive night club in Tokyo, Japan. We returned to Boston for six months and then went back to Tokyo for a six-month encore.

The extensive travels through America, Japan, and Europe, the three cultures where we were living, working, and so fortunately exposed to, enabled me to expand my thoughts and interests on "Difference" and what that actually meant.

I eventually discovered the power of difference, and found that its scope of understanding was within an individual; and that it mattered greatly to not be ignorant of this, because *difference* is a precedent to *discrimination*.

Each country where we traveled and worked had their own identity, their own nationalism and unique differences in global power, people, and culture. This was fascinating to me; I had lived and thrived on only the American experience and its ongoing social, political and cultural dramas, and as a traveler in foreign countries, one does not actually experience the dramas that are happening in other countries every day, all day. I wanted to delve deeper into the countries, peoples, cultures and differences that I experienced; knowing that I would become "more of myself" by engaging and interacting with the local peoples, so that they too could see and feel my differences. As an American who was an American only by virtue of his passport and accent, nothing else mattered. In the foreign countries where we traveled I was seen or identified as a black-American artist, a novelty, and as an invited guest; which was all fine and good; but there was much more to me and my differences that I wanted to share with the many interesting and fascinating people I met and exchanged a few honest words and laughs with. "Let's hope to meet again" would be our parting words. And in some cases, we did meet again in later years; "coincidently."

Throughout the global tours with The G-Clefs, meeting people, seeing places and the "Wonders Of The World", I continued my method of self-evaluation which had become my habit by this time. Often in my travels, I would have a "déjà vu" moment, as many people do when they think, "I know I've been here before!" A reflection or a "flash-back" would occur at a tourist site, at a street corner, in a café, at a river's bank, or at the market when meeting someone and while in conversation I would say to myself, "I know this person!" This innate intuition surfaced when meeting a very special person by chance, and throughout the course of a few general conversations embedded with honesty, somehow would conclude with the understanding and the mutual consent that, "He or She, knows me too!" This connection with two people or a group is *absolute*; the *affinity* is there! "How can this be, and why?" I had more questions than answers. These were the types of frequent and consistent thoughts and flashes that prompted me to further evaluate my reasoning and questions by considering the memory and the knowledge of reflective events that had occurred in my previous Cycles. One in particular happened in London, The United Kingdom. But the narrative begins with a humble and sincere wise man who also lived in the Roxbury neighborhood. "Jack" was a Spiritual Reader at that time, and throughout the years since and to this day we've been very dear friends.

It was 1967 and the G-Clefs were about to embark on a national Doo-Wop Tour; simultaneously, my confused mind was "touring the universe" looking for some concrete answers. A friend who was also of an inquisitive nature, suggested that I have a spiritual reading from the wise man of Roxbury. At the reading, he wanted to hold the copper bracelet I wore on my arm. "Is this special to you?" he asked; before I answered "Yes!" he closed his eyes. He slowly turned and fumbled with the bracelet, fingering it with soft touches, and then lovingly cupped it with his strong brown hands, saying nothing. Suddenly, his eyes opened wide! "Oh, you don't like the cold weather!" he said, "I see you someplace, but where, I don't know...and you're always cold, man!" His eyes seemed to pierce the bracelet as he continued; "There seem to be many children surrounding you all the time, but you endure this cold place because of whatever it is you are doing there!" He paused a few seconds with a slight eye squint, "But doing what exactly, I don't know; that I can't see," he seemed to be saying to himself. With a mild bit of skepticism, my words of opposition to his "cold weather" comment were, "No way, that's not possible, Jack! The G-Clef's tour is national, this is Summer! There's no cold where we're going!" His eyes looked up from the bracelet to scan mine, and I couldn't help myself. I was compelled to stare directly into his deep, dark eyes filled with "distance" and "transparency" when an unforgettable thick silence was suddenly sliced with his words. "I didn't say 'when' this is to happen, my brother; I only see it 'happening'!" And then his eyes shut tight as he added,

"And, I know that somehow you can understand that!" Although puzzled by his words, I somehow did hear them clearly, and understood the depth of what he was saying; but, hearing them vaguely from somewhere deep in my mind and spoken without words, I felt a cool wave pass through my body and heard a clear "sound" of understanding.

"Jack Miller" continued on with the Reading. "Ah, yes; I see something interesting here," he said. "The earth we walk on; you are afraid of! You know, dirt, earth, sand, mountains, and yes, also the ocean!" (it terrified me to hear the truth of his words). "And I'll tell you why," he said. Jack didn't move a muscle. I sat there relaxed, but spinning with my thoughts of *"Afraid of the earth and dirt* and..." Jack interrupted my thoughts, and raising his voice, "Volcano, Earthquake, Southern-Greece, is what I see!" Jack's pause seemed timeless. "Hmm, yes... a tremendous earthquake hit that area, man!.. You were killed in an earthquake, suffocated by the earth!" he continued. "Do you understand what I am saying?" he asked me with a soft tone in his voice. "Yes, and...no" I answered;... "Are you talking about past lives, reincarnation, and stuff like that or something else? Because then, if that's what you're"....Jack leaned forward in his sofa-chair to meet my eyes. "Good, my brother, good; yes you understand." I too leaned forward from my sofa-chair, our eyes meeting even closer. "I do?" was all I could say slightly above a whisper, and with a face of absolute doubt! He kept his eyes to mine for another timeless moment, rolled out a personal laugh as he pulled back in his chair and reached for his pipe on the small table by his chair. The fragrant aroma of his special tobacco and the fluffy clouds and curls of smoke stimulated each of senses with mild relaxation. Slowly I could feel myself easing back to comfort in the deep sofa-chair and its throne-like shape, lying my head back against the headrest to think and to absorb this mysterious moment of "hearing and feeling" a familiar reality that I didn't see but somehow recognized; and at this very moment, it suddenly snatched me off this planet to "Someplace Else." Both of us, wrapped up together in a silence that again had no time, was broken with Jack's parting words to me; "What you understand now my brother, you will understand more of later, when all of this unfolds to you through your extraordinary life experiences as an artist. It won't be until then that you will really understand!"

The recall of this spiritual reading from Jack came to me nearly three years later; It was in 1969. The G-Clefs were performing in London, U.K. during the upheaval of terror and fear that shocked, gripped and slandered America's landscape: The Assassinations of Dr. Martin Luther King Jr., and Robert F. Kennedy. The great American cities of liberty and justice burned with hot fires and the wide streets overflowed with angry rioters.

On this particular day, The G-Clefs were free from an engagement and were relaxing together, watching the riveting news of the American crisis on the television in the lounge of our hotel. The lounge was thick with gloom, anger, sorrow, and shame. "Those bloody Americans are idiots" said one Englishman who witnessed our national disappointment. "Hey, man! When we gonna go eat?" said one of the members of the band who broke a silence of about one minute after the television news presentation. Upon hearing the *click*, when a hotel clerk turned off the television, it was unanimously agreed that we would all go eat. Disgruntled and tired of our English diet of Fish & Chips, British fast foods, and plates of tasteless, bland meals offered at the many hotels and roadside restaurants where we stopped during our tour, we decided to reward ourselves with Greek Cuisine. We had decided this because earlier that day the bass player and I were strolling the streets of Bayswater, the area of London where we were living then, and as we walked, we both were attracted to *The Acropolis*, a small Greek restaurant. "This is where we have to eat tonight! I think all the guys like Greek food, don't you think?" I questioned him. "Let's go in now and make a reservation for tonight!" Before entering, I could hear him behind me proclaiming his desire for this taste and stating adamantly, "Hey man, if they don't come, it's you and me!" He and I were bonded in friendship, music, and the arts; and he was an extraordinary acoustical guitarist and my side kick during our Bohemian Hippie Harvard Square and Hootenanny fun days! (my nickname then, "Giovanni" was his and another friend's moniker). So, our close friendship has always been real, honest, and loving.

Entering the "Taverna" as the owner called it, was like falling or stepping into a small Greek village restaurant filled with vines of garlic and wooden barrels of wine, a few tables, and the delicious aromas of herbs and spices from the bountiful Mediterranean area. The owner, a handsome Greek man of maybe 35-40 years of age came out from a back room. He was about to greet us, but stopped where he stood, awed, motionless, and not saying a word. His thick black hair and smiling eyes were prominent. I could feel his constant stare at me and my every move as "Gene" and I, unexpectedly surprised, were admiring what we were seeing of the rustic Greek village decor from the moment we entered and without uttering a first "Hello!" Instead, in my excitement, I forcefully blurted out "Wow! What a beautiful restaurant!" to the owner who was just standing there, as if his feet were glued or nailed to the floor boards. He closed his eyes and then gracefully bowed his head, looked up at me with fixed eyes and smiled. "Hello!" I continued, "We came in to see if..." He interrupted me, raising one hand in a peaceful gesture and spoke his welcoming words with a gentle Greek accent. "I am sorry gentlemen, but now we are closed; but thank you for coming in and appreciating the Taverna!" he said, wiping his hands slowly with a small white cloth and taking a step or two towards us. "And, my American friends, to say this is a 'Restaurant'? No No No!" he said; as he pointed his index finger upwards, raised his thick black eyebrows and lifted his chin at the same time. "*Parakalo*" he said in Greek. "Please, you must say; wow, this is a beautiful 'Greek Taverna'!" he said modestly, with a smile and natural pride. "We will open tonight at 5 o'clock."

Gene and I made reservations for nine seats for dinner and left The Acropolis and it's delicious aromas behind, discussing as we walked, that "He never did ask for our names, nor did we ask his!" I stopped Gene going forward. "Should we go back?" I said. "I mean, we need to know his name or he needs to know ours, don't you think?" He, less anxious and puzzled than I, shrugged his shoulders, saying calmly, but with a reluctance, "Hell, we don't need to walk back, man! Why do we need to know his name? We don't really! And he knows that nine people are coming for dinner, so, he doesn't need to know our names. "Hey, that's a set deal man, I think. Come on let's go home." I agreed with him, but we didn't have much of a conversation on our short walk to the hotel. Gene's logic hadn't erased my inclination and want to return back to the restaurant and why I was suddenly becoming anxious about that, perplexed me.

Waiting in the hotel-lobby for a couple of the other guys to join us for our Greek dinner was a quiet, somber wait; The television news had affected our usual talkative and high energy group. "Oh, come on, let's go!" I said anxiously; "They can walk-it! It's just up the street!" Of the nine-membered group (5 vocals and 4 musicians) seven of us left the hotel and began our 10 minute walk to The Acropolis Taverna, cozily tucked away on a small side street in the Bayswater area of London. We were strolling slowly so as the delayed two guys could catch up to us, and being American tourists, seeing street sights that caught our attention as we talked and casually strolled. "Whoa! Check out that building!" said one of the guys. "That looks like the *S.S. Pierce Building*! You know, on the corner of Harvard street and Beacon, in Brookline!" A classic old English-style building of Tudor architectural design. We stopped talking when we realized we had finally reached the Greek restaurant and proceeded to go inside.

"*Oriste,* my friends, welcome!" said the owner as we entered into his candlelit Taverna with Mediterranean aromas that filled our nostrils and heads with the anticipated satisfaction due to come. He cordially invited us to take our seats at two lengthy tables that were laden with cheese, olives, bread baskets and small white candles, already dripping with hot wax. "Sir!", I said to him; "I'm sorry for this, but we still have two other people on their way to join us, so we'll… he interrupted me; "No problem, my friend! So, there will be nine altogether, no problem!" As he was about to turn away from me, I said, "I'm sorry, you don't understand what the problem is; earlier today I made reservations for nine!" He faced me directly. "You said seven, my friend, but no worry, no problem! Come, sit, I have been waiting for you and your friends!" Saying this, he then happily hurried off, instructing two of his staff waiters to assist us, and leaving me baffled and disconcerted. Adding two extra chairs I know was not a problem; but, saying that "we reserved for seven", was for me, a problem.

Taking a seat across the table from Gene, I quickly noticed that his inquisitive eyes were upon me and his face pasted with a frown. I sat and paused a moment as we both eyed one another and was just about to speak, when he leaned forward towards me. "Don't freak out man, let it go!" he said above a whisper. "Hey, I know we told him nine, but let it go! He'll bring a couple of chairs." Those at the table sitting closer to us could hear and see Gene and I making big hand gestures discussing a conflicted issue; but left us to ourselves as the waiters were placing small glasses on the table for the coming wine. Gene continued; "I heard him tell you that we said seven, right?" I quickly responded; "Right! Damn! Now Gene, you know that man has got my Mind bent and twisted, right?" We both laughed until our eyes met again; and during that pause, something very deep inside of my mind prompted me to sincerely say to my *Soulmate*, "Thank you my friend. You're always there when I need you!" Gene broke out in laughter as he pulled back in his chair and began his signature gesture of cupping his hands, rolling and twisting them, as if he had just come out of the washroom; and in his natural Italian accent he said, "Hey man, this all sounds Greek to me!" This aroused laughter between us that captured the attention of the other five guys who were being poured a light tan colored wine in their small glasses. Gene, put his index finger to his lips, and motioned to me "Shhh… the owner is coming!" As the owner was in small talk with his waiters about performing their duties, I could not keep my eyes off of his every move, thinking, "This man is weird! Why has he not yet brought two more chairs and set the table for the two other guys?" Not annoyed, but really curious, I was just about to lean forward to let Gene know what I was thinking, when I felt the powerful presence of the owner standing tall behind me, and then felt the weight of his hand on my shoulder. It was a heavy hand with a fearless tremble that slowly brought my body to attention and upright.

"Styn-Yamas!" He loudly shouted out the strange word. "In my Greek language, that means Cheers, Health, and Happiness to all of us here tonight! And to thank my new friend here." He softly squeezed his fingers and rested his palm gently on my shoulder. And to thank his handsome musician friends for coming to dinner here at *Taverna Acropolis*, not, restaurant, please, "Parakalo"!" He explained briefly with humor and raised his small glass of wine that the waiter had just filled. "Let's toast and drink to the beautiful music you make for all people to be happy in the world!" he said, lifting his glass to his lips, sipping, as we all did. "Oooh! Shit!, Aaagh, no way!" The boisterous sounds of distaste came from the wine-sippers, some even spitting out their first gulp in clean white cloth napkins and letting it be known they did not like what they were drinking! "Aaaah, yes!" said the owner, "This wine is called *Retsina*. It is a homemade Greek wine from my village on the island of Crete and is a special taste that has to be acquired my friends. Come, drink! After one or two more sips, you will be fine with the Retsina!" he said proudly. With due respect, we struggled through our tasteless wine toast and thoroughly enjoyed the delicious dinner of fine Greek foods and sweet desserts. The other two musicians never did show up; nor did the two additional chairs.

As we were all satisfied, in good spirits and preparing to leave the Taverna, all saying thank you and goodnight in English and in Greek; the owner announced an invitation to us to return later that night after 11:pm if we'd like to hear some authentic Greek music played by the musicians who would be arriving at that time. The invitation was immediately turned down unanimously because the next morning at 7 a.m. we were leaving Bayswater for an evening engagement in Leeds, a small city requiring 3-4 hours of road travel. As we were exiting the Taverna, Gene and I were the last in line to leave when the owner stopped us. The expression on his face was intent and serious, quietly piercing my body with his weirdness; his dark chestnut-brown eyes never leaving mine. "You must come back tonight, my friend, I want you to," he said earnestly. "I am your friend, *Thassos*, I know you. I know how you like to feel, my friend. And tonight's music from Crete will make you feel very happy. Come!" he said. "The stories and the music you hear and feel tonight will make you want to dance, or cry sometimes; it is Greek!" His big laugh and the intrigue I guess, convinced me enough to secretly eye Gene, just to get his solid "I'm always there" approval, and to confirm that he too would be able to handle our 6 a.m. wake-up call!" Thassos instantly got the "vibe" that Gene and I were on. He turned to Gene and said, "And also you my friend, will love the guitarists tonight! They are your kind of musicians! Every note and string their fingers touch, tells a story. They play "Real" music! Come!"

With agreement and anticipated excitement, Gene and I left *The Acropolis* and hurried in the streets to catch up with the other guys who were silly-fun drunk, jovial and satisfied with their unusual early evening dinner, and because it wasn't the usual fish and chips or tasteless fast food we had been eating most nights. The few minutes it took to reach the other guys ahead allowed me a moment to question Gene with the thoughts that had followed me out of the Taverna. I turned to him and asked, "How did Thassos know that you played guitar?" Gene didn't turn to me at all, he just threw his words out there; "I don't know, man!" he said; reaching in his shirt pocket and pulling out his cigarette pack. "Like you say man, that cat is weird!" He then quickly added with his unique wit, "Hey, maybe he looked at my string-cut calloused fingertips and thought to himself 'Ahh, a guitarist!' I don't know man, I don't know!" We said nothing more to one another; but in our silence, my deep concern was, Thassos *is* weird! How did he know?" Gene and I caught up with the other guys; but these thoughts continued to follow and play with me all the way into the lobby of our hotel.

Fortunately, in those days long ago in Europe, television entertainment and programming did not exist after 9 p.m. therefore; no bad news to see and hear tonight! The drunk, happy and satisfied bunch of music makers all went directly to their rooms for a good night's sleep and a very early 6 a.m. "Resurrection"! The plans for Gene and I to meet later in the hotel lobby at 11 p.m. to return back to *The Acropolis* were being discussed, but also my personal thoughts were that for the next couple of hours, I could relax and prepare my thirsty mind to hear real music, dance, and see weird Thassos. I smiled as I packed my bags for Leeds.

CHAPTER FIVE

Following behind Gene, as he opened the door entering the Taverna, we heard the music come pouring out and we walked into the smells of herbs and spices and a gathering of happy people. Some were dancing and some were sitting in candle light and thick cigarette smoke, enjoying their intimacy and the dark corner that shadowed privacy. The waiters gladly welcomed Gene and I as one gestured with both hands for us to "Please wait!" and then hurried off. Seconds later, Thassos appeared from a back room; his face delighted upon seeing Gene and I standing there and his serious dark eyes sparkled and illuminated his broad happy smile. He stopped there in place and immediately flung his arms open wide, closed his eyes as in prayer, lowered his head and began to move his body, dancing with himself, (from within himself)! The musicians seemed to understand his mood, and suddenly the "Real" music began to be heard. Thassos moaned words and sounds that seemed to erupt from emotion, resolve quickly and then explode into hand claps, bodily rhythms, and forward steps, as his dancing steps and agile body slowly arrived next to me. "Horepsime!" Thassos said boldly, "Let's dance! Dance with me, my friend!" Captured by surprise, his dancing spirit and the admirable request, my only thought was to stop thinking and just do as he did! I closed my eyes and also flung my arms open wide, feeling my body move first and soon dancing with itself, from within! This is when I too exploded into a dance with Thassos! Like two wild animals meeting for the first time, slowly stalking one another in a rhythmic dance with an eye-to-eye discussion of the anticipated next move. "Come, my friend, this is

Greek," he repeated two or three times as we circled one another waiting for the other to trounce first.

A crescendo of rhythms from the musician's Tabula drums and the stringed *Bazouki* and guitars rapidly heightened to peaks, exhilarating our dance to a sometimes frenzied moment! The small group of wine filled happy people on the dance floor loudly cheered, whistled and shoutted "Bravo!" as they watched and clapped their hands with every rhythm and beat. Step by step I followed Thassos' every move without thinking about it as he followed mine; and his eyes were always shining with a smile. In frantic quick moves towards him I would lunge, he would leap! I would crouch, he would kick! We were two magnetic energies in a magnificent display of challenge, power and presence to one another; there for all to witness the triumph of masculine dare, challenge, and dance; unrestricted and untouched by the conventional thought, of "Why do men dance together?" A question we were now answering.

During the last movement of our dance together we were face-to-face and eye-to-eye from one another, but still apart. We both spread our arms open wide in a salute of gratitude, and slowly danced towards each other until our bodies touched; chest-to-chest, shoulder-to-shoulder, and our arms aligned and stretched out, palms touching. Consciously I understood and felt that he had positioned us into the form and shape of a human crucifix. The left side of our faces laid flat against each othe,r sliding in sweat and body heat like I have never felt before! In his language, he whispered in my left ear, "Efaristos Polli, Filemou!" (Thank you, my dear friend!) With our heads lowered to a bow, we joined together at the frontal lobe of the brain slightly above the forehead. Our two bodies remained stationary there as one, dancing in a slow tempo sway from side to side, flowing through each other and feeling "the quiet" coming to us, and hearing the diminishing sounds of musical strings, rhythms and a distant single voice in song, faintly finalizing our dance together. Somehow it became known to me that this was not my first encounter with the Greek movement of dance. I knew that "I have danced this before"!

Thassos and I held each other close for a long moment without a spoken word; only heavy breathing. Finally releasing each other from the embrace, I noticed that his face also was lined and streaked with wet dripping tears. Somewhere near my ear, he whispered again, "Efaristos! Thank you, my old friend." It took a few seconds for me to emerge from this surreal bubble of surprise, sweating and breathlessness and to notice Gene across the dance floor, sitting with the musicians and conversing as he finger plucked strings on a treasured "Bazouki", a popular and predominant instrument played in Greek music.

"Hella, Krasi, Parakalo! Pare To Filemou Etho! Kei Towelettes!" I heard Thassos' voice bellowing to his waiters; "I tell them to bring you some wine and towels," he said, as he escorted me to some chairs where we could sit together, in a shadowy intimate corner of the Taverna. "Now, we must talk!" he said. He began unwrapping from around my neck the soaking wet scarf I was wearing; He held one end of it in his hands and began to wipe my face dry. "Do you think you know who I am?" he asked bluntly, and in my face! "Do you *See* me, my old friend? Can you remember me? What is it you feel?" he asked and waited for answers, fixing his eyes to mine and wiping my brow. I did not look into his eyes as he wanted me to; I couldn't, there was only a blur and a haze to see through as if his face was appearing to me in a fog. "I don't know anything,

Thassos; I don't even know who I am at this moment!" I said to him. Then, purposefully resting my heavy head against the wall next me, "I know nothing man, I know nothing," I murmured. Reaching forward again to wipe my brow, he began to question me; "Can you remember me, the earthquake?" he asked. I was tired, drained of energy and impassive. I answered slowly, reluctantly, and with doubt, "I remember nothing! I only can "feel" you, or "something" I don't know!" There was a silence that prompted me to open my eyes, to see him smiling; and his eyes were gratefully "pleased" with my answer.

"Have you ever been to my country, Greece?" he inquired; but only received a slow shake of my head "No" for an answer. "Never to Cyprus?" he continued. I opened my eyes and lifted my head to face him; "No, never!" I said. "And, 'No!' to anything else you want to ask me about this stuff, man! I can't; right now, I'm still looped and spinning from the dancing, the wine, and your questions! Thassos, I have no energy to think, except that I think I should be going!" I said, and rose to my feet. "It must be late now!" He offered his hand to mine for a shake that very soon became a tight grip, saying, "Yes, yes, my friend! You must go, I know. I will see you after tomorrow, or in a few days when you return from Leeds! No problem! I know we will see each other again before you go-back to America." I agreed with him; although, he didn't know that The G-Clefs were departing London soon for Tokyo, Japan.

"Yes, my friend," I said. "I have to get some sleep before tomorrow. I'm tired, I feel drained, like the life has been sucked out of me!" I said truthfully. I got Gene's attention from across the room and motioned to him to come over to our table to make our hurried exit; he came right away. Quickly, from off the table, Thassos picked up the large tin pitcher of Retsina and began to pour wine slowly in three glasses as he turned his face to Gene and I, and spoke in a serious tone of voice. "Believe this unusual story my friend; and, one day you will…once you go to Greece!" His pause was long, transparent and empty of time, until he took a sip of wine, exhaled, and spoke again, telling his story.

"You and I are childhood friends from many years past on the island of Cypress, where we lived and perished in a catastrophic earthquake! As you continue to live your life, from this moment on my friend, 'go back' in your mind. Then try to remember me and the time when we always played together as children and we were happy in the Sun! The earthquake separated us until now, my old friend; Believe this!"

An instant flashback recall came to me of the Spiritual Reading I had with Jack Miller three years before, at his home in Roxbury! I remember him saying to me: "And you have a Spiritual Guide, his name is…" Jack paused, closed his eyes tightly and then uttered, "Agnostine." Strangely enough, the name was somehow familiar to me, as if I had known it all along. I looked down at my hands holding my glass of wine, my eyes staring hard at the small, light tan-colored pool of Retsina as Thassos continued; "Can you feel, in a strange way my friend, the truth of you and me, and of what I say? This morning when you came in the Taverna door with your friend here, I remembered you in Cypress! "When" that was, I don't know! Ahh, but your eyes and your heart are still the same! I can see that and feel that!" He again paused, looked to Gene and I both and blended a thoughtful chuckle to himself to say, "I also am one not to believe such things sometimes; but this one is true! I say that because my heart feels good to see you again, my friend." He picked up his glass of wine and took a big gulp without a flinch and kept looking at me with an endearing light of love in his eyes. I'm not too sure if this light of love was for me, or for the answered "Truth" he believed in and had been waiting for, which had finally materialized for him! The answer to the question he had held throughout his life had arrived; I could see that, because the answer was in his smile of acceptance. Yes, it was clear; Thassos was satisfied. He was wiping small teardrops from his eyes with my already soaked scarf as he began to stand up on his wobbly legs.

He then said sadly, as he was holding the scarf above my head and carefully wrapping it around my neck, "It is now after 3 a.m. I know you must go! But, go with good and happy memories of *Taverna Acropolis!* And, when it's time for you to go to Greece, go my friend, go home! "Kalinikta, Filemou!" "Yes, Thassos my friend, goodnight!" I said; and we left.

The entire evening made Gene a happy man. "Even though I'm Italian, I must have a lot of damn "good" Greek in me!" he said jokingly; and then added, "Because man, that was too much! I was like, 'There!' Shit man, I was 'There'! His emphasis on *There* had us again laughing hard! As we were wine-tipsy, silly and casually strolling back to the hotel, Gene burst out again "And whoa!" he slurred from his twisted tongue; "Is Thassos weird or what, man!" I wasn't too sure how to answer him, so I didn't. "Hey, hold-up," he said, "I want a fag!" I couldn't believe what he had just said! I looked at him sharply, and then suddenly we both burst out laughing! At that time, the British had coined the slang word "Fag" referring to a cigarette. Even then, at that time in our ominous social history, for an American ear to hear one ask for a "Fag" is not what our ears wanted to hear! Gene pulled out a cigarette from his pack, held its end between his thumb and fore-finger in front of his face! With his body slightly "bobb'n and weav'n" he stared at it, and spoke to it. "It just ain't right calling you something you ain't!" he said, with a tone of sadness. As he was lighting my cigarette, my thoughts were: "A word, or term, used without conscience, just struck me as being insensitive!" Blowing out my first-puff of smoke I said directly to his cigarette, a remembered childhood-riddle. "Sticks and stones may break my bones, but names will never hurt me!" I said, as any taunting ten-year old would say! And moving my face closer to it, I winked an eye and said; "And, we won't let them do it, baby!" We both knew, that to laugh at such ignorant humor was a silly thing to do; but we did it anyway!

We stopped briefly for Gene to adjust his belt and to light up his "Fag"; The cigarette was dangling and hanging from his lips, as he was squeezing out words from one open corner of his mouth. "You don't think he's weird anymore, huh?" His words were accurate, and surprised me! "I don't know man," I said to him; "If he's weird, then I'm weird! Maybe he's just different! You know, like I am and, like you are!" I asserted as we continued to walk. "It's not that he's weird man, it's *how* he did what he did that's really weird!" I said. "He damn well knew that we said nine and he claims that we said seven And, after telling him that two others were coming, he didn't set the table for two more or bring chairs! I think Thassos knew that they weren't coming, Gene; but, *how* did he know that?" Gene and I were silent for a moment until he said, "Yea, that was strange! Then he asked you to dance! Whoa, that was crazy! But nice; beautiful, really!" He snatched a quick puff from his cigarette;.. "Man, you guys really got down in it! Shit man, I have known you for years, and I have never seen you dance like that before, damn!" As he snatched another puff from his burning cigarette, I thought for a moment before carefully saying, "I never have!" because I wasn't sure of that myself! Tonight, on the dance floor was just so familiar to me and my feelings, that my comment to him was, "Maybe, I have"!

Our hotel was in sight before I could say any further words to Gene; and we had not even realized that we had been strolling in a London drizzle of light rain and had approached the hotel "a bit dampened" as the British would say.

Standing in front of the door to our rooms we stopped and looked at each other before going in. "Thank you, man," I said to him, for all my reasons; "I'll see you in the morning; Goodnight!" He stood there doing his signature hand rub. "Yea, it was a good night! O.K. man, Ciao!" he said, using the Italian word we both loved using. Smiling, I said to him, "I'll see ya in a minute!" Our doors shut quietly at 4:45 a.m. but for me it was a sleepless night with profound thoughts of all that had occurred that night at the *Taverna Acropolis*.

The "takeaway" from this little narrative, my wise young people, and those of you who are "ageless" is that, "If you are in search of "Whatever", and your need is that great, then be *alert* and be *wise*. Your most significant resource to help you "Realize" yourself, your identity, and your surroundings at a particular time in *The* Life, could be your next-door neighbor, your family member, your pet, your friend, or a stranger you may meet on any street corner or path that you may travel in the world. And of Gene; my genuine dear loving forever-friend, brother, and "side-kick" for well over 50 years; he passed away or came to his end here on the planet about eighteen-years ago. But; "Did he really go-anywhere?" I Don't Think or Believe So!" This chapter is being written only because he has been with me *Here*, present in his beautiful and loving Spirit as I write, now! He has been guiding me through every moment of writing this chapter with his words and laughter; and "Being There" for me, to capture "The Honesty". So, In my truth, all that I can say is, "He is *here* for now…should anyone ask!"

CHAPTER SIX

During the first engagement that The G-Clefs had accepted to perform in Tokyo, Japan, I had taken seriously ill upon arrival. Due to a severe bronchial issue, the first three weeks of performances had to be cancelled, as I was totally disabled and bed-ridden in our large exclusive Tokyo apartment that towered above others in the district of Akasaka.

I mention this foretelling story because it precedes the turning point, or the "Change" and self-imposed challenges that I had undergone to find **ME,** and this illness is what introduced me to Hatha Yoga.

The distinguished Japanese Impresario that hosted The G-Clefs in Tokyo was a fine gentleman of nobility and knowledge, and was highly honored and respected throughout the country. My illness concerned him greatly; and, I believe, not because of the performance cancellations, but because of his fine character. How the procedures and details of my care were arranged, I know nothing, and have never asked; nor do I know why I was not hospitalized; but instead, a specified healing method was applied to me within a bedroom of our apartment. These questions were never asked because I had no concern then, and still don't today. I had become healed, and my trust in the Impresario Mr. Matsuyama and his management of all things endured and left me with no questions. I was told after the healing, that he came to visit me at the apartment a few times, but never entered the room where I had taken ill.

The bedroom was always candle lit and quiet, and floating in the air, a light fragrance of scented oils which would sometimes awaken me from an unconscious sleep. One person usually, sometimes two, sat there conversing in Japanese. At any time of my awakening, I was always incoherent, dazed and in a mental fog, and without the memory of ever speaking a word. There's very little that I can recall of this specific treatment of healing; except for the final week when consciousness slowly came back to me, and the moments, day or night when I would awaken and find myself netted and bound tight in an unusual body position that restricted me from any and all physical movement. Within my "Netted Cacoon" of recovery and occurring conscious moments I'd ask myself, "Why am I bound and caged like this? Who are these people here? And where are my brothers?" These were my rambling thoughts, meshed with the fragrance of scented oils and the occasional sightings of the Japanese healers who would come in and out of the room with a bow to greet one another and a bow to depart. My dormant memory and lack of knowledge of the details and specifics do not allow me to tell you what actually transpired during this mysterious practice of healing; except for that final third week. Thereafter, when my healing was completed, we began the first of our many performances at the exclusive *Club Mugen,* in downtown Akasaka, Tokyo.

The G-Clefs returned to Boston to family friends and fans after an engaging six months in Japan. One early afternoon shortly after our return, my sister and I were enjoying our friendship in talk and stories; we had missed each other very much. Throughout the past years of our sibling relationship, we were always extremely close in heart, like one! Always together, we attended the same co-ed highschool, enjoying the same friends throughout our early teenage years, until I became a famous G-Clef, leaving her behind in my travels. She married young, like many of her girlfriends in the early

1960's. This time period was pre-onset of her 4th Cycle, or one or two years thereafter.

"What are your plans later; I mean, like early evening?" she asked me. "I don't have any, really, why?" "Oh, Arnold," she began; (calling me by my original birth name) "You should come to my Yoga class tonight! I just started a couple of weeks ago and I love it! It's really interesting you know! It's hard for me, but for you it would be easy!" she said. Now, I had not a clue of what she was talking about, therefore my mind was already making evening plans of finding some "Real" enjoyment elsewhere! And I knew well that a solemn, quiet stretch-class of all-sized bodies bending and twisting was not in the picture! There was nothing "Real" in that, for me! I had to stop her from her usual excited "ramble" of things that she enjoyed most in her day, and then she would just keep "babbling" on! "What are you talking about?" I asked her, "Body-stretching on your back? And falling asleep when you're supposed to be *thinking* or something!.. No, I don't think I'll be going!"

Although she was busy in her gadget-filled kitchen, I knew that she was listening carefully. She stopped her busyness for a moment, put both hands on her hips, and smiled, admiring the fresh vegetables we had just picked up at the local market. I continued, knowing that she heard every word. "What is a Yoga class? I mean, I should go there to do what, and why? What do you do in the class?" I asked her, as her eyes focused downwards on the vegetables being chopped. "Oh, it's great!" she replied with enthusiasm and then quickly turned her glowing face to me with her eyebrows raised in excitement! "Oh, we do slow exercises and stretches and breathing and thinking - it's what they call "Meditation" stuff you know." "No,

I don't know! And, what should I be doing while you guys are doing all this "Stuff" may I ask?"

Standing at the kitchen-counter, she abruptly stopped her action of chopping vegetables; and holding the knife in one hand, she turned and looked at me with an expression on her face that made me feel like an idiot; "You join us, or you just sit and observe," she said calmly and direct like a middle-school teacher; her eyes sending a signal and a measure of discipline. I said nothing more. She went to the stove to resume stirring her sauce and began to chuckle her thoughts aloud; "And sometimes we'd have to hold ourselves from laughing because somebody there is always farting!" she said with a laugh. "And Sri, our teacher from India, disciplines us to not laugh, but it's hard not to; Damn!" She and I laughed a lot about that and other things that afternoon; and we ate a delicious lunch as more stories unfolded. Finally we left for her newly loved Yoga class and the benefits that she wanted to share with me. Her genuine enthusiasm and delightful approach made me feel the joy of us being together once again on another one of our life-altering adventures but this time it was all hers. I felt our childhood "Oneness" again, and was persuaded to go. Not knowing what I was getting myself into, I had chosen the option to "observe" this intriguing class of silence, movement and softly spoken words in English and some in the Indian language of Hindu! The language attracted me with its rhythms and vocal sounds that blended with the recorded background music of celestial harps and the aroma of sweet incense. The class was being held in the basement of a beautiful old church in the town of Newton. My sister knew well my attraction and interest in Cathedrals and quaint old churches, so it was somewhat of an easy win for her to get me there.

Sitting on a standard folding chair that you would find in any church basement, my eyes roamed the room, admiring the old wooden structure and décor, and glancing at the students in class lying on the floor looking like they were sleeping; but that was the "Meditation stuff" that she spoke about, I assumed. Suddenly, they began to move their bodies in the postures of Yoga, which were called *Asanas*. Sri, the lean dark brown-skinned teacher spoke softly. He stated the title and spoke words defining each of the instructed postures. I heard his voice only faintly, sitting in the dark secluded distance; but suddenly his voice became more audible when I heard him say: "In sequence; The Plow, Fetus, and Sun Pose!" I heard no more words from Sri, as suddenly I went into a mental flashback, a glimmer, a recall of Japan: the bedroom the healers, the oils and the "Netted-Cacoon"!

Again, his gentle voice sounded, "Now, slowly relax, breath naturally and in your moment inhale deeply, exhale, and move into the Fetus posture." I heard the words from "somewhere" or "someplace beyond" because my mind was being occupied in clarity by a vision of myself netted and bound tightly in the fetus body position; and once again, my eyes saw through the netted cocoon, the candlelit room, and the dancing shadows on the wall of two silhouetted human figures; one sitting against the small table of oils, and the other hovering over me. And somehow I knew and felt that his or her hands were just on me, touching my body, arranging its position, and faintly seeing their fingers twisting and turning to adjust the fine, thin netting. The vision that occupied my mind startled me; seeing how my fragile body had been placed, crouched and rolled into the Fetus body position of the Yoga posture that I was now witnessing and experiencing here in this church basement!

There were four embryonic/fetal positions that I also saw in this bedroom flashback: My body laid on its left side, a sit up position, laid on the right side, and on my back; all four body positions placed, bound and netted. The interior of the basement, the students, and Sri's distant words, suddenly all appeared to move together hurriedly and simultaneously in a rapid staccato-movement or rhythmic effect comparable to a strobe light, pulsating and flicking brightly, and all fused together and funneled into a total blur that eventually faded into nothing.

The next thing I remember was my sister's hand on my shoulder and her concerned voice asking me, "Are you okay?... My God, you're sweating! Are you sick?" Feeling her sitting next to me and seeing the worried look that masked her face with fear, I quickly replied, "No, no, I'm fine!" and added, "I just got dizzy for a minute, I think."

The 20-minute car ride returning to Boston was a quiet one. I sat next to her in the passenger seat feeling exhausted as she drove with a few words while maneuvering through the traffic. It was not until later that evening at home when I discussed with her the Yoga class and the unusual experience that occurred in the basement of the old church. And due to my sister's incessant provocation, I did finally go on to register for the Yoga class.

Due to The G-Clef's sometimes out of town performing schedule, it was nearly impossible to attend class once a week, so whenever I was in Boston and able to attend, I would be there with interest and commitment, learning the body postures and feeling the beneficial effects of Hatha Yoga and its Meditation exercises. Eventually, the habit of practice and its disciplines became a part of my every day routine, and eventually I incorporated into my everyday thinking.

The 4th Cycle (22-28 years of age) is loaded with the personal dynamics, struggles and "Changes" that are required to establish oneself securely, with confidence fortitude and self-esteem. It is the Cycle that makes it known to yourself and to others, "Who you are," "the person you'd like to be" and being aware of what your immediate plan is to live *The Life* as **YOU** think it should be lived! Select your priorities from the options you have to choose from, and then "Act" on that plan, don't just think about it! And if you don't have a solid plan of substance, you'd better get one!

The constant turmoil, self-doubt, "fun", and social activity that occur in this Cycle, all happen quickly and without warning. Soon you may realize that you are now into your 5th Cycle" and without a "Plan." "Be Real!" If you're not sure of "Who you are," look in the mirror! The reflection you see is **YOU**! And if you don't like what you see, "Change it!" And what you see there that you do like, "Improve on it!" It takes exercise and practice to develop absolute "Self-Identity, "Confidence," and "Character." Young people, hear me: "Let No One Tell You Who You are! **YOU** must define that!"

During my perplexing 4th Cycle and my dedicated engagement with Hatha Yoga, I discovered that the routine Meditation practice eventually became similar to a mirror in that it was "reflective, honest and personal." One early evening during this Cycle, I was in an unusually calm and peaceful Meditation; (often, it would be restless with rambling thoughts that took much discipline to curb). During this particular evening's unusual Meditation, the quiet was intensely silent, and the dark nothingness I was seeing appeared to be just a depth of blackness; a vacant space. Suddenly, this vacant black space burst into a bright glow and became completely filled with the bold and vivid colors of orange and yellow, whirling and churning in a translucent fluid motion! I was startled at first, but was interested in seeing more. I repeated "Relax, Relax, Relax" to myself several times, breathing slowly with paced inhales and exhales, until finally, relaxation came. I had never seen such strong, bold, radiant colors emanating with such beauty! This colorful liquid-like motion circled and churned and whirled in beautiful designs and soon began to boil and bubble, throwing off a warm alluring heat to my body that I felt coming at me and also that I wanted to go to or be a part of. Then instantly, it all burst into the "Sun!" A huge round ball of hot, flaming orange and yellow fire, framed and encompassed in deep blackness! Swirling in circles and boiling! Once the orange-yellow flaming sun made its ultimate spin, and stopped its motion, another realm of my "Being" became conscious and the perception of a new kind of "Stillness" surrounded me! And seeing the Sun before my eyes and feeling its heat, I was conscious and aware of myself in the Meditation and with the singular thought: "Is this a fantasy, or a mind game of some kind?!"

Within this vision - its stillness and my awareness - I suddenly noticed and focused on a tiny black dot that appeared in the center of this glorious orange-yellow Sun, fixed and centered like the bullseye of a target. The tiny black dot was slow in its swell, but in its own time swelled into the shape and form of a human figure! At first, it began to slowly move its body-like shape in a natural movement; as if it were touching and feeling its own limbs and body with its hands for the very first time. Then, the faceless black, human figure began to shape a dance for itself with movements that flowed smoothly and just as soft as the willful motion of the translucent fluid that it appeared from; "dancing, sometimes joyfully and quick and sometimes wistful in its own rhythm and time! A "He" or a

"She," I don't know; but I do know that a black "Dot" became an "It" right before my eyes!

What I was seeing in this Meditation, Vision, or Fantasy, was astonishing and crystal clear: "A black-silhouetted figure dancing against the blazing Sun!" It stopped its movement once, paused, and then two tiny, red dots suddenly appeared on its black face, as if it had eyes out of which were shooting two thread thin laser beams of red lines to my eyes, penetrating and directly meeting mine. I knew that I was seeing "Me" and almost instantly I also understood that the black dancing figure was me against the Sun; and I "Connected, Identified, and Accepted" this. Seconds after that, the two red beams of light and two black dots slowly disappeared! The silhouetted black figure dissolved into nothing, and the blazing Sun fizzled out quietly until it too diminished into the unframed blackness.

Thereafter; my yoga practice, its ideology, and my personal experiences peaked my interest to learn more of **Me** and "What makes me tick!" I began to consider serious study, and continued to exercise this original method of self-evaluation that has become a conscious thought for me to develop and apply; and "Why?" Because since that specific Meditation, "Something-Else" happened to me, or "Someone-Else" with "red-eyes" impounded who "They" saw! I don't know; but this new wonderful and unusual sense of "Being" began to arouse and stir within-me an awareness of difference within the thoughts of who and what I am; and my thinking what was negative of myself became positive, and strangely, that felt good! What was good for me and what was not good became crystal clear; and I began to take notice that although for some others, to feel good or to feel bad all day every day, didn't seem to matter to them; it did to me!

Prior to self-evaluating, I had never thought to differentiate or measure my day with the forces between these two magnetic energies of "feeling good or bad." I adopted the mere importance of Living *The Life*, as my priority-motto of the day; "How" I should live it, and the subjective reasons "Why." The "Unknowing" and strange thought of me "Being Me" was no longer strange! This Cycle, for me, was to evaluate and harvest the bountiful fruits of my successful work in music and the industry, and to evaluate my desired and achieved aspirations along with the unrealized dreams that became realized.

And of most importance to me, was the role I played within my family story; being the youngest of six boys and the most stable within the The G-Clefs at keeping the vocal group organized and at handling all the business matters. Yes, even the family became a part of my deliberate scrutiny to my destined path of discovering **ME**. Was I happy, then? No! Was I totally satisfied? Yes! Satisfaction came by way of the fact that I was taking "Action" upon my "chosen" commitment and my responsibilities; and this brought about a strong sense of self-confidence.

After a period of about a year's time of consciously evaluating myself, I began to realize that, "Yes; I am happy!" I would not have known or learned how to navigate through the upcoming next Cycle had I not undergone this evaluation! The "Realizing" of who I am, and what I have accomplished and achieved at this point in my 4th Cycle, brought to me "a place that I call *Happiness*;" and that is because of the selected "Positive" evaluation results that "allowed me" to move forward! No longer merely *thinking*, but instead *acting* to develop my work in the Arts, to develop myself as a powerful magnetic human being, to reach out to those in need of understanding honest love and direction; and also, to be "Free," and to be able to act upon my choices, whatever they may be!

This is the Cycle that "separates the men from the boys," and "the women from the girls!" A young man "stops toying with his life and playing with the boys," and a young woman "sheds her giggles and doubts to plan her future." One cannot ignore, avoid, or escape, the multiple "Changes" that occur during the 4th Cycle; they can only be challenged by these changes.

At that time, my intended and passionate thought was; "Now that I have established myself as a person of 'Choice,' I am able to trust my choices!" The evaluation and its process provided me with a grounded self-confidence that surely challenged **ME** to "Trust myself if I dare!" I had a choice: My dare was "To be A fool or to be **ME**." Is it because of "That place in my Mind I call *Happiness*," and my trust of self-confidence and *choices* made, that I allowed myself, and actually did 'Dare'?" I believe so.

Maybe it is because of my obsession with the multiple ideas and theories of "Time" and my experiences, that I have come to believe, that *Happiness* does exist! But it is not merely *discovered* nor is it *gifted*. The two facets of this brilliant diamond is that "It is *Realized* and It is *Earned*." And before that can happen, one must have the desire to embrace and learn the understanding of humility, sacrifice, love, humor, and foremost, humanity and *The Life*. And once it is learned, we must try our best to live within that state of being or consciousness on a daily basis. That is when you will know, that *Happiness* does exist, in a place or within a space of your understanding. What is being offered to us to seek and find happiness aside from religion, our relationships, children and delusive careers? It is the abyss of our gluttonous consuming habit of "buying happiness" to satisfy our monetary wants whenever we are feeling *dispirited* and *down*, causing the overwhelming factors of stress, anxiety, and cost, to those of us who cannot afford this route to *Happiness*! But still, we buy and buy again, hoping to affirm and celebrate that we are no longer sad, depressed or dispirited! This illusion of fulfillment for many of us is a mental disordering of priorities, and is simply a "bandage" to soothe our wounds. Therefore, those of us who are *self-determined, confident, wise* and *challenging*, can consider following the "Whatever it takes" route or way to happiness; thereby avoiding the dismal abyss of *buying* and the aforementioned conventional routes to seeking and finding your happiness! For one to follow the "Whatever it takes" route or way to happiness, one must be self-determined, must evaluate and track the specific positions they are in at this time in their lives and consider the trail of: "Where I've been, Where I am today, and Where am I going/or Want to go." A trail that many supporters have helped you pave, but this new one is solely on **YOU**! My wise young people, you must remember that *The Life* and **YOU** are treading on a "Tightrope" of a fragile and delicate balance of these two realities; and it is **YOU**, lovingly carrying *The Life* on your back! And the attempt to walk-it demands *Faith, Dare,* and *a thread of Acceptance.* Above all, be alert!

The last half of the 4th Cycle is a period in the self-evaluation process that one must give full attention to because it is a critical point of "Determination" as to the direction that one needs to take or adhere to at this formidable crossroad or turning point of *The Life.* This period of the Cycle that one must endure, "will challenge every fiber of your body and every honest thought, of the real needed 'Change' that you will undergo." But maybe, by this time in your very young life you are already or likely to be, "Trapped" or lured, by the conventional routes to happiness because of your already decided personal commitments and possible substantial goals! Already trapped by marriage, children, career plans, or... "Whatever"! Its o.k., no need to panic! But I advise you to evaluate your present position your passions and goals as to "Who You Want To Be, and Where You Want To-Go!" I mention this little narrative because of the actual route or "Trap to Happiness" that I was into during this Cycle. The dedicated and committed performing artist that I was "back-in-the-day," was not the initial passion of my soul; I was a fortunate young man, successful, talented and fascinated with my work in the music business. But there I was "Trapped", in the sweet nectar of its lifestyle and glamour. And the "Inspiration" of my soul's passion was being ignored or denied daily, being distracted, consumed and interfered with! And although "living" each day in the glory of a "real live dream," my sublime passion within waited patiently for me to escape this elusive "Trap" that interrupted the true and personal attitude of my desired growth and development, for and towards the needed focus and studies to discover **ME**. This was my soul's passion then. When I did finally "escape," and evaluated the "trap-syndrome," I realized with acute clarity that, "Happiness was not out there, but here, within **ME** and where **I** am."

For those of you who are honest, and find that you are being caged or are in a position of being "Trapped" by a plan that you have already made, let's be "Real" and confront the fact that some newer adjustments will have to be made in your case. "Newer plans" of your trapped position will have to be "arranged differently" and the original plan will have to be "Let Go." It is a critical time for you to "Trust" **YOU**! It is the moment in your life to believe (or disbelieve) in your self-confidence and your abilities; and you must make the attempt to dare! The discerning "In Your Face" honest truth and confrontation that will occur is an absolute requirement for those who are *strong-willed, courageous, confident,* and *fearless,* in this battle of the conventional thoughts of *Happiness,* its attainability, and its "Permanence". This profound challenge and method to self-evaluate is for those who comprehend the words I write and have the "need" to explore the superlative wonders of truly establishing self-identity and free choice; and also, who are wise enough to know that they have their own personal key to the "Trap-Door"! I advise **YOU** to use it. Remember to try and anchor this explicit advice somewhere within your orbit of everyday thought that "this is final!" This is the "Do It Now or Never!" Cycle. This is **YOUR** self-owned responsibility! And for whatever reasons actions are not taken (but without guarantee), you may possibly have the second and "last chance" at the onset of the 5thCycle.

CHAPTER SEVEN

Unexpectedly, "The Dance" became the "New Change" in my life. It became the *New Passion, the New Purpose, and the New Horizon*, for me; And I would have never known, had I not dared. It was in 1971, a mid-September day in Cambridge Massachusetts. I had begun classes in social studies of an extension course being offered at Harvard University. By this time of my 4th Cycle, the exploration of self-identity and adventure to find **ME** continued. Art school, theatre school, social studies, The G-Clefs and the family and wonderful friends still didn't satisfy my "Need" for purpose and being. The G-Clefs had completed their successful engagement in Japan, and had decided that Boston would be their established base and they would accept engagements blanketing the East Coast thereafter.

I had left the study hall and began my walk across campus towards the Charles River. Blaring rhythms were dancing in the air and being pounded out loudly on drums, bells and shouting, chanting voices; enough so to make me stop and listen to find out where this blare of music was coming from! I followed the rhythmic sounds to a large gymnasium with its doors flung wide open, exhibiting an "Afro-Jazz Dance Class" for spectators and all passers bye to see and join in if they liked!

"Ooooh! You must come in my brother and join us with all that you've got going out there!" a beautiful brown-skinned young lady said to me; touching her scarf to her dampened face that was as keenly-chiseled, as I had seen in the art paintings and imagery of Pharaoh's ancient Egypt. Her exotic eyes were the color of chestnuts and finely shaped like those of a Siamese cat. Reaching out her hand to me she said, "Hello, my brotha, my name is Nana."

I had been standing at the open doors in front of the other enthused spectators and apparently, from within the class, she could see me and my body moving accurately and following the rhythms being pounded out on the African drums.

She came to me and invited me in. "Oh, no thanks," I said to her, "I'm just watching." She took two steps closer and got right up in my face! Her warm insistent voice convinced me of the truth. "You're not watching, my brotha," she said, "Look at you! You're *dancing*! Now, get in here!"

Halifu Osumare; Master teacher, scholar, and author was conducting this organized, highly-spirited dance class of pulsating energy and sweat. Her most recent book of dance knowledge (published 2018) is entitled "Dancing In Blackness, A Memoir."

I witnessed an amazing display of physical abilities! Earthy, and raw, warrior-like primitive body movements; quick, dashing, leaping across the gymnasium floor and jumping high into spaces never touched or reached before! I watched, mesmerized, as inspiration manifested in its highest form: *Spiritual.* Halifu's voice was masterly, always encouraging their efforts and praising the pride and power of their high achievements; and often she'd scream out at a proud "YES!" at you if you excelled in her specific given movement. To observe wasn't enough for me, and "Nana's" Siamese cat eyes could see that. She kept prompting me to participate, saying, "Halifu's waiting for you, my brotha!" After two or three of her prompts, my shoes came off so easily my bare feet to began their moves across the floor to join Halifu and her novice dancers. No trembling, no fear, "just do!" as I did with Thassos at the Greek Taverna, was my last and only thought. She welcomed me into the group simply with her long arms outstretched to me and her long nimble fingers and wrists rolled inwardly, beckoning me to dance. With the drums pacing in a slow, syncopated rhythm, I moved with the rhythm into the dance circle and then to its center for a solo dance. An "ecstatic wave" swept over me; "Cool, feeling like a new kind of 'love' unfelt before." I could feel my body absorbing it, and taking in something "Fresh, New, and Nourishing."

Every muscle from head-to-toe suddenly became energized by this loving wave, sparking the fire within to ignite and make my body glow with the desire and feeling to *naturally* gyrate, bend, stretch and dance to every rhythm, beat and sound it heard! Never had I felt like this, nor had I ever felt so "Free" to do what I was meant to do so naturally...Dance! Thereafter, my life was totally consumed day and night 24/7 with classes and the study of Afro-Jazz dance, it's music, my yoga practice, and The G-Clefs.

Soon, "I was dancing," and became one the principle dancers in Halifu's newly organized dance company of Afro-Jazz dancers, poets, and musicians. I felt blessed and grateful to have the opportunity to be amongst a company of such talented artists who shared with one another their artistic skills, their passions and loving friendships; along with the hard work that we produced together from our long moments of *Joy and Love* and all derived from and for, the elusive "Spirit of The Dance." The company's concepts on dance, cultures, and peoples, were always brilliantly executed, choreographed, realized and performed; but that being said, "at the end of the day," nothing excited or thrilled me, as much as the performances did!

Waiting backstage or in the wings for my cue to make an entrance onto the stage with the corps of dancers; eight to ten professionally-skilled drummers and percussionists would push the dynamics of their rhythms and songs from the lowest of tempos to mild and exhilarating great heights! They would be shouting out "Ilanga, Ilanga" repeatedly, as I was dancing with my body and Soul, in a solo performance.

One day at rehearsal I asked Victor, a drummer from South Africa. "What are you guys always shouting out when I'm dancing?" "Aaah, yes!" he began;" 'Ilanga' is a word from the country of Zimbabwe, and it means 'The Sun'" he said. "So my brotha; when you come onto the stage, we must shout "Ilanga" with force and in a strong powerful sound that's stronger than the drums!" He laughed and raised his voice slightly; "And, why do we do that… because when you come onto the stage, you light it up maan! You make it bright and shining like the sun! We like that very much!" he said warmly, with a flashing white smile on his black tribal-scarred face. "You do what the Sun does to people; You make them happy, smile and feel good, maan!" Victor said. Eventually, the entire company and friends referred to me as 'Ilanga.' Halifu decided to base the company in Oakland, California. After a year in Oakland; and between The Dance and The G-Clefs, I had to "Decide, Dare, and Do" the necessary. I legally had my birth name changed from Arnold A. Scott to what it is today, 'Ilanga' (one name only).

I returned to Boston from Oakland to announce to my family and The G-Clefs that I would be leaving for "Somewhere" in due time. That thought of "Somewhere" was in Europe. I knew that I had to begin the pending process of emotional and physical "Detachment" from family, The G-Clefs, and friends; This was my major concern, because throughout *The Life* and my career, they all have always been my ultimate support. I must declare, that because of my "Understanding" and studies of the Hatha Yoga ideology, I was able to detach from my major concern and diminish the thoughts of my "Selfishness." I Understood and accepted, that at this pivotal time of my life I had completed my role duties and responsibilities to my family, The G-Clefs, and loving friends; and as in my usual travels, the actual "physical detachment" was to be temporary, and the "emotional detachment" would have to be learned in time. And as well; I knew that I had to "establish a balance" within myself, and *not* enhance or encourage any remaining residue thoughts of Ego, its influence, and its unwelcomed "Selfishness." Six months later, I left the United States to live in Europe "Somewhere" to work my artistic abilities, meet peoples of the world, be adventurous, and discover who this "Ilanga" guy was. He has quenched his thirst of all passions and desires, earned "Happiness" and is still in the pursuit of "Something-Else."

As a professional singer, dancer, choreographer, actor and model, I felt confident enough to find work in my extensive trailblazing career and efforts in the Arts; and due to the organizational responsibilities I had taken upon myself to operate and maintain The G-Clefs career, my administrative skills were also an asset in my bag of tools. So, I was professionally prepared to do whatever needed to be done, and mentally prepared to do it well, and without the anxiety and fear of not succeeding. My personal preference was to be alone, to be unknown, and to "Become." It was my desire to embark on this new life adventure and hurl myself into the "Unknown" strictly in pursuit of "Self;" it had nothing to do with anyone else. I admit that although I worked hard at a balance, a slight residue of "Selfishness" remained.

I left the United States without work references or European contacts purposely to begin and establish my own network of friends and associates. I settled myself in the interesting city of Amsterdam, The Netherlands. At that time, it was the mecca in Europe for artists who came from around the world to be free in spirit and to seriously do their work. Soon after my arrival, I began to circulate within the artist's community and became very selective and discriminating of my new associates and any soon-to-be-new-friends.

Arriving in Amsterdam in the month of June enabled me to investigate the city throughout the Summer months and decide whether to go to Paris, France or to remain there in Amsterdam and wait for September's business cycle to begin. During the Summer vacation months, most schools and businesses were closed. I remained in Amsterdam, exploring the city's unique architectural design, the ambiguous Dutch thought, and felt that the freedom of artistic expression did exist here! I Settled in, renting an upstairs room from a wonderful elderly Dutch couple who had the table set for three and dinner "promptly" at 6 p.m! Aside from my intuition, this was my first signal of regimentation and compliance that I was asked to undergo here, and I decided I had to immediately defend my personal independence and lifestyle! I Explained to both of them that I could not be a part of this traditional Dutch nightly dinner ritual because "first of all, I'm a dancer, and also do Yoga," I said politely. "We don't eat dinner like normal people do! We eat a lot - and good wholesome meals - but only when we're hungry, and that could be every couple of days!" I said in a matter of fact voice. Lynn and Dick sat still in their chairs, their wrinkled-skinned faces frozen and pasted with a baffled look of bewilderment, a puzzle of confusion, and said nothing. "And the second thing is," I continued,

"It seems that the food here doesn't agree with my digestive system. It's like raw meat, tasteless and bland! I guess it's good, but not for me, my stomach or my mind," I said as tactfully as I could. Dick said something to Lynn in their Dutch language which she told me the next day; "He's a good man, not crazy, but he's very strange!" was his remark about me. She agreed with him; but nevertheless, being a reasonable and humorous woman, she laughed; and we all learned how to live together under the same roof with the mutual understanding that "Differences" can, and do work by listening and observing.

Three weeks after my arrival in Amsterdam, my dear, wonderful Mother passed away at 70 years of age, burdened with the illnesses of Parkinson's Disease and Alzheimer's, she left. The evening I received this devastating news, I had arrived home about 11 p.m. after being out networking with friends at a social hang out called the "Melkweg," an infamous multi-media and performance center located in the "Leidserplein," a well-known city square that is a throbbing heartbeat of Amsterdam. As I approached the house where I was living, I noticed the parlor lights shining through the windows. This was unusual because "lights-off" at 10 p.m. was Lynn's standard rule; for her, the night was over for both of them after the television programs ended and signed off at 9 p.m! Only a small night light would be left on in the downstairs foyer for me to make my way through and up the stairs. I entered the house, climbed the narrow stairs and noticed that their bedroom light was still on; and as I stepped into the parlor they were both sitting in their separate chairs staring out the windows into the dark night and lit street lamps of the roadway we lived on called the "Middenweg" located on the east side of the city; (so vividly-clear and indelible is this night's lasting memory).

"Wow, you guys are up so late!" I said, shocked and surprised, and still slightly buzzed from an earlier hit on a joint, but I continued. "I won't disturb you here, I'll just say goodnight; I'm going upstairs to do some Yoga; and don't worry, Lynn, I won't forget to blow out the candle!" Every morning, another Lynn-ritual; she would ask me if I had blown out the candle from the night before. "Wait!" Lynn said softly; "Your sister Karen called, and wants you to call her when you come in; It's about your Mother." I said quickly, "Oh, okay; I'll call her. My mother's health has been failing a bit I know, so this is all about that! I'll take my bags upstairs and come downstairs and call her!" There was only one telephone in the house, which was located in the parlor. When I returned about ten minutes later, Lynn and Dick were still frozen in their chairs, sitting up erect and still in their pajamas and still staring out of the large bay windows, as if they were witnessing a glorious 6 p.m. sunset!

I heard no words being exchanged between them as I was in the kitchen boiling hot water, preparing for a cup of tea. I entered the parlor slowly, balancing in both hands toasted bread, tea and my daily agenda book, when Lynn immediately said, "Hey, will you call your sister so that we can go to bed!" Surprised, I took a chair to sit, "Oh, you guys don't have to stay up! Karen and I will be chatting for awhile, I'm sure! I'll tell you in the morning how things are! And besides, there's nothing more to see out those windows! You old guys know that on this side of Amsterdam the streets have been folded up now for hours!.. Go to bed, it's almost midnight!"

Dick turned away from the window and looked at Lynn. After a long pause, her pale sad-face looked over to me. "Ilanga," she said; "Your mother died today, and that's what your sister wants to tell you! And, she said it was okay if I told you when you came in! Dick and I are so sorry for you because we know how much..." I interrupted Lynn; and being in a complete state of shock, I blurted out nonchalantly, "Oh, that's okay with me, thanks! She's been ill for so long now, just suffering and enduring it all with no complaints; She'll be fine now, that's for sure!" They both were "stunned" with what came out of my mouth and just stared at me, as I lifted my cup for a sip of tea. Peering over the rim of my large cup, I could see that perplexed look of bewilderment again on their faces, this time expressing sincere concern; and I knew that I needed to say "something" to assure them both that they needn't worry about me. "Believe me, Ilanga is fine!" I said, "So don't think that I'm not! You guys go to bed! I will call Karen and make my flight arrangements to Boston, and let you know tomorrow when that will be!" Jokingly I added, "And don't worry, my Spirit will still be here with you guys while I'm gone," I quietly chuckled; they didn't. I began to engage myself into making the Boston telephone call; and as Lynn and Dick were slowly leaving the parlor, they were conversing in Dutch, quickly sharing words back and forth and most likely, discussing my unusual state of mind!

Suddenly I was alone, and before dialing the telephone, I could feel myself bracing for an emotional conversation that would keep me awake and up for the rest of the night. Karen's telephone rang and rang but there was no answer. While sitting there waiting to call again later, naturally, thoughts of my mother and her life, her children, and my dear loving father, who passed away seven years earlier was all that I could think about. These thoughts stampeded and rambled through my mind for the next half an hour, until I tried again.

"Oh, Ilanga, I knew you were going to call about now", Karen said. "I'm sure that Lynn told you about Ma; didn't she?" I replied "Yes" and waited for her saddened voice to continue; "We're just getting back from the morgue now, so I'm about to start dinner; but I'm glad you called now, because tomorrow we'll be going to the funeral parlor to make some primary arrangements, so your timing is good! But, when do you think you'll be coming in?" and she tagged it with "Well, that's if you're coming to Boston!" It was her tag line that suddenly made me think, "Why did she say that?" That is a thought and words that only my mother would say to me. "Of course, I'm coming in! Why would you even say that craziness?" I bluntly asked her. "Well, you know," she said quickly, and paused… "You're just arriving there and settling in, and knowing you and how you do things when you focus on something, networking and stuff, things come together for you very quickly! I'm just saying, that to come here may interrupt everything you're doing there now and preparing before the work really begins for you in September, you know." The words I was hearing were clearly from her mouth, but her voice and tone had suddenly changed, it was different, it was now that of my mother's! "Are you there?" she asked, after my long silence. Again, she asked, "Ilanga, are you still there?" I answered with the need to attest to our bonded honesty; "Karen," I asked; "Do you believe, Ma is dead?" Waiting for an answer, I heard nothing. It was my turn then, to interrupt her silence with "Are you there…?" "Well you know," she said, "You and Ma have a special thing about all that stuff. That's why I said, "*If* you're coming in!" Do what you think is best, and let me know. If you don't come, we'll be fine," she said convincingly; and then ended with a tearful sound in her voice, "Ilanga, we understand!" We didn't need to talk any further but before hanging up the telephone, I needed from her the answer to my question. "Wait, don't hang up!" I said, "You didn't answer my question! Do you believe that Ma is dead" is what I asked you, but you didn't answer!" Her instant reply was, "Oh Ilanga, don't be silly!" But again, with my mother's sound and voice and words that she would say to confirm a mutual belief, which would actually mean, "Yes, I believe that too, dear!"

Because of our explicit bond of trust, I expected the reply from Karen to be a "Yes or No" answer! But, that didn't happen; she didn't give me a direct yes or no answer! But as my mother and Karen both knew, "Jibberish" and a million questions would pour from my mouth, and about to prepare dinner, she didn't have time for all of that! "Well, my sister," I said; "You know me and my silliness, and I just don't believe she's dead, that's all!" Karen's silence meant that she was waiting for more "silliness" to come forth - and I knew that - so instead, I let it go and I threw her a curve-ball and said, "Okay, I know that you've got to run, so let me see... tomorrow I will check on flights and everything and I'll call you in the morning, Boston time!" Abruptly, she said, "Oh, good! I have to go now, I gotta do dinner; and tell Lynn and Dick, 'Thanks'! Okay, we'll talk tomorrow. See ya, love ya, bye!" Her hasty goodbye left me knowing that our conversation was over, and anticipating the long night alone and the emotional thoughts to come, I said "Ciao!" and hung up the receiver slowly, ending the Boston call to my sister.

Climbing the stairs to my attic room quietly with soft tears flooding my eyes was a difficult climb. Its only purpose was to get

me from where I was to where I wanted to be; alone and away from
the opaque and disturbing downstairs-reality.

My yogic-behavior had me lighting candles, trying to do Asanas
and meditate to no avail; it was impossible to concentrate. Sitting at
my desk, I pulled out my usual writing pad to write "something" or
"anything." I was becoming anxious; I needed to have an immediate
focus, so I began writing a letter to Karen; why, I don't know. As I
was putting words to paper, my mother's loving presence suddenly
entered the room. There was no visual apparition, but all within me
became calm and I could sense her "Presence" there, next to me. The
frustration and struggle to find the right words and her presence,
caused me to stop my attempt to writing more.

"You don't need to come see me, you know that," I heard her
voice calmly saying. "I am here, with you now; if you go, this is what
you will see." My wet eyes opened to a sudden beauty! "My mother
was resting peacefully in a casket, her skin glowing with health,
and a smile on her face that revealed the traces of her time here with
us and how she loved every day of it!" Immediately I shut my eyes
tight from what I was seeing. It was a brief vision, unexpected, and
seemingly beautiful in its own privilege, that vanished when she
began to speak again. "What you have just seen with your own eyes,
is what you will believe if you go," she said; "But what you believe in
your heart is where I am, silly!" After that was said, I felt that she was
smiling; warm, knowing, and with a nature of unusual intelligence.
And I could feel that somehow "she knew that I understood that!" I
waited to hear more, I needed to hear more, I thought. I waited, but
she was no longer there with me; she had gone. I continued writing
long into the night and it was well after daybreak before I blew out
the candle and thought about closing my eyes for some much-needed

sleep. It was not until noon that I awakened to find papers and all of what I had written lying on the desk. My letter to Karen, I found out later, became the Eulogy read at my mother's funeral in Boston.

A couple of hours later, I went downstairs to make the impending telephone call to my sister. Lynn and Dick had finished lunch and were sitting in the parlor; he gazing out the large bay windows and she, pretending to be reading the news-paper. "Goedemorgen!" I said. It was one of the first words I had learned in the Dutch language, meaning "Good Morning." Lynn had a sarcastic sense of humor in her style of delivery and said, "Het-Neuw, et Smeerdags, youngen!" (It is now the afternoon, young man)! and continued, "You were up late! Your light was on in your room when I went to the bathroom this morning; you didn't sleep?" In my haste, I said to her quickly, "No, yes! I mean, this morning I did; Now, I have to call Karen to let her know that I'm definitely not coming to Boston!" I then went over to the telephone to make my call. Dick's English vocabulary and understanding was not as keen and sharp as Lynn's and he slowly turned his puzzled face to her and raised both his hands in frustration, "Ik begriep et niet! Wat Zeckt he?" he questioned. "Oh Dick, shut up! You don't understand anything!" Lynn snapped at him; "He said, that he's going to call his sister now and tell her that he's not going to Boston!" And then with her sarcastic eyes fixed on him for a second or two, she lowered her lids and slowly plunged her face back-into the newspaper and again pretended to be reading. As I was dialing and overhearing their guttural Dutch quibbling, I began to think to myself, "Ilanga, you and your madness have jammed the minds of these two wonderful people long enough! Maybe it's better to find a new living situation, fast!"

"Goede Morgen," sister love!" I said to Karen. She busted out laughing at my Dutch greeting, chewing on a bite of food at the same time, I continued; "Oh, you're still having breakfast, so I won't hold you; listen, I'm just letting you know that I won't be coming in. After a long night of thinking and writing I've decided not to go." I paused to hear from her; "Oh, okay," she said with the bite of food still in her mouth. "Well, you know what's best to do. I'll let everyone know that you're too busy, and... don't worry, we all understand what you're doing there." The Dutch quibbling had stopped, and I noticed Dick and Lynn listening intently as I continued, "Yea, I know; everyone understands and knows me, but Karen, my real concern are the kids (my young nieces and nephews), I want to be there, only for them; they are as close to me as I am to Ma, you know!" She replied softly, "I know, I know." "But listen," I said; "I'm leaving the house now and going to the Post Office! I'm mailing you a letter that I wrote to you last night. I read it when I woke up a couple of hours ago. Wow, it's strange; but I feel good, not sad, and... I'm fine!" I said with honesty. She believed and trusted that I was fine and that I was doing the best thing for myself. Before she hung up the telephone, she assured me that she would do her best to bring comfort to the family and friends because of my absence; and the letter I sent was decided by the family to be the Eulogy. Still to this very day, I have not read that letter again, nor have I ever given it a thought after that! Apparently, I dismissed it from my thoughts the moment it was sent. The soft, sad tears that trickled down my face that delicate night, never happened again that way; That was the last time the sadness and grief lived with me for one long night. I did not like that feeling; but it was there within me; and it was necessary in order for me to release my sweet, sweet mother.

The stories that I am writing here, are not fantasies or fiction, but "Realities" that I perceived through my five physical senses that I consciously co-exist in every day. "It's been a lifelong thing." For those of you who are reading these words and are able to relate to my differences in conventional thought, perception, and maybe, even to some of my experiences (even one, for that matter!) you are "There" also, every day, all day, existing "Elsewhere" and "Here" as well."

Believe me, it's okay to give that a thought now and then, if you haven't yet; and if you have, be more conscious of it, more alert, and try to follow through with the thought, its process, and the evaluation from its root to "the very moment" now! I suggest you consider the one profound question that you need to ask **YOU** and that is, "Why is it, that 'This' is happening to me, now?" I assure you, by critical self-evaluation, self-love and honesty, your personal questions will be answered in time.

CHAPTER EIGHT

September 1975 came, and I began my work teaching and developing my afro-jazz dance technique, learning the Dutch language, living and being "foreign" amongst new friends new and different kinds of people - all appearing to be living harmoniously together in a new "Old World." After my first year of residency there, I had established myself well with the dance community and found a productive rhythm to follow in my everyday work and play. From my disciplined practices of dance, yoga and meditation, I became more focused, centered, and balanced, to finally arrive at the surprising knowledge that "I was in charge"! It was now my life to live, my own show, and that "I was the Director and the Producer!"

This new knowledge, being separated from the egotistical values of self, I felt had to be applied with my genuine natural persona, humility, honesty, and of course, with a smile! It was **Me** that had to represent "Ilanga" all day, every day! Naturally, I had to question myself and my intelligence; "Was I psychotic?" My answer, "No; just "Realized"!"

The 3rd and 4th Cycles demand the need to recognize and explore the *beauty* of all things people and places; not the *ugly* that exists within us and around us and that can be seen or experienced at any time or anywhere! Therefore; It is because of *self-evaluation* and the fact, that by this time in *The Life* we already know the importance of *choice, consequence* and *acceptance*. I discovered within the year, that the *ugly* of Amsterdam was parallel to its *beauty* and abundance of artistic value; therefore I chose to explore its beauty, and to accept and protect myself from its ugly.

The technology and social media that we have today did not exist during these Cycles; The landline telephone cables and Western Union telegrams were our only mode of instant communication at that time. For many travelers such as myself, either of these two options were a financial expense that I had to consider and demanded "serious" emotional self-control before choosing whether or not to communicate! "There was nothing more heartbreaking than knowing that I couldn't make a telephone call that day and had to wait in forlorn anguish and frustration to speak to and hear a distant voice of a family member or a loving friend. The "physical detachment" that I had to undergo had been totally accepted by this time; but the dormant and stifled "emotional energy" that I was unable to detach from engulfed my every day. This burdensome energy I had fortunately channeled into creativity and innovative displays of my work in the Dance, and other art works that I became heavily engaged in throughout Amsterdam, Brussels and Paris.

Aside from an emergency, placing a telephone call to the United States was always a second thought; corresponding via letter writing and post cards was "the way to go!" I found this emotional outlet to be the main and most reliable source of communication for the personal touch that was so desperately needed at certain times.

Detachment from my family and friends in the United States did trouble me that first year. "Nothing and No One is Yours!" is a profound quote from Paramahansa Yogananda, author of *Autobiography of a Yogi*. My family, loving friends, work, and living a "positive" life, would be my daily emotional concern; and often during that year, there would be days or nights that this ever so wonderful feeling of "loving" would come to me and to "that place" I've earned called "Happiness." But the loving feeling would not last long; eventually, the "negative energy" of honest "Emotional Attachment" would surface! Immediately, I'd stop all motion, reflect, and hear his words, again; "Nothing and No One is Yours" always brought calmness to me. His discourse on Ego includes this lesson of detachment, and "Why."

I will emphasize here; "These are the only two Cycles" that are full of signals, red flags, opportunities, and great possibilities, for those who can recognize within themselves the need for *Self-Identity* and/or *Self-Evaluation.*

An alertness and a "heads-up" is required at all times to be receptive and open-minded to this new and abundant flow of natural, positive energy that **YOU** alone have conjured-up for yourself and it is surrounding you daily with whatever information and guidance you may need. It is "There" within you, waiting for you to tap into it! With this exercise you can mentally condition yourself to receive this physical energy. You may be asking; "How will I know, or What will I feel?" when this new source of natural positive energy is surrounding you, asking you to self-evaluate, reflect, and analyze, for self-identification. This is an excellent "loaded" question that certainly deserves an honest answer; but, "it's not for me to answer." It is a question that **YOU** will answer "Honestly" and soon enough! The "Mirror Exercises Method" that I have included at the end of this Chapter is a method and a simple daily discipline that I encourage you to exercise and to experience. This is precisely what you have to do to find the absolute Truth and Essence of "That answer."

Although the interests of each particular individual will vary, I myself found that Amsterdam has a lot to offer a tourist or a newcomer who intends to live there. There are attractive lures socially and culturally throughout the day and night that can be entertaining as well as a danger to one who is naïve or vulnerable enough to be sucked in and caught in a web of dangerous activity with others who have made the choice to challenge and dare. It is also a city that offers and allows anyone of character and self-confidence to "ignore the ugly" and excel in your purpose of being "There."

A few days before my mother had Passed, Lynn had been very helpful. She knew of a person who operated a community center in a district called the "Beijlmermeer" just outside of the city's center. She had arranged a meeting for me with the person responsible for hiring staff for the activities being held for children and adults; my first job interview in a foreign country! The interview was cordial, the English language was a requirement and my professional presentation was a success. Explaining thoroughly my work as a dance instructor, how I would interact with both child and adult students, the technique of Afro-Jazz dance; and my intentions of permanently residing in Amsterdam, at least for an entire year. A mutual agreement transpired from that meeting, and I was to begin my new job there in September. Leaving the interview, I had only one thought on my mind; "to acquire reliable Percussionists."

Just in-front of the "Plenix Community Center", I caught the public transport bus heading back to the city's center, which was a bumpy and winding zig-zagged thirty minute ride. Before nodding off to sleep with satisfied thoughts of the interview, and my needed search for Percussionists, I felt my head being bounced up and down by "rhythmic" road bumps. Suddenly I was compelled to listen and give attention to haunting, but soothing, persuasive, percussive drums tempos and rhythms; sounding and gently playing in the background of my mind.

I awoke to the face of the bus driver standing over me and nudging my shoulder; "U moet heir weg, meneer!" he said. After hearing this Dutch-phrase many times riding public transport, I clearly understood that he was saying, "This is where you get off, Sir!" Upon entering the bus, I had told him in English where I was going in the city's center, and that if he knew the whereabouts of a small jazz club called the "BH" or "Bim House;" and that if he could stop anywhere near there and let me off, it would be fine! He said that he knew of the place and fulfilled my request by stopping nearby and calling out to me, "Meneer; this is where you must get off!"

On this unusually sunny day in Amsterdam, I was loitering about the city's streets admiring the Dutch architecture and the famous waterways or canals that are vital to the businesses and people who thrive on the genius of the Dutch waterways systems and their vital functions in The Netherlands. Traveling the narrow side streets and the miniature walking bridges that often crossed over small stagnated canals, I was in search of "The Bim-House," a supposedly small jazz club hidden or tucked away somewhere on one of these narrow winding streets located in the Market District, and I had heard that The Bim House was open in these early afternoon hours featuring a musical jam session and hosting the various local musicians of Amsterdam's jazz scene. Sounds of lively swing music was pouring out of one large rooms housing the performance stage and a long wooden bar, flocked with boisterous drinkers. There was also a smaller room adjacent to the entrance door which provided snacks, juices, pinball machine entertainment and a space for intimate conversations.

My immediate attraction was the performance stage and the ten musicians "jamming" together and struggling with the notes and rhythms that make and aspire to the music of jazz. I was sitting on a stool that I pulled away from the noisy crowded bar to a side corner of the room, absorbing this fine music, alone, and thinking that it was somewhat reminiscent of "The Jazz Workshop," a nightclub in Boston. Because of my "G-Clef" experience of clubs, sociability, and awareness of environment, I felt at home, comfortable and a familiarity here that made me think of my friends and family in Boston. After that hour-long jam session, another group of musicians were embarking onto the stage for their rendition of jazz music as I proceeded to wander away and explore the smaller room. Here, delicious flavored juices were being drunk, hashish joints were being rolled, and many small conversations were going on simultaneously.

I heard five different languages filling the room: Dutch, French, German, English and Surinamese, a mixture of Dutch and Cantonese that I had never heard before. Standing next to me at the juice bar, busy rolling a joint, a young brown-skinned man of about 18 years of age was in conversation and laughs with, I assumed his friend, speaking this language that had a Dutch influence. I was fascinated with his nimble fingers, quickly maneuvering their way to a perfect cigarette roll like I had never seen before! He took notice of my fascination, looked at me, and stated in English, but with a natural latin flair, "You are American, yes? I mean, you don't look American, but I can tell that you are!" Quite surprised at that comment, I answered "Yea; from Boston!" He held up his rolled effort in front of my face, "Nice, heh?" I had to agree, it was a work of art! The three of us laughed as he asked his friend for a light in Dutch, "Hept je een fuertje?". "Where are you from?" I had to question him; "You speak English so well! And that was Dutch you just spoke; but what language were you two speaking before that?" I asked. "Surinamese", he said; "I am from Suriname, South America!" was his proud answer. "He too!", making a finger gesture towards his friend standing next to him. "Oh nice!" I said "You are men of the Latin tropics!" I didn't know anything of Suriname, except for the fact that it was a small country somewhere in South America. It was later in our conversation that I was told it was a part of the Dutch Antilles colonies, and was granted its independence in 1975; the same year I arrived in Amsterdam. "This is my friend Punt, and I am Glenn," the young man said. "And you, your name?" Punt asked me bluntly as he reached his hand forward making the offer to share the joint with me and continued; "Here! Do you smoke, maan?" Punt asked in his Dutch-Surinamese accent; I answered, "Well, I never did until I got here three weeks ago... so, yea; thanks!" Admiring Glenn's exquiste work of art between my fingers he quickly interrupted my fascination; "So maan, what's your name?" Punt asked. "Oh, I'm sorry!" I said; "My name is "Ilanga!" as I took one hit from the joint and passed it on to him. "Oh, a nice one," he said; "Ilanga, nice-one!" he repeated. Within an hour's time, Glenn, Punt, and I discussed ourselves and discovered that we three were dedicated to music; Punt a bassist and Glenn, a novice Percussionist. "A Percussionist?" I loudly asked Glenn, and I followed that outburst with the story and purpose of my being in Amsterdam, The Plenix Center, and the search for percussionists to assist me in the dance classes that would be beginning in September. As I was thoroughly explaining to him and Punt how I would be using the percussionists in the dance classes, their structures, and how they are incorporated with the afro-jazz technique and the technique of Hatha Yoga, the facial expressions of both, were of interest to me, because they were so different. Punt's expression was that of "good news" and Glenn's was that of "pending fear, when I asked him if he had any interest in partaking in this year-long commitment. "Oh, Maan!" Glenn said apologetically and convincingly, looking me straight in the eye. "No, maan! I can't do that! No, no, I'm not that good! I'm just learning how to play! You're a professional dancer, maan!" A shadow of sudden disappointment must have flashed across my face, because Punt, a professional musician and member of "Solaat" a well-known Band based in Amsterdam, could see an opportunity for his friend's "dream of lifetime" suddenly fizzle, and he also understood well my own disappointment.

"Hey, maan!" Punt said, and making a gesture towards Glenn; "He's good! he just needs to learn some professional things, and he can be very good, if he..." Glenn interrupted, his face lit up by his "safety net" of self-confidence and Punt's acclaim of praise and approval. And from our conversations of his minimal, but definite trace of footprints in the garden of music, it was enough for me to know, that he had been walking that path to become a Professional. Then Glenn's face brightened even more and he said, "No problem, Ilanga!", he said; "I have friends who play congas, jembes, bongos, and bells, maan! I can speak with them and, maybe they would like to do it!" He ended this innocent plea with a beautiful smile on his face that read, "Believe me!" There was something about the sincerity in his warm sparkling eyes, his genuine honesty, and spiritual nature, that somehow stirred within me, my reliable Intuition (a.k.a. "gut feeling") and the knowing, that I would get an honest answer from him. If asked; "Can you play a beat! Can you play "clean" and keep a solid steady rhythm?" Without a thought or pause; his direct-answer was, "No maan; not the way you would like it!", and he then quickly looked to Punt for an affirmation on that.

Punt's up and down head nod told me that he agreed, but added; "No, he's pretty good but not strong with confidence yet, you know!" Punt, tightly squeezed his lips on the end of the joint, passed it to me, lowered his jaw, curled his lips into an oval shape, and exhaled rhythmic puffs of perfectly shaped circles of smoke rings. His eyes watched each puff of smoke until it faded thin and dissolved into the air. "He needs somebody like you, maan; he needs you!" Punt said; "A Professional!... you know what I mean!" And then he flashed at Glenn a wide smile of supportive friendship, showing his one gold tooth that I hadn't noticed before now. I didn't respond to Punt's comment; and for about a minute, no words passed between the three of us during the thick silence until Punt asked me, "Another juice?" and pointed to my empty glass. Saying nothing to Glenn, Punt walked over to the juice bar; purposely leaving Glenn and I alone, together in an even "thicker silence"!

Glenn, saying nothing; began to assemble his "art supplies" and roll another one of his "works of art." My thoughts were still harboring Punt's words of Glenn; and feeling sure enough of myself to say to him, "Glenn, I want to hear you play!" But within that moment, and before I spoke these words, the percussive drum rhythms that I was hearing on the bus ride began to sound again in my mind, but with more energy and passion! For me, this was a signal to speak; "Glenn, I want to hear you play!" Staring deep into his eyes and within him, I could tell from his facial expression that my words smashed in his face, hard! But ignoring this look of sudden fear, I continued to say "Can you join me at the Plenix Center one afternoon next week! And, bring your drums!" He immediately stopped his "artful roll" and slammed his eyes into mine, pleading; "Ilanga, I don't have any drums, maan," he said and paused. "O.K.; I have a set of small bongos, two heads, that came from a toy shop, maan!... I can't!" he pleaded. To hear "that" from him, for me, wasn't enough! My voice raised; "Bring those!" I demanded! "Or any old pot or pan with a good sound to it!" Glenn could see that I was serious and he burst out laughing! "O.K., maan! I'll think about it!" As Punt returned to us with our juice drinks and placed them on the table, Glenn and I told him what had just transpired between us and Punt's gold tooth flashed at me again, but he smiled much wider, and longer this time! Upon leaving The Bim House, we exchanged our telephone numbers and planned to meet one day the following week. Unexpectedly, that glorious day had blessed me with two new friends and a loving friendship that I cherish to this very day, some forty-three years later.

Because of the Summer vacation period, it had taken a week to make contact with the Director of The Plenix Center, regarding a date and time for an available rehearsal space. Once I did, the day came for me to call Glenn to inform him of this good news; ironically, it was the same day that my sweet mother passed away, as yet unknown to me.

It was just about noon when I made the call to Glenn and I could hear in his sleepy voice that I had awakened him, as his response was slow to recall "who I was and why I called" until I reminded his sleepy brain to recollect our meeting from the previous week and of our appointment to rehearse. "Oh yah-yah, Ilanga!" he responded with total recollection; and because of the vacation period, he was surprised that I was able to secure the rehearsal date! "Can we meet tomorrow afternoon?" I said to him, "at 3:00?" He hesitated, he stammered; "Well, ahh... maybe! Okay, I'll be there Ilanga; I like you, maan!" His voice revealed every touch of fear and doubtful confidence that any eighteen year old boy or girl would have. I reached out to him as best I could by saying, "Relax, my brother; You will be just fine for me, I'm "almost" certain; but we'll see tomorrow, now won't we?" That triggered his confidence enough for him to say, with effort "Yah maan, yah!" I believed what I had said; and he tried to believe it too; but actually didn't.

Hanging up the telephone receiver and exhaling a sigh of relief, I looked up and noticed that Lynn and Dick were pleased with what they could hear of the conversation between Glenn and I, and of what had transpired with The Plenix Center negotiations. "Bravo, Jongen!" bellowed Dick from his comfortable leather chair; and I, picking up new words here and there, easily replied in Dutch, "Ahh, dank U Wel, meneer!" As usual, Lynn's sarcasm sprayed across the parlor from the dining area where she was arranging her traditional weekly bouquet of fresh cut flowers. "Oh, Dick, listen to Jesus speaking very good Dutch! Bravo! she shouted; an American is finally learning!" They both had a good laugh; but not me. More annoyed than upset that she had referred to me as "Jesus" and, that "Americans were dumb"! Respectfully I said to Lynn; "I love that you guys are laughing because that's something good! Let's all laugh; but, "at what" and "why" are you laughing?" "Honestly, I don't know what you guys ate for lunch, but I am not Jesus"! And believe it or not Lynn, Americans can learn anything." Her sarcasm flared immediately, "Oh, come on! That's only if they want to!" she said, carrying in both hands her crafted Delft designed vase of flowers and briskly walking to a table near Dick to put them down. "What good is learning anything if you don't know what to do with it? They confuse everything!" she said, as if she was talking to the bouquet, and not to me. I got up from my chair to leave the parlor, deciding not to say anything, except, "O.K., Ciao! I have things to do upstairs; cleaning, and pulling some things together for this meeting tomorrow with the percussionist, and also to get in some time to do a bit of meditation," I said, and began to hurry out of the parlor. Dick chuckled at first, and then looked at Lynn, "Jesus is busy today!" he said, and continued enjoying his lonely chuckle. I had to stop in my tracks, and at the parlor door I turned around to say, "And, what's with this "Jesus" stuff all of a sudden?" I said with a tone of annoyance. Lynn, reaching for the newspaper and calmly taking her seat for her make believe read, buried her head in it and said, "Oh, stop it! Nothing, nothing! Dick thinks he's a comedian! Go upstairs, you're busy!" I did; I went upstairs and left the weird downstairs conversation where it all happened, downstairs! Tomorrow's afternoon meeting with Glenn preoccupied my thoughts as I prepared myself with the tools for work: dancewear, music, tape recorder, and the scribbled notes I had written and intended for him that were ideas for the class. Later in the afternoon I left the house with a packed bag of work tools and thoughts of my mother, her funeral, my brothers and family, all coming with me. I Quickly went down the stairs, saying only "Daag" ("Goodbye!") as I passed the silent two in the parlor, down to the foyer and out the door!

During my many walks and exploration of the antiqued city, done to gain familiarity - while networking at the same time - I met Benjamin Felixdal a well-known and well-established classically-trained dancer and choreographer who, during one period of his professional career was a principle dancer for "The Nederlands Ballet

Company." We first met in a street café located in the Jordaan neighborhood of Amsterdam. "Excuse me, you're from The States, aren't you?" he asked. I was slumped over a book, sipping on my first usual late-afternoon cup of "Cappuccino-Koffee" when Benjamin tapped my shoulder and politely excused himself. I turned around to see him standing there next to my table and said, "Yes, why?" and I instantly began to "check him out" accessing his vibe presence, demeanor, eye contact, words used, etc. This was my usual character search whenever I met a person for the first time, there in Amsterdam. At once I could feel that he picked up on my defensive vibe and said right away, "No, no, there's no problem. I just noticed that when you came in that you were a dancer; I am too!" he said. "I lived and danced in New York for a few years; that's how I could tell that you were from The States! My name is Benjamin!" He then asked if he could join me at the table. "Sure, have a seat," I said to him, "I am Ilanga;" and added as a precautionary measure, "I will be leaving shortly but, please sit until that time!" He did, and mentioned that he had seen me once before sitting at a café with friends in the Leidserplein and wanted to stop and introduce himself, but didn't want to interrupt. "I knew that I would see you again!" he said; "Amsterdam is a small village!" An interesting-looking young man, I thought; totally comprehends and speaks fluent English laced with a formal Dutch accent, my age, working in the same profession, and a good-character vibe, "Why not!"

Our café conversation comfortably flowed into at least three hours of discussing The Dance, The States, Boston and New York; It felt and sounded so good to hear again and exchange the New York City dancer's fun slang and use of words! We had good laughs and interesting stories of other dancers we both had known in New York, training at Dance Theater of Harlem or at the Alvin Ailey school, and finding that we had very much in common. We agreed that our time together here at the café was of value to both of us in so many different ways and most-likely, meant to be! And we both, somehow feeling and understanding that "there is a scope and depth to our meeting one another here in Amsterdam that is yet to be nurtured and known," and that being here together today is fate; "This is not a Coincidence!"

Empty cups of Cappuccinos pushed aside to a far corner of the table, along with a couple of Brandy glasses that Benjamin had emptied is when I noticed the time. "I think that I need to start heading out of here, my Brother! It's not late but, I just need to get going," I said. His eyelids were a bit lowered by now, but he said without slurring his words, "Yes, yes, me too! But wait, I'll roll one last joint for us together and we can exchange our telephone numbers Ilanga, because we have to keep in contact! I think we've still got a lot to talk about! And also, you must come by my dance studio!" he said. "It's on a boat, sitting on one of the canals not far from here!" To his surprise, my first reaction was my loud outburst, "On a boat!" I could not fathom the idea of a dance studio being on a boat unless it was a cruise ship or a very large yacht! Benjamin explained to me that it was a small boat that he had converted into a small private dance studio to personally train selected students for a dance company that he would be organizing in the coming school year.

Benjamin looked at his watch; "My God!" he said, "it's almost 7 O'clock! I have a rehearsal tonight at 8 O'clock with a duo; twin girls whom I think may be my future proteges," he said with pride. "You're welcome to come with me if you have the time!" he said, lighting the last joint.

The cautionary "red flag" of danger that would often wave at me when a first meeting and invitation such as this happened, didn't signal, and I considered the invitation to go with him. And when he blew a long stream of white smoke from between his lips and said; "And, you can leave whenever you like, because Tram-line # 17 (The Trolley) will take you directly to the Middenweg, where you live!" I liked what he said, and felt no anxiety or thoughts, warning me that "this wasn't the thing to do"!

We left the café and began our walk to his studio on a boat floating on a canal. "How can you smoke two joints, have two Brandies and still walk straight and run an 8 O'clock dance rehearsal?" I asked him as we walked; "Oh, Dit is niet normaal!" he adamantly said in Dutch, and then in English; "I don't usually do this." But this is our Summer break, no classes, time to be free and "Be"! Also, I think meeting you today makes me feel good to do this! We've been talking, laughing and "traveling" without leaving that café! If we hadn't met, I would be home or at the studio working on the rehearsal notes; (you know the routine Ilanga) and the usual 24/7 "Passion" that lives inside of us artists, every day!"

We both walked in silence for a few steps, before he happily continued; "And tonight, the girls are dancing, I'm not! So I'm fine to conduct a rehearsal, demonstrate, then sit down, tap my baton on the floor for tempo, observe, and scream my ass off if I need to, from the chair. You know, like the bitchy Russian Ballet Master from The Bolshoi!"

We both staggered and howled in laughter for a good five minutes without taking a step forward! We were holding onto doorstep railings, rows of parked bicycles, and anything else standing, that could hold us up from falling on the brick street.

Still, at our sauntering pace, we finally arrived at Benjamin's boat-studio floating on the canal. At one time, before he had taken it over, it was a large cargo barge. He had gutted it and turned it into an open space large enough to choreograph for himself and work with not more than four to five dancers at a time. There was also a small office space, just large enough to fit a desk, a telephone, and a folding chair!

The rehearsal with the teenaged twin girls, Deborah and Daphne, went very well for him that evening. I admired his control of the work he designed and applied; being twins, the concept was of mirror reflection and elusive imagery. He was alert to each and every choreographed movement and demanded absolute precision from both girls who were being groomed and disciplined as protégé potential. In a certain section of his piece, he had them both mirrored as they balanced equally on a one footed Pointe; held powerfully strong for at least 10 seconds without a muscle or a twitching nerve to be seen! And he, sitting erect in his chair was watching this marvel also without a muscle or twitching nerve to be seen. He was intensely focused, engaged, and used explicit and precise word delivery. One would never know that he had "knocked down" two brandies and two joints within three hours, two hours before this remarkable rehearsal! I felt fortunate to be a witness to his classical skills that proved his notoriety in Europe and the dance world.

Benjamin tapped his black baton on the floor with three loud tempo beats! For he and his students, this clearly signaled a "dancer's break"; which is to rest for ten minutes, and most importantly, "not to forget what you just learned!" At this break I decided to leave; his studio clock was reading 9:35 P.M. "Wow, Benjamin; Bravo!" I said. "How fascinating your classes must be; thank you for this," the words coming from my heart and mouth so easily. "Ahh, Dank je wel!" he said; "Thank you for coming! So, what do you think of the studio?" he asked bluntly. Slowly wrapping and adjusting my signature scarf around my neck, I had to be honest and say only one word; "Brilliant!" His smile in return was also one of brilliance; and now, also shimmering with Dutch pride. While our eyes met I asked him in friendship, "Do you have a preference to be called "Ben, Benji, or..." He closed my question immediately by saying proudly and with a flair of elegance, "I am Benjamin!" "Of course you are!" I said to him with my smile. Before leaving, he said to me with a bit of excitement in his voice; "In September, I will be opening a very large studio with a Café-Bar; you must come by for a Cappuccino! We've got more to talk about!" "Sure, give me a call when it happens and I'll get there!" I said; and left the boat-studio for my pensive walk to Tram Line #17.

The "Take-Way" from this slice of the narrative, my wise young people, is that "what I discovered in Benjamin, is myself!" We were so relative in our self-identity, confidence, character, age, and choices made, that just like his creative choreography, we "Mirrored" one another in so many ways; and all this was discovered in a matter of a few honest hours together! It is because of this method of self-evaluation, analysis, and thought process, that I realized how valuable to both of us those few hours were; coming together that afternoon and early evening, along with four cups of Cappuccino-Koffee, two Brandies, two joints, and our honesty, all bonded together and encapsuled in a moment of truth that existed for us "To Be," "Realize," and "Act"!

This outcome of our relationship would have never occurred if he and I were not "self-identified, confident, determined, prepared, and honest"! If one is self-knowing, wants the qualities of life, and wants to excel, I advise that he or she must "Act" within the parameters of the 4th and 5th Cycles. There is no time for "delay!" Banish all thoughts of fear and any advice given to you that perpetrates fear; remember, that fear is only "a thought" so why think of it! "Alternative-thinking" plays an important role in the arena of thought; you must step "outside of the box" and process your thoughts of fear, and you will find that it is you who creates fear, and it is **YOU** who conquers it!

Tramline #17 screeched and howled its steel wheels for a short while, winding its way roughly through the night life and streets of Amsterdam to the Middenweg, where I lived. Arriving at the house and taking notice of the windows and the house lights still being on so late at night flashed a "red flag"! Dick and Lynn should be well into sleep by now! As written previously, this was the night of my 11 P.M. arrival home when Lynn had told me that my mother had passed away earlier that day; and when I went upstairs to light a candle and write my sweet mother's Eulogy.

My scheduled afternoon rehearsal the following day with the novice percussionist Glenn, was my priority; but aside from that my thoughts were of my family and the loss of a great woman.

The rehearsal studio at The Plenix Center was available to me any time after 12 P.M. and I arrived shortly after that. I was prepared; clothed in dancewear, with scribbled notes, a cassette tape recorder, a lit candle; trying my best not to be distracted by these haunting restless and lingering thoughts of Boston. "Nothing and No One is yours" came to mind! But I needed to focus on dance before Glenn arrived at 3 P.M.

I do not play piano; I do enjoy sitting at one and tinkling with one, two or three fingers on the black and white keys, which is what I was doing on the grand piano in a far off, dark corner of the studio, waiting for Glenn to arrive. I turned on the tape recorder to make a test for volume; and not being completely focused, I "accidently" left it on! I was doing my usual "tinkling" on the piano for about ten minutes, when suddenly a "wave of unsurmountable emotion flooded my vulnerable and unguarded mind, and I felt the drips of soft, wet tears falling down my face; not of sadness, but of "Something Else!" I found myself "not tinkling" but using both hands and ten fingers, playing and composing music that came out of nowhere! A one-fingered tinkle slowly and gradually evolved into a rhythmic rhumba tempo that was trying to ascend to a climax, but then didn't. The musical movement diminished again to a solemn meditative mood of tranquility and transcendence. My tears began to fall harder, yet without hurt and without a grieving pain! I was not in control; there was nothing I could do but let my fingers play! Helpless, mindless, and possessed, a melodious rapture suddenly began to creep into the movement as if it were coming from darkness, or a place that it didn't want to be, and began to spiral upwards! "Dance" is what it became, or is what it felt like! It moved and swayed and flowed with a passion and a sweet freedom! My fingers were dancing with the black and white keys, and then I saw a vision of myself dancing with Christine, my dear Mother. That's when I learned that tears never stop falling when you want them to; they just keep falling and falling and falling. Following through to the music's end, we stopped dancing, and I released her from my arms. But then; her powerful presence and beautiful physical form reappeared! She smiled at me, gave a slow gentle nod, and then suddenly, she left again. I wiped my eyes, took a deep breath and got up from the piano bench, and seeing the little red blinking light on the tape recorder signaling that it was still on and recording, I turned it off.

It is amazing my young people who are yet to measure true value; that this special cassette I've titled "Meditation to Christine" recorded forty-three years ago, is still in my possession! A family treasure, far beyond what I could ever imagine! And at this very moment, it is playing and sounding in my ears clearly, and sometimes even making my body quietly tremor.

I noticed the time, that I had about forty minutes before Glenn's arrival. I was mentally drained and physically exhausted from this "musical-meditation," and I needed to re-energize whatever energy was left in my body for this rehearsal. I turned on the cassette player again and put in a special cassette of music I had edited for classes, forcing myself to get into a bit of silence and Yoga to calm my anxiety. The first fifteen minutes of the cassette tape was tranquil music and thereafter, the rhythms and tempos of afro-jazz music began. This enabled me to absorb myself into the timeless moment of the music with body warm ups and dance stretches during the remaining time before Glenn's arrival.

Well into the music and my space, I was starting to dance full out, with my body "feeling" the musical moods dictated by the various tempos and rhythms. The musical dynamics would accelerate, evoking a sometimes "frenzied and wild" movement when hearing a powerfully high and exaggerated musical-phrase! Suddenly, "the rhythms I was hearing and dancing to were not in sync with one another, nor was the timing! Obtrusively, it kept throwing my timing off and the usual easy flow of movement kept constantly being interrupted by beats I had never heard in this music before!

The studio was at ground-level with panoramic wide-framed paneled windows, allowing views of green shrubbery, small trees and the outdoors. I stopped dancing to listen more closely to this obtrusive rhythm but it continued. I turned off the tape recorder, but it still continued! I was panting fast and hard from dancing and leaned against the piano to relax a bit. I took a few slow, deep breaths and then turned myself around to face the windows. Surprise! The obtrusive "other" rhythm I was hearing during the dance was Glenn, tapping his house keys on the window pane! Sometimes he was tapping in time, and sometimes not! I went to him at the front door. "Oh, man! Sorry; I forgot to unlock the door!" I said to him as he came in carrying his toy bongos and wearing a big wide smile on his face that couldn't hide his fear. Drenched in sweat, still breathing a bit heavy, and happy to see him and his bongos, I wrapped up quickly with a couple of dry scarfs and greeted him with a sincere wet hug. "Thanks for coming, it's good to see you! But, no pots or pans?" I said jokingly. We both laughed. "No!" he said seriously, "My rice pot didn't sound that good, maan! I tried to borrow some Congas from my friend, but he has a gig today, so I had to bring these," he said, lifting the bongos he had tucked under his arm. "Perfect!" I said; "They will work fine! Relax, find yourself a chair there by the piano and I'll explain and go over some written notes with you." I sensed his natural sensitivity and could feel that my professional presence possibly could be intimidating, so I tried my best to relax him from that; but Glenn had his own remedy for his new-found nervousness! "Do you mind maan, if I roll a joint to relax while we're talking about the notes?" he asked with a genuine respect for me I think, more so than for the studio. "Absolutely, go right ahead man! Blow those nerves away!" I said; hoping these words would help bring some calm. Digging down deep in his brown leather shoulder bag he came up with a tin box of "Samson Tobacco" rolling papers and a small block of Hashish. He broke off a small piece, lifting it to his nose and smelling it, "Ahh, from Turkey!" he said with such satisfaction! He started rolling, and stated, "Maan, looking through that window at you dancing! I could feel and see that you were really just "out there" with the Spirits, maan! Yah! I tried tapping on the window in rhythm and stopped because I could see it didn't work too good for you. And what's this music you're playing and dancing to? It's nice!" His thin nimble fingers continued rolling, wet- tonguing the edge of the paper; and I started talking.

"The music you're listening to is one of my specials! It is the musical score from the "African Ballet de Guinee," A touring dance/theater company that "blew my mind" Glenn! About six years ago they performed in Boston; The only thing I knew about them is that it was an international African dance company, and at that time I was very much into the cultures of Africa. I tell you man, it was the most spectacular performance of musicians and dancers that I've ever seen in my life, even until this day, honestly! And, believe it or not, I wasn't even into dance then, I was more into a music and theater scene, you know?!"

The African Ballet music had ended as Glenn lit up his long Amsterdam joint. I got up from the piano bench to change the cassette to another very special one from my treasured dance music collection. The music began just as he had taken a long deep "Turkish" inhale! He went into a heavy rolling cough, his lungs clogged with congestion! He kept coughing until he was able to say,

"What! Ray Barretto?" and coughed some more. "You're into Ray Barretto, Ilanga?" I answered, "Oh man, Barretto and the rest of the giants! Willie Colon, Celia Cruz, Tito Puente, and all that! Oh Yea, Glenn, this is the music I love and need and work with in my classes and choreographies; as well as jazz, Brazilian, Reggae, and music from many different cultures!"

Glenn was listening well now, smoking and becoming more relaxed as my words continued, "But, *The Drum* is what inspires my dance and my concept. Whenever I hear one drum or one hundred, the sound of its pulse just seems to take mine along with it! I don't know why Glenn; I hear the drum speak, I guess; I hear the words of life and living in every beat, man!" So, I think *this* is what ignites the spontaneous spark in me to dance! I don't know; it's like I hear the words of the drum saying, "Dance with me!"

He passed the joint to me; "Here, you want a hit of this?" he asked. "No, not now, maybe later after we finish rehearsing; I'm already buzzed from dancing!" I quickly replied. "Okay!" he said, still offering the joint to me; "I know maan, I saw you! But here! This is with the Turkish drum, you know, another kind of beat!" Both of us laughed and I accepted his offer knowing that it would help him to relax from his fear, be much more comfortable with me, and as well, to help me to be less formal. Glenn smiled at me, vigorously rubbed his palms together to warm them up, and said, "Thanks maan!"

He started to lightly finger tap rhythms on his toy bongos as Ray Barretto's music "Cocinando" filled our rehearsal space with its rich sounds of Latin percussion and voices; his fingers tapping precisely to the rhythms he was hearing. Our minds, now dazzled and dipped in "Turkish Delight" I asked him, "Do you know the "Juajuanco rhythm?" and quickly added, "I know you're just learning, so believe me, I'm not expecting too much! Basically, I just need to hear your "feel." I need to hear from the drum just how much love for playing you have; if there is true passion there in your heart, or something that you just like to do! You understand what I'm saying?" He took a last hit from the joint, squinted his eyes tightly and did a local search for an ashtray to put out what was left of the Turkish delight.

"Heptje hier een asbak?" he asked me. I didn't understand what he said, but I knew what he was looking for. "Wait, I'll get one for you!" Walking across the studio floor to where I knew some ashtrays were, I could hear Glenn begin to incorporate his own rhythms into those of Ray Barretto's. I walked across the floor with his rhythm and listened. I didn't walk back with the ashtray, I danced to him, only to find that he had already crushed the joint on the floor! His eyes were closed, and so as not to interrupt his musical trance, I picked it up in rhythm and placed it in the ashtray. I could feel a sense of excitement stirring within my body and danced my way to the tape recorder, gradually lowering the volume to off.

Glenn didn't even take notice of that! His head was bent low, and his big brown "1975 Afro-Style Hair" was just shaking and bobbing up and down to every beat; and it would fly backwards when he'd throw his head back, lifting his chin to show a smile or a grunt! His afro hair style hair was in a cleanly cut round shape and so much bigger than his face! Sweat began to dampen his forehead, and mine as well, from witnessing his passion; I listened carefully, followed his lead, and began to dance, to "his word"!

His sounds were good; they were steady, often clean and precise. Within certain phrases of the rhythms or beats he heard, he'd accentuate that moment with a moan or a loud grunt; I was listening, he was "talking"! His fingers banged out a swift rhythmic riff that made him throw back his head and big flying afro hair and natural primitive screams escaped from his teeth and broad smile! Instinctively, I acted on impulse as he was bringing his head forward slowly, "I bowed to him, closely enough for the frontal lobe of our brains to meet, just above the forehead; as I did with Thassos at The Acropolis Taverna in London. Then I darted away and took to the center of the floor and became tribal in form and thought; picturing myself in a village, circled by dancers and people, and hearing a hundred drums harmonizing with toy bongos!

I leaped high like a barefoot warrior, and when I landed, I heeled the earth hard with a good thump, as if I had conquered! My body had no restrictions; knee-bends, fly kicks, winding torso and body-rippling contractions that caused my shoulders to rotate and my arms to swing like roaring fans! Glenn's rhythms were like hot fire, and I was dancing like an impetuous flame! The speed of his fingers revealed every passionate word from his soul to let me know his deepest desire; "to be the music and the drum" and I heard every beat and "word" telling me that this was the instrument he would use to execute and to deliver his words, and his deepest desire!

Bringing the high dynamics of his musical message to a plateau of mutual understanding, he then resolved our wild frenzied moment to a low of warm and sultry soft rhythms; and my dance and movement led me from the center of the floor to where he was sitting and dripping wet with sweat, where he continued playing his soft rhythms. I too, drenched in sweat, stopped my subtle movements about ten feet in front of him to say, what he wanted me to say; which was to "Watch very closely, my body and every isolation you see that I make with each limb, joint and muscle!

Capture that isolated body part with a beat or beats that identify with that specific isolated movement! If you see an isolation that requires an accent such as a head roll, shoulder rolls, feet, etc; I need accents! You are not to be in a musical trance with eyes closed; you are to have them open, and always alert to follow the dancer! I will isolate both shoulders, maybe one; from my toes to my head, I will isolate a limb, a joint, a finger, hands, hips, knees, feet, or a foot! Your discipline is strict! You are to follow the dancer!" I said sternly; "Does that make sense?" I asked.

Glenn slowly nodded his head up and down with his gentle smile, understanding, and saying quietly, "Yah, maan!" It did make sense to him. We underwent a series of isolation exercises about technical points and their purpose that he grasped quickly with understanding and the acceptance to learn more. I admired his intelligence, his will and his action.

The clock was reading 5:30 P.M. and my studio time had expired; Together we left The Plenix studio and jumped on the bumpy bus over winding roadways heading for the city. We didn't talk much during the first ten or fifteen minutes of our bus ride, we were quiet; both in a daze, gazing out the windows to the flat landscape of Holland. Hanging on the edge of my mind were thoughts of the piano, the musical meditation and Christine.

I turned to Glenn; "Do you play piano?" I asked. "No, maan!, Just a little," he said; and then asked, "Do you?" I stammered and was searching for the truthful answer; "No, I don't," I said, with a pause and turning my head pretending to window gaze; "But, today I did!" I explained to him the piano experience I had, and recorded, before he had come to the rehearsal. "Oh, maan, let me hear it!" "Yes, I will do that one day," I said. "No, let me hear it now!" he said with tones of excitement in his voice, and reaching deep down into his brown leather bag, he pleaded, "Come, maan, give me the cassette! I have a 'Walkman'!" He pulled from his bag a new electronic device I had never seen, and explained that it played cassette tapes. I reached into my bag and passed the recorded cassette to him. "I got this a few months ago in Berlin," he said, "It's so cool!" He slid the tape into the Walkman and inserted the earplugs into his ears to listen.

I remained quiet, window gazing, and he remained quietly listening until he said, "Maan! You said you don't play! You play piano! This is like, classical, maan!" Saying nothing more, he lowered his head and continued to listen. I continued to window gaze and then a couple of minutes later I turned to him to speak but saw tears were trickling down his face as he looked at me. "You said, she died last week, Ilanga?" he asked. Not giving him an answer, consumed by my thoughts of "seeing" her today, I continued my window gazing. "This is beautiful, maan! She must be alive in Spirit, cuz your mother was right there!.. Yah; I can feel her in this! Her Spirit is right there with you, and in this music!.. It's making me cry a little too, because my mother is spiritual like yours, and she also is not feeling-good in her health, you know. I love my mother like you do maan; but I know that soon she has to die too," he said, with his own tears still trickling down and resumed listening to the music's end. When it did, Glenn returned the cassette back to me and wiping his eyes, said in soft words, "You are strong, Ilanga. You don't seem your mother just died last week. "You don't look sad, maan, and I know you are, because I hear it in your music! I hear your heart sad and crying; but you seem happy, playing the piano and I can hear that too!"

I could not reply to what he said; I was stuck and lost in my thoughts, thinking that this young boy doesn't know me!... or, does he?" We only met once, a week ago for three hours, had one brief telephone conversation, and today in this exact moment of time, it seems he knows me, my nature, and my "Being" and I know his! And now, we are here together in Amsterdam. We are "ageless" and "Time is only Present"!

Being frozen in these thoughts of *The Life*; and of *what we know and don't* know about it, and my extraordinary personal experiences, enabled me to "realize" again the endless "Cycles" of things, and that "There's so much more"! We were both lost in our thoughts and did not speak and by the time we arrived at our bus stop in the city, I had come to the conclusion that Glenn's profound and insightful thinking must have come from his beautiful mother also.

The Bim House was featuring an early evening jazz-trio, as Glenn and I could see and hear as we entered. After my friendly greeting to Punt, he introduced me to a couple of he and Glenn's friends, also musicians in the Band, "Solaat." "How did it go today, maan?" Punt asked me, wanting to hear from both of us; quickly shifted his eyes to Glenn, who flashed a big smile of satisfaction and said, "Nice, Maan," and holding onto that smile and pulling out from his leather bag, his tin of Samson Tobacco and his now smaller block of Hashish, Punt looked at me in question and waited for my comment of the afternoon's rehearsal. Unable to reply because I was briefly distracted by the thought that "joints are everywhere" here, every day all day and night! How do these people get things done, I thought! And then I replied to Punt, "A fabulous day! Yes; Punt, my brother, and man, I Thank you for it all!" His question was answered; but he wanted to hear more! He threw a puzzled look at me, and then to Glenn, who had already completed his newly-rolled "work of art" and Punt looked at me again as I said confidently, "I think I've found my Percussionist!" Punt's gold tooth was clearly visible; It shined!

And now my dear reader, the "Take away" on this metaphor of "beats and rhythms" that are included in the melody of our narrative, is that; "Here is a "Wise" young boy/man who was into his 3rd Cycle when he and I met in Amsterdam. The tremendous amount of fear that he created within himself, and the stress that gripped him for a long week of nail biting and sleepless nights, toyed with his Mind! Compelled by an instinctive passion to become a real percussionist, and amidst his fear of self-confidence and incompetence; he was still confident enough to listen to "Himself," his intuition, his "gut feeling"! An intelligent young man, he was able to evaluate the position he was in at that time in *The Life*, and act upon it.

His Past: a 14-year old boy arriving in Amsterdam from Surinam, South America, with two older siblings. **His Present**: An independent 18-year old young man on a mission of survival, without harm or damage to himself or to others. Every day and night, in the streets, cafes and clubs of Amsterdam, he became a part of the music scene, exploring and stimulating his passion "To Be." And then, his first opportunity to become "More" suddenly arose! A challenging decision to be made within a week; daily, in a mental state of limbo…"Do I dare? and If not, then what?"

His Present: He knew very well that it was only "Today"! Which is the reason for his fearful immediate decisions. **His Future:** He will own it, he will flourish, and he will find *Happiness* "There" because he understood that the future is his choice, beginning tomorrow! He *evaluated*, *dared* and *challenged* himself and his created fears.

He *realized* his present position, *decided* and *acted*! Glenn had made a *wise choice* to attend the rehearsal at The Plenix Center; He reluctantly committed to being there, even to the day of the phone call; but, he *acted*! And this action was the "Key" that he himself turned to unlock the door to the surprising and opaque opportunity to indulge his passion, even though his intelligence offered him other choices.

From that rehearsal day, and forward for the next twenty years, he became "Glenito" my major Percussionist, a super-professional who went on to become one of Europe's most celebrated and sought after Percussionists.

The technology we have today of cell phones, computers, tablets and "everything at your fingertips" we did not have "Back in the day"! Glenn's approach to discovering his passion and realizing that it was one-on-one contact, hands-on experience, years of foot work, a smile, and good self-presentation! These were the only tools he had to work with; and along with his chosen environment, they *inspired* and *motivated* him to *act* upon self-improvement and his higher goals!

Today, in our imaginative wonder-filled and global age of amazing achievements, excitement and often, delusional entertainment, it is the undeniable "head in the sand" devices such as cell phones, laptops, etc. that have become the deterrents keeping us from relying upon our essence of self-responsibility! These devices will explore, navigate, contact, do the foot work, and even "Think" for you! We have become a species of human beings who have lost the delicious appetite for self-discovery, and sadly, have abandoned the "Natural Creative Energy" within each and every one of us, to be responsible for becoming the **YOU** of **Your Choice.** Our naturally beautiful, costless, wireless energy is wasted and unused because of a keypad that has hampered and tarnished our natural thought processes by obstructing and inviting the lack of our genuine imagination.

To witness the abysmal sight of our everyday, all day social and personal existence, and if you are in any public environment, for a "Timeless Moment," lift your head from your cell phone or laptop! Your eyes will see the blatant deterrent "there" in front of you, for **YOU** to honestly access and summarize; and if you like, make a choice to value this moment! "Click-Off or Shut-Down" your interfering devices, make an effort to "Relax", slowly breathe in a long deep inhale and then exhale slowly to its end, until you must inhale again. And as you are breathing slowly, and "feeling" your body and mind relaxed, make an effort to calm your restless thoughts on one specific thought: "*Gratitude*"!

Allow that word and thought to sit there in your mind to jell for a moment or two, just "thinking and being" very grateful that **YOU** are aware and conscious of "*It all*," and that every day you are trying to be wiser and to *Become* the choice **YOU** make!

The new and "Wise" young women and men of today must consider and not forget, that "we are solely responsible for ourselves"! Dependence upon others, and their unlimited support is an ambiguous invasion of this truth. It is your responsibility to set the limits on extended support systems such as parents, relatives and friends. This high-achievement of personal quality is a gift from you, to **YOU**!

Yes; it is an unusual perspective on how to view yourself, if you want to look at it that way; but never abandon or underestimate your *Potential Abilities* and your *Personal Power*. Even though you may think, or maybe even believe, that you have limits, you don't! This is where **YOU** step in, by *Choice* to measure your limits, (even after "whatever attempts" have been made otherwise, and with determination!) This **YOU** who steps in now, is a **NEW YOU** whom you haven't met yet! And, together, as one, honest choices will mushroom and better decisions can be made. "Knowing" your potential is the first step toward explor-ing your abilities and capabilities! And here at this new plateau, **YOU** will *feel, know,* and *understand* the volume of your personal power. Believe me!

The 7-Year Cycles of Self-Evaluation offer alternative ideas to the familiar and more conventional norms of *Being, Purpose,* and *Choice,* and expose how the effects of your external social environment outside of yourself determine who **YOU** are! Therefore; a very important question to ask yourself is: **"Who Am I?"** In the next section I am offering a method of daily exercises that I encourage you to practice and experience in order to find the *Truth* and *Essence* to the question: **Who Am I?**

MIRROR EXERCISES

Preparation Exercise:

Whenever you have 5 minutes of free time, day or night, stand about 4 feet in front of a full-length mirror, reflecting your whole body, and most importantly, gaze at the most revealing source of your Nature and Soul: your **Eyes**.

- Inhale deeply, hold the breath 4-seconds, and then exhale with a rush and give your body a vigorous shake, including shoulders, arms, hands and fingers, legs and feet; and then slowly come to a gradual Stop! Resume normal breathing.
- Absorb the image that you see in front of you. This is the **YOU** whom you most identify with and that needs to be *totally relaxed*. Standing in a natural body position, relax your shoulders, arms, hands and facial muscles, and slowly inhale and exhale in relaxed, normal breathing. **Repeat this whole exercise twice**.

Note: To breathe properly: Straighten your spine and let your abdomen and lungs function naturally and at their full capacity. Comfortably, and in your own natural rhythm, breathe deeply and slowly, using eight slow-paced breaths. Inhale through the nose and exhale from the mouth, lips slightly parted. Use this pattern: Inhale: 1...Exhale: 2...Inhale: 3... Exhale: 4...Inhale: 5...Exhale, etc. At the end of 8 slow, deep breaths, inhale deeply, holding the breath for at least 8 seconds, and then exhale slowly; keeping your eyes on the image that you see in the mirror in front of you.

THE FOUR PERSPECTIVES/ EXERCISES FOR "SELF-IDENTITY"

After a few minutes of practice with the Preparation Exercise, you are ready to try to visualize yourself in the four separate *Perspectives*: **YOU**, **ME**, **I/Ego**, and **THE LIFE**. During visualization, remember to keep your body relaxed.

Body Posture: Stand in front of a full-length mirror, the back/spine upright, stomach muscles held in tight. Concentrate on breathing from the lungs and upper chest area.

1st Perspective is **YOU**: See your physical body, which is reflected back to you in the mirror. Imagine yourself as an objective Observer. You are the *Controller* and *Owner* of yourself and the *"Overseer"* of the other three perspectives.

2nd Perspective is **ME**: Looking straight forward, focus intensely on your own eyes while keeping facial muscles and body relaxed. Say to yourself, "This is me, this is who I am." This is who I have recognized and known as **ME** my whole life.

3rd Perspective is **I/Ego**: This is the part of me that governs my *Emotions*, my *Character*, my *Personality*, my *Vanity*, my *Self-esteem*; how I react to events and situations in my life. Asking **YOU** to assess **I/Ego** can be challenging.

4th Perspective is **The Life:** This is the life you have lived from birth to the present. The **YOU**, **ME** and **I/EGO** have all been present in every moment of your life. Every action, thought and feeling have all been present. Try to remember, without judgement, how you have lived your life at each stage, taking into account your actions, thoughts and feelings during each of the **CYCLES**.

Now try the Mirror Exercises using this technique:

- First, see yourself as **Perspective #1 YOU,** the *Controller* of all perspectives.

- Next, see yourself as **Perspective #2, ME,** but this time imagine that **ME** is the obstacle that prevents the discovery of the genuine **YOU.** This eye-to-eye contact is a Q & A between **YOU** and **ME. YOU** will ask the questions and **ME** will provide the answers. Be prepared that it will often not be an honest answer. **ME** is an ambiguous and challenging hidden personality that has a close relationship to the **I/Ego.** Examples of questions for the Q&A could be as follows:

Are you an honest person? In what way?

If you are not honest, why not? How do you feel about this? What do you like or dislike about your honesty and/or your dishonesty?

Do you procrastinate when thing have to be done? Why do you always wait until the last minute to do these things?

Does being alone trouble you? Or do you prefer being alone?

Focus on issues that are important to you, such as family, personal relationships, school, career and life goals.

Keep your breathing slow and your eyes focused during the Q&A. Let **YOU** ask the questions of **ME**; keeping in mind that **YOU** is looking for honest answers from **ME**; answers that emerge from deep within the soul. It may help to remember a profound quote from Socrates, the ancient

Greek Philosopher who said: **"An unexamined life isn't worth living."**

"Thinking" with your eyes closed is what we're doing here, and **YOU**, The Controller takes charge. The challenge to these exercises is to hold a few seconds of concentrated Focus on the images and thoughts that are of importance to you such as work, school, life goals, relationships, and family members. Ask, "How can I see myself differently, and also be able to recognize, enhance, and see clearly my *Purpose*, *Choices*, and *Challenges*?" The answer is to follow through with these daily exercises of "Self-Identity" and "The Four Perspectives" if not daily then at least three time a week.

- Next, see yourself as **Perspective #3, I/EGO**, which has its own voice that demands to be listened to, and its own needs that want to be recognized.

This is the irrational part of your brain that governs actions and feelings such as selfishness, vanity, self-importance and narcissism. **I/EGO** feels that it is the most important aspect of your identity and often can be very confrontational and devious. Terrible things have been done merely to serve powerful Egos that were reckless, uncaring and out of control.

Let **YOU** ask **I/EGO** questions such as:

Do I consider myself better, more attractive or smarter than others or less attractive, not as intelligent, not as good? Why do I feel this way and what makes me feel superior and/or inferior?

What do I want to achieve in life and what actions can I take to make these dreams come true? Do I feel strong and confident or weak and unsure?

How far would I go to achieve wealth, success, love, power, fame? Would I act to achieve this even at the expense of others? Why or why not?

What if my family, friends or a love interest don't support me in my dreams? Should I ignore them and do what I want anyway? Why or why not?

These are big questions and the answers will determine the course of your life!

There will be times when **YOU** will need to take charge and make a Command to **ME or I/EGO**, that a serious change needs to be made; and that needs to be determined by **YOU**!

Once this is exercise is completed, close your eyes, and remembering posture, keep your spine straight and stomach muscles held in tight. Inhale comfortably, breathe deeply, and try to visualize **Perspective #4.**

- **Perspective #4, The Life,** is not an entity in your life, **YOU** are the entity in **The Life**. The truth is: "The Life will always be here, but you will not!" *Objectivity* is the focus in this Perspective. Therefore, read and hear clearly that

YOU are simply an entity; as a curious butterfly would be, fluttering about and absorbing only life's sweetness, until its destined end, or new beginning; and if what you see is maybe not to your taste, likeness or feeling, then you just flutter away quickly because there's no reason to stay. **The Life** Perspective and its *"Reality"* will always confront **YOU** with "Up In Your Face" *Honesty, Fact,* and *Choice,* which is for **YOU** to scrutinize; not **Me** nor **I/EGO.**

Within the evaluation process of **Perspectives #2** and **#3** be aware, that If **YOU** cannot believe the honesty of **ME** and **I/EGO,** then **YOU** must ask again and again, until **YOU** receive a satisfactory answer that "Feels" true. There can be no question of doubt! Be direct and demanding! Remember that these two entities do not define your character, they only "represent" the character of **YOU**! This is the moment to be as imaginative as possible.

Try to visualize **YOU** being in a scene, a video, a landscape or a movie. The choice: You can be the Director or you can simply be one character in a cast of millions, acting in this new movie called **The Life**!

Be as objective as **YOU** can possibly be, see this scene for what it is; "a temporary wonder of deliberate fascination, Ego entertainment, and so much more," to allure, entice and distract from your purpose of objectivity! Therefore, these visuals are only for **YOU** to scrutinize, asses, and to discern its truth to make an honest decision if need be. Maybe, at the present time a definite decision needs to be made to improve upon your personal character and/or to enhance your quality of life such as a housing move, a career direction, a relationship issue, the care of someone in need, the personal demon within, etc. As difficult as this may seem, try your best to visualize and clearly see into the *Reality* of this fourth Perspective exactly as it is, not what **Me** or **I/EGO** think it is! If **YOU** are honest in your decisive choice, the outcome will always be a positive for **Me** and **I/ EGO** and will work in harmony with **YOU**! The practice of these exercises establishes an identity and a needed *"Trust"* between all three entities; A mutual bond that is required to achieve the essential personal purpose of *Self-Evaluation*.

This collaboration can prevent and resolve many of the problems that the two entities **Me** and **I/Ego** can create together when they are "in cahoots" with each other to cause many everyday problems for **YOU**!

It may be often that **YOU** will have to exercise the authority needed, and *Take Charge*! Exercise this by listening to the Needs and Wants of Ego and its **"I** this" and **"I** that" rhetoric; and also by being diplomatic and honest about a disputed issue of disagreement. But you must remember, this is not about negotiating or consideration. It is only **YOU** who has the ability and position to tactfully create and have an open dialogue with Ego on an issue, by wisely de-escalating it and resolving it to an end with the established fact of *"Who's in charge!"* Consider this to be a strategy game about *"Position"* and what it can mean in the process and development for **YOU** in all of your other three Perspectives.

This position that **YOU** have taken in the relationship can establish a "*Trust*" that will eventually lead to the unanimous understanding of authority that **YOU** are the neutralizer and keeper of balance for all three Perspectives.

Be Noble! young people of intelligence, and with your dreams, **Be Wise!** Guard them well and learn well your personal and natural gifts of *Imagination*, *Creativity*, and *Self-Potential*, so that you too are able to live *Your Choices* and "Earn" *Your Place* of "Happiness" and to honestly experience the "Awesome Wonder" of **"The Life"**.

ACKNOWLEDGEMENTS

Gratitude to all my family, friends, colleagues and strangers with "The Love" inside of them; those "In Need" and those whom I've yet to meet.

Special Thanks to: Bibi Cross-Nicolosi, Editor Eda Marie Gunderman, Keeper of Records Patrick Maloney, Back cover photo and cover design.

My undying gratitude goes to Jack Miller, Spiritual Guide.

Ilanga
July 2019

TRANSITIONS

One must travel the land and the waters of the world whenever possible to understand its "purpose" and most importantly, to know that it is here for us to discover and extract from it the global wealth and power it offers. It is by way of travel and by encountering diverse peoples in the world that we are able to discover and understand "our purpose" within it. Whatever "more" there is "of you and for you" is not only within yourselves; it is also acquired from the external environment that we may presently find ourselves engaged in.

In *Part Two* of this unusual narrative, I will clearly explain global power and its importance to the "more that is of you and for you." Travel with me and ride on the rhythmic words of Part Two so that you can comprehend – as I did – the dire Importance of **Self-Evaluation**. That is, if it matters to you at all!

CYCLES - PART TWO
The Seven-Year Cycles
of Self-Evaluation

ILANGA

CONTENTS

──────── CHAPTER ONE ────────

Determination is the only key to
Successful Achievement.

We are now beginning the New Year, January 2019, and the President of The United States is presently being scrutinized and investigated on the "Russian Investigation, Obstruction of justice, and Corruption charges." The political climate is tense, the earned state of Democracy is threatened, the United States of America is once again recycling the turmoil of its own "back-in-the-day" cycle of racial bigotry and injustice; and the global harmony that was once attainable is seemingly no longer to be in "our time" here on this planet. My young people who are reading these words; "Happy New Year!" and "Happy future!"

A few months ago during Autumn in October, I was at a street cafe in Boston Massachusetts enjoying a circle of friends who were in conversation about music and the arts, when I became momentarily perplexed by a question a young lady who was in our group asked me. She was an eager Sophomore studying Theological studies at a local university. It was our first time meeting one another and we were having our own side bar conversation together, discussing the efforts and task of writing and how difficult it can be at times. She was a talker, and was rambling on about an exam paper due in two days that she hadn't started working on yet! "Oh God, it's due on Monday!" she said with frustration several times, dramatically rubbing her face roughly with both hands and running her fingers through her long, unruly blonde hair. Her guilt about her habit of procrastination was obvious. In between her rambling, now and then I was able to wedge in a few words of my own about the discipline it takes to set aside a certain amount of time each day to write a self-help book about memoirs and self-evaluation. I assumed that I had her undivided attention and interest as I continued explaining the effort, time and energy that I put into writing, and that it's not to be "put off" for the next day. "Up every morning, seven days a week at the crack of dawn like a farmer isn't easy you know! I don't think about it, I just do it!" I said to her, "It's a strict discipline that eventually becomes a routine or, as I call it, 'a good habit.'" She took a quick sip of her beer, and I could see that she was vaguely listening to my continuous complaint of routine. "Hey, it's a difficult thing for me to sit there in a sedentary position writing words for six to seven hours a day! Up until last year, I lived my life as a dancer; leaping, jumping, and actively moving my body seven days a week! And now, every day and some nights for the last year, I've been bound to a chair and captured by time to sit still and write. To become an author is challenging for me. This is not an easy change of lifestyle for a dancer to make! Each and every day it requires effort and perseverance!" I said, and found myself rambling on as much as she had done, but I continued anyway, "And presently, I am exhausted from sitting in a chair, tired from effort and the physical need to "get-up-and-dance," but not yet. At the conclusion of writing my manuscript, and at the end of publication, then I will rest by stretching and exercising my lifeless body every day for its health!" I assumed that her interest and attention was "there" with me; but suddenly it occurred to me that she wasn't actually listening to me at all; because, whenever her head was up and out of her hands - her squinting eyes staring distantly through the cafe's glass window - she would then suddenly pull herself together with a quick shake of her head and tousled hair, glare at me, and with a frowning face of anguish painfully say, "It's due Monday!" She just seemed to exhaust herself with her own thoughts of guilt while supposedly listening to me. Her last hair fling of the two-thumbs-and-eight-finger-run-through ended with both hands holding her hair back from her face; nose wrinkled and eyes narrowed. But it was what was candidly bolted out of her mouth, her comment and question, that stunned me. "Self-evaluation! Are you serious?" she asked, "Who in the Hell wants to evaluate themselves, and why?" She paused, left her mouth open, and with her frown and squinted eyes in question, she glared at me and said nothing more. Her question totally baffled me! Even though I had long been interested in writing a book on self-evaluation, l had never given that question even as much as a thought before.

We both stared at each other until I broke the silence with my definitive reply;

"Well, maybe it's not about "wanting" to self-evaluate, but more of a "need" to, especially for a person such as myself who prefers to analyze and evaluate myself; and maybe there are those people who are in search of their own self-identity, or who have difficulty with self-motivation, confidence, perspectives, and future planning. There are young folks out there who are like that, you know," I said. Her eyes un-squinted to their natural beautiful almond shape and suddenly revealed a deep calm, letting me know that she "heard something" and so I continued, "and also, self-evaluation is a helpful tool for one who is curious and consciously motivated to be the person that "they" themselves "choose" and "want to be" for productivity, self-satisfaction, and with a purpose, to live *The*

Life!" I then asked her; "Don't you think that during some period of this person's growth and development that it's possible that he or she may feel that they are not going "forward" in whatever they're trying to accomplish or achieve? And rather than going forward, they are seriously stuck in a rut, and living a cycle of bad habits and yearly stagnant routines! Maybe a young person like yourself does have a "need" to know "why" and "what" are the obstacles and challenges that are preventing the attainment of their personal goals and achievements. I mean, don't you think that you should be thinking about that?" I asked. Her eyes carefully roamed my gray hair and then traced my age-lined face more carefully with her thoughts, which I read to be that she "heard" something else within the words I spoke; but "what" she heard, I don't know. She stopped her stare; "I gotta go!" she said abruptly, and once again with both hands grabbed at loose strands of hair. I heard only the tag end of her anxious voice saying, "I have to go home!" Within ten brief seconds, Janine gathered her loose items from the table, shoved them in her knitted shoulder-bag and quickly grabbed her glass and swigged her last drop of beer. "It was nice meeting you," she said as we clasped hands, "and, the only thing I can say is, thank you!" She left me with a warm smile, got up from her chair and began to maneuver her way from the table and group of friends. "Bye everybody, I gotta go!" she said, along with individual goodbyes and a "ramble" of words about her exam on Monday. It appeared odd to me, that from the moment I had asked for her thoughts on if a person in need should evaluate themselves, it was not more than five minutes later that she was like a full-spread winged Ostrich "flying" out of the café doors! Our group's laughter of Janine's dramatic exit echoed behind her as she left, and together in our laughter, we left it at that! But my thoughts lingered, "Did she actually 'hear' something in our conversation? What did she leave with? What was her "take-away?" She left us with a smile on our faces that lingered for a long while; and with me, she left her tangled thoughts. I have not seen her since; but of that group of gathered friends, a few have seen her and say that, "She's fine, and working hard at school!" Hearing this news of Janine had given me the good feeling that maybe "she did hear something!" An intelligent young lady concluding her **3rd Cycle** (15 to 21 years old), who is "in need" of *Self-Evaluation* and doesn't know it! Her future goal to obtain a PhD. in Theology is in jeopardy because she "honestly doesn't know why" she chose this field to study and make her professional career. And it is this way with many of us in this precarious position of the **3rd and 4th Cycles!** Although her interest had always been world religions, without insight and *Self-Evaluation* she had declined to consider her other options: interests that have now surfaced and are provoking thoughts of doubt, causing her to become indecisive and having an emotional effect on her personal behavior and her enthusiasm for her studies in Theology.

This little narrative of Janine that I have written has a touch of what I had mentioned in *Cycles, Part One*, that the "coincidence" of meeting someone is often "not a coincidence at all" but maybe the meeting has an undisclosed or hidden "purpose" that is to be revealed later in time. That meeting of a few hours in the afternoon had a significant purpose for her: She "understood" and "realized" that something within her was disturbed and needed to be "acted upon immediately!" And for me, the purpose was to "recognize" that need, and speak! The only "coincidence" was that we both had mutual friends who wanted to come together for an afternoon to share our friendship.

Janine, and all those who are fun-loving, challenging and daring young people of "invincibility" living in the adventurous **3rd and 4th Cycles**, are at the peak of their intellectual abilities but are nevertheless clueless as to what's ahead for them in the coming Cycles thereafter. They have yet to "arrive" and fully believe and comprehend the fact, that for them, "reality and real life begins" as they approach their **5th Cycle** (Ages: 29 to 35). They can only grasp a hint of what's ahead for themselves; and that's "if" they are intelligent and consciously observing their adult surroundings and being "aware" that "something else" is happening in their lives other than "what is!"

These aspiring young believers are able to see a blurred vision of the **5th Cycle** and the possibility of their "dream" being realized; and they begin to understand and begin to "act" with incentive and with this exciting new force of *Determination* which is *The key* (an energy), that enables **YOU** to open the door to your Dream! *Determination* is the principal energy of commitment within the **5th Cycle** as I have clearly defined in Part One. These intelligent young believers who are dreamers of "their dream," living in the tumultuous **4thCycle** of their life, and whom are struggling with personal and external challenges, have eventually come to their "mark" in time to make a "definite choice" to do "something" of self-worth, value, and purpose! It is this brief moment of precious time to step into their own "Spotlight" on the stage or platform of *The Life*! By taking up this personal challenge to "act," they will be in their own spotlight doing "something" that is worthy of themselves! And, with the "unknowing" of, whatever that chosen "something" is, they will discover soon, that this is their first "indelible" mark of personal choice in "real-time", and that it "matters most" and remains that, for the duration of their lifetime. But, while undergoing this challenging process of growth and development, they are eagerly looking forward to their **5thCycle** of *Determination* and soon to be naively discovering that in "real life" everything isn't "awesome!"

──── CHAPTER TWO ────

Knowledge: "Things known or learned."
(M. Webster)

Once the "gift of knowledge" is known and well-understood, it then needs to be valued, shared, and *applied*. Those of us with intelligence who are lucky enough to be receivers of this privileged gift, know well the vast properties of "thought" that are caught, tangled, and untangled in the mysterious web of knowledge. We conceive with imagination, the rapture, passion, trust, love, and understanding, and know well that these thoughts funnel through and lead us to believe in the possibilities of "higher achievement!" And we, the receivers of this precious gift know that the experiences, challenges and choices that come in its beautifully unwrapped gift enable us to charter our course and direction! This gift of knowledge has enabled us to determine "where we are today" and "where we want to be tomorrow!" No matter what **Cycles** are lived after the **5ᵗʰCycle**, *Determination* remains, and is still **"the key"** that one turns to open the door to move "forward."

And because of these "things known or learned" we proudly carry this knowledge with us into our productive and applicable **6ᵗʰCycle** (36 to 42 years of age). Single, partnered, coupled, or married with a child or children; this becomes a time to incorporate and share the wisdom of all your past five **Cycles**.

It is time for the cultivation of *Accrued wisdom, Self-Evaluation,* and *Assessment* and to apply this personal success and *High Achievement* with the same sincere passion and determination, that has brought **YOU** to this wonderful place that "maybe" you could call "your happiness!" But your young "wisdom" cautions not yet! This wonderful place, "happiness" does not belong to you, it is earned by **YOU**! And now, with a sense of your already recognized and established innate "intuition", **YOU** listens carefully. It is during the **2ⁿᵈCycle** (8 to 14 years of age) that we learn increments of "love" and the fundamentals of its many facets; first pets, family, and then friends. And by the time we close our **4ᵗʰCycle** (22 to 28) we have learned that love has many other facets to embrace, include, and take with us as we bravely move through our **5ᵗʰCycle** and into the productive **6ᵗʰCycle**; where "things known or learned" are produced and applied. We also have learned and nurtured by this time, the "need" to share; "sharing" is from love. Taking this action "to share" is an action of offering and accepting honest love, and sharing fulfills that "need" in this specific **Cycle**. Suddenly, the combination of "things known or learned" and "your wisdom", prompts the need "to educate." Teachers become better teachers, lovers become better lovers, and for Moms and Dads, the need to educate their child or children becomes a practical obsession and the "thing-to-do" because sharing is motivated by "the love" that we have learned to be the source of our "being" and a way to happiness, for all concerned.

Evaluating all that had transpired thus far in my career of music theater and dance, I decided in 1975 to close my "determined-to-be-me" **5ᵗʰCycle** (29 to 35), with the impetuous-thought of leaving the United States and living abroad, "somewhere" in Europe… maybe Paris, France! During the early and mid-1970's, the magical "Flower Power" movement of love, peace and happiness fizzled away peacefully, leaving us only with the prophetic music of Bob Dylan's "The Times They Are A Changing" and the lament of Otis

Redding's "Change Is Gonna Come." America was still sweltering in the swill, stench, and lasting residue of social-injustices and ablaze with an impeachment process for the then-President of the United States, Richard M. Nixon. And presently, in 2019, "here-we-go-again" with the country's "back-In-the-day" re-cycling of America's social and political history frightfully ablaze! The threat to abandon democracy is raging once more, and can only be salvaged by the young vote and the determined meager vote of the remaining elders who have "been there and done that!" Just as it happened then, it is happening today in "real time" to our aspiring, intelligent, wise young people. The "stench" and "effects" of the toxic environment that is engulfing the country today, also blocked, distracted, or stifled the dreams of many young "Dreamers" back then, in the early 1970's!

My "dream" or quest to "live free or die" or "die to be free" prevailed in my thoughts, that "here in America" the possibilities for me "to be me" and to *Produce*, to *Apply*, and to *Educate*, were really not a possibility at all! It was because of my "young" wisdom, that I rescued myself from the plight of America's state of conditions: to be stifled, limited, caged, and mistakenly defined, was not "my choice"...it was America's choice for me!

By this time, my professional career as an artist had already been established, beginning as a sixteen-year-old teenager in 1956, and being a member of The G Clefs, an infamous vocal group of five members from Boston Massachusetts, singing the American music of "Doo-Wop, Rhythm & Blues, Jazz, Soul, and Pop." And along with that glamorous and "sparkling" high life and continued success in the music business in 1971; my potential and natural talent at dance was surprisingly exposed to me. My intense studies in dance and Hatha Yoga "crystalized" my personal artistic vision, and I could instinctively feel that "it was the "new" form and passion for me to produce, apply and to educate. Shortly after this fresh awakening, "My Choice" was decided: I was to become a professional Afro-Jazz dancer and would perform with "Halifu Osumare's Dance Company" in Boston and in Oakland California. This new and remarkable learning experience of "the dance" teaching classes, and also being personally committed and obliged to the already contracted singing engagements with "The G-Clefs", did not interfere with my "intuitive" plan to leave America in 1975; "It was destined to be."

The last six-months before my departure in May of that year was of preparation; organizing my professional career Portfolio of photographs, bio, resume, etc; (the technology of Social Media communication did not exist then!). And being diligent in my efforts to get my official business in order by filling out name-change documents to change my birth name from "Arnold Anthony Scott" to only one name, "Ilanga." The sweeping thoughts of detachment from the G-Clefs and my family and friends were my biggest emotional hurdles to overcome; and also during this time before departing, the "bitter-sweet thoughts of selfishness and liberty" played their game with me daily, and neither dance nor meditation could quiet their noise.

I had a thirst for reading then; a thirst that I learned to quench and satisfy with words from those writers who captured my imagination with their honesty. Nineteenth century American author, philosopher, abolitionist, essayist, poet, and naturalist, Henry David Thoreau was one those authors. As an adventurous, naïve boy of fourteen years, I discovered a touristic cabin site where he once lived during his rebellious and non-conforming years of civil protest. I was approaching my **3rdCycle** (14 to 21) and riding on my junk-made parts-pieced-together bicycle, constructed by the hands of my genius oldest brother. It was during one of my exploration adventures to "Somewhere" cruising down a small winding road, that I eventually discovered the natural jewel hidden deep in the woods of Concord Massachusetts; "Walden Pond," located about twenty miles west from where I lived in Roxbury. Mine was a congested neighborhood of tenement buildings, shops, families, lots of trolley cars, trucks and "noise and every day buzz'n" within the city limits of old historic Boston. Since that first impressive day of "wonder," Waldon Pond is where I took refuge from the city's environmental noise and learned of a new word and a new place called "Sanctuary." Often, my hand-made bicycle would get me there, sometimes not! It was not until my **3rdCycle** that I got my driver's license and first car; and always on the passenger seat next to me would be a book to read, note pads and pens. I would make frequent trips to my personal Sanctuary in Concord just before the early sunrise hours of the morning; or sometimes I would go early afternoon and leave there hurriedly before the rush hour traffic on Route 2 began, heading east or west. Often, I would go to Walden Pond after a G-Clef's night club performance held in Boston or another local vicinity, and after the 2 a.m. closing of the night's fun and noisy club - and the spontaneous after party that always seemed to follow - I enjoyed these festivities with patience, because I knew that daylight was coming soon.

One early sunrise morning in Autumn, I was sitting on a mound of gold and orange-colored leaves that had fallen next to the old cabin site. Nestled in silence and wallowing in peaceful thoughts while reading a very profound essay by Henry David Thoreau, one sentence jumped out at me with enough power to "move my soul" to a place of thought it had never been before: "The world is a canvas for our imagination!" From that insightful and timely moment, roving about within my personal space, I could feel a presence; an energy of support that surrounded me, causing an epiphany of really "understanding" completely the author and the environment! His words, his presence, his power of information came down on me like rain, like a shower of "divine" realization! "Henry had given me the canvas to paint my world as I imagined it and I did a preliminary pencil sketch drawing of my life as I saw it to be now in the present and also in the future. I painted lavishly with color, the dynamics of movement, and even included my personal signature. It became a completed painting and work of art within a matter of minutes! With that one sentence, he had personally delivered to me: "the imagination to see it, feel it, and become it if you think you can."

Even at that age, on the brink of my **3rdCycle**; I could "feel" with my intuition that living abroad was a part of my future; and in that moment; "Knowing" that my life had to be of travel and of seeing the world; and to actually "paint my-own world" is what I "Imagined." And I decided, why not?! Throughout those years of my youth, my frequent visits to my Sanctuary and to "Henry" allowed me to become close to his "Spirit." I felt his mysterious presence and knowledgeable guidance often there at Walden Pond (and as I have heard, many other devotees "feel" this as well at times) and my personal attachment to Henry David Thoreau, his works, and thoughts would be a lifelong spiritual connection of loving friendship for me.

My insatiable thirst for reading stems from the "spark" of childish curiosity that flourished and prevailed within my inquisitive **2nd**Cycle (8 to 14 years of age). My interest began from the pictures and words of primary school books, children's bible stories, and holding up a newspaper to my face to pretend I was having a "big-read" as adults do; mimicking the intensity and postures of my father and mother who were avid readers of books and newspapers. And also, because all five of my older brothers were typical, active teenagers, movie-goers, and had lots of girlfriends, there were always glossy-covered magazines in their rooms that showed me flashy photographs and the glamour of Hollywood movie stars and their stories, along with a few words that were easy enough for me to read, (but really, understanding nothing at all!) And often, curiosity would get the best of me, and I would delve into my older brother's school books; these schoolbooks were different from mine. The titles of each book always read in big bold letters, "Geography, Math, Health, American History," all with beautiful photographs of the world and the country; and drawings of how organs and things looked inside of your body along with visual illustrations and hand-drawn diagrams of lines and numbers and all the things that fascinate us in our **2nd Cycle** of *The Life*. All that I imagined and read in my brother's school books were so much more interesting and fun to me than the comic books, newspapers, or that 12-inch small circular glass-screen "Thing" with many glass tubes and black wires dangling from behind it, that my genius older brother had constructed by himself and had called it a "Television!" Another "new" word and a four-syllable sound that fascinated me! He was a serious teenager, exercising his brilliance and young wisdom; studious and with a mind of ingenuity that was always soaked in his monthly magazines that were titled in bold letters, *"POPULAR MECHANICS."* His days of fun were filled with technical creativity - he could work with or fix anything that consisted of wires, gears, nuts and bolts! And with his small tools he repaired the urgent needs of the family's toaster, radio, clothes iron, and any broken electrical appliance in our household. My older brother Reggie's teenage-days were not filled with play such as board games, Baseball, Football, street-games, movies, or girlfriends; and music just didn't seem to interest him as it did my other four brothers. All of this **3rdCycle** activity for them was an everyday-all-day natural thing to do! But he was a loner...and being the oldest sibling of seven, and strictly disciplined, he often would undertake the role of father to me and my younger sister. Whenever the play with my sister annoyed me or I found it to be boring, I would sit with him quietly in his space, at his junk-cluttered and private, small work table in the corner of the one bedroom that slept six boys. I watched him; his mind and fingers always being busy with wires and small shiny tools that glimmered and caught my eye. He knew that I loved "whatever" he was doing; and because of my active bustling child-like energy, it was an unusual thing for me to be "sitting still" for hours, and especially to be focused on wires and tools! But somehow, from within his young wisdom, he also knew that I knew that he loved doing it! To him, doing this together was our "Fun"! We bonded, and we never separated from one another since those days of our unlikely togetherness, during my **2ndCycle** of explorations and learning of the two factual "energies" that he said we live with every day, and that we need to learn and know about: "electrical" meaning, "technology" and "creative."

"These two energies together, will change the world someday when you are older," he said. Of course, it was much later in the years that the "Information Highway" (the internet) appeared to us and it was not until then that I understood these profound words and the intelligence that he shared with me and did so with such love and guidance, always.

As it happens with all inquisitive boys and girls in this joyful explorative and risk-taking **Cycle**, and with the ability to read well; I too, in my own time of silence and the study of things, suddenly became aware of the fact that learning something new was always going to be happening every day! I learned a big word one day that had four sounds, or four beats to it: *Comprehension.* This word had a power and a rhythm within it that I could sing with in confidence to myself repeatedly; and I would dance sporadically as I sang! At school, I had learned that the beats I heard in the word *Comprehension* were called "syllables". Thereafter, more "long" words were learned with four and five syllables that I could sing and dance to; and sometimes, "perform" with passion in tempos fast or slow depending on the word and its meaning. The new long words I learned each day were my fun and play when I was alone with myself discovering, creating, and shaping the person who I am today.

It was at a Saturday morning catechism class at the Catholic school that I attended when the teacher - a Nun in Habit - was questioning students on a variety of lessons learned that were now being reviewed. She had asked me to explain, "Who Jesus Christ was, and what does He mean to me?" "Oh, He's my friend!" I answered abruptly..."and, you say, that "He was" but Sister, I say, that "He is!... He isn't dead!" The classroom instantly erupted into soft giggles that she ceased immediately with one clap of her hand, and then cupped them close to her breast. "Yes, go on!" she said, and remained staunch in her demanding posture. The classroom was silent, all eyes were fixed on me, waiting for me to continue. "Well, "I can't see Him like I'm seeing you and everything! But I see Him; we play and talk together lots of times!" I said without a flinch of doubt, and added easily, "And I think, that he always was, and always will be! I stated proudly the words I had read in my catechism book, and in my innocence truly "believed"! Sister Mary Martin de Porres smiled, and said, "Rightly so!" and waited. She could see that I had more to say; and because of my rigorous training in Catholicism and my religious family upbringing, I confidently rambled-on a few more seconds of my story, about "How Jesus' mother Mary gave birth to Him, and that He had two-fathers, but God was the real one! And, that "His other father Joseph was the *real* one on earth." I continued rambling-on with certainty; "I think He's a big teacher who's not alive, yet is, and teaches everybody in the world about love! And that He loves children more than anything else!" Sister Mary Martin de Porres in her black & white Habit looked at me with delight, peering over the rims of her granny-style eye glasses! "Well, young man" she said happily, "Your comprehension of Jesus is very good! It is very much like mine," she stated proudly, satisfied that her work was being done well. Her pointed words assured me that I too would be going to Heaven if my comprehension was like hers, because she's a Nun, and will *definitely* be going to Heaven when she dies! and I felt good about that; but hearing that word *Comprehension* had me running home after class to ask somebody I could trust to give me an honest answer - like my older brother or my mother - to explain exactly what that big long word "really" means. I was not satisfied with Webster's dictionary definition, "to understand" just wasn't "enough" for me...there had to be "more" to the word *Comprehension* than just, "to understand" I thought!

Because whenever I danced spontaneously to its rhythmic sound and four beats, I did not understand the word; I simply understood its vibration and what it did to me! I "felt" that there had to be "more" to that word, than "understanding"! I asked my brother and he told me that it means, "you clearly understand everything you're talking about;" and my mother's answer was, "Well dear, you really don't understand anything at all, until you comprehend it!" Those two answers to me were just a big "puzzle of thought" and I preferred to continue "singing" the four-syllable word and enjoyed my play and dance with its rhythms, while walking-a-fence with precise balance; and being a high wire tightrope walker in a circus rather than to trying to use it in my every day vocabulary! For me, its meaning was "limited."

Within a very short time afterwards, I had finally and totally understood the word *Comprehension* by way of the three distinctive words I had learned from my older brother Reggie: *"Energy, Electrical,* and *Creativity"* and that "somehow" the three were connected to one another as one and yet each had their own *Purpose, Power,* and *Identity,* as I understood them to be, as a twelve-year old child. And his emphasis on the fact that "Now that we have this vital information, and know what to do with it, we will not be able to live without these three energies!" This part of his theory, days after, had me bouncing many questions of "Why?" to him and off of his wonderful brain that stimulated my every move and inspired me so.

Is it a question of "coincidence" that these three words that resonated the sound of life to me then, are still echoing in my mind and ears today, now, living in my **12ᵗʰCycle**?" Maybe! My **6ᵗʰCycle** (36 to 42) of *Productivity, Application,* and *Success,* in my works of dance theater and music - as well as within the ideologies of theology and studies of various Yoga paths - have proven to me that I was "destined" to hear those three words of "wisdom" then, at that time in my life! And, to be hearing them with a measure of intelligence and the "natural wisdom" that is innate in every child "learning" within their **2ndCycle** (8 to 14)! Once I had accurately learned the big word "comprehension;" its depth, vast and complete definition, and "what it meant to me" I came to the realization that, the idea of *coincidence* had nothing to do with "what happened then" in my **2ndCycle** and "what was happening now" in the **6thCycle**! I understood, accepted, and "comprehended" it to be a "matter of fact destiny"!

Also, my entire **6thCycle** of *Productivity, Application,* and *Success* was living and experiencing *The Life* in two foreign countries: The Netherlands and Greece. At this particular time, I was residing in Amsterdam, The Netherlands, learning the language, the Dutch culture and its people. Why the choice to leave America, live abroad and "become"? It was because I intuitively knew there was more of me and the world to learn of, and it seemed to be a natural thing for me to do, and, of course there was my usual challenge and daring attitude of "why not?!"

Single young men and women of this **6thCycle** have already made their choice **"to be who they are,"** aware of what responsibilities they must undertake, and **"Know"** that they must **"act now!"** For some, this deserved Independence is by choice, reason, fearlessness, and without boundaries. They are "un-trapped" from the norm of being "trapped" within the cage of conventional thought. And for others, who are in a serious mutual relationship, marriage, or a partnership, within this Cycle, the choice of Independence is not the approach or path to take towards their **7thCycle.** For them, that "choice of independence" is being analyzed and digested when they are alone in their scheduled free time; thinking positively, and being "almost" satisfied and content with an "assured" and "determined" future. And most likely "this choice" has been taken simply for the reasons that without the financial means and the support from others, the struggles and personal hardships of "living with Independence" can be truly frightening.

The dogma of religious and social conventional thought has us believe that it is our nature to bond ourselves to one person and to share in the joint pursuit of happiness, and to cling to the assurance of "hope and trust" as the blueprint for their future Cycles together.

The primary search for that "oneness" begins during the **4ᵗʰCycle**; the college or university years, the first serious job, the social circles they join and the ambitions prayers and desires. This presupposed search for joint happiness has hopefully ended in success usually by the conclusion of the **4ᵗʰCycle** (22 to 28). For those who have found the "*One*" for a marriage or partnership, this constitutes a personal sacrifice of independence; and yet they embrace the amiable conditions of love and endurance with a future plan of togetherness, pursuing an oath to joint happiness that begins in the morning of every day and ends with the two cuddling together at night, whispering about their wishes and "oneness." But for some others this is not the outcome; and yet they too had the ambition and desires, said the prayers, and responsibly made all the attempts and self-sacrifices to succeed and find the "*One!*" but somehow "that just didn't happen!" The reasons why are of their own account of course; and often they claim to have been less fortunate, and fall into a realm of despair and emotional negativity that can disrupt and interfere with any positive thoughts of going "forward."

Little do they know, that at this "significant" moment of time in their young lives, a hidden or unrecognized "turning point" has happened to them! Whether it occurs at the beginning, middle, or at the end of a Cycle, the "turning point" is there to be recognized, acknowledged, and "acted" upon! And the "disappointed" but courageous young man or woman must learn now, that it is the time to reflect, analyze, and "seriously" self-evaluate. If you haven't yet done any of the "Mirror Exercises" I suggest in **Cycles I**, please try one! I think that the exercises would be helpful to you at this time; and remember..."the *Dare*, the *Challenges*, the *Choices made*, the *Successes*, the *Determination* the *Perseverance*, that **YOU** have accrued so deservingly from the previous Cycles were the substantial and reliable support factors that got you to the plateau to build your dream upon!

You may feel prepared, so that when that *"One"* comes whom you want to live your life with in the coming future, you feel ready to submit your share of the "joint-plan"! Yet although the plan was intact and going well, an issue of mutual conflict arose and caused a divide, and it seems as suddenly as "the one" came, that *"One"* has gone! You may consider all the past efforts, achievements and accrued wisdom, along with the ambitions, hopes and prayers and the thoughtful preparation and planning all wasted. And even for some of the most courageous and strong, this can quickly become a "why me?" disappointment of the reality, that that *"One"* came, but still; "It just didn't happen!"

The "acceptance" of this "turning point" becomes the new challenge, the "new forward" to go towards; and most importantly, for the "new you" to become! Consequently, it is **YOU** who confirms the "acceptance" Not the *"you"* you just left behind!

It happens, that two can come together, and it all begins with a dating experience that evolves into the idea of "*Oneness*". And, it could be a period of some years together that jointly they are discussing the proposed mutual blueprint of happiness that they are planning to live for their next Cycles together. But as it can happen, a "break-up" ensues, and the painful inevitable "separation" occurs. This causes an eruption of emotional energy that surfaces, disrupts and distracts. These emotions determine your next moves, which are inevitable. But to *where, how,* and *with whom*; or just *alone?* Fortunately, the only "positive outcome" to this dilemma is strictly "your choice;" and keep in mind that the honest choice **YOU** make is "the only way out"! "This" is the "turning point" I speak of.

"How did this happen to me?" you may ask, and "Why?" It could be due to circumstance, situation, or joint ego-related issues, such as obsession, loss of affection, maybe a touch of jealousy, possessiveness, a "misunderstanding." Or, it could possibly be the "non-comprehension" of the "honest words" that bond and weave through our lives daily: *Truth, Trust,* and *Commitment,* all to be examined by **YOU.**

There is a positive outcome to this "turning point" that happens to one who undergoes this traumatic experience: the accrued personal values of one's past *Achievements, Character,* and *Determination.* They are the reliable recovery factors and the source to make this necessary turn in *The Life*! A life changing turning point that is to be decided by a wise "choice" amid the emotional trauma, fast changes, and the now critical and perplexed situation. This is not the time for soothing rationale or a "middle of the road" position! "Drive yourself quickly into the fast-lane!"

It is the time for definite "action" not deliberation! Should immediate action not be taken, one welcomes an onslaught of daily negativity, mental depression, and the risk of letting go all that you have worked for throughout the years of wonder, efforts, achievements, and values, that **YOU** accrued with diligence during the 5th**Cycle**, and those prior! And when or if this is your situation my young people, please... "Tap the Wisdom Within." One must remember to "never forget" that the "Dream" that occurred in the 4th**Cycle** was the source, foundation, and sole purpose of getting up in the morning and "Rising to the *Dream*" and the daily disciplines, efforts, and personal reasons for doing so; and each day learning how to drive this dream and "Train of Thought" in the right direction!" We must always try to remember "how hard it was", to keep this "Train" on its track during the 4th**Cycle**! Never forget "where You've been and how you got there"! Analyze and appraise that; and consider the fact that the only "power" and "wisdom" that drove that Train through that entire 4th**Cycle**, was **YOU**! Now, isn't that a beautiful thing to "know" and "believe" for the rest of your life? No one can take that personal value away from you; that is, unless you allow them to! The question that needs to be asked here is, "Should an *Obstacle*, or "another person" have the power to derail that "train of thought?" I don't think so! Only **YOU** have the *Power* and the *Wisdom* to keep that train on track and heading for the "New Destination" that has been chosen by nobody else but **YOU**!

The two most dynamic and critical **Cycles** of *The Life*, are the 4th and 5th. The drama and theatrics of our *Dream* seem to subside at this point of dream-making. All that needed to be accomplished has been, the direction to go forward is set, and *Comprehension* engulfs you with an understanding that comes with a calm acceptance of...

"So, that's how it is!" This pinnacle of the on-going *Dream* concludes at the end of the **5ᵗʰCycle**; Anxiety transforms into deliberate *Action,* and in balance with *Acceptance* and the *Comprehension* of it all, because **YOU** have decided, what's next to be done.

Nevertheless; whatever the outcome of our efforts amount to, single or partnered, and with "self-trust" and the "need" to produce and apply, we confidently begin our journey onto the **6ᵗʰCycle** determined to do and become more. This is motivated by the Force and the Power that **YOU** have acquired in the previous **5ᵗʰCycle**! The "Realization" has come to **YOU** that you are now a young man, or young woman; and the games that boys and girls play themselves, with one another, with friends, or family, is a game no longer to be played. And it is at this point within the **6ᵗʰCycle**, my intelligent young reader is when "Young Wisdom" prevails! This is what introduces and produces the remarkable and triumphant "turning point" in *The Life* to be *Evaluated* and *Realized* for your coming and noble future.

"This" my dear young brothers and sisters who have arrived at this success, is personal "high achievement" and is the reward for all of your "realized wisdom" and your efforts so well accomplished, amidst the numerous obstacles distractions and deterrents that happened "coincidently", or possibly "destined" on your way to "becoming"!

— CHAPTER THREE —

The Heaven and Hell we hear about could be here on the grounds we walk on.

As a Single black man experiencing his **6ᵗʰCycle** (36 to 42), with no expectations from anyone but myself from and with a determined but unknown and "visionless" future ahead of me; I was still discovering myself, and what was most interesting and most important to me in my everyday life. Another word of power that intrigued me at a very young age, is "Joy"! When I first heard its sustaining one syllable and positive sound, I began to "feel" and totally "comprehend" this happy word, "Joy"! Also within my interests, I had discovered that within each day there would always be a big or small surprise! It could be a good one or a bad, it didn't matter! The idea and thought that within every day of our lives there will always be an element of surprise fascinated me! And I could not dismiss toying with the anxious thought, that "something" would always be there for me if I was fearless, daring, and believed that an inevitable "surprise was waiting just around the corner wherever I was in the world"! And "joy" can be found in a simple thought, an instant sight, a personal contact, and can be "appreciated" if we allow ourselves to think of it in that way! There would never be a "joyful" day for me, had I not listened to the sound and felt the power of that word!

My **6ᵗʰCycle** flourished with creative energy to do "more" and to continue with what I was achieving with my successful work in dance at this time in my life. The two significant events that "sparked" and inspired the spirit of African dance within me were: a performance in New York City, *Les Ballets Africains* performed by the *National Ballet Dance Company of Guinea* and in Boston, a powerful and impressive performance by the *National Dance Company of Senegal*! Both of these events occurred during my **5ᵗʰCycle**, and what I had "seen, felt, and desired" then, and from what my eyes were open to, I decided to let go of the music scene, become a dancer, and dance "hard", like those impressive performers exemplifying the highest standards of dance by way of their nature and their vision of African dance theater! Classical Ballet and Contemporary dance were of course still of interest to me but... not to dance! But rather, I wanted to extract from these dance forms what I was able to in design, technique, and the extensive physical body work required to become a "hard-working" dancer. It was the "Jazz Dance" form that captured me.

The disciplines, the practice, and the vigorous daily routine required in dance and the practice of my ardent studies in Hatha Yoga inspired an urge within me to develop an unusual technique in Afro-Jazz Dance. But for me to combine these two vital lifelines of dance and yoga at this time, was only an "idea" that I was not yet ready or able to apply. It was best to only plant the "seed" of this idea for it to grow, be nurtured, blossom, and eventually be shared; "But not here in Boston," I thought, "nor anywhere in the United States!" At that time in the dance evolution in the American dance world, one had to study dance within the boundaries of its glorified garden of limited conventional thought; Classical Ballet, Contemporary, and the happening trends of intimate social dancing such as the Waltz, Ballroom, the Charleston, the Lindy Hop, and Swing! Latin music from South America dominated the radio airwaves, and the listening audience living in major cities across the country suddenly were dancing in style to the vibrant music of the Mambo, the Cha Cha, and Tango! This national "dance wave" of Latin music and its content of African percussive sounds that induced spontaneity in dance and song, influenced and inspired me greatly, to do "more".

The "American Jazz Dance" form had just been accepted to become a part of the American dance culture, and was on its way to becoming an institution. Because of my background in the soulful music of Jazz, Doo-Wop, and Rhythm & Blues, and my natural ability to move, Jazz dance attracted me as did Latin dance and Latin music. My music career of fifteen years was still ongoing but it interfered with my "new career" in dance and my desire and commitment to do more; and consequently, I was beginning to feel pressure coming at me from both of these external forces, causing me to make a "turning point" in my professional life. I desperately tried to balance the rehearsals and nightly gigs with the G-Clefs - often local, sometimes not - with the intense daily study and training in dance.

Add to this, the dance performance schedules conflicting with The G-Clefs' performing schedules. This balancing act lasted three to four years and I realized I desperately needed to analyze and evaluate this...so I did! I had to escape from this reality, this "trap" that stifled my "imagination of being"; and so my next action was to *Dare* to follow the dream that was dancing in my head.

My **6ᵗʰCycle** of *Productivity, Application, and Action,* led me to become a professional Afro Jazz dancer, teacher, and choreographer of dance theater; and it successfully took place in the 16ᵗʰ Century old city of Amsterdam, The Netherlands for a five-year period from 1975 to 1980. Later, it was "destined" that I would live and do my professional work in Athens, Greece until 1985; but for those five years, I was residing and working in eclectic Amsterdam, a magnet city for "the curious, the wanderer, and the tourist"; I began to realize after a few months there, that "I too, was all of that!" But the awareness of my spiritualty also separated me from all of that and had me thinking, that however or in whatever way one perceives the word and their vision of "Hell", one actually doesn't know the secret of its existence until they have actually been there.

My perception of Hell is what my eyes are seeing and what my mind is intuitively feeling; which is the need to protect my soul! A daily reminder of this secret, the impact of these surreal visuals, and the need to always be alert, was the constant thought that kept me conscious of my strange new environment.

The Hell that I speak of, was the five "productive" years of living in this thorny environment in the "wonderful but precarious" city of Amsterdam, with the sensible Dutch people and the manicured, flat and sunless landscape of The Netherlands. And yes; the selective words I've chosen here, *Productive, Hell Thorny, Wonderful, Precarious, Sensible and Sunless* hopefully describe the daily existence of what an honest man or woman experiences while living *The Life* in a quest for truth, and using it and wisdom as a guide. And who also is a fearless explorer, safe with "self-trust" and the zeal to "win"! Amsterdam offered a mix of confrontation and battles that only a *Warrior of Truth* could decipher, confront, and survive. A battlefield of surprises was waiting around every street corner; but not always of "Joy"! Therefore, "this" too had to be cautiously deciphered, because "anything or anyone at any time" could be there waiting for you; to battle or to love. And I humbly confess to you, my dear reader that there were a few times when I did call on God's name! I had learned thus far in living *The Life*, that when in need you call on "Who's got your back"! Indeed, I "tapped-into" and used that wisdom because it was there for me! The daily attacks upon my *spiritual, moral, and ethical values* were massive at times! Often they'd be overwhelming enough for me to actually think of leaving Amsterdam! But I somehow knew intuitively that to remain here was my personal challenge; and to leave Amsterdam would be to defeat my "purpose" of being there. I was producing, applying, and materializing the "dream" and as well, calmly in constant pursuit of my earthly "being"! Nor was I perplexed about this battle of love and hate for this threatening environment of attractive, enticing pleasures and charm that could swallow any vulnerable soul that is simply wandering through the romantic canals and streets of the city and prone to fun excitement and daring-do! An array of alluring vices are incessantly looming and being offered, displayed, and camouflaged in many forms that can be customized to suit any appetite for a new delight. The arts and worldly cultures are featured here in Amsterdam for art lovers and lovers of people, brilliant diamonds, fashion, cafes, social activity, and the international ambiance of humanity. And in many cases, the pleasures, the gifts, and an invitation to a special event is all there for one to buy or exchange for something - or themselves - via a bartered agreement of some kind.

Unlike Athens, Greece, New York, Los Angeles, Paris, Bangkok, London, and other major trendy cities of the world; in Amsterdam one can sense and experience the "feel" of liberation, its powerful energy, and its ability to shape and transform a person or a society from the limited knowledge of themselves into their full potential and possible capability once the "exposure" to and the "understanding" of this useful, sensible and dynamic power called "liberation" is unleashed. And I do believe that for one to truly "comprehend" liberation, one must "dare to be!" The Dutch people are wise enough to have learned throughout their inhumane history of colonization, the sacred words of Scripture, "deliverance from evil" and the law of nature itself "To respect human beings and all living things!" Maybe through a cloudy window of remorse, they could see that some degree of absolution or rectification had to be made! I don't know how that actually happened; but maybe they too "called out God's name" in their time of desperation, needing to deliberate and barter these measures of their historical "soulless" activity!

My fascination and interest with the Dutch culture and thought, and the "rectification" that has been made from their inhumane trials through the centuries is their stance and position upon voicing the rights of "freedom for all." I disagree with vindication; but I admire how they found a way to smoothly side step, what would be an "obstacle" in the path of any country's growth and development: the dark past history of insensitivity and deliberate human abuse. Somehow, the Dutch people managed to dismiss these moments in their social history as an "obstacle" and "moved on" to firmly establish a new frontier in global relations. They discovered that within their tiny little country, it was possible to socialize the people; especially with their well stabilized bureaucratic-mandates, plausible social system and rigid cultural and social traditions. The idea of "duality" worked well in Holland, and within that fabric of "Dutch-Thought" a clever loop hole was found for them to deliver, and to exercise, the *Morals, Values* and *Truths* of human life that they abandoned so long ago. And finally "absolved" they were then able to raise and wave proudly, the deserved flag of leadership that spearheads the global humanitarian "rights of freedom".

In this amiable country of The Netherlands, a clear window of "freedom" is always open for the world to see and experience if they care to; especially for those who are just "curious" to experience the unusual logic of Dutch thought. And also, for those who are in "want or need" of lessons to "respectfully" *Learn, Exercise,* and *Experience*, the sensations of "sensuality" and "pleasures" offered, and are available to them on any given day, at any hour! Here in the Netherlands, one's sexual fantasies can become real, alive, and "tangible"! The "Right of Freedom" is allowed for the "sensual touch" and a "flesh to flesh" rendezvous can be experienced anytime; a barter of delight on offer to be purchased and a wonderful opportunity and delight for those in need of such pleasures! "Here in the land of wooden shoes, tulips, and Delft Blue," the blessing of "World Music" is heard and worshiped throughout the country; Wonderful international musical sounds are heard in cafes bars and restaurants all day long. The "Joy" that I find in this "Dutch-Treat" is that this new world music and the profound message of how life is being lived around the world is being heard loudly and is genuinely understood and accepted by the people. It blatantly provides a vocal freedom and musical platform for global artists to leave their country of strife and struggle, perform here, and proclaim their voice of freedom to listening ears by becoming the common thread of social thought and bonding collectively for social justice!

It was at this time that the prophetic words "electrical creativity" that my older brother Reggie expounded upon became more clarified. I finally understood twenty-five years later, more of what he actually was saying to me! This had become the era that ushered in the gift of "creative technology." After radio, television, and the jukebox, came the onslaught of 8mm home movies, 8-Track tape and 60-minute music cassettes, and music videos that blanketed the global market and instantly connected the international artistic expressions that Reggae music had so wisely prophesied. This World Music is the rhythm and the throbbing heartbeat that is thumping today in every major city around the globe. Here in Amsterdam, the dance halls were filled with beats of reggae music and euphoric aromas of marijuana, inducing the "Love-Vibe" in Jazz clubs and cafes, all featuring live bands to celebrate an unusual liberty and the "timely moment" of an unusual experience! It could be for a day, a week, or however long a visitor may be here. This environment of the daily sensual pleasures of drugs, of music, of harmonious energy, and also, depending on the company of friends or associates, was like having your very "first-ever-time-of-fun"!

But for some, the first time becomes "endless" and the "fun" soon abandons one timely moment for another. Then slowly, "fun" drifts off on its own, leaving one "all alone out there" on a fragile limb that threatens to snap and break (and often does) leaving one to fall hard into a Zombie pit of lifeless and fun-less human souls that "fun" has abandoned, causing them to suffer and wonder why. I can still hear the laments from those fun-less Zombies:

> "What happened to yesterday's giggles?
> "What happened to me?"
> Am I caught in a "Trap"?
> Will I ever be "Free"?
> Please, "Somebody" help!
> I am so desperate!
> I need to find "Me"!

A gripping and seductive environment this was then, that could destroy, impair, or interfere with any young man or woman's adventurous life and future if their inner-strength and constitution was one of weakness. It was after about a year of living *The Life* in Amsterdam when I began to recognize the "Hell" that I was living in, complete with the various vices that have caused so many of those weak- minded souls to be caught in despair and hopelessness. But, this "Hell" was of no threat to me! I was intuitively guided and because I didn't allow these traps to catch me, I felt protected and safe!

I could not leave Amsterdam because I had already invested too much of myself, time and finances. It was a fact that my theory of the Afro-Jazz Dance/Hatha Yoga technique was being nurtured, developed, and accepted; and I was very sure that being there and taking *Action* on my dream was "my purpose!" It could be that due to my "inner-strength" and "spiritual constitution" there was never confusion or doubt while I was engaged in this self-inflicted war of values! My personal *Conviction, Identity,* and *Purpose,* aligned with the weapons of inner-strength and spiritual constitution in my defense, and I, dueling with the circumstantial enemy of "place and time" was desperately fighting for their separate survival. Without either, I would have failed. Both "Amsterdam and I" were in a constant daily challenge for the "Power to Be" and I *Knew, Accepted, and Believed* that to win "I had to conquer!"

It had taken five years for that turbulent battle to come to an end; and when I was certain that it did, I felt an epiphany of "cleansing" from the soul tarnish of what I believed to be a personal blatant "spiritual war." I attest to that because of the "unusual and inexplicable" incidents, the meeting of certain people, and mysterious events that occurred "coincidently" during those wonderful and productive five years.

As I mentioned in *Cycles, Part One*, during the first month of my arrival in Amsterdam my mother passed away in Boston; and from the day I received that heartbreaking news, there was a week or so filled every day with a sweet blend of constructive and meaningful, vibrant "positive energy" supporting me in my deep grief and in the solemn days ahead of me. This fresh and new energy that kept me afloat from sorrow was due to the words and thoughts that I was receiving and the initial feedback and response from those whom I had spoken with in regard to my work and stay in Amsterdam. Their unanimous advice to me, was to "remain here"! They had convinced me that my stay was a lucrative opportunity for me to explore and to continue to invest more of myself, and above all "to not yield to defeat"! "This" was the positive energy that I could feel swirling around me every day; but it was entwined with another warm flow of substance that some people would consider to be negative, "strange" or "uncanny"! It derived from my ominous decision to not attend my mother's funeral in Boston. The polarity between these two energies - positive and negative - in a circumstance such as this is minuscule, and one must find the point of balance within this slim crevice of sanity and be strong or else become a part of it. The chemistry or mix of these two energies can be disturbing and mentally unhealthy if dwelled on daily. There is no knowing; no outcome or answer to the questions of the "uncanny" nor, to the absolute mysteries of "life and death"! I had to dutifully "come-to-grips" with this dilemma quickly; or else I would surely lose *Myself* and become tangled in a web of useless thought, and lose the *Dream* and the *Purpose* of being "there" in Amsterdam! Whereas the "positive energy" that swirled and spun within my orbit, "grounded me" to act and follow through with my everyday plans of meeting friends and colleagues and networking within the art community. I needed to go "forward" and not be a slave to negativity, stuck in a doldrum of wasted thought. I firmly believe that on our path to "somewhere" each one of us at some point have the experience of these positive and negative energies simultaneously entwined; and also have grounded themselves to do what I had done; which was to *Act*! But I must add that realistically, the "uncanny" is not a negative energy, it is simply one of difference and of "unknowing." Young people may not now, or not yet, have a complete "understanding" of themselves; or may believe themselves or this uncanny energy to be negative. Nor, is this uncanny energy "strange" as many people believe it to be! It is an energy that is to be used as a tool for better understanding of self and the fears that limit us, the origin and nature of things, and an escape from ignorance. In its playful secrecy, it can tease and lure us to the "unknown" to discover and learn of this energy's existence, and that, "nothing is strange" once its origin is understood. After that week following my Mother's death and a few days of my personal dilemma, in the Fall of 1975, immediate negotiations were underway to begin a year's contract to teach fifteen dance classes a week at a community center located just outside of the city in a diverse district called the "Belmermeer." Now that the prospect of work was no longer a main issue, I had made some closure on my mother's passing; sidelining my grief with the help of hours of meditation and prayer, only allowing the many memories of her that could make me smile. I now had the months of July and August to relax from that emotional drama by making time to explore Amsterdam and eventually discover and join the community of artists and also meet new friends.

The piercing of my right ear happened the following month of July. It was an unexpected, self-imposed body mark of a lifetime, and the only one. It was one of those frivolous late nights of winding down the fun among a small group of new friends who had known each other for barely two weeks; but admired the natural qualities and honesty that we discovered in one another. The four of us recognized our individual differences of culture, politics, family upbringing and social background. One of this group was from New Zealand and she had "un-trapped" herself from the city of Wellington. She was a curious, intelligent, dignified, "uptight and very serious" young woman, midway into her exciting and "determined" **5thCycle**; and was now taking "action." This being her first time in a city such as Amsterdam and arriving "face-to-face" with the realization that in Wellington she had become this complex "mind-bended" person, and didn't like who she saw! She was determined to change that, "here."

Amid the raw background of this quaint old city, She found herself to be a prissy-prude, as we all did, and often we would quip jokes about it and therefore; we appropriately named her "Lady Austin". She approved of this playful moniker because she too felt that she had the qualities and touch of a "Duchess" and of royalty! In a short time, she arrived at the understanding of the delightful humor that others would grasp in this juxtaposition of thought that was a trigger for our friendly laughter! This novice dancer, actress, poet, writer, and dreamer, exploring herself and Amsterdam and living "her big dream" to someday be an honorable published author; is in fact today, in Wellington New Zealand, just-that!

During these past forty-four years, she and I have continued our rapture of loving friendship; watching one another on our individual paths to success, and encouraging the growth and development of our individual dreams and the "seeds" that we sowed and planted together in Amsterdam. We followed-through with the nurturing, love and deep passion that is required for a fruitful and abundant harvest of an honest and a lasting, loving friendship. What I am saying is that this is just a simple metaphor of "how a dream can be realized and also how absurd" it is to say, that she and I met, by mere "coincidence"!

Ian and Jeanne, the other two that Lady Austin and I were with on that late night of frivolity were both already well into their 4ᵗʰCycle (21 to 28). The two were compatible, living together for the first time as a couple in an attic apartment that romantically overlooked one of the quaint canals of old-city Amsterdam; They were smart and wise and never talked of marriage. Ian was from Alberta, Canada; his round angelic face lined with a thin sandy blonde-colored moustache and locks of curly hair. He was a serious, well-controlled and insightful young man. And whenever he laughed or broadly smiled, his green eyes would sparkle and shine bright like emeralds; and his nature, always quiet, observing and thinking, with plans to someday create a living "dream" with his beloved Jeanne! Ian was responsibly experiencing the "Oh, I-get-it" 4ᵗʰCycle lesson, that "Everything Must Change!" He had left his humble Canadian roots to attend a small university in Seattle, Washington, where he began to dream his "dream." Jeanne was born in Hawaii and living in Seattle, and they met at a small university and became friends and planned a dream together. She was a beautiful brown-skinned young lady from Hawaii, of Asian-American descent, and was never without a smile or a facial expression that revealed her newly found happiness with Ian, and her ageless, peaceful wisdom. In a group conversation, she always took a "back seat" position, listened, and allowed her Asian-shaped brown eyes to watch and observe, her smile revealing that she enjoyed being in this position; it was her place.

I include this significant narrative because it is truly, the "defining moment" that my theory of **Cycles** began. The date was July 22nd, my original birthdate; although it is officially documented as the 23rd of July. This is due to the small village in Cape Cod and the Midwife's delay to register "Baby Arnold" at the Town Hall of Onset, Massachusetts. It was unknown to anyone in Amsterdam that this was the day of my birth; an occasion that I never cared to publicize.

The four of us; Jeanne, Ian, Lady Austin and I had been together throughout the entire evening. First being at a Café with other friends, smoking joints, having beers and laughing, and then we dashed off to a discotheque; it was time to dance, hard! The winding down of our late-night escapades had taken us to Ian and Jeanne's attic apartment. The hilarious laughter and conversation that we were having during our 3:00 a.m. walk was about body mutilation, facial scars indigenous to tribal cultures, tattoos, and ear piercing. "That is something I would never do!" I said; "I'm not into body mutilation for myself… but, I like to pierce ears!" and adding, and trying to not slur words, "Oh man! The many ears of others that I have pierced in the past years, and how I enjoyed doing it!" I said proudly. "And, I was twelve years old when I did my first piercing! Of course, I was assisted and taught by my favorite cousin, Duckie. She is the mother of my infant Godchild Pamela, whose ears were both being pierced then; and is today living with her pierced ears and her "found" happiness, within her **10ᵗʰCycle** (64 to 70). "Well, then, Doctor Ilanga!" Lady Austin said boisterously with a slight slur of words. "Do mine! That's right, you heard me! Do mine! I want my ears pierced tonight! Yes, I *Dare* to pierce!", she said prudishly and with a pride that she owned. The Duchess tightened her neck scarf, took a few steps ahead of us, and with her chest carriage held high; she strutted her self-confidence. We fell over ourselves with laughter; the three of us planting unsteady feet, stumbling and mimicking the proud strut of the "Duchess of Wellington," tipsy from wine and the false courage it induced, strutting in her high stiletto heels so blatantly dramatizing her own courageous decision! "Lady Austin!" I screamed, "Your wish is my command!" She abruptly stopped in her tracks looked over her shoulder at us, tightly knotting her neck scarf and lowering her eyelids halfway, "I'll see to that, doctor!" she said; and then slowly turned her head away from us and stepping forward proudly with the absolute "determination to do" that one acquires in the **5ᵗʰCycle**.

Jeanne and Ian's attic apartment was always a cozy warm place to be; shadowy and isolated; and from its many windows, the view from above overlooked the tiled rooftops of the city. And, as it was in most apartments or studios that housed the creative artists who lived in Amsterdam at that time, our homes would be graciously adorned with "good garbage." Fine furniture of quality and design, imported from all corners of the globe, "found" in the streets, discarded and left as "trash"! During the dark weeknights and very early mornings after 2:00 a.m. is when the "good garbage" could be rummaged through and obtained; and only on specific nights, on certain streets and in various neighborhoods! It was not an unusual sight to see folks walking the night streets, leaving the cafes and discotheques to scurry on a mad hunt, prowling the city; and not unusual to see scavengers with bureaus on their backs or tables and chairs clutched and dangling from their hands! Bicyclists who were suddenly walking and had given up their ride to a sofa in need of a home. Kitchen tables and chairs, would be well-balanced and strapped tightly to the bicycle by any means necessary! To most of us impoverished artists living in the community and furnishing an apartment or a room, finding "good garbage" was like finding a pot of gold at the end of the Rainbow in the actual form of a "dusty old treasure" at the end of the night. Ian and Jeanne's attic flat (apartment), was hippie-style comfortable, sparsely furnished with their found treasures of "good garbage".

Jeanne clapped her hands together to make an announcement; "Listen you guys! At the university Ian was considered "the Canadian master" all over the school because he rolled the biggest best damn joints ever! she said, with the flair of a booking-agent! So; he'll do that, and I'll get the beer and wine! "And Doctor," she said before darting away and cupping her hands to her chest; "for the ear surgery, what can I get for you?". My needs, were to have a needle, a flame to sterilize it, distilled alcohol, a basin of water, towels, and many ice cubes. "No problem, doctor!" she said; "they're coming up!" "Well, let's get on with this, quickly," I heard Austin whisper audibly to herself, building a bigger mountain of courage. During the intense 15-minute ear piercing procedure on both ears, Austin, who sat erect with both hands clamped to the seat of her wooden straight-backed chair, eyes squeezed tight, was petrified! Standing and hovering over her, the three of us and our six eyes were fixed on her ice-numbed earlobe, the needle to puncture, and on her face, red with color and ridden with fear. "Ooh, I hear it!" she said a couple of times. I asked; "Do you feel anything?" She opened one eye wide, to say with a dash of sarcasm, "Don't you know the difference between the words "hear" and "feel" man? You're not listening! Now I know that I said distinctly, "I hear it!" she said, and closed her one eye. This caused a moment of pause in the procedure for the four of us (and also her) to howl with laughter. Whenever she spoke, her delivery was heavily laced with her New Zealand accent, that somehow to our ears, came across sounding like a "lesson" and was always enjoyable to listen to.

Jeanne was standing next to me on my right side, and Ian was facing me, standing behind Austin and her chair with his two hands pressed on both her shoulders to stabilize and brace her trembling body. "How come you never pierced your ear?" Ian asked me, as I was holding a needle in my right hand, while the fingers of my left hand vigorously rubbed Austin's left ear lobe testing the possible numbness. I lifted my head to face Ian and his deep emerald-colored eyes. "Oh, I don't know," I said, shrugging my shoulders; "I never had reason to, I guess; and I'm not into body piercing, scarring, and tattoos, anyway. So, yea, I'm "earringless"! Ian squinted his eyes and smiled; "Yea, but I can see that you'd look really cool with one!" he said. "Oh, I don't know about that!" I said; "just because you look cool with yours, doesn't mean that I will look as cool as you!" His smile got broad with a chuckle and I gave him a quick wink and began to resume Austin's procedure. "Nurse Jeanne, I need a short piece of thread for these holes, so that they don't close up", I requested. She quickly left; "Yea, sure," she said, "Job well done, Doctor!" Austin was relieved; sitting still in her silence with her eyes calmly closed, and with a satisfied smile and just loving herself for her bravery and achievement! Her body had shed the trauma and was now totally relaxed and motionless. "Bravo, Austin!" I said; "Bravo!" Jeanne handed me the thread that I cut into two smaller pieces, needled, and dipped, into a jar of thick petroleum jelly to help glide them smoothly into the newly pierced holes in Austin's thin and boneless ear lobes. "After a few days, the healing of the wounds will begin," I said very professionally "playing hospital" and Jeanne being inspired, instantly joined me. "Yes, Doctor; I am listening, please continue," she said. "Good!" I said, and went on to say; "Then, I will remove the threads and replace them with a short piece of broom straw, cut to about a half inch in length that she'll have to lubricate with this jelly daily! And with her fingertips holding both ends of the straw, she needs to push that straw back and forth on each end, slowly and carefully. She'll need to remember that, so as not to aggravate the wound, or invite possible inflammation! And, after that I think she'll be good to go," I said with a skillful certainty. Austin sat still and quiet, waiting for the plunging straws to come. The three of us were also still, just standing there quite serious, and looking like professional doctors (without face masks), hovering over our survived patient and eyeing each other's achievement and success, as if we had just finished major surgery in the ER! "Thank you, Doctor, how splendid!" we heard Austin's voice quietly say, as she raised herself from the chair and headed straight for a large floor pillow, crawling over on her hands and knees. We heard her quietly murmuring words to herself saying, "It is done, Austin, it is done!" These were her last words before she reached the pillow to lay her head down to sleep.

My anticipated long-winded exhale came with a slow sit-down on a small arm-chair next to where Ian and Jeanne were sitting huddled together; as the Canadian Master spoke and began another roll of a joint. "It's weird man, you know, that you pierce ears and don't have any holes yourself! And earlier you told us that your brothers in the singing group, The G-Clefs, had pierced ears! And you said that onstage "you all wore a brilliant G-Clef stud in one ear as your symbol!" Waiting for my answer, Ian lowered his eyes to focus on rolling the joint and on wetting the line of the thin paper. Jeanne laid comfortably against Ian's hunched-over back for the "roll up," while her thin smile of anticipation was also waiting for the answer.

"What's weird to me Ian," (I said in jest to lighten-up our serious moment), "Is to puncture myself with another hole in my body when I already have five! Let's be real, man! One big one for my mouth, two in my nose to breathe, the penis's exit of liquid satisfaction from its tubular tunnel of love, and one for my ass! And they are all "functional" if you don't mind!" Ian's eyes opened wide from the images that he imagined! Amid our blare of laughter, Austin "playing possum" and pretending to sleep, burst out with a witch's howling cackle and shriek of laughter. "I can pierce your ear, if you like," said Jeanne, taking the joint from Ian's stubby fingers and using the dainty fingers of her left hand to dangle his earring hanging long from his left-lobe. "I pierced his!" she said quite proudly, and then taking a long inhale from Ian's perfectly rolled joint, waited for another answer from me. She exhaled slowly a long single stream of white smoke, and saying at its tail end, "And, If I do, then you'll have "six functional holes" to boast about, if you like!" The laughter she got from us was big, along with a beer spill from Ian's knocked over bottle! "Yea!" was my immediate response, "But, that sixth hole does nothing but sit there! I mean, what function does it have but to fill a hole and show an earring?" "Well, maybe that depends upon the earring being shown!" said Ian, bending over and cleaning his beer spill with a napkin. "You know; like the G-Clef's earring you talked about, and that yours was a clip on!" His simple words instantly had my mind spinning the wheels of thought, and I said; "Yea, I know what you mean, my brother!" and suddenly I got swept away in a drift of meaningful thought, leaving him and Jeanne to themselves for the following three minutes that seemed to last much longer, and easily felt like an hour to me. In this imagined hour of timeless thought, quickly the wheels turned faster and spun me away to only one realm of thought; "That maybe, there is no beginning and no end to "anything" at all! And because of the continuous rise and setting of the Sun, followed by the Moon's rising and waxing and waning and the ocean tides, we gave the day its name, and added the night to end the day!" It was humans who decided to take those three cycles of nature and their natural movements and consolidate them into the time frame of a twenty-four-hour day, so that all living things may duly "comprehend" this cyclical movement of time, concept and theory, and continue to function as they will.

Once "anything" begins, that "anything" becomes an absolute "energy" beginning its cyclical movement. The start of a day, the first day of school, the birth of a child, the excretion of bodily waste, the start and end of our daily breakfast, lunch and dinner! Needless to say, our daily routines, our weekly calendar; including the monthly or yearly bills to be paid! "Everything" and "anything" is in constant movement with time and is an energy of measured **Cycles**! An idea is an energy and its first beginning is just a thought! It is a "spark" of something new that is about to become movement and then will follow through with more thought and a process of development; and then soon, blossoming with the possibility that "this new idea can be physically realized"! And, let's hypothesize that for some reason this new idea has to be delayed, postponed, or isn't ready yet, and needs to be "put on the back burner" for a while! This can happen, but "to kill an idea" cannot happen ever! This new idea is not dead or forgotten, but rather, it quietly lays dormant in the pot on the back burner, waiting to emerge by a sudden and "triggered" recall! What is to be remembered is, that this new idea in the pot is only to be stirred a bit, with added spices of thought, covered, and then placed again on the back burner to simmer, and soon, maybe "become"!

Also not to be forgotten is the fact that this idea (energy) has already "begun" its calm movement and flow, and is now unstoppable in thought. Remember that you have created and released its own independence; it has its own *action* and *purpose* and it is **YOU** who controls the flow!

Once an idea manifests, "it can never be killed or extinguished" but can become "recycled" after being taken off the back burner and it begins another cycle of continuing development. An idea is an energy of unending passions linked by rings of emotion, people, places and time! Thinking alternatively, and with swift analysis of my life experiences, I summarized that everything and anything living or dead is an energy of measured **Cycles** and it is up to **YOU** (in the mirror) to know, understand, and comprehend, "where a Cycle ends, and when the next one begins"!

My thoughts rambled, until Jeanne's restless body movement of uncurling herself from Ian's, startled me and quickly interrupted my imagined hour of "**Cycling.**" Standing and giving herself a much-needed yoga stretch, she said, "I think you need more wine" and reached for the bottle. "Oh yea; absolutely! I answered.

And being still hinged on the Cycle's conversation with myself and reaching-out my hand to Jeanne to carefully grasp my glass of wine, I quietly made the insightful comment; "I think that, should I ever pierce my ear, Jeanne, I would like to see a "gold hoop" earring filling that hole! And maybe, when I look in the mirror every day, it will remind me that everything and anything that happens in *The Life* is about **Cycles!**

"Whoa, man, that's beautiful!" Ian shouted out, leaping up and raising high his fresh bottle of beer; "Let's drink to that!" Jeanne lifted her bottle, they guzzled and I gulped from my glass of wine. Ian's face was bright and flushed with excitement from hearing my thoughts on a piercing. He moved quickly, adjusting his large floor pillow to sit comfortably; and the "Canadian Master" began his skillful roll, again. The three of us had no words to say, we were quiet, as each of us "drifted" and were suddenly "distant" in our own space of thought. The only movement in the room was the twists and turns of Ian's fingers managing a perfect roll. Sitting there, the quiet instantly became a vacuum of thick silence for at least twenty seconds! It had a movement and I could feel its powerful impact on us. This brought an immediate recall to mind, and I managed to wedge through its thickness until I was able to whisper loudly enough for them to hear; "When a silence is long and thick like this, and if there are three or more people in conversation, and suddenly the talking abruptly stops; my mother would always say, 'It is when the Angels are passing by and that this special silence is to be acknowledged and respected'". The silence remained until the sound of Ian's cigarette lighter clicked, before he asked; "What else would you wear in your ear as your symbol? You know; I mean like, would you wear diamond studs or other things?" There was not even a pause between his question and my answer; "No!" I said adamantly to Ian who was listening carefully, and Jeanne likewise. "I don't think that I want or need a meaningless symbol of identification stuck in that hole, should I ever have one! And if I did, I'm sure that it would only be and always be a gold-hoop earring! Maybe it being there will actually fill the hole with a meaningful function and not just as a dangling ornament; and every day when I look in the mirror, it's there to "show" me its purpose, which I think can only be to remind me that "everything goes in cycles" and "what goes around, comes around", If you know what I mean, I said. I liked that thought, and also how the words sounded in my ears.

"Ooh, that's nice!" Jeanne said, and was about to say more, but Ian interrupted; "How cool, man! There's your "reason" to do it!" he said with great emphasis. Jeanne agreed with him, and passing the joint to me, continued her previous thought; "It's nice! It's so perfectly you!" she said, crossing her arms and tilting her head to one side. Her waist-long silky black hair framed her face and genuine smile. I exhaled, slowly oozing-out a long streaming flow of cloudy white smoke, and felt a release, a "letting-go" of something other than cloudy white smoke! The blockage of the thought "to never pierce a hole in my ear" suddenly became "unblocked" and, I liked the new thoughts that were circling in my mind; I liked the conversation we were having, and its content; and actually, liked it well enough for me to say to myself convincingly, "Yea! Why not!"

Raising high my half-empty glass of red wine, I said, "Okay guys, let's pierce now!" A husky cough and a cloud of gurgled white smoke came blasting-out of Ian's mouth; and Jeanne's round face beamed and gleamed like sunshine! I said to her loudly as they raised their bottles of beer; "And Jeanne, you're going to do the piercing!" Her voice squealed high at first, and then melded into an excited, "Holy-Shit!" Lady Austin leaped up from where she lay, and bellowed to be heard, "I heard that!" quickly coming over to join us. "Do I hear a "dare" Mister Ilanga?," she asked sternly, and standing high above my reclined body with both her hands positioned rigidly on her hips, said; "People, must I refresh my glass of wine and partake in this 'profound and prophetic' legacy-to-be?" She answered herself instantly with a quip, "Yes, I Must!" and dashed for the bottle of wine, as Jeanne dashed away for another basin of fresh water; both on their separate missions.

It was my turn now to sit in the straight-back wooden chair to relax, breathe slowly and contemplate the reasons "why" and endure this procedure of self-torture. Jeanne began tugging at and numbing my right ear lobe with freezing ice, and Ian had relocated his floor pillow to sit opposite me, sitting crossed-legged in the Yoga lotus position and smiling warmly to witness this, my new experience. "Hey, Jeanne!", he stated; "You're numbing the wrong-ear! It's the left-one that needs the hole!", Ian said with a flair of dutiful masculinity. Lady Austin again quipped, "Oh, come on man; does it matter?! Let's get on with it!" Jeanne released the ice from my lobe, relaxed herself, and calmly said to Ian, "He" decided this ear, Ian; this is *his* choice, man, not yours, or anyone else's, don't ya think?" she said sarcastically, emphasizing her question with a tilt of her head! Her pause and intense stare at him lasted a few seconds before she resumed the piercing. Ian's face that was once of question and concern, was now a face that suddenly became wiser, and had embraced a shower of "enlightenment" or had come to a full circle of personal "understanding." "Touche," Ian said to Jeanne. "But you know how it is in *The States* for guys: If you're "Straight" it's on the left ear, and if you're "Queer" it's on the right, that's all!" he said objectively. "I don't live in The States, Ian; I live in the World!" I said to him, and with an acceptance of this new cyclical beginning, I allowed Jeanne and the jelled-threaded-needle to glide into the new hole to begin and end the procedure. Not looking at Ian, Jeanne gently said, "Thank you, Ian!"

After the gleeful viewing of my newly-threaded-hole from the three, there were many gasping "oohs and ahs" that followed. We reclined ourselves and refreshed our drinks. And after the Canadian Master rolled up once more; he picked up his small Native American drum and began a slow, soft tap on its skin with his thick fingers. The rhythm sounded good to Jeanne; and with her bottle of beer in her hand, she got up and slowly began to dance with her arms, hips and smile, as if she was on an island in Hawaii. "Well now; that's the thing to do; isn't it?" said Lady Austin, and got-up to join Jeanne in her dance. Ian kept beating his drum and loving his slow-paced rhythm, and with his eyes closed, the girls danced. I knew that he could hear my words to him; "Ian, if you are upset or disagree that I wear an earring in my right ear, don't be! And I'm saying this, because I think you're too wise to be caught-up in that stale old American thing, man. Allow "them" to believe that; and you, just continue being Canadian **YOU** and "Let that go, man!" He abruptly stopped tapping his rhythms as Austin and Jeanne continued to dance, but Jeanne "scolded" him by just saying his name, "Ian!" at the top of her voice, "Why are you stopping?" she asked. "Indeed, continue on, man," said Austin; "Ooh, it was just getting good! There's certainly no-stopping now, Ian!" she said, dancing in continuous movement, and spilling red wine from the now half-empty glass she was holding awkwardly in one hand. "Surprised" that he had indeed destroyed a joyous moment of rhythms and dance, Ian responded quickly, "Oh, sorry!" and began beating the skins of his drum with a new up-tempo rhythm so the dance could begin again. He then talked to me with an apologetic tone as he continued playing, more relaxed and less involved with the rhythm while holding a steady beat. He continued, "I mean; I stopped playing before because I wanted to say to you that I heard all of what you were saying and I agree with you! And no; I don't think like "they" think, man! It's just that, well you know, you're gonna have to deal with a lot of bullshit and verbal abuse and you're too cool for that, you know what I mean?!" His steady drum beat became unsteady and I could hear and see that Ian was becoming annoyed. "And I don't like it that all of that bullshit is gonna come down on you! It hurts me, man!" he said; "This is like wearing a "label" or it's like waving a "flag" of identification no matter in what ear an earring is in!" This thought flustered Ian, and it stirred a slight anger; his stop of the next drum beat was instant! "This is real American bullshit and it pisses me off!" he said in disgust. He rested his drum, placing it next to him, and continued; "And as Lady Austin says, does it matter, which ear it's in? Hell No!" He sat firmly on his floor-pillow and folded his arms across his chest to think about what he had just said and decided instead, to pull out his small blue package of Samson shag tobacco and roll a cigarette.

I admired Ian's honesty; a young man with Integrity, and one who has "nobility" locked into his future. His face lit up and his green eyes gleamed when I said to him, "And of all of this trifling and useless thought of an earring in the left or right ear; you Ian, are going to be the balance for me in this new experience that I will be going through in The States, of putting myself through "self-identification and bullshit"! And whenever a stupid incident of bullshit happens, I will think of you and the long earring pierced in your left ear, dangling and showing Jeanne's love! And, the shiny gold-hoop earring that I have, will be "showing" me *Cycles* hanging from my right ear! My "joy" is, Ian; that each time I am verbally abused, I will always think of the fine balance that you and I have together, 'in thought, and as friends'! So, no, don't worry about me, my brother; for me, the right ear is fine!"

Ian's smile broadened reflecting on this happy thought, as I "snatched" the joint from his fingers and saying with dramatic and honest force; "And actually Ian, I have no concern what "anyone" thinks about me, except my family and friends!" Then I slowly inhaled a stream of white smoke from the joint "that wasn't a joint" but, smooth shag-tobacco.

Lady Austin halted her dance and with one steady hand holding her glass of wine, said; "Oh my; I heard that, Mister Ilanga! "No concern, mind you! Would you "dare" to say that again, as I am here, waiting in my stationary pause!" I did, and with over-the-top exaggerated "drama" we all laughed loudly! Ian grabbed his drum again and began beating its skin with another level and force of energy; and Ian's tempos and rhythms (which had escalated to a high frenzy) grabbed me and beckoned me to get up, take the last big gulp of wine, carry the newly-made joint with me to quickly puff and pass on, and join the now frenzied "wild-hip-shaking dancers" as he played!

Soon enough, the sunlight of the new day seemed to come upon us quickly, showing itself through the fabric of Jeanne's salvaged curtains that she scored from a "good-garbage" night in the neighborhood. It was an "unusual sun-lit morning" in Amsterdam, so we decided to borrow Jeanne's sunglasses and head out the door to the early-morning-bakery for warm bread and croissants.

This little narrative is credible and very significant to the creation of my theory of the *7 Year Cycles of Life* and *Self-Evaluation*; but, there is a heartbreaking wound to this little narrative that is still open, and that lingers with me; and it is that neither Lady Austin nor I, ever did see Ian and Jeanne again since they, or we, left Amsterdam! But, maybe we will in our next cycle of the afterlife together! Well, that's if they believe and live for that also.

CHAPTER FOUR

Careful, words matter – a child is listening.

The **6th Cycle** (Ages 36 to 42 years of age), comes with the need and the desire to establish the "purpose of being and doing." This awakening is an absolute, and has the need to be decided upon and established. *Who you are as a Person*, the *Career, the Profession, the Partner, the Nuclear Family, the Goal or the Dream*. And because of those chosen and committed "responsibilities" it leaves only a small margin of opportunity for the inclination to "dare". One cannot chance to "dare" with so much at stake in the **6th** and **7thCycle** (Ages 43 to 49). To take risks in these two crucial Cycles can be detrimental, and truthfully, immature. Unless one is a single person, he or she still has the independence to "dare" and take risks, and be selective without a bond to anyone else but themselves and to their "purpose."

Once the purpose has been decided upon and established, the "vision" of its possible reality opens wide and expands for a desired plan to be implemented and "acted" upon. We are continually designing and applying new strategies to navigate and pursue the purpose. A new Mom is determined and strives hard to become a "Mother" and a new Dad (also determined) is fearless in his quest of becoming a "Father" and is primarily focused on the family's welfare and future. For the new Mom and Dad, this has become their "new purpose in *The Life*," above all else! No matter what the goal, dream or purpose was prior to this new-event, it is no longer! Once-possible achievements or realities have been pushed aside for the "new reality" of an infant child in your arms. This new reality is the tangible result of "your seed," "your creation" and is now your *primary purpose*. The powerful "realization" of this "new reality" and "new purpose" comes instantly to Mom and Dad after the moment of the infant's birth, when this new life energy is held and caressed for the first time. It is a specific moment in time when one totally "comprehends" self-creation, love, personal evolution, and responsibility. One who is single and childless in *The Life* may comprehend this as well, equating this juxtaposition if his or her "purpose" is being responsibly upheld, acted-upon, and realized. For Mom and Dad with a child or children, or for the childless, single person who lives with a child or works with children and youth, the responsibility to care for and "to educate" becomes clearly understood. The honest truth and facts of the purpose prevail: to do the job well with commitment, passion and a measure of love! This is the golden key to the child or children's future; and without question, Mom, Dad, or Guardian, are to be held accountable. They are the significant ones in the child's life, the ones who decide the teaching and the education. "What matters" and "What does not," "What is a dream" and "What is a reality"! A child must learn, that she or he will not always be a child; and this needs to be introduced to them within their **2ⁿᵈ Cycle** (8 to 14). It is important to ask a child, "What do you want to be when you grow up?" but the most important question is, "What kind of *person* do you want to be when you grow up?" This is the Cycle of self-exploration, awareness of adult characters and their behavior; and the Cycle of "figuring out exactly where they fit" within their circle of family and friends. By the time they've arrived to their **3ʳᵈ Cycle** (15 to 21), they have "figured it out" and have begun to shape and visualize the "person" that *They* want to be; (which is often not the person that Mom Dad and the Educators want the child to be!) Yes; We admire how "now" they are grown and have come unto their "Own" and have "Their" new ideas; but, as I previously mentioned: "An idea, is just a new thought that is sparked and evolves into a movement to be processed and developed, before it can manifest into a reality"; and in this Cycle, age is ignorant of process. The intelligent young girl or boy may have a "new" idea, but it is not yet ready to be implemented and because of that, reasonable advice is given; but at this age, the advice is well heard, but interpreted into a childish "gloom", a big disappointment, and a "natural" misunderstanding. And from the whining voice of naivete, shouts the infamous cliché "Oh, you just don't understand me!" or, the silent "shut-down" treatment of solitude, after the "leave me alone" is strongly stated! Often, some of these "precious gems" fall into a "trap" of bewilderment and confusion; embedded with low self-esteem, "just chillin'" and preferring to stagnate for a period of time. They dare not risk the valuable attempts to "believe in themselves" or seek the motivation to go forward rightly into their new and soon- approaching, challenging and complexed **4ᵗʰCycle** (22 to 28).

This is the importance of *Self-Evaluation*. One needs to Know oneself. He or She needs to ask themselves, "How did I take on this shape?", and "What did I experience?" and "What is my "take-away" from all of this?" and "Now, what do I do and where do I go with it?" This analysis and insight enables us to find the *Truth* of ourselves from within, and not from external sources which can often cause confusion due to the barrage of "untruths" being learned. When one evaluates with thought, experiences, and environment, one discovers a new plateau for themselves, and a "new idea" from which they can go forward; and "to go forward" is something that we all must do! Therefore, the question that I ask for finding the truth, is: "How else can we learn to be and do something better?" We will never know unless we learn how to analyze and *Self-Evaluate*.

I can only answer from within my own discovered truth; and I need to say, that without self-evaluation to go forward meaningfully and strong determination with *Purpose* must be there to motivate and cause the thrust to "Act"! The energy of *Determination* that we establish and learn in the 5th**Cycle**; its *Power* and usefulness during periods in the following Cycles is the energy that we must commit to when we are lost in doubt and stagnation and can't move forward! Yes, we all understand and know the definition of the word "determination;" but to actually "comprehend" its *Energy, Power*, and its *Impact*, one must first undergo and experience the **6**th and **7**th **Cycles.** Prior to then, we really only "understand" it to a certain level.

Every loving child born deserves and is due education and every knowledgeable Mom and Dad go beyond themselves wanting that to be of quality! The dedicated and sincere teachers of children and youths go above and beyond themselves to provide quality education, but often are prevented from implementing quality due to obstacles provided by the already established "Educators, Politicians, and Parents," who cause interference with the ongoing argument and discussions about "What is quality education?" Therefore, it is the primary responsibility of a "Self-Evaluated" Mom and Dad, to teach "their" truth and values to their children, from their own personal experiences and knowledge and the environment in which they live; otherwise, the children will only learn "otherwise!"

How sad it is for a child to not learn the truth of themselves, the family and the environment. Consequently, to "undo the untruths" that have been learned in their primary stage often could take a lifetime (if at all) to undo, untangle and to realize that what has been learned is not of truth! It is only natural for a child to absorb what they hear, see and feel; and "a moment of happiness" can quickly change into a moment of "hurt" simply by a word or by something that they see! This is a critical moment; and it is within this narrow space of time that the adult has the opportunity to explain and share the truth of the happiness felt, or say words that can make it easier for the child to understand, "the happiness that has gone, and the hurt that brought about tears".

Words matter and that is because they too have an energy and a purpose, and that is to make a person take action in thought or deed. A child can understand the words of truth or untruths that the adult speaks, by their own natural instinct; and soft-spoken words of truth have the positive energy of *Enlightenment* and harsh sounding words of untruth, have the energy of *Doubt*. This, can cause confusion and a conflict with innocence; a disturbing place for any child to be wandering in without an adult's hand to hold. By nature, a child can see and feel the actions of every adult, and to a child, every adult is a teacher! Therefore, words and action matter greatly!

Those of you who are parents, teachers, children's advocates, and are of the **6th** and **7thCycles**, have most certainly witnessed a child's happiness instantly change and suddenly come to tears, by what their innocent eyes have seen or tiny little ears have heard. Adults understand completely and with passion, the words of truth and the essence of "where-I'm-coming-from." They also know the difficulty of administering such values within today's prolific environment of social untruths, adult lies, "fake news," video games, and other deterrents that obstruct a child's natural yearning for the truth of themselves by what they hear and see.

My advice to Mom and Dad and we Teachers who need to see and feel the efforts and results of our work and want to witness our personal achievements and success; is to rely on your own *honest intuition* and *personal truths.* The already acquired *Determination, Action taken,* and your undisputable *Beliefs, Values,* and *Self-Confidence,* is what your child receives from you. It comes from your truth, knowledge and Love, and when administered with the purpose of educating, you will be able to "See, feel and witness" all of your wonderful efforts as your child/children, transition into the 2nd and 3rd **Cycles** which is when they too should be introduced to the tool of *Self-Evaluation.*

It is because of the womb, what it produces, and the "gift" of a loving Mother that that I have an affinity for *Mothers.* From the moment that she lovingly conceives, the embryonic process begins, and in that instant, **YOU** become! You are there with her, both, holding on to one another "forever." Her natural love, fortitude, determination and vigilance is as constant and rippled as the ocean's tides. She sees, hears, and feels for her child what no other person can! And if a mother should ever have to leave her child to someone else, usually it is because of a dire situation of practicality or a mental health issue (this is not a Mother's nature, but a Mother's grief). There are two days on our yearly calendar that are of great importance to me: The day Jesus Christ was born - the most special child - and the annual celebration of Mother's Day. When I see a mother and child together, the image is symbolic of the diverse Icons of "The Madonna and Child" that I have seen on display around the world. It confirms to my eyes and my soul that pure love still exists, and it gives me "hope" that that kind of love never becomes extinct due to the amount of selfishness and greed that is so prevalent in the world today.

I also have deep respect, honor, and admiration for those Dads who are obedient to their Namesake: Father. Fatherhood is a "big-shoe-to-fill" and a man can only wear these shoes when he is no longer a boy, and realizes and accepts this truth. Only then can he become a "Man" and be a "Father" to his child; and in some cases, it takes a strong and challenging wise Woman to give assistance to him who needs to "fill-the-shoes" of Fatherhood, Manhood, or both. The Man who can also fit the shoes of Motherhood as a single parent, is a "Super Man" in his dual role of new discoveries that encompass new fears, lingering doubts, and often questionable guidance. "What does a Mom do?" is his weapon of thought in his quiet battle to "Win"! There is no surrendering this responsible position of duality that he undertakes; all challenged daily, with his thoughtful weapon of devotion and an endless love!

Being a childless and single man throughout my life was by "choice" decided during my teenaged 3rd**Cycle**, of friends, fun hormonal explosions, and the excitement and thrills of being a cool-dancing Doo Wop singer in the G-Clefs! By the onset of my 4th**Cycle**, I had only given a thought to marrying (and it went no further than a thought!) It had no energy, movement or purpose, as an "Idea" would have! It was a serious thought to be considered; but "to marry" was not my idea, it was hers! The reasons to marry and its purpose suited my friends and my brothers; but I understood clearly at that time - once I had concluded the challenges of the 4th**Cycle** - that "it was not my purpose" nor did I have a good reason to marry! During that era of conventional thought, it was the "norm" to marry; but I wasn't interested in following the norm!

I understood then, that the position I had taken on marriage, having children, and to planning a family dream, was simply to analyze and evaluate the choice I had made: to not partake of but rather, to "only observe" the roles of the Mother and the Father! To be either, was not of my *Purpose* in *The Life*. I had begun to self-evaluate in the midst of my **3rd Cycle**. This is when I became more aware of my environment, the differences in people, and of myself. To "listen and observe" became a discipline that I had to learn and develop for years thereafter. It was not until the onset of my **5th Cycle** that I began to understand, comprehend and accept completely my choice and the position I had taken; and I became determined to find out why.

Presently, I am two years into my **12th Cycle** (77 to 83), and throughout these many years I have remained a single man. I am a Brother to six siblings, a genuine Uncle of concern for each and every Niece and Nephew, a Cousin to many, and friend to all those who befriend me. And for well over fifty years, I've had a purpose, to teach the many children and youths, who every day "communicate" and teach me the importance of "pure and honest love" in its most innocent and natural form because, they are only "of this" original nature until they reach their **4th Cycle** of *Changes* and learn the many other colors of *Love*. They discreetly signal their quiet needs with a whisper of their truth, teach, and show me all of the reasons why I must give back and teach them in return. This is their primary lesson of "fair exchange." How important it is for them to harness that lesson of honest love and ride with it throughout their entire life! And to never forget, to show and reveal their truth. I have always felt that my rapport and relationships between children and youth are, and must be, a "fair-exchange" and it is because of this, that daily, I bask in the bright Sunlight of *Happiness*! There is not a day that goes by without listening to and hearing a child's voice, or a young man or woman's voice in need of a truthful "something" and they want and deserve the truth! To deliver that truth is my responsibility to the children and youth of our time, and to those who are approaching the **6th Cycle**, and the Cycles thereafter.

It was because of my independence, personal experiences, my environment and self-evaluation, that I made this certain "deliberate choice" to remain a single and independent man and embrace all children with the pure and honest love that they thirst for and need to receive so that they too will be able to give back! This deliberate choice was decided upon during my **4th Cycle** of "changes" and with self-promises to remain so throughout my **5th Cycle** of adulthood (29 to 35).

It is not until the **6th Cycle** (36 to 42), that some of us arrive and should be aware that we are now "crowned" as an actual "adult." Grown-up, mature, and responsible! We have "arrived" and are wise enough now, to understand a child's needs; and if we think that we don't know, then we must ask!

We all have been a child, and eventually we become a young woman or a young man! We already know a child's need, hurt, and happiness, and we know the needs of a youth in need because, we all have "been-there-and-done-that"!

> Bitter are the tears of a child;
> Sweeten them.
> Deep are the thoughts of a child;
> Quiet them.
> Heavy is the grief of a child;
> Lighten it.
> Soft is the heart of a child;
> Embrace it.
> (Anonymous)

This verse of truth is an "Idea" of "what to do with love"; and is a gentle reminder to ourselves that this is an Idea and a responsibility that is never to go on "the back burner" during our specific "actions" being taken in the **6ᵗʰCycle**! What keeps me on my toes and alert is whenever a child or anyone younger than me stands before me with their need, or asks something, I am always able to assist, just by "being there" for them, to listen and to hear their story. The support and comfort they need is there for them, even if it's only for that moment; but It is often that their silent cry falls on deaf ears, or that no one else is there to hear it! A child can only "hear see and feel" an adult's immediate response to their need; and if the response is positive, the child is receptive to dialogue. Should the adult's response, by body gesture or facial expression have a shade of "unconcern" or should their verbal response have a tone of negativity, such as, "I'm too busy, we'll talk about this later!" or "I'm on the telephone, go to your room!" The child is "listening" and he or she, "feels and hears" these hurtful words instantly! We must always try our utmost to remind ourselves "to listen and to be there" and to be attentive because this is when a child is introduced to the value of "Trust."

Now that we've become "adults" and somewhat established we should have a *Purpose* a *Plan* and a *Vision*, that is now being charted to navigate through the following **Cycles** thereafter. This is the "success" and "high achievement" of the **6ᵗʰCycle**, and it has been accomplished by **YOU!** As adults, we should now be "responsible" and able to confidently apply and share our gift of knowledge; which is "to educate"! And what to do with this accumulated knowledge that we now have? Generously share it with those who are younger and in need of positive strength, power, understanding, and love.

This is what "responsible" adults do! There are those however, who are in their **6ᵗʰCycle** and have still not "arrived" at adulthood, and are not yet ready to be completely "crowned" as an adult due to their own personal experiences that caused delay in the process of their growth and development. Some may not ever "arrive" due to their ignorance of ever becoming!

And then we have the "adult" who has made the attempt to establish and succeed in their *Purpose* by collaborating with someone else such as a friend, a partner, or a marriage to someone whose *Purpose* is likewise; but suddenly, the intended collaboration fails! This failure could be possibly due to the will of their own **EGO,** the immaturity of the partner or merely by circumstance. This is not unusual, nor is this the time for discouragement! There is still, that one-last-time opportunity for the "disappointed" to capture the realization and possibility of "re-establishing" themselves and their "new purpose" during their **7ᵗʰCycle** (Ages 43 to 49). "A half-century of age" accumulated and being lived successfully by the everlasting source and "determination" of the **5ᵗʰCycle**. This not the time to give up but to "go forward!" And you must know and believe during this intense and crucial time of self-survival suddenly happening in your life, that there is only *One Positive* and *Supportive factor* to help you to go forward, and that is **YOU!** You are now alone again, but well-prepared "to start anew" and rewardingly, a sense of "wisdom" surfaces that you seem to *Comprehend, Believe, and Know*; and it has surfaced to guide you through it all! How wonderful it is to know that, and to "act!" The already accrued values of your *Purpose* and the energy of your *Determination* is still there and therefore; you must recall, recognize, and address this valuable and positive thought and action. This is personal and this is your only supportive factor. This is the last opportunity to take off from the back burner that other "Idea" that you had left there to simmer! And external support? that is now secondary. **YOU** already know the measure of effort it will take to go forward, and **YOU** already know the consequences should your "Ego's" choice be to just "stagnate"! So, it is **YOU** who must recognize this opportunity, and must make this choice wisely! **YOU** (in the mirror) are the only one who is able to access the recall and dynamics of "what happened." And, if you are still in the "pursuit of happiness" analyze well and objectively and, *Self-Evaluate.* This is your first step "to go forward"!

And my humble advice to you, my young and ageless reader is; by all means, "don't sweat the effort." You already know what must be put into this challenge of "rebirth" or "starting over," so stressful thinking, would only be wasted energy! Remember well the past. **YOU** have already "been there and done that" so why sweat over something of which you already have knowledge? "Effort" is an attempt and it is a discipline that you must be mindful of, but also, don't forget that this discipline needs to be considered and pointedly addressed by **YOU** and "your" intelligence and not by the influential **EGO** that can swell into false pride and dominate positive thoughts. "To attempt" with an energy of negativity is self-centered and allows that negative energy to flow evenly, thick, and without ripples, straight in the direction of ignorance.

The 7ᵗʰCycle (43 to 49) is the "try again" Cycle; one more attempt to succeed in your now, "new measure of high achievement" that was once attained, but was interfered with, and now must be regained. "Whatever happened, happened"! It is no longer happening in the present, and will not be happening in the future. That is, if **YOU** (in the mirror) are able to release the tormenting "stagnant thought" of what happened and realize, that this thought is deeply harbored in the limbo of your **EGO's** hurt and its own disappointment! You must remember that these are "two separate entities" and they are in conflict with one another. It is **YOU,** not **Ego,** who needs to take control of this dire situation that has you stagnant and not making a move forward. This adverse situation may welcome mental depression and is a sad place to be in, if in the 7th**Cycle** your dream has been deferred.

By releasing this harbored thought of "what happened?" it affirms the fact, that **YOU** have successfully perceived that the **EGO** is the cause of this "blockage" and **YOU** have found your distance between "it" and are now able to scrutinize, analyze and prepare yourself "to go forward" in thought and action. For some of us who undergo this situation during this Cycle, there is no escape from or letting go of this every-day-all-day overwhelming thought of "what happened" and Why?" And the danger is, that "treading on this dark road of thought" paved with limitations and visions of future despair, is destined to be full of self-destructive forces. The "positive energy and action" that **YOU** embrace today in the present, will not erase those harbored thoughts; but even the smallest attempt to "let them go" by **YOU** deciding your fate, will foster "new ideas" and "new energy" and will gradually help you to ride on and flow in the direction of "Go-Forward"! Be *Aware* of who you are today, be *Confident,* be *New* and "regain your high achievement"! And again, you will feel the "wonder and joy of self-love"! But, please don't forget to be grateful to whomever or whatever made this possible; it might just be **YOU!**

CHAPTER FIVE

Party games are fun...if you know it's a game.

Being who I was; a well-established artist, singer, dancer, choreographer and teacher, with a unique art form that revealed my natural-talent, personality, and professional abilities that were of personal and cultural value, and also proved to be lucrative, allowed me to live *The Life* as I deemed it to be; "a daily adventure of alluring curiosity!" And also; "Why Not?" think of *The Life* in this way! As an adventurous, international world traveler and lover of all cultures and peoples, to "book a flight to anywhere" was my choice! And whenever possible, exploring and totally being in the nature and environment conducive to "my nature, my Soul, and my Spirit." This always "left the door open" to the opportunity of choosing where to live in the world; be it a village, town, city or country, it was my place of residence and where I called, "home."

I had been living in Europe for ten years before returning to the United States in 1985, and America had transformed itself within that decade! A "new" culture had emerged from social riots, Watergate, and folk songs; It was President, Ronald Reagan's "New and Happy" U.S.A.! The theaters along Broadway dazzled their audiences with musical shows that sparkled more than ever with brilliance! "Blockbuster" films and videos were being viewed by masses of people standing in long lines at the box office of crowded, large spacious Cinemas, housing attractive and tempting food courts and "push-back" seats of comfort! Disco dancing, its music, and its vibe, had America on its feet, up late nights, and "Partying hard" until sunrise; and the President of the United States had welcomed the dullard "Hollywood Celebs" to once again walk the red carpet with their usual glamour and dignity; but now; with more lights and bigger and brighter spectacles! More cameras, stage gadgets, and more "infamous" designer gowns on starlets; surprisingly accompanied by men's bright plumage in the form of tuxedo lapels in tapestry and floral brocade!

My departure from Athens Greece and my arrival back in America once again, was "shocking"! After the first month of joyful greetings and settlement, the first wave of "Culture Shock" washed against my mind; and I could "feel" that the tremendous impact of this shock would remain with me for as long as I was here! I felt as if I had stepped out of an "Old World" known as Europe, and walked into the "Trap of modern times" again! "To patiently endure, is the bow that ties a gifted package of Dreams and purpose." This was the sweet thought that I held onto tightly for two years; along with the sour thought of what I had left behind: The monumental ancient relics, cultures and age-old traditions, loving friends, and most importantly, professional independence! The thought of all this "Wonder" in exchange for glittering tall buildings, enormous football stadiums, and millions of people, was the sour thought often triggered by what my eyes were seeing. Nobody cared about anybody they were passing; rudeness, oblivion, pretentiousness, and personal space dominated the sidewalks! And without missing the irony that on every street-corner, a small Christian church, jam-packed with followers; or a showy "Megachurch" stretched out along a flashy boulevard and housing a congregation of worshipers by the thousands! This "awakening" of my "new" everyday reality came to me after a year of planning to leave Athens Greece and Europe.

Although I had been very successful with my company, *Ilanga's Jazz Dance Theater* and other dance works, my appetite to evolve as a knowledgeable artist never ceased! And, because of my ten year absence from doing any career work in the States (except for flying in from Athens or Amsterdam to do a "G-Clef's gig" and then returning home) somehow it just didn't satisfy my appetite enough to become more of "what and who I am"!

I "awakened" to this "new" reality with the fortunate opportunity to live in "The City of Angels" (Los Angeles) for two years; aka the "Hollywood fantasy." And with the onslaught of fax machines, pagers, weird television sitcoms, tall shiny buildings reaching sky-high in a dirty orange colored cloud amid a baffling roadway system of sprawling highways and byways congested with trucks, large cars and too many exits to find one's destination! I was in "La La Land" the film industry to learn the makings of a film. This was my interest upon leaving Athens for Los Angeles; not the Hollywood glamour or the spotlight. Nor did I have any ambition or desire to become a screen actor, a film star, or another rejected talent, grimly walking the "boulevard of broken dreams" or "schmoozing" day and night with the high hopes of "being seen or discovered" by a Producer or Talent Agent. On the contrary; I wanted to learn what was it like to be a film Director, a Producer, a Producer's Assistant, a hard-working crew member, or more specifically, a Screen Writer for television and film. To learn "hands-on" all the components of filmmaking was simply another "new" experience for me to evolve and "become."

But, as it is "life happens!" and after a few months of being a novice "component" of the industry, I was offering every talent and ability I had to merge with this "bizarre" way of living life every day and night of the week in chaos, where all is hurried! The severity of time and its every moment is crucial; and there is no end to the "schmooze-parties" hosting blustery Egos and the "wanna-bes" who dream of having a "Star" cemented in a sidewalk on Hollywood Boulevard! And that could sometimes only depend on a Producer, Director, or "whoever" has the "casting couch" available.

As a Producer's Assistant, one does, what one is able to do. I had the opportunity "to do" from being a choreographer on music videos and for a film that I can't remember the name of, to being an on-set "gopher," a location scout, van driver, and whatever else the Producers saw fit to have me do. The valuable information, guidance, and lessons that I extracted from this every day madness of life in "La La Land" fascinated me with many attractions and thrills! At times, I saw and felt that the activity "buzz'n" in this sprawling city of excitement was like that of an enormous amusement park or a big circus without a tent! It was always alive and rushing with an unstoppable force of continuous creative energy that was manifested and so prominently displayed in visuals. I saw characters of their own design and artistic expression parading in the streets, tempting my gawking eyes! Breathtaking images in film and on stage, with an output and overflow of creative energy, constant and quietly "zooming in the fast lane" twenty-four hours a day!

It was all there for those who "thrive" on such demanding energy to succeed as a film mogul, a TV or film star, a crew member, a costume seamstress, a hair and makeup artist, a stunt person, a screenwriter, or for anyone else who dreams of working as a professional in the film industry.

The few months soon became a year of being a novice component within this spinning "Wheel of Fortune" of a city; that, to some eyes and ears, I appeared to be and often felt to be a "Novelty" or a possible "Alien" that just landed in L.A. from some strange world "out there"! And because I had been living in Greece and the Netherlands for the past decade and not speaking the English language daily and fluently for years; my words were often mispronounced or totally forgotten! It was difficult to remember a word that I hadn't heard from anyone or spoken myself in these past ten years; and whenever I would forget a word, it would be easy in an instant for me to just make up a word that sounded like the correct one. And when I would be called out on this, and given the correct word; I would just say, naively, "Oh yea; That's what I meant!" and simply continue on with the conversation! Walking along the wide and congested sidewalks of L.A. in the blazing hot Sun with a long colorful scarf loosely draped around my neck, and along with a gold hoop pierced earring in my right ear; I deemed myself to be a "character of artistic expression"! But on a stroll down the boulevard of Venice Beach, I was undoubtably unnoticeable; just another character!

Those few months quickly passed and soon became a year of insightful realization as I was learning more, doing more, and "Becoming" more; I also had become more conscious, aware, and in-tune with the environment and its chaotic creative energy. But the more I adapted to the many rhythms of the city, its offerings and lifestyle, the deeper I got myself caught in its caged "Trap" of glitter and gold! And again; It was because of intuition, analysis and *Self-Evaluation* that "Salvation" arrived to me; and this is when I came to the realization that the "Man in the mirror" had to escape before he too would be caught! And for years to come, captured in a weird daily delusion of "what the everyday should be about" and secretly pretending that "this was *Happiness*" I just could not see myself living in a gilded cage "trapped" and nurturing a lifestyle of "plastic," succeeding only in becoming another "Hollywood character" walking down Wilshire Boulevard, wearing a colorful scarf, and in search of a dream that he knew, had much more potential of becoming a living-nightmare!

The west coast's world of movie making and television sitcoms, and the many "out-takes" of a day's work when the Director and Producer finally decide which scene to select for the "authentic performance" that has been captured in the lens of the camera, is the aspect of the business that had me thinking of the emotional effect that this concept and finished product of "technical creation" would have on me! And because of this in-depth thinking, I was led to consider the alternative-thought aspect of the business: the thrilling "live-on-stage" performance and energy that my *Mind, Body and Soul* absorbs and thrives on, relentlessly, and with passion! If I was to be living this celluloid-provoked lifestyle, I would need to include the dynamic energy of the live performance with its *spontaneity* and the expected adrenaline rush and "butterflies" that flutter in the pit of the stomach of every stage performer before each live performance! This is the capture, and also the rapture that artists ponder and endure, as they are applying their make up in the quiet of their dressing room, or standing in the wings of the stage waiting to be thrust into the spotlight! Ultimately, all of this became overwhelming and I decided that it was time for me to leave America once again. After those two years of lessons well learned, however, I did not return to Europe or Greece; I needed to abandon the fantasies of La La Land for "something else" and therefore decided that my next country of residence, was to be Mexico.

I ended up in Cancun Mexico, and was winding down my 7th**Cycle** and at the threshold of my 8th**Cycle** (50 to 56) when this fresh new wave of realization came to me: that by taking away the best of what I had experienced in L.A., leaving behind all that was worthless and of no value, I was able to dismiss or erase from my mind the prickly thorns and abrasiveness of L.A. And the difficulty that the city's residents must endure - the pressure, stress and self-sacrifice needed to "Succeed" I could leave behind; making my arrival in Mexico a welcome, new "joy" and my decision to stay was filled with peace.

My time in Mexico was a retreat from the modern times and spinning wheels of progress that incessantly grind in the shiny cities of America and Europe. Living in a calm and stable rhythm every day in the beautiful and natured world of Mexico for a year, was so unlike the "scramble" and "dizziness" of Los Angeles! It was a much-needed retreat from an overdose of high energy, and the foreseeable thought, that "this trapping could be endless"!

I enjoyed working hard in Cancun more than half of that year, teaching creating shows and meeting new friends; and often, finding the right moment in a day's time to swing in a hammock beneath the shade of a tree to shield myself from Mexico's hot tropical Sun. But it was the sudden departure from Cancun that left the most impact on me! I had received a telephone call one morning regarding a work contract to be implemented in Amsterdam; and from that day on, I made my preparations to return to Amsterdam, The Netherlands, for a three-year work project. This was an unexpected proposal, and daily, my thoughts of departing from Mexico and releasing my year's embrace of its natural passion, warmth, abundant beauty and fair-exchange, was like one who is leaving the cherished lover the morning after, infused with a personal smile of gratitude.

A collection of significant recalls came to mind, the one being of most importance because of its definite prospects; and that was the meeting with Mary Sherwood in Cancun. It was on an early sunny morning at a family-owned restaurant that I often frequented for a Mexican breakfast before the 10:00 a.m. dance class that I had to teach at a nearby studio. The restaurant's outdoor-terrace opened at 6:00 a.m. and always welcomed me to a shaded table where I could spread my books, work-papers and notes to plan the class and the day's agenda. Also, It would be a ritual for me to pull out of my canvas tote bag, my essential (back-in-the-day) "Walkman" and fill my ears with the sounds of music. The cassette of Spanish music that I was listening to that morning, was the voice of "Rocio Durcal"; a famous female vocalist popular in Spain and the Latin-American countries. I was obsessed with her voice quality, tonality, and diction; and listened daily, hoping to learn how to pronounce Spanish words correctly, and choose the right words for a language rich in verbal sound, rhythm, and passion. Before arriving in Cancun to do my work there; I spent three months in Mexico travelling along its west coast, from the U.S. border of Tijuana city down to the glistening beaches of Huatulco Bay, south of Acapulco. Often, I would be riding a crowded bus filled with cigarette smoke, chickens, children, and families. Sometimes, at my leisure and adhering to my wandering thoughts, I would walk for miles and days; and at night, sleep on a beach in a swinging hammock, "Walkman" in hand, music in my ears, letting my eyes play with the stars and anything else that moved "strangely" and questionably, up there in darkness. Frequently, the need to "leap out of the hammock and yield to the dance would "attack" me by impulse, and that's what I would do until I was satisfied with the dance and the natural "union" and feeling of "oneness"! And when that was over and I felt "complete" I would then saunter back to the hammock, crawl into it, arrange a feather-weight scarf over my body, and patiently wait to catch the glorious morning sunrise that would brighten the day as it slowly rose and lit up the dark blue Pacific Ocean. The blistering hot sunny afternoons would try to catch me but I escaped by walking in the cool and dark shaded woods and our hide-and-seek game of play would end at the time of day when I decided the chase was over. Then I would set up a campsite on a mountain top, hang the hammock and begin a new game of play; one of chasing an orange sunset that would close the day to almost-blackness, knowing that when it sets and goes someplace else to shine, the chase is over and there are no more colors to play with. Suddenly, within the already quiet space surrounding me, there is always a "time-slot" of silent stillness that looms and is sparsely filled with a measure of waiting and anxious anticipation"! This stillness and its silence, even quiets the crickets and talking night birds; and it doesn't last very long - its clarifying message is brief - revealing that it too has its purpose, which is to enter quietly into this realm of space that we see and are in. It then staunchly commands its presence and remains in its transparent darkness for our anxious and waiting eyes to watch and be a witness to its glory! This happens as it does, because it wants us to be keen and take notice of its *Black Beauty*, its *Independence*, its *Purpose*, and its *High Achievement* as it enters and commands the radiant colors of the Sun to quickly dim to a soft orange glow and fade-away, so that its "determined" black presence can be seen, felt and listened to as it engulfs the vast space we are in. In this way, it quietly "becomes" a daily ritual "time-slot" which hosts a prominent and audible whisper of "still silence" and bears a lasting message that leaves one to wonder, to listen to the silence and to clearly hear a definite and undoubted affirmation that beyond even this "Divine Magnificence" there is more! Lying still in my mesh-rope Mexican crafted hammock, and "feeling" the Universe within this gap of peace, my eyes would be against the sky, and I would watch and feel the slow movement of the earth's wheels rolling grinding and turning, beginning its new cycle for a brilliant and spattered starlit sky. It would be just me and the Universe together, our natural selves speaking to one another with our mutual understanding of this divine magnificence, all happening within an unusual silence that one can only hear on the top of a mountain, alone.

Was I ever safe from harm, prowling banditos, or from the large packs of wild dogs preying and roving about, that could surround me at any time showing their biting teeth and hanging drool? No, never was I safe from sudden danger! The only protection against possible harm, was that I always wore a head scarf or bandana; and tucked-inside would be concealed, a small peeling knife that I could reach for, should I need to raise my arms on the pretense of surrender. I was alone in my wandering and travels with only my "packed" head scarf, a backpack and the music of Rocio Durcal my only companions to guard and protect me. There was nothing more to me than this! My traveler's checks and passport were the only valuables that accompanied me on this tabooed jungle journey of rivers, streams, and mountains. I was confident that I was safe on my fearless travel across the narrow-necked land of Mexico, from the west coast to the east's Gulf of Mexico and ultimately to my destination, the city of Cancun; located in the state of Quintana

Roo, on the east coast of the Yucatan Peninsula. Arriving at the Gulf and its shoreline village of Tulum (which is approximately eighty miles south of Cancun), I lodged for three days in a small family-owned Pension (A Bed & Breakfast). When I was shown the living space and my accommodations (which included a "real bed, a real hot shower, and real food that would be cooked on a stove top), I was excited to realize that this was really going to be happening!"

After an early evening family dinner, which was delicious, simple and informal, and served with genuine Mexican hospitality as the only guest of the Pension, my very tired and listless body collapsed and laid itself down to rest in peace for the next ten-hours of "real sleep" that was undisturbed even by crawling insects and the crackling sounds of bushes being rustled by nighttime animals on the prowl. It had been a while, since my body laid itself down on a mattress, in between clean sheets, and my head resting on a "real feathered pillow"! Before retiring to a comatose sleep, I had intended to write a few lines of grateful thoughts in my travel journal; but most likely, that only happened in a dream, because the blank white page of my journal remained blank, with only a written heading" that read, "Tulum!" I had awakened at daylight just before the hot sun was about to rise, and quickly decided that a fresh morning walk and a few stretches of my now well-rested body was the first thing I should do.

I felt the "excitement" and "flair" that I could continue to be "Me." It had been six-months now, that I had "dismissed" work; needing to be a "butterfly;" free, alive, independent, and non-professional! And surprisingly, I didn't miss the work that I was born to do and loved so very much! The long hours of work along with the socializing and all the clamor and glamor of L.A. had worn me out! One's life work should be "to give energy" not to drain what is there. The days and nights had me listening carefully to the voice of "Intuition" telling me that my body, mind, and spirit, needed a "recharge"! And consequently, I had to leave the "sparkle" of Los Angeles for the mysterious "wonder" of Mexico. Since arriving in Mexico, my body had been draped in scarves and beads! I only wore shorts or tight jeans when necessary, for bus travel and chilly cool nights; and for a three and a half-day trek through the woods, jumping over and falling in running streams. Finally, the moment had come for me to shed that attire for my own. At Mamasita's Pension when I woke up on a fresh morning and started to dress, it felt so good again, wrapping and tying around my waist a large scarf, blazing with beautiful colors and hanging down long and loose, rubbing against the flesh of my legs and thighs. I flung another scarf around my neck and draped it across my shoulders, exposing my half-naked lean brown body. I jangled with neck beads, my arms choked with bracelets, my imitation gold hoop earring dangling from my right ear! "Feeling tropical? Absolutely!" Feeling native, nomadic, and oh so "complete," and as natural and raw as the sunless morning itself! But, facing the full-length mirror and adjusting my seriously "packed" head-scarf; I looked at myself for a good five-seconds with slight astonishment. "What an ornament!", I said twice, staring and laughing at myself. I slung my long-strapped canvas bag on one shoulder and laden with my Walkman, Rocio Durcal's music, and a large towel, I was definitely ready for "Something."

I stepped out of the screen door onto Mamasita's front yard of cut, wild grass and weeds and clucking chickens, all divided by a foot path that led to the dirt road that I casually walked down while listening to the sweet songs of the morning birds and inhaling the drifting fragrant scents of Nature that seemed to follow me. I paused in my steps to power up the old Walkman and plug both ears, letting the rhythmic Latin music and the voice of Rocio Durcal's "Amore Eterno" envelop me, my body sauntering, and swaying in tempo, flowing in a motion that allowed me to "feel" the dance in my walk and in my every step. I had been told by Mamasita, that I would have to walk the dirt roadway for about 200 yards and that it would lead me to the beach and the green waters of the Caribbean Sea. As the narrow dirt road winded and twisted, I saw just behind a large bush of blossoming flowers, a posted sign with a hand-painted arrow showing the sandy path to the beach. I then passed through a shady cluster of tall brush and wind-blown trees that created a darkened tunnel, coming out at the end of the path which opened itself to soft white sand, the green sea, and the grandeur of the ancient Mayan Pyramid of Tulum, Mexico! It's not difficult for me to explain exactly what my eyes were seeing at that splendid moment, nor the trembling in my body and the brief loss of breath! Nor am I afraid to tell you, that I began to weep; and then, I cried, I cried hard. Why such emotion, such drama, and such a physical reaction to this spectacular sight of hidden secrets? I think it was because it triggered and exploded within me, an acute sense of *Relativity, Time, Place, Humanity,* and the *Universe* itself! The sensation electrified me with a "joyful energy" that I had never experienced or felt before! This was a "new" Joy! I understood what my eyes were seeing, but instantly, the word *Comprehend* came to mind. Yes! This is "Divine Joy," the message and "The Word" that swelled and bubbled inside of me; and to be able to see this and stand there with open arms of gratitude was a revelation. I fell to my knees, buried my face in both hands and cried even harder. I am not ashamed to explain what my eyes saw, the epiphany that ensued, and the physical reaction that erupted from being a witness to this ancient knowledge and how it has produced such lasting and magnificent beauty; with its incomprehensible statement of *Time* and how it is measureless. But, as I sit here now and write of this personal event and its lasting impression upon me, I have to think to myself, to anyone else who reads this, or listens to this story, how difficult it must be to absorb and comprehend the power and magnitude of this wonderous sight and be in compliance to its truth, if they haven't yet" experienced it! And also; There are moments when I sometimes think of those of you, who like myself have had or do have such experiences! And in their own personal and insightful way, who have also discovered an unusual piece to life's puzzle of time and existence, found its value, and have included it in the ongoing quest for their happiness. I'm sure they have; or they would not have found that piece of the puzzle, and recognized it for what it is; which is that it should be questioned; and is simply there for one to acknowledge, and to fit that piece into their own personal puzzle of life that each of us must try to figure out and work on.

On my knees, with my face buried in my hands and sobbing quietly in my "Joy," I was gently tapped on one shoulder. "Miss, do you want I get help for you? You not feel good?", said the voice of a middle-aged man who told me later that he was the security guard, protecting this sacred property on which rests this majestic Mayan Pyramid.

Rising to my feet and wiping my face dry with the end of my available scarf, "No, no, thank you!" I said; "I am good, I'm good, thank you!" His wild locks of hair and moustache were a silver shade of white. His face was gentle, and his skin was smooth, like expensive brown leather; and when he smiled, his lips parted, revealing his warm smile and the newly indented facial lines of early ageing. Standing next to him, I could see that he was not as tall as he appeared to be, when I was in the sand on my knees and looking up at him. His body was small in stature, appearing youthful, healthy and strong; but also exuding a magnetic energy that captured my attention. "Oh, perdoname!" ("Oh, excuse me!") Bernado said humbly in well-spoken English garnished with a Mexican peasant twist. "I think you was a lady!", he said. "But no, amigo, you are a man! Perdoname!", he said apologetically, holding both hands close to his chest. I offered him a forgiving smile of understanding, nodded my head and said, "Yes, I am." He began to explain with sincere apology, why he had thought that; "Yes, I see now that you are a man!", he said, and added quickly, "But, I see you on the road coming here, and you are walking like you are dancing, you know? And now, I see you in the sand crying like a lady", he said with honesty. I gave a laugh and said to him, "Well, I am a dancer, so that's what you must see in my walk on the road, I guess; I don't know!" He kept nodding his head up and down as his squinted eyes gave a swift scan of my body, and said, "Si, Si, I see!" Bernado wanted to hear more about me, and I wanted to hear more about the "Mayan Pyramid from one who has lived his entire life with it, there in front of his eyes every day! He told me he has remained in Tulum because of this Pyramid, and the magnetic force that "compels" him to protect it.

He and I sat together in the sand, side-by-side and talked, while witnessing a spectacular yellow-orange sunrise splash its first morning light against the ancient Pyramid of Tulum! We watched the first rays of orange-sliver slowly rise up to its peaked height, swelling into a huge circle of golden-orange splendor, sending a wide, shimmering beam of yellow-orange light skimming across the sparkling green waters of the Caribbean Sea, caressing Bernado and me and the Mayan Pyramid! The hour or so we spent together telling stories, laughing and talking of his work there as a security guard since he was a young man, enabled me to believe that he knew everything about the Pyramid that I wanted to know. Bernado preferred no other work, because he felt that this is where he belonged with his family; and his "purpose" and life's work here on this sacred land where he was protecting the Pyramid of Tulum. "When I was a very young boy", he said; "My eyes were always on the Pyramid, amigo! On the way to school every day, when I was playing football, or no matter wherever in the village I was, and no matter what I was doing, amigo; 'tambien' ('always') I want my eyes to see the Pyramid!" He leaned towards me closer to reveal a life-long secret. "Before I marry my wife, and we were young, he began to say, and lowered his voice further, we make our first love, here, 'there' on top the Pyramid!" Bernado's eyes again squinted with a long reflective thought. "I did not like that, what we did!" And quickly excusing his wife from his guilt, and turning his head to me with his face close to mine and his brown eyes wide open, added, "Not what *we* did, what *I* did, amigo! You know, how the 'hungry hombre' is," he said roughly and then laughed. His pause was long, resting on his thoughts of guilt and that night of their "fun." He held a steady smile and his brown eyes were glazed with deep thought as he overlooked the sea until he was able to speak. "No, my friend; I did not like that we were having our love 'there' on the Pyramid!" He paused a second or two; "No, no, my feelings were not good that night because we did not go there to do that! Believe me, amigo!" he said, asking me with his eyes to trust his words. His word did not strike me as a plea, but rather resonated in my ears to be a true confession of torment and a personal guilt in his heart and soul that he has lived with for many years and had finally found "me" to confess this to and unburden his heart. I listened as he continued, "Amigo, we go to the top only to see the new Sunset that day!" he robustly explained, convincing me of the truth; "And when the Sun finished, the night came to us!" Bernado's voice softened, he relaxed himself, his face smiled and his eyes gleamed! "Amigo, I was holding her hand," he said; "And, I bring it closer to me, you know, and when her hand touched me here (gesturing to his genitals and clutching one hand tightly to his other wrist and fisted-hand.) It was hard and strong, amigo, like this"! he said, and gestured toward his clutched-wrist; "Big and strong like that tree over there; and she made me forget that we were 'there' on the top and made me to forget all about the good thinking, like 'this is not a good thing to do, 'here.'" Bernado paused a few seconds and the expression on his face changed quickly from an anguished frown to a pleased, warm smile. "I opened my pants, my friend, and I held her hand there; yes, she wants to pull her hand away, but no, I hold it tight on me for her to feel with her soft fingers what is hers, amigo! I give to no other girl!" "Mucho loco" ("very crazy") she makes me with her touch and her very strong love, amigo, he said, "And one year after, we marry, over there on the sand, near that tree!" He was relieved and now unburdened from his teenaged trauma of having sex on top of the Pyramid! Finally, he had told his secret story to someone after all these years; and I could see that this needed catharsis of this life-long secret was a good feeling for him. I tried to believe myself, that I was not astonished by his honest words and detailed experience of his "joyful" moments; but I was!

His true confession and delivery, was a "man-to-man" communing. It is a genuine trait in most men when there is an undeniable trust in one another; because otherwise (generally) a man's overpowering *Ego* forbids him to confess; Well, you know, Bernado!" I said; "You think and believe that you and your girlfriend's night of love was a bad thing, but, was it really? Maybe now, you should try to think differently about that beautiful night and all that has come from it!" Bernado reached in his pocket for his cigarettes, listening. I continued; "Maybe, you have to realize and think of all the good that has come from that night! I mean, if you are a happy man now with your life and with the girl you loved and married, I think that's a good thing; but maybe why you think this to be a bad thing is because you believe that by holding her hand "there" you forced her, or made her do this! But that's not true, Bernado; she wanted to do that! She knew well, that her touch "there" would excite you and her willingness was to please only you; and this is a "woman's thing" to please. She could have said; "No, Bernado." She could've gotten up and left you there alone; but no; she liked what you did with her hand, because what her hand was feeling and what her mind was thinking, is what you yourself have already said that; "what she was holding belonged to her!" And, my brother, everything else about you was hers, including the feeling in your heart, the sounds of pleasure she heard in your voice and how your body moved for her just by the touch of her hand! She loved that moment too, man; just like you did!" Bernado hardly puffed on his cigarette which was now one long ash. He sat there, just holding on to it between his fingers. He was still, sitting with his chin resting on both knees, with his eyes squinted tight and fixed on the Pyramid, but he was listening.

"Who knows?" I continued to say; "Maybe her thinking was that, if she pulled her hand away and let you go that you would go, and maybe never come back! You know what I mean? She liked that you held her hand there and if she had any feelings of guilt, you freed her from those feelings, by pulling her hand even closer! This helped her to feel and understand that it was the 'thing to do' to please you both and for the two of you to have this pleasure forever!" I paused and asked him, "Do you know the meaning of the word, *Guilt*? He turned away from the Pyramid and looked at-me. "Si, yes, I know," he said, turning his face away from me to gaze again at the Pyramid, and saying; "My church makes me think that I know the meaning of that word guilt because I feel it!" he said with a frown of anguish and confusion resting uncomfortably on his face. I did not expect those words to come from his mouth and I murmured to myself and then said carefully to him; "Well, maybe then, you can understand why you feel guilty and think that it was a bad thing to do! Anyway man, I think that it's a deliberate 'Church Thing' to make one feel guilty, and maybe now, in these few short minutes that you and I have spoken of this, now you understand so much more! Who knows, Bernardo; but what I like best and feel good about right now is that your 'understanding' is now different, and you 'comprende' that Church thing! And if that is true, my brother, I must say, 'Bravo!' because when I leave Tulum, I will be happy with this feeling knowing that you are now 'Free' from that long ago teenage 'trap' of stupid guilt!" We were both looking outward to the sea as I spoke, and when I turned my face to him I could see he was listening.

Bernardo didn't look at me, he kept his gaze to the sea during our brief pause and quietly said; "I always think of that beautiful night, amigo, 'siempre'!" He said nothing more, pensive in thought; but somehow, I could see clearly in his glazed eyes his teenaged thoughts of recall and thereafter. "How do you think your life would be now if that night didn't happen?" I asked him; because a slight and satisfied smile had slowly crept across his face, revealing his innermost thoughts. I wanted to hear more about him, that beautiful night, and what he thinks and feels about how it has affected his life today. He still didn't look at me, he kept his gaze, but said, "It is good for you to see the Pyramid again, isn't it, amigo, "dismissing my pointed question. I instantly picked up on his quick change of body posture and a "let's not discuss this" vibe that I respected and understood; and therefore, I decided to answer his unrelated comment. "Yes, my friend," I said with irony; "I agree, it is a good feeling to see the Pyramid but this is my first time here seeing it! I never even heard about Tulum until I saw it on the map and arrived here last night," I said. He finally turned his face to me with his eyes saying something, although he was saying nothing. With our eyes locked together I saw in his eyes that he was now somehow free and "un-trapped" from the cage of guilt that he had locked himself into for many years. He then turned away from me and remained in his silent and delightful reverie, and holding on to it with his steady smile, I said, "I can see that you are now in some kind of peace with yourself, Bernardo. At your church, did you ever speak with anyone about that night, and how you felt about it?" I asked. And, within his still gaze and deep thoughts, he eventually turned to me, saying; "Si; At my church we have confessions with a Priest. It was a good talk, amigo; but he still made me feel that what I did was wrong, and a sin! I knew that already, yes? But, I did not feel that to be true, amigo! So, yes; I stopped with the confessions; and after that, I only talked with God here, at his Pyramid!" Bernardo's face suddenly brightened and his smile got wide. "It was good talk, my friend; It made me marry young, and to have the nice life I have today with my wife and three children! I am happy with this, amigo!" he said, and turned his face away from me, to the Pyramid, saying, "And still; It is only God, I talk to!" Bernardo sat silently, satisfied that he had found his happiness there in Tulum with his family and the Pyramid. It was certain, that from our intense conversation, he felt redemption, and realized that he himself was the obstacle to the truth and he then "accepted" his ignorance. Our silence together, was "sweet" and I say that because as still and thick as the air was, the fragrant scents of morning flowers making their first bloom of the day somehow managed to find a way for silence to yield to this sweetness.

We sat with our eyes on the Pyramid, admiring its grandeur, its size, its flat top and skillful architectural design of stone, and I asked him, "How did you two get to the top of that? How did you climb all of that?" I questioned him in amazement and a bit of doubt. After a thoughtful pause, he faced me; "You don't know?" he asked in surprise. "No! How would I know?" I bluntly answered; "I just told you that this is my first time here!" Bernardo's eyes squinted and then his questioning face suddenly changed into a childlike expression of his "surprise" and the revealing of a wonderful hidden secret, that caused him to raise his voice and to burst loudly with excitement! "Do you want to see how, amigo?" he said, and briskly jumped up to stand on both feet! Looking up at him from my seat in the sand, my eyes scanned his attire of jeans and a simple white cotton shirt and thong sandals on his feet. "Oh, no!" was my instant reply to his "obviously" absurd question; due to a quick flashback of the "ornament" I had seen in the full-length mirror getting dressed three hours before! It was an absolute, No! I too stood up tall with my bare feet pressing deep in the sand; "Look at me, man!" I said adamantly; "I can't climb up there with "all this" on! "No, my friend, I answered, "But I will go with you and stand down here and watch you climb!" But Bernardo acted as if he had not heard a word, "Come, come! No problem! You look good!" he said, and turned around and quickly started his walk in the sand, ahead of me! Following behind Bernardo to an upward incline of wind-blown trees, we arrived onto a plateau of a thick wooded area, pathless, and with an array of brush that kept snagging on every hanging scarf that was dangling from my body! I had to make numerous stops to release snags, with a tug here and a pull from there, and eventual tears! "Come, come my friend!" I could hear Bernardo's voice about twenty meters ahead of me, and by the time I caught up to him he had stopped, beckoning me with his hands to hurry; "Come, see!" he said excitedly, making me hurry.

There where we were standing on the edge of a cliff, was the massive Mayan Pyramid about fifty feet below us! It sat majestically, with grace in its ancient character, on the sandy shoreline of the vast emerald-green waters. The early morning Sun was warm against my face, and it seemed that everything on earth was still, except for the green waters and the thumping beats of my heart still racing inside of me. Not a drift of soft wind carried a fragrant scent where we were: alone up there in the majesty and stillness.

"This is where I come to speak with God!" Bernado said seriously. I said nothing to that and the silence followed us on our descent down the steep cliffside that edged close to a tier level of the Pyramid. A heap of dead, broken and falling wind-blown trees had tumbled down from the top of the cliff's edge to below, and I could see that, for years this rummage of wood, packed and lodged tightly between the Pyramid and the cliff's edge, was solid and impenetrable. This provided a rugged but feasible way to reach a level of the Pyramid that would bring us up to the flat top. The ancient stones of hard rock and gravel on the high climb to the top bruised cut and hurt my bare feet with every step; and the dangling neck beads and scarves were totally disarrayed and abused by the time we arrived at the top. Above our heads stretched the cloudless blue sky and below, a long stretch of white sand beach ending at the emerald green waters of the Caribbean Sea. I stood there in awe, taking in the breathtaking view, of another "high achievement" of the Creator's nature; and I remember feeling humbled and grateful in that perfect moment. Bernardo and I sat in our world of stone and sky for a short while, discussing *The Life* and other meaningful things.

His gaze was fixated on the sky (like it had earlier been fixated on the sea) as if he was looking for something; but more like "waiting" for something! I was about to ask him, "What is it that you see out there in the sea and the sky?" when he interrupted my thoughts and out of his mouth came "strange" words that baffled me; "When you come back here again, I think that you will understand more, the Pyramid, and you, amigo," he said. I looked at him gazing, and thought without a doubt, that "This man is reading my Mind!" I sat there watching him; carefully listening to my thoughts, all the while holding his steady smile.

The big orange Sun was now changing its colors to a golden yellow and beginning to throw its morning heat against us and the new day. Upon leaving, we noticed the beach far down below was being occupied by the arrival of a few sunbathers as the Sun's heat was brewing fast. "There will be many people down there today," Bernardo said. "Si, amigo, they will be there all day to enjoy the beach and swim in the ocean. Some never see the Pyramid; and if they do, they only look at it one time and say, "Ooh, with their eyes big and then they forget it's there!" We both understood that; and he chuckled, saying, "But, they will go after the Sun finishes its work and the night comes. Here in Tulum, and in the black night, one gets to see another gift from God; This is when the sky opens, amigo! And it's the only time of the day when one with a thirsty Soul and with eyes wide-open, can stand here and see what falls and comes from the heavens! This is when I start 'my' work, until the Sun comes again in the morning!" Come, we must go now," he said, and looked at me with a pleased smile. His poetic words had been spoken in a musical tone that had me smiling; even though the twenty-minute return back to the sandy beach across the heap of dead trees, and up the steep cliff was gruesome! And the ramble through the trees and pathless brush was another continuous snag, pull and tear of a scarf ordeal! At the beach, we sat again in the sand beneath the shade of a large green bush before parting from one another, discussing Bernardo's "secret way" to the heavens. Many more sunbathers had arrived, and the hot, yellow sun welcomed each one to bask in its glare of bright light, heat, and the burn that each bather would feel soon enough. We both stood up on our feet for a mutual embrace of our new friendship. "You are here at Mamasita's I know!" he said. "I will see you again before you go from Tulum, my friend! I know this!" Bernardo placed his right hand over his heart, gave a quick nod of his head and left; leaving me with my thoughts of him as a man of honor and respect, and one I know I would never forget.

My walk and pace back to Mamasita's was slow, and also with my rambling thoughts of what Bernardo was actually "seeing" in the green sea; and of his clairvoyant reading of my Mind. While I was on the top I had already decided to return to the grand Pyramid tonight at Sunset!" My walk ended at Mamasita's, but one thought remained; how did he know that I would be returning to the Pyramid? It didn't disturb me as much as it just made me "wonder" at our strange encounter, and about our ignorant-selves, who only have a tiny clue of "what's going on" in the sky and on the earth; and "what else" is out there swirling around continuously day and night in the Creator's magnificent Universe!

My decision to visit the Pyramid that evening was discussed at Mamasita's breakfast table, sitting there with her three children. I was telling them of my Sunrise visit to the Pyramid site earlier that morning, (excluding my secret adventure with Bernardo). "Oh, Mister Ilanga, go! You must see it at Sunset!" said Rosita, Mamasita's well-schooled English speaking eleven-year-old daughter. "When I went there at Sunset, everything was beautiful!" she said, as her little brown face beamed brightly with her new 2nd**Cycle** wisdom of discovery. "You can feel the magic all around," she stopped abruptly; "Not 'feel it,' but you 'see' the magic all around, mister Ilanga!" she said apologetically, and continued; "Not like in the morning, that's a different Sunset!" she said and then quickly turned to her mother and whispered Spanish words. She turned and faced me again with her soft whispered correction; "I mean *Sunrise*, she said, and covered her mouth with both hands to suffocate an "oops" kind of giggle. I replied, "Yes, I will go for the Sunset and I will tell you tonight before you go to bed what I saw! Maybe I will see what you said that you saw; 'magic and everything beautiful!' And maybe also, because I am older than you, I might not only 'see the magic' but maybe 'feel' it too!" Rosita looked up at me with the eyes of a skeptical adult as she tore a warm tortilla in half and slowly lowered her tiny eyelids saying, "Maybe!" My morning, midday, and until late afternoon were spent walking and roaming the village of Tulum; Its street markets, and its community of happy faced people passing by and eyeing the "ornament" with their smiles and whispers. And as Bernardo had done in his youth; I too, was wandering the peasant village with my eyes on the Pyramid throughout the day and at every street turn, corner, and angle, wherever I roamed, and having thoughts of his stories all magnified and clear. The clear *Comprehension* accompanied me throughout my walk.

After an early evening dinner at Mamasita's, I gathered my thoughts and dressed "properly" for the tangling brush and pathless way to the edge of the steep cliff and the bridge of dead broken trees. I tightly tied my "packed" head scarf and stuffed my canvas bag with essential music cassettes, scarfs, bracelets, jangling beads and a flashlight, preparing myself for an extraordinary "dance with the Sun" before it leaves Tulum today, to rise and shine someplace else tomorrow. Stepping out of Mamasita's screen door, dressed properly with tight jeans, a long-sleeved cotton shirt and shoes, I casually walked down the dirt roadway to the beach, knowing what to expect for the next fifteen or twenty minutes of my life. I ventured upwards to the incline of wind-blown trees, the plateau and pathless wild brush. The steep cliff and accessible bridge of dead wood leading to the Pyramid was not as difficult to arrive at this time, as there were no snags pulls and tears to deal with from the hanging scarfs and dangling beads, making it easier to maneuver. Preparation, had made the big difference! The bright yellow Sun was just beginning to fade into its soft welcoming orange glow when I arrived at the Pyramid and its flat top of archaic stone. Hurriedly, I changed from the "properly-dressed" to the "Ornament" attire once again, and began selecting the most appropriate music needed for me to dance my "dance of gratitude – a soulful offering to the Creator, for whatever and all that I am." And what I saw, felt, and believed at that moment; and on that blessed day I knew that "I am here, to celebrate *The Life*"! My obsession and affinity with nature, sacred places and all things sacred (such as the place Bernardo mentioned; "Where the black sky opens, and things fall from the heavens") has me dancing "secretly" in countries around the world! I have found myself making soulful offerings on mountain tops, on the sacred soil of Mt. Olympus, and on a full moon night, dancing on the temple of Acropolis in Athens, Greece! Once, also on a full moon night, I did my dance of gratitude within the Great Pyramid of Giza, Egypt! That came about due to a network of friends there, and specifically one who was in security management and by chance on detail that hallowed night. I will never forget that amazing night; as I had imagined myself being in Egypt someday, riding on a camel, and galloping my way to the Great Pyramid! Never would I have thought that that "fantasy" would materialize into reality. The fact that it was not a Camel, but a fast-driven Jaguar automobile that sped me along the sandy road crossing the Sahara Desert to Giza as the Moon was rising, made no difference in my fantasy.

Chasing a Sunset, waiting for a Sunrise, hugging a tree, or being hypnotized by a spectacular full moon, have always been the priorities of my global travels. This obsession has always given me the inspiration to do and see "more"! And why not? There was one incident where a hilarious mishap occurred during one of my "performances" (a dance of gratitude) that I was inspired to offer to a glorious Sunset which was truly spectacular! I was "dancing with my joy" on a large, flat boulder that jutted up from the sand, half of which sat in the water close to the shoreline. I was aware of the possible slight danger; but I was lost in the dance and in total ecstasy at dancing in beautiful Big Sur, California, U.S.A. In the midst of my undulating movements, I mistakenly tilted and fell into the Pacific Ocean! I emerged, unhurt from the ocean, got up on the rock again, caught my breath and joined the company of friends I was with, in big time laughter!

Why such an obsession and affinity with this self-imposed ritual of "gratitude"? This question was finally put to rest during my **6ᵗʰCycle** by evaluating how often these impulsive and sometime planned rituals have occurred in my life, and how they made me react and feel, physically, mentally and spiritually! And also, that I needed to have this extraordinary universal relationship with "matter and all living things"! The answer to that question, the realization and the affirmation that came to me in the **6ᵗʰCycle**, was that I was a very blessed man! Not a "strange" man, or a "deluded" man; just, *Blessed* and *Gifted*, with the *Love* and the *Infinite*!

The huge ball of Sun was setting and blanketing Tulum with its deep orange colored light; splashing onto the Mayan Pyramid, and upon me, "ornamented" with dangling scarves, beads, bracelets, Walkman and earphones, plugged in both ears, filled with music! I danced with such *joy* and *freedom,* feeling so "complete" and humbly offering only "the best of me" to the Creator! I danced and danced, like a Whirling Dervish; and at one moment in a spin, my arms were outstretched wide and reaching high, and suddenly I felt and envisioned myself caressing in my arms a huge orange ball, dancing with it, and then lifting it high with both hands, and throwing it back up into the sky! The sky then flung the ball back to me and I flung it back again. Our dance and play went on and on, until one time when I threw the orange ball back, "the sky missed its catch", and the ball kept rolling away! I guess it rolled itself to "someplace else" to rise again for "someone else" who was in need of its soft, red and inspiring morning light.

It rolled away and left me with a touch of daylight; just enough to change quickly from my dangling "Ornament" attire into my "proper" dress, and flashlight in hand, I headed for the darkened pathway through the woods and home to Mamasita's. The dirt roadway was filled with my grateful thoughts as I walked along through the darkness in peace, and thinking; "Once again in *The Life*, this eminent "dare" and impulsive "action" that I have taken tonight has resulted in a long day's work of conquest and "high achievement"! This thinking, enabled my "mind, body, and spirit" to feel their individual strengths and "Purpose"! I strolled through the front yard and onto the narrow path to the Pension door with a steady smile on my face and a bit of anxious thought about telling Rosita just how beautiful "everything" was, and that, "I did see, but, also could feel, the magic" that she had spoken so eloquently about! The smile remained with me as I walked through the door, tired but energized and refreshed!

The following morning began with a surprise at Mamasita's, hearing Bernado's laughter and distant voice as I left my room and headed to the dining room for breakfast, again, dressed as an "ornament" of new colors for a day's walk in the village. I greeted Bernado warmly, interrupting his conversation with Mamasita. "Oh, Amigo!" he said; "I was just telling Mamasita how beautiful you danced last night and how nice it was to see the Sun and you together dancing! And I tell to Mamasita, it was like a movie for my eyes to see; like a story, you know, amigo!" Mamasita rambled off a quick one-line sentence in Spanish and they both laughed very hard. "Mamasita says to me, you are a movie!" The three of us laughed, as I took a seat opposite him at the table. "You saw me last night?" I asked him with surprise. "Si, amigo! It is my work, to see you," he said proudly. "But never do I see any other people do what you do, no! My work is to see banditos and hungry young lovers in the dark, you know!" Mamasita chuckled to herself and spoke her words jokingly, and in English; "Si, this is why he likes his work!" she said. Bernardo was not upset at this insinuating comment, he just laughed along with her! I could sense that these two had been friends for many years with mutual understanding and support for one another; and because I admire greatly, endearing and enduring friendships, I asked them, "How long have you two been friends?" "Oh, amigo, she is my sister!" Bernado said; and flashed a broad smile of love to her. "She is my baby sister, I have two," he said as if he himself was surprised! He raised from his chair, leaned over to her for a big squeeze, and with love, planted a kiss on the cheek of her face. Wiping her cheek from Bernado's wet lips with the back of her hand, She said, childishly slapping his forearm. "Si, mi hermano, Bernado!" His face beamed with love. I recognized that solid union and I missed my baby sister greatly.

That bright, hot sunny day was spent walking the inland of Tulum and its tropical landscape; the village and its markets, shopping for fruits and hoping to pick up a new tourist map of the east coast of Mexico. I would be leaving for Cancun the following morning, dressed as an "ornament" for the eighty-mile hike north along the coast of the state, Quintana Roo, before arriving at my ultimate destination, Cancun, to become a "professional" again; These next couple of days would be the last of this personal adventure and exploration. The next move was a "no brainer" decision to simply roam its astounding examples of Nature consisting of small coastal villages, white sandy beaches and the soft, green waters of the Caribbean Sea.

I was breakfasting with Mamasita and her three happy children when I suddenly realized that for the two days of my stay here, I had not seen or heard "Papa"! I was about to inquire, but instead, asked about Bernardo. "He comes now, after-work, maybe," she said, sliding her chair back, bending low, and picking up the napkin that had slid off her lap. "He does not know, you go now! I did not say to him, you go today!" Mamasita said, and continued with a tone of sarcasm. "He no listens to everything, so I no tell him everything!" She looked at her children, busy eating and talking amongst themselves, and tapped her temple with her forefinger, and her other hand cupped next to her mouth and shaping her lips to softly whisper "Loco"! I smiled and I didn't know why, until It evolved into a steady grin.

Saying "adios" to the children and squeezing Mamasita with a big hug of "Gracias," I could feel that our meeting was and always would be a wonderful memory of happiness for all. Leaving Mamasita's and stepping through the screened door for the last time onto her weedless path to the dirt roadway, I turned left, going in the opposite direction from the beach, and thinking that I might see him, ending his long night of work, in search of banditos and hungry young lovers, but I didn't. I never again saw Bernado; but maybe he saw me, walking my dance on the dirt roadway north, to Cancun.

It was not until high noon when the heat and light of the Sun blazed its brightest that I decided not to hike any further. In the past hours I had been dwelling on alternate thoughts of Bernado and Mamasita. These vague and questionable thoughts were temporarily dismissed by a quick plunge and a cool swim in the green water, a lunch of fruits, and a sit beneath a large sprouting bush offering shade and camouflage welcoming me to relax and feel refreshed. I found these thoughts however, to be persistent since I had left Tulum, and when I unloaded my travel bags and began to prepare lunch, I was thinking: "Were they brother and sister, or husband and wife?" Bernardo was certainly an honest man, I had no doubt about that; he was not a liar. But his playful humor was childlike, fun and innocent! At the breakfast table, when I saw him last, the genuine love and chemistry between he and his baby sister was as "honest and real" as the relationship between my sister and I. But now, my alternative thought was that it could be that they wanted to have "fun" with me and play a "guessing game"! And I knew well the secrecy and trust within the game of "baby sister always follows big-brother" was a game played in our childhood and often carried over into adult games of play, "just for the fun of it" and the harmless "fun" was the "adventure" that was sure to follow. Baby sister, already knowing that "this is going to be fun," was willing to risk any harm or danger because big brother will take it on, should anything go wrong!

And so, I thought there was a good chance that Bernado and Mamasita were husband and wife, just playing a harmless "party game" with themselves, and including me in it! And me, being the very gullible tourist and only guest at the Pension, was part of their fun moment; and in the delight of meeting this authentic Mexican couple and being innocent of their harmless fun, I realized that they were entertaining not only me, but themselves as well!

The personal "Party Games" or "Scenarios" acted-out, understood, and played between couples of this nature is an exciting adventure and vital stimulation to a relationship that enjoys playing a harmless game of fun. But the dark side of this fun game and how it can become an ordeal of horror was portrayed in the classic 1960's film, *Who's Afraid Of Virginia Wolf*, which showed the raw dynamics and chemistry between the legendary actors, Elizabeth Taylor and Richard Burton. The original play was written by the prolific American author, Edward Albee. This film impressed me greatly during my **4ᵗʰCycle**, and cautioned me to be aware of the harmful "party games" that an "adventurous" couple can play with innocent and gullible people who only came to the party for a little fun. And at that time, being in the music business, my social life was very active with networking, parties, meeting people, and adventurous game playing couples (often playing games unknown to the guests).

I never came to a conclusive thought about that day, or any day thereafter, whether Bernado and Mamasita were "brother and sister" or "husband and wife with three happy children"! These restless thoughts drifted away along with the fragrance of the blossoms hovering above my head, their scent swiftly being blown into the soft breeze and smells of the salty green Sea. Soon, all of this mental activity eventually subsided and left me calm enough to wiggle and snuggle my body deeper into the soft, white sand, feeling my heavy eyelids closing, and allowing my wandering mind to "travel onward to someplace else" for those well-deserved restful moments.

── CHAPTER SIX ──

Always watch, look and listen, ageless
reader, something's coming!

Living in Cancun within its "El Centro" area; the city's small downtown center of daily authentic Mexican activity, I saw on display the daily lives of the families and residents who lived here in "The Center." It didn't take me long to became active and engaged with the artists, dancers and musicians who lived close by in the adjacent neighborhoods, or "El Barrios" as they are called, and many soon became my very close friends. There were staff workers, laborers and professionals, most of whom were working in the tourist business and servicing the many small hotels in the area as well as servicing the larger and numerous hotels lined up in a row like elegant dominos along the beach's shoreline, tall and sparkling brilliantly beneath Cancun's hot Sun! "El Hotelera" (The Hotel Zone) is the exclusive area located on a peninsular strip of land about two-miles long, attracting and hosting thousands of tourists from around the world, daily. The Hotelera is the area where the elaborate *Intercontinental Hotel* stands tall. This is where I worked, proving my artistic abilities in any capacity that was called for, which was choreographing weekly fashion shows or beauty pageants featuring the local Mexican beauties. On Sunday afternoons, the main Ballroom would be generally filled with elderly, rich, white gentlemen with grey hair, big round bellies and large eyes, gawking at every parading beauty they could snatch a glimpse of, before getting an elbow nudge from their wife or "Holiday Mistress!" My work there at the Intercontinental Hotel often included my presence as a "Novelty" at the elegant, large swimming pool on some hot sunny afternoons; socializing and informally entertaining the hotel's vacationing guests with pool side laughter, small talk, games, and the renowned "Conga Line" dance around the pool to end their afternoon of pool-time fun before hurrying back to their lavish rooms to prepare themselves for evening dining and entertainment.

I had already done this type of work during my previous years living in Athens, Greece while working in the tourist business; choreographing and performing in shows on cruise ships sailing the Mediterranean Sea to Mykonos and Crete where sophisticated western-style "Discotheques" were lauded. Within the city of Athens, (the "Mega" tourist trap!) much of my work consisted of catering to tourists at the elegant Athens Intercontinental Hotel. Needless to say; "satisfying, pacifying, or engaging with" the privileged tourists who expect and demand what they are paying for, is not an easy job! And, let me make clear to you my ageless reader; about this work, I am not complaining, I am "explaining"! Yes, the tourist deserves a fair exchange!

For those who work in this exciting and lucrative business; The days and nights are all about wearing a "pasted-smile" on a disgruntled face! And make sure that your eyes are always bright and clear and that they are smiling too; yes, even when there is no tip! In Cancun, the enjoyable poolside fun and activities at the Intercontinental Hotel, the beauty pageants, beachwear fashion and fanfare were not the "glue" that would hold tight, the all day long and night "pasted smile and clear eyes" for long! These thoughts and my innate intuition flashed "red flags" to not establish myself as "Mr. Novelty" here in Cancun! My only two options were to stay here and spend most of my days and nights wearing tight jeans, shorts and a pasted-on smile" that in time I knew would eventually "crack!" And of course; I instantly imagined myself in Cancun and in "El Barrios" on a futile search for a Mexican scientist who formulated a "permanent glue for a pasted-on smile!" And if that didn't happen, then my second choice would be to go and immediately book a flight to Los Angeles for the infamous "pasted-smile facial surgery!" Aside from my work at the plush Intercontinental Hotel; also located on the Hotelera strip of land was Cancun's suave cosmopolitan discotheque "La Boom." The "go-to" prime destination for "hip" young tourists and "the place to be" if you needed or wanted international-flair trendy fashions certain to be noticed among the glamorous and pretentious, sophisticated Mexican Jet-Set; rubbing shoulders with global celebrities who were also there for the same reasons! My one-month project at La Boom discotheque was to choreograph an internationally attractive discotheque show that would sustain throughout the Summer tourist season. I proposed the concept of utilizing fifteen members of their staff of twenty-five; presenting the young, vibrant and hip waiters, waitresses and bartenders, to serve and dance to Michael Jackson's "Thriller" and "Billie Jean" as the featured attraction, plus solo cameos for those who were "dancers" and lovers of Michael's music. It was a tremendous success for the discotheque; and did sustain that season! But, La Boom's policy of discrimination against the young, hip Mexican youth of "El Centro" bothered and troubled me. The constant reflections of the past years of living in America and being caught in its web of discriminative policies showed its prickly ugliness when I also recognized it at the La Boom discotheque. Although I had not lived in America for the past thirteen years, I still recalled the oppressive feeling of being caught and tangled up in thoughts of bitterness and resentment. The civil activism I had thought was a thing of the past for me was alive again. This was as real as the "American Dream" itself; and now, this abominable reality was happening to me again! But this time its nightmare appeared differently to my eyes and stirred a nausea within my stomach. The racial divide within the vicious web of Mexican discrimination disturbed me greatly, because for the first time I experienced the horror and reality of "brown against brown." It was nasty, and seemingly every day was predictable. The thought that I would be wallowing in this sludge all day sickened me even more! To be of positive mind was certainly a daily task to endure and something that had to be "worked-on" all day.

It was not long after the opening of the show and its success that I left the nightly excitement of discotheque La Boom, because by this time, I had acquired close friendships with artists young and old who also lived in El Centro; the dancers, musicians, and colleagues from the two dance studios where I was happily teaching classes. They too had heard about the dazzling show happening on the Hotelera strip at Discotheque La Boom; and also wanted to be greeted at its door by "Zombies" that welcomed you in! But, my friends, they couldn't - they were not allowed to enter! They were not sophisticated enough to be among the elite! Nor did their bodies smell of "expensive perfumes or colognes and nor was their evening wear trendy and fashionable, made of the exclusive fine-quality fabrics that were worn, and obviously "expected" at Cancun's alluring jewel of entertainment, "La Boom." To enjoy a night out dancing and socializing, my preference was to go where the brown and sensible, hip white people generally congregated in El Centro. It was a small, family-owned Bar/Discotheque called "Cats" and it had an intimacy and an ambiance of welcome and friendship, with the exclusive sounds of Reggae music and the smell of "Weed"! This is where the brown artists and their friends of any color, size or shape could enter; and they congregated nightly in their "love vibe" wearing "whatever" and just "Jamm'n"! Consequently, it was sad for me to hear nightly, their many stories of rejection from the infamous La Boom and the chic restaurants on the Hotelera strip of land. But because of my analysis of this troubling situation, and the evaluation of my core nature principles and beliefs, I was grateful to my parents, teachers and educators for providing me with the abilities that allowed me to recognize this hateful and moral crime of discrimination. And I was also grateful to La Boom Discotheque that I was fortunate to be in a good financial position with the independence to make a choice suitable to my nature and principles. I had a "well-paying gig" and a $500 cash bonus for work well done! I needed no more than this to make the "needed" change of this toxic daily environment and lifestyle. So, within a few short weeks of time frequenting "Cats", I never again returned to the Hotelera with its extravagant luxury and its pretentious display of wealth and ignorance. I no longer had to be day and night in tight jeans, shorts, or a "disco-outfit" with its flashy night-time sparkle! Never did I go to the Hotelera dressed as an "Ornament" because I would have never gotten past the "Zombies" at the front door!" The dangling Ornament-attire was only acceptable, admired, and respected, in "El Centro" and the adjacent "Barrios"; and tight-jeans or shorts and "one-dangling scarf" were worn only for special occasions such as a garden party or a wedding! And always at these affairs and according to these people, I was considered appropriately dressed, which I always felt that I was!

I spent the remaining three hot summer months in Cancun where I taught my last scheduled dance classes at the two studios in "El Centro." I enjoyed my friends, danced Reggae at *Cats* and travelled the Yucatan Peninsula. My hike from the west coast to the east and my days spent in the old cities of Puebla and Oaxaca, were inspiring enough for me to see the old city of Merida and the other Mayan pyramids located in the area of the Yucatan.

By "coincidence" or "accident" or by "circumstance" I met Mary Sherwood, an elderly agile, frisky and alert gray-haired woman whose height was not more than five feet and four inches tall. She was a white American tourist and member of the Massachusetts Audubon Society who was in Cancun for a few days "watching birds." She came one memorable day for the very early-morning breakfast at the family-owned restaurant I frequented often for a healthy Mexican meal. Sitting alone at my big table beneath the shade of a tree and preparing notes for my ten a.m. dance class, plugged into my "Walkman" and totally satisfied with a finished breakfast, suddenly I was tapped on my shoulder. I turned around and looked up to see this elderly woman with her tray of breakfast and a smile on her friendly, deeply-lined face. I unplugged my headphones to hear her small voice saying "Buenas Dias! Do you mind if I join you here at your table?" she asked politely making a gesture with her breakfast tray as to where at the table she wanted to sit. Then she hurriedly dashed to the chair at the end of the table opposite me, and sat! Struggling with words that she had grasped here and there from her newly bought tourist book of the Spanish language, she was able to piece together a sentence courageously, but with hesitance. Her tiny beaded eyes looked directly into mine; "No, hablo, Espanol, muy buen!" ("I don't speak Spanish very well!), she managed to convey to me, and then quickly added; "Are you from here, do you speak English?" "Yes, I do!", I answered, as my eyes quickly scanned the sunlit terrace, noticing that all the tables were empty of customers. Mary noticed my quick scan and added gratefully, "Oh, thank you!" as she plunged her fork into her scrambled eggs. "Our table is the only table with shade, dear! And also, from this angle of the terrace, I can see that tree over-there; I'm a "Bird Watcher!" she said proudly, fringed with a bit of eccentricity. "This is June, and they say, the bird I'm watching for is somewhere here in the Yucatan!" she said; quite disturbed and feisty, and with her shifty eyes scanning the table for cream and sugar. She spoke rapidly, boldly waving a spoon back and forth between her finger and thumb to emphasize each word spoken. "They don't know what they're talking about, I think! Every year, they say the same "BS";… "Oh, Mary, he's in the Yucatan in July!" This is the third year I've been here looking for that little rascal!" she said, lowering head and vigorously stirring a spoon in her coffee cup. I wanted to ask her, "Who are "They?" and "who is "The Little Rascal"? although I assumed that "They" were the experts within the "Audubon Society", and "The Little Rascal" was a very special bird that her eyes were searching for! I also had the urge to let her know in a gentle way of her rudeness, but my words were too slow emerging. Mary's action was fast; her fork went into the scrambled eggs for a second plunge, and after her chew, she continued; "I can see you're quite busy. I won't disturb you dear, you go right-ahead!" She had said the word, "Dear" again and I began to think about that, as my thoughts wrapped around the word and its beautiful sound that has been absent from ears now for so many years. Only my mother said that word to me; no one ever dared call me Dear except for her! The warm, peaceful sound of that word was gentle, it resonated and stayed with me all day. As Mary had noticed; I was busy, and so I continued my work as she had suggested.

Trying not to be impolite or isolated from her presence; I took out my ear plugs and continued working on my class notes. She had not disturbed me, but often I was distracted by her unusual behavior. During her final bites of breakfast, she would raise her small face from her plate whenever she heard a prominent morning-bird song, quickly grab her binoculars from off the table, lift them to her eyes, and slowly scan the trees and the blue sky! Her ultimate passion for "The Little Rascal" and her raw instinctive behavior fascinated me. She had finished with her breakfast and was sitting with her binoculars in hand, but I could feel her eyes fixed on me, and she wanting to engage. Lifting my head from my spread of written notes; I cupped one hand to my ear and pretended to be listening for something. "Well!" I said, "I guess that little bird has finished his song!" I turned to her, and her squinted eyes were still fixed on me. "That was a She" Mary said sternly, and immediately followed that with, "Where are you from?" You speak very good English! I'm trying to figure out from your accent, exactly what tropical foreign country it is you come from! Is it here, Mexico?" Somewhat surprised; I answered, "No! I am an American! I am from Boston Massachusetts, originally, but I haven't lived there for many years!" Her facial expression changed from the serious face of an investigator to the delight of a child who has just met a new friend at the playground. "Oh, I'm from Concord! What a coincidence!" We're neighbors!" she said, her face lit up with surprise and joy. "So, that's why you speak English so perfectly! I was thinking that maybe you were from here, or some Caribbean island, South Africa, or someplace, but, not from America, dear! And certainly not Boston!"

I could sense her relief escaping from the language struggle that she had thought was about to ensue. "It is a pleasure to meet you," she politely said, and quickly sipped on her hot coffee. But then Mary's voice raised to an erratic burst; "Whatever in the Hell happened to your 'I-paaked-my kaah-in-the-Haaved-yaad' Boston accent dear? it's not there at all!" We both laughed and made quick jokes of it with a common understanding. "Oh, I probably lost it by not living in Boston for over twelve years now," I said. "I've been living in Europe; Amsterdam, Greece, and now, here in Mexico for the past few months. When I was In Boston last, about a year ago, many of my friends and family there had commented on my accent also! I guess that it's learning different languages, maybe, and how that in itself can change the various ways of your tongue movement, your mind, and the many things that probably cause one's accent to develop as it does, don't you think?" I got no reply and we were silent together for a few seconds, until I heard from her, "Hmm, that's interesting!" She placed her binoculars on the table, leaned forward towards me and lowering her voice to almost a quiet whisper said, "Well, that one calls for a discussion now, doesn't it dear!" When she said this her face softened and her total disposition changed. It was in how her voice sounded and how she shaped her words that I sensed to be of a "motherly" tone, with an interest in hearing what her child has on his or her mind.

"My name is Mary; Mary Sherwood!" she said, reaching over the table to offer me her strong, thin white hand for a friendly shake. "So good it is to meet you, Mary!" I responded; and to avoid a barrage of questions, I added, "How nice that I hear your last name! I am Ilanga, and I have just one name only!" She said nothing and her eyes held steady in their "squint" during this long pause of emptiness that prompted me to say something, anything, to divert whatever thoughts she was having, away from a "name change" conversation! "So, Mary, someday, we'll meet in Concord, and there we will discuss what learning different languages can do in regard to one's accent," I said. I will meet you at my most favorite place of childhood; which remains a favorite still today!" The squint of her eyes narrowed as I leaned forward, closer to her face; "Walden Pond, I'm sure you know it well! I know it well too. Let's meet there someday!" I said, believing that we would.

Mary's "Dr. Jekyll & Mr. Hyde" transformation was instant! Her aged face brightened with a young delight! "Oh yes; that would be wonderful! I would love that! My work is there at the pond in the woods; I am an Environmentalist and Preservationist of Walden Pond! My work there is to keep - and excuse my French - those new young bastards who call themselves "Developers" from coming in there and destroying it!" Mary's face and thoughts suddenly flashed with anger and annoyance; "You'd better get there fast, I tell you," she warned sharply, "Because you won't recognize Walden soon!" She was very annoyed by these interrupting thoughts but found a way to relax from them with quick sips of her coffee and a glance now and then into the trees above her head. In her new calm, her eyes softened, as did her words, and she looked at me and quietly said "And when you come, Ilanga, I will tell you of its history as I know it to be, of its secrets, and of Henry David Thoreau, who I'm sure you're familiar with! We could have lunch at my home and spend a wonderful day together; what a brilliant thought and plan!"

After our brief discussion about learning different languages and its benefits, her knowledge of the birds that fly, and of my long-time friendship with author, Henry David Thoreau; I noticed the time had flown, and suddenly I had to leave Mary. "My dear new friend," I said, "I have to go and teach a dance class now; but I'd really prefer to stay here and continue on with our beautiful meeting!" As I raised up from my chair hurriedly to stand and gather my spread of notes and Walkman, I could feel her eyes squinting and fixed on me. "Dancing, huh?" she muttered to herself quietly. I said not a word, and continued to stuff my belongings into my long-strapped canvas bag. She got up from her chair to stand tall in her height of just over five feet; "You're an interesting young man," she said, eyeing me up and down from head to toe and taking notice of the total "Ornament" on display of hanging scarfs, bracelets and beads standing before her! "Yes, quite interesting," she repeated.

We embraced each other in this new and genuine friendship that I knew we both felt, that had ignited in only a matter of a couple of hours. "Mary, give me your contact information there in Concord!" I said; "And when I visit Boston again on my next trip from Amsterdam, I will give you a call. I am sure that we will meet again, and it will be there with 'Henry' at Walden Pond!" I referred to Henry David Thoreau because during our lengthy two-hour conversation, our words were mostly of him, our affinity with him, and the unusual relationship we both have with our dear author friend Henry who died in 1862, right there in Concord, Massachusetts during his 7th Cycle at the young age of forty-four. "Look," she said, thoughtfully, "I leave for Boston tomorrow afternoon, but I would like for us to meet again before I leave. Today is not possible, now that you have to go and dance!" she said, and again, giving me the total "once-over", adding; "And I'm sure beautifully, with all that on dear!" Mary's jest and bit of sarcasm ended quickly with her flair for eccentricity, saying, "And also, I leave in an hour for the city of

Merida! I have some bird friends there, "flying all over the place" and we're meeting there this afternoon and early evening with the hope that "we can get that wandering flighty "little rascal" to join us!" She paused, and then said with enthusiasm and the intent to be heard, making a swift hand gesture with her bony pointed finger aiming at my face, "But listen, tomorrow morning…!" Her pause and thought caused her finger to shake radically, and Mary's small beady eyes narrowed with a penetrating stare. "Can you be here again, the same time? and saying no isn't going to help anything!" she said definitely. It was obvious to me that during our discussion, "something" had "triggered" in her mind, and Mary had an unresolved thought. "Yea; I can be here! I have a class at this studio again at 10:00; let's do it!" I left her standing there with her eyes fixed on me as I walked away, crossing the large terrace to the exit gate. I turned my head around to see her wave a frisky goodbye and I did as well as I continued to hurriedly "dance my walk" to the studio.

The following morning was as sunny and bright as the day before, and Mary was already there at the restaurant, sitting at the table beneath the only tree that offered shade. Seeing me arrive at the gate of the terrace, she quickly left her chair to stand and joyfully swing both arms high over her head in a happy welcome, making small quick steps to meet me half way across the terrace! After our friendly early morning hug, she held my hand tight as we walked to the table to sit. She repeated twice; saying, "Oh, we've got a lot to talk about! I've had this interesting thought that came to me during the bus ride; "It lingered with me all night and yesterday, all afternoon in Merida! I was thinking that…I interrupted her abruptly, saying, "Oh, Merida! How was it? And did you see your flying-friends?" I asked as I unloaded my canvas bag of notebooks, etc. onto the table.

"I'm not talking about Merida right now!", her serious, impatient voice "snapped" at me. Mary paused; and then immediately switched her bitchy attitude and tone of voice. "Oh, it was wonderful, dear, thank you; and I did get to see a few of my new friends there! And you know, that 'little rascal' did show up with his naughty self! So, it certainly was worth the trip from Concord to here!" Her pause was a bit longer this time, and the sparkling excitement in her small, blue eyes softened to a calm. "But, we'll discuss that another time! What I have to talk about now, is much more interesting!" This comment came with a tone of apology; and it appeared to me that her hasty, intrusive demeanor tamped down from its high energy and began to flow moderately due to her habit of reaching for thoughts of relaxation that she attained by taking a deep breath and a slow exhale. Mary noticed that I hadn't yet sat down and was about to sit; "Oh, I'm sorry dear, sit down!" she said as she waved her thin arm high to beckon a young waiter to our table. "Order your breakfast, it's on me! Listen, she said, leaning forward towards me from across the table, 'Have you ever heard of *Earth Day*? It's a campaign now being launched in America. It's an environmental event to save Mother Earth!" She then quipped jokingly; "No! You wouldn't know of such a thing, living in this beautiful jungle!" I replied; "No, I've never heard of *Earth Day*!" She leaned in closer and said; "I know; that's why I'm telling you!" she said, and began to thoroughly explain its meaning and the intent to celebrate the earth for one day, nationally. "Well, Boston is to be the first city in the country to launch this campaign; the exact date for this to happen isn't yet settled, but the committee is shooting for a Sunday in April, I think in 1991!" She paused and continued with a serious look on her face; "Let me tell you; in Concord, Massachusetts I am a member of a progressive environmental committee, it's called *Walden Forever Wild.* There is an interesting group of smart young people working with me and they are dedicated to saving Walden Pond and the surrounding climate from our encroaching environmental crisis!" Mary stopped her flow of words, turned her face away from me to rapidly blink her eyes and envision a quick thought, then audibly said to herself, "But, "we'll see about that now, won't we!" This new committee is now all young people. They are the fresh new scientists and developers of our time, Ilanga! But, unfortunately - and it's sad - they just don't have the *Passion!* She solemnly reached for her coffee cup as this new thought appeared to agitate her; but after a sip of coffee, she briskly shook her head to "wake up" from her pensive thought and continued; "But anyway, that's neither here nor there; let's talk about us, we're more important!" Mary reached out her hand to admire and play with the bracelet of beads dangling from my wrist, and began to speak again; "You know, when I arrived here the night before last, when the airport bus dropped me off here at my hotel just around the bend, I knew that this is where I would be coming for an interesting breakfast with my lovely, feathered friends here, and not 'back there' having a boring hotel breakfast and 'silly' tourist's conversations! That's why I travel alone. I just knew that this was the place where I would start my day; and then coincidently, you and I meet! Well, 'coincidently' is maybe not the right word; but I must say, since meeting you, Mister Ilanga," she said, beaming a smile of understanding; "You and I sitting here at our shady table having our interesting talks of your vibrant, young life, your social activism, your dance and your music has been all quite fascinating; but, my favorite part of your stories is about your childhood journeys to Walden Pond on your bicycle and your enduring personal relationship with 'Henry,' his work, and his purpose!" The words that she spoke next were wise, and they instantly transformed into a soothing liquid of wisdom to my ears that was slowly being poured over my Soul as she continued speaking; "This to me, seems to be a lifelong passion of yours that will go on and on, maybe, *Forever*, Ilanga!" Her brief pause allowed more of her 'liquid wisdom' to pour over me and I was starting to feel even-warmer. "Perhaps our meeting here this time and our acquaintance is not by chance, but has been and will always be a *Forever Thing* for You, Henry, and me!" It was then I heard a bird's song and her eyes quickly looked up in search of her feathered friend, hoping for a glimpse of the elusive "rascal.'

"Perdoname," the waiter said placing my tray of breakfast on the table as my thoughts went to Mary. "Gracias amigo!" I said to the waiter as he left Mary and I alone to continue speaking her thought. "I've been thinking," she said. "Listen to this. What do you think the possibilities are of you coming from wherever you are living in 1991, and performing your exotic "earth dance" there, at *The Pond*; sort of your tribute to 'Henry' and your personal contribution to the celebration!"

We both stared at one another for about five seconds; she waiting for an answer, and me with no answer and many questions! This lovely eccentric old lady has gone mad, was the underscore of my thoughts. I said nothing; but as if she were reading my thoughts, she waited and folded her hands together on the table and said: "Oh, no answer? I know what you're thinking dear, because I'm thinking the same thing; yes, we've known each other for only twenty-four hours, and only what you know of me, is that I watch birds; and only what I know of you is that you dance; and I believe, beautifully, or else this idea wouldn't have come up!" She unfolded her hands to clutch her coffee cup and sip her coffee slowly reflecting on a thought; but decided that she hadn't finished talking yet and after her sip of hot coffee, she murmured, "Ahh, that's good!" and continued; "My goodness; within a matter of twenty-four hours, at least 'three or four of them' have been absorbed with you and I sitting at this table, and we've 'blah-blah-blah'd' about every necessary thing only for this idea to happen (if you think about it) and it's all because of our dear friend Henry! Oh, I'm sure that he has something to do with this; he's still working. And I know, my thoughts of him and this idea sound crazy and far-fetched, but it's not, dear!" She said, gestured with her head and repeated, "No; It's not!"

Mary braced her elbows hard into the table to lean a bit closer to me. She was close enough for me to see the details of age; and how years of hard work, passion, and wisdom had carved deep lines of *The Life* into her small face! Her beady blue eyes peered over the clutched coffee cup as she sipped. "Listen," she said, "After our *very* interesting meeting yesterday, I was thinking about you as I was on the bus to Merida all afternoon; and by the time night came, half of it was spent on thinking about, "How will I convey to the committee this unbelievable true story of your visits from Roxbury to Walden Pond on a bicycle as a young black boy, first of all," Mary said, and adding another twist of truth; "That" might be difficult for one from Concord to believe!" she stated and followed it with a chuckle. "Well, some members of the committee and the community think I'm a mad old woman anyway! So, for them to 'hear' something like this from me is not the first time, dear! It's just that they haven't yet seen the old woman actually be "mad"! They can't conceive what 'real madness' is! That's how backwards *they* are!" she said, becoming more flustered and accelerating the anger, continued her rant; "And, this new committee of so called 'experts' who are not yet even fifty years old, devastating and bulldozing an earthly treasure and anything else in their sight older than they are, including me! You know what they learned in school? How to destroy, not to preserve! That's what this old lady thinks, anyway. They're too fast trying to get to the future or, oh I don't know... they're young and... Mary stopped herself from exercising her long-time personal rant of frustration with the committee and its newly proposed direction. I could feel and see that this was a cancerous thought to her and it deeply affected her. She paused for a moment or two with her eyes squinting in deep thought and continued saying, more calmly now; "Having a young black dancer like you welcoming this new historic day with an 'Earth Dance' at the pond is just what we need in Concord, and I can't see why it can't be performed right there at the same location where we plan to have the morning's tree-planting event," she said to herself convincingly and added; "I think that this wonderful idea definitely has to be realized for Earth Day-91 in Concord! Oh my goodness, half the night I was awake with this idea and how to execute it; until I finally went to sleep!" she said, and leaned back with a big sigh into her comfortable chair to relax from the intensity of the conversation.

"So, what do you think? Is it a good idea, a bad idea, can you be there? I need to have some answers now dear, because the committee meets next week, and this is an idea I want on the table right away!" Mary reached into her straw-bag and said with defiance, "I told you already that these kids are fast! Well; they'll see just how fast I am!" Hurriedly she pulled-out a note pad and pen, lowered her head, and began writing her contact information for me. "So, what's the deal, dear?" she said calmly without looking at me. "I know, I understand! Take a deep breath! You need guts to make an on-the-spot decision like this; but then you've got guts or you wouldn't be staying here!" She handed me the sheet with her contact information and adding sternly, "Here, this is me…and your decision is?" She sat back in her chair, with her eyes never leaving mine, and waited. "My decision is yes!... Of course, I will be there!" I said without a doubt. "This is my work, this is a job!... But, don't you think that we've got a lot to talk-about before I confirm, and you accept my decision?" I questioned her. "Like what?" she asked me quickly, and with sincere naivete that actually surprised me. "Mary, we've got to talk about real things such as financial compensation and contracts, rehearsals, travel expenses from Amsterdam where I will be living, and that's only what comes to mind right now! This is important stuff, Mary!" I said to her firmly. She sat up in her chair, disturbed, and her body movements were quick, looking for something on the table for her hands to fidget with. She found her glasses, but never put them to her face and only removed them from one location to another as her eyes overlooked the table with her rubble of papers and maps spread in front of her, searching for something else to toy with in her restless state. Finally, Mary found the beads dangling from my wrist bracelet and the tense and tight muscles of disturbance on her face relaxed into a soft and quiet smile. She leaned her body towards me, hunching her boney shoulders and said softly; "Ah, these are beautiful. West-African cowry shells." Touching them with one finger to swing back-and-forth, her eyes fixed on each swing, she said almost in a whisper, "You know, that paper work and professional BS; don't worry about that! That'll be all taken care of! The 'kids' will take care of that!" She lifted her eyes to mine, releasing the cowry shells from her fingers and folding her hands up to her face to brace her chin. "Do you really believe that you and I need to have a written contract for this to happen? Well, Mister, I don't!" she said solidly, and then quickly changed her tone; "My goodness, this contract has been made long before you and I ever knew of Walden Pond!" What she was saying astounded me! "So, what does that mean?" I asked her. "Are you saying, that this is going to happen with or without a written contract because it has been 'written in the stars, or something'?" Our eyes never left their fix on one another until she said;.. "Do you and I need a written contract for this to happen?" I ask you dear, and that's a simple yes or no answer!" she said directly tilting her head to one side. It was in that brief but beautiful pause that I could feel this new bond of friendship that she and I had established in just twenty-four hours; and it felt honest, it felt good. I too braced my elbows on the table, folded my hands up to my chin with a quick head tilt, to align with hers and said, "No, dear Mary, the answer is no. You and I don't need a contract for this to happen!" And somehow strangely believing that, I managed a twinkle in my eyes; but I couldn't help from saying in jest, "Come on now, Mary; don't you remember that the contract between you and I was written and signed even before Walden Pond. There was no paper to sign and no committee then, but damn, woman; can't you remember that we signed it in the stars?!" Mary's hands unfolded and her jaw dropped a good two inches as her voice began revving up into a strong, hearty laugh that threw her backwards into the chair! And I, seeing her immediate response, laid my face on the table, slumped over my notebooks and rubble of papers! "Oh my!" she said after her recovery from laughter; "You are a 'hot-ticket' you are!" You hit the nail right on the head, mister!" Mary sat up straight in her chair, planted both hands on knees and just kept looking at me with a genuine smile on her face. She understood. I too sat up and folded my arms across my chest. I felt relaxed, holding and exchanging my long smile with hers; I too understood. And again I could feel the mysterious bond of friendship that Mary and I had established between ourselves…maybe, so very long ago.

We both sat there in the quiet, and it seemed as if the settled silence and the early sunny morning belonged to Mary and I alone. Our silence was long, and consequently, filled with an unusual *Trust* that was sealing and confirming the verbal contract, that her proposed "Earth Day idea" and my "Earth Dance" at Walden Pond was going to happen in 1991. "There was no-doubt about that!" Suddenly, Mary's tiny body "jolted" and her ears perked up to hear a singing bird that she thought she had heard! Her swift move and reach to the table for her binoculars was a clear sign to me that she heard a song being sung. She waited; her body remaining still and tense, holding the binoculars in both hands, ready to lift them high at the next sound of a note or flutter of feathers that she was anticipating to hear. Her motionless posture and "old lady" stance had me smiling to myself, and she caught me, saying; "Chuckle if you want dear, but I swear I heard a…" Mary stopped, her ears perked up once more, listening! "Quickly," she hurried away carrying her binoculars and the remaining words with her, and stepped out onto the wide-open space of the terrace, looking up and into the trees and the Mexican blue sky. I held onto my long smile. When she returned to the table, we both knew it was near time for me to leave for the class that I had to teach at 10:00. Making a move to gather the mess of notes, books and wrinkled papers in front of me to load into my bag, I said to Mary, "I will contact you when I come into

Boston, which will be sometime in the next month or so. I will be visiting my family before I begin my new life again in Amsterdam, so, you will be hearing from me!" She slowly loaded her straw bag with her rubble and mess; "Oh, I know that I will, dear," Mary said quietly. Together, we both slowly walked across the spacious terrace to the exit gate with our arms locked and in a silence all our own. We embraced each other closely, again, sealing and confirming a "forever" friendship. "Stay young, young man!" she said, as she released my hand, smiled warmly and turned away to walk in her direction, opposite from mine. I pulled my Walkman and ear plugs out of my canvas bag and stood there to watch her walk her slow footsteps up the path to the bend where she would be making a left turn to her hotel. I knew that she would stop there, to make a boney-armed good bye wave, and she did. I threw both arms up high for a big wave and shouted out, "Ciao!" loudly for her to hear. Turning around to walk the path in my direction, I turned on my Walkman and plugged in the ear plugs to hear the traveling sounds and voice of Rocio Durcal lamenting her song, "Amor Eterno." The ten-minute walk to the dance studio in "El Centro" allowed me enough time to digest in my mind and rest the thoughts of Mary Sherwood. 'I have a class to teach' was my next thought, and 'without a class plan or notes' was my second thought! But I was feeling good, assured and *confident!*

In April of 1991, the first national *Earth Day* celebration did concur in Concord Massachusetts. The *Walden Forever Wild* committee hosted the spectacular event, featuring the *Eagles* band's front-man, Don Henley, with a Sunset performance. Mary Sherwood's tableau and *Tribute to Henry David Thoreau* did manifest for her, and for me as well; dancing on the shore's edge and waters of

261

Walden Pond! That morning, my body felt ethereal and feather-light! Leaping high from the water, to claim its own space and individual purpose. How strange my body felt; like it left me. It danced in in its own space, flowing and fluid as if I weren't embodied in it. My physicality and my mind had abandoned me; I could only see myself shaped and formed into *Spirit*; trying to *comprehend* all that was happening simultaneously with *Matter, the Moment and Me*. It was factual, it was "Real." I was dancing and filling Walden Pond with my tears of happiness unequal to that of any earthly exalting joy. My meticulously planned choreography transformed into an improvisational dance of sacredness that "demanded and willed" my body to lift itself off the earth even higher! It was not a performance for me, or for an audience; but somehow, it felt to be more of a "Ceremonial Rite." And somehow, through my blurred-vision, I did see Mary Sherwood standing there, intensely watching; holding in both hands a tree-bulb to plant in commemoration of me and my family, who were also there. My sudden and deep "connection" to Mary, our spiritual relationship, her passion and obsession for "Henry" and his works, became very clear to me at that special moment! Yes; we three were bonded somehow, in some other time, somewhere, in a forgotten, lost or unknown dimension. A *Divine* and *Possible Spiritual* contract manifested into a *Human* contract by-way-of *Coincidence*? How profound this thought was, that lingered and rested with me. It was the only thought I left with on my flight back to Amsterdam that same afternoon; I never did get to see Don Henley's Sunset performance.

September had arrived, and October would be the month of my departure from Mexico to Los Angeles; It was there that I had been living and working for two years prior to my Mexico retreat. Before leaving the city of Santa Monica (west of LA and situated on the Pacific Ocean), I had packed and prepared my load of luggage that would have to follow me first to Boston and then to Amsterdam. Therefore, the month of September was about organizing for my departure from Cancun and the making of final appointments. I stayed busy tying up the loose ends of my business contacts in El Centro, arranging final dates for the private and studio dance classes that I had yet to teach, which consumed much of the time I wanted to spend socializing and enjoying the passionate "Adios" and "Goodbyes" from and to friends whom I would not see again after September. I was running to them whenever I could because many of them were performing artists who had their sparse "gigs" outside of El Centro, in Cuba and other places that would prevent us from seeing one another again until…who knows when? I accepted this fact, knowing well that this would be the primary and heartfelt thought that we would all be thinking about on that saddened moment of leaving each other.

The September day that I decided to leave Cancun is a day that I will recall ever since "it" happened and will never forget! And to this day, whenever I see a stormy black cloud against a bright sunny sky above my head, it signals to me the threat of a serious storm brewing! The warm tropical hard rains that would downpour on Cancun daily often shared the blue skies with huge bubbles of floating white clouds that would glisten a clean shiny-white whenever and wherever the bright Sun would flash its light against them - absolute "eye-candy." Those of us with "imagination" who are fascinated with the spontaneous and fast-moving joy of "Cloud-Reading," would create images and stories from the shapes, formations, and movements of each cloud. But this day, September 10th, with its daily twenty-minute tropical rain storm was different than other days! The sun was bright and the clouds were bubbled and white, but there was an unusual energy churning and sizzling in the sweltering heat of Cancun on this particular day. "Something" chilling and strange was "swirling" in the hot air, in the trees, and in the songs that all the disturbed birds were trying to sing! I was listening carefully and watching the stray dogs scattering in confusion as I walked my way to the dance class that afternoon. This constant buzz of energy I could feel and almost hear was disturbing to me as well, and caused an anxiety of fear and uncertainty that I had never experienced before! But, because of time, I couldn't stop in my tracks and think about it because I had a class to teach; and also, I was thoroughly prepared with a class plan and notes of a new choreography that I was excited about. And this was the day that I was to present this new work to the class; so, I had to apply my focus to "that."

"Tia" was a young beautiful dancer, twenty-four years old and mid-way into her **4ᵗʰCycle**. She was a member of a cultural *Folklorico* Dance Company and also a student in my class. Tia was also an efficient, professional flight agent working full time for Air Mexico Airlines. We had become close friends during my time there in Cancun, going out together with friends, dancing, eating and always having a good, fun time; and often serious talks. Before class had begun, she and I were discussing an award of promotional achievement she had received the day before from Air Mexico. She was thrilled, happy and full of excitement telling me of this great news. "Let's go out tonight to *Cats* and celebrate!" I said. Tia agreed and stepped closer to me, whispering quietly; "And Ilanga, let me know if ever you have a problem with Air Mexico or whenever you need a flight to L.A. or Boston. Maybe I can be of some help."

She quickly took a step back and struck a flamboyant dance pose and flashed a Latina "Hollywood Smile" proudly saying… "Because sir; I am now in an "official" position to personally assist you, Mister Ilanga,' she said. We laughed, hugged each other and went into class. About thirty minutes into my class of Yoga, dance technique and body stretches, I advised the students to rehearse and work repetitively on the final choreography I had set for them. They were to have a studio performance before my departure due in two weeks. I was observing the rehearsal and slowly walking through the group, making corrections and giving verbal notes, when suddenly my entire body from head-to-toe began to feel flushed with a tingling sensation and rush swiftly moving throughout my body and nervous system with a slight feeling of "shock" as from an electrical current! Suddenly I wasn't feeling well; and I saw the studio and the students began to wave and sway in a rippling motion. I sensed the same agitated feeling of fear and anxiety; the strange, swirling energy that had swept through me as I walked my way here! The students noticed my immediate disconnect, and as the room blurred, I excused myself saying, "I need to sit!" I sat down quickly and instructed the group to continue. "Dance harder, and sweat!" I said loudly, and sat back on the wooden bench to relax. I sat there and proudly watched while my students faithfully followed through with the choreography and my instructions, noting their growing desire to learn it quickly so that they could actually "dance it." It was an effective deterrent to the thoughts and physical disability I was presently undergoing. The tingling of electricity and anxiety had subsided, but it left me with the intuitive thought that 'I must leave Cancun, immediately!' I intuited that immediate action needed to be taken.

The class ended with all the concerned, hot and sweaty dancers gathered around me; and seeing that I was "fine" and in no need of assistance, they left, leaving Tia and I alone. She was concerned and watched me closely. "I know that you're going to say, you're fine, but are you really?" she asked. "Yes, I am fine, really!" I said as we gathered our personal items to leave. "But, guess what, Tia; I need a ticket, one way to L.A. and Boston!" I said without looking at her, not wanting to see her response. "Oh, that was fast!" she quipped, "Sure! Just give me the date in October when you want to leave, and I'll see what I can do. When in October do you think that will be?" she asked, throwing her bag over her shoulder as we walked across the studio floor. My reply shocked her; "Immediately, or as soon as possible!" I said; and looking directly at Tia's face to see the expression change from concern to a complex mix of sudden surprise, sorrow, confusion, and a frown of unexpected disappointment, collectively grasping for an answer. She paused our footsteps for a couple of seconds to say something, but she didn't; except for, "Let's go!" I could feel her deep anguish and overwhelming confusion. "It's an emergency!" I said. It was the only thing I could say, because I didn't know myself what the emergency was! I only knew, that it just was!

We exchanged no words exiting the studio. She was quiet and pensive with thought, and I the same; except, that my quiet thoughts were of Tia's hurt that I felt exuding from her body as we slowly walked together. A hurt and anguish that had caused her "once happy, dancing body" to change its attitude and posture, and to now be walking with a lethargic slump! In my quiet, it was as if the deep hurt and sorrow within me had eyes that were seeing a once real "joy" instantly being crushed and shattered by my **EGO**'s selfish "whim"! And she, with her professional knowledge and pride unquestioningly accepted the "emergency" but walking next to me still hurting from the "why?" this was happening, and the uncertainty of fact that yields to the formidable question that faced us both: "Will we ever see each other again"? We continued walking without words being spoken, and I was trying to follow the many thoughts that were leading me into an arena of analytic thought and questions yet to be answered; "Will Tia ever learn the answer to "why" I had to leave Cancun, and whatever the "emergency" was, would she believe it? Will I ever learn the ways and means of **EGO,** who and what it is, and how can I differentiate **IT** from **ME**? It has its Purpose, and I have mine! And, my *Purpose* in life is certainly not to cause hurt, destroy love, and to live each day on the whim of Ego or its mood!" Feeling overwhelmed, selfish and feeling this painful moment that I caused to both of us simultaneously, stirred my in-depth thinking of Yoga's scientific and proven message of "detachment" and its vital lessons of mental balance in the quest of "Independence." I must once again review and exercise detachment, I thought, as I slowly walked, trying to "not walk with a slump like Tia. It was not until we arrived at the usual crossroads that would send us in our separate directions, where the outdoor Café was on one corner, where after class, we would usually sit for coffee and chat. Since leaving the studio and walking together in our thick silence, we had not spoken. "I can't sit with you and have coffee," she said without reluctance. "Tonight, I must go home and cook; Carlos is coming over for dinner! She was engaged to Carlos; and their plan to be married in December was their romantic dream. "Oh, nice!" I said with a sense of relief; because there was an unusual vibe of honest awkwardness that I'd never felt with Tia before now! And also because of the lingering and disturbing thoughts of what had occurred in the afternoon on my walk to the studio, my disorientated minutes in the dance class, and my **EGO**'s immediate decision to hurt Tia, I wanted to be home alone. I needed to relax and "think about the day and all of what I had brought upon myself!"

The "intuitive decision" to leave Cancun immediately, also brought up the hurtful thoughts of, "what do I do now?" to bring comfort to all those of my friends and students whom I have exchanged loving friendship with, and was now leaving so abruptly! Such a hurt, hurt me as well; and I needed to be home to think about "our" hurt, and to call on God's name to help me find "which star to reach for now, and how high" in order to snatch a glimmer or sparkle of comfort needed to share with my dear friends whom also would never know the reason of my departure. It was soon after I got home when the thoughtful conclusion came to me that the decision was "selfish" but the "intuition" was honest. "And, give Carlos a big "Hola" from me, Por favor!" I said to Tia, and making a hand-to-heart gesture, attempting to dispel or break our unusual awkwardness. "Oh, you know I will!" she said with a bright tone in her voice and a beautiful smile. Before turning away from me to leave, she took in a deep breath, exhaustively exhaled, paused, and said seriously; "And, I will see what I can do for you!" I watched her walk away with her sadness; and I took mine with me in my heavy walk home heading in the opposite direction.

It was two days later that we had our next dance class; which happened to be the first and last class that I so "sadly" taught in Cancun. Before class had started and the students were gathering in the studio, Tia pulled me aside and into a corner to say; "I have a flight to L.A. that leaves tomorrow morning at 10:00 if you want it," she said, with reluctance; and the first wave of thought that swiftly washed upon me was, how blessed I am that this remarkable young woman has always "been-there" for me since the day we met, when she wanted to organize a dance class! And never once since then, has she ever come to me with a negative attitude. She has always been positive, and in the beauty of her generous spirit; never did she reveal her many disappointments. Tia interrupted my wave of thought saying in a professional manner; "And if you don't want it, or can't do it tomorrow for some reason, there's nothing I can do for you until next week because of an approaching storm, and all flights are suspended until we get further notice of its path!" 'Next week' I thought; 'I can't! Not next week; It's too late!' I did not hesitate another second to respond to her offer. The intuition, premonition, and the annoying anxiety that had being stirring within me for the past twenty-fours prompted my instant reply, "Yes, yes! I'll take it!" I burst-out, somewhat loudly! Tia's facial expression remained calm, and with her "professional plastic smile", she responded without emotion. "Well then; It's final!" she said; "Meet me tomorrow morning at 7:30, at Air Mexico; with luggage, and ready to leave at 10 a.m. for L.A.! And when you arrive, you are to see and speak with our agent, Cassandra; she will take care of your flight to Boston for whatever date you'd like to depart; any questions?" I had never seen Tia in her professional role as a flight-agent; She was unlike Tia the dancer! With a tone of sadness that I was now leaving her, I answered quietly; "No." Only she and I knew at that moment that this would be the last dance class together in Cancun. We could only eye one-another's emotions and I thought we both remained professional. "Come, let's go dance!" I said. Tia's smile was genuine; "Si Maestro!" And we did!

We began our class with Hatha Yoga and a brief Meditation with all fourteen adult students preparing themselves to dance hard, sweat, and be happy together! They proudly showed me their highest achievements thus far in their effort to learn and perform the new choreography with the spicy music I had chosen for the dance; a hot, energetic score of music by Jazz giant Miles Davis, that he aptly titled, *Bitches Brew*! I've always thought it to be "dancer's music" and that it was thirsty for a "sizzling hot" choreography! Yes; "We danced!" The two-hour class had us sweating and steaming from dancing hard, stirring the pot of "Bitches Brew's" hot energy! And at its end, I pulled Tia aside and said to her quietly, and trying not to disclose the pain in my heart; "Tia, I must tell them now!" "No! Don't do that!" she said, and interrupted me with a stare. "I will tell them at the next class, Ilanga; because right now there are too happy to hear sad news, don't you think?" she asked, and went on to say; "You have given us what you came here to give; and you have done what you came here to do!" Tia said, with her eyes floating in tears yet to be dropped. Looking at her, my eyes too began to fill-up; but I couldn't hold back the first drop, which led us to an embrace. We folded into each other, burying our heads deep into one another's shoulder. "Gracias Amiga! Gracias!" my soft words whispered through her hair and into her ear, filling it with sincere gratitude. I could hear Tia repeating several times in my ear, "Si, Si, Si!" sobbing quietly, and said twice, dutifully; "Yes, I will tell them, I will tell them!"

Thereafter; I was left alone to feel that the early evening was going to be of sadness and blanketed with cloudy emotion. The lonely walk home was slow, "slumped", and with the disturbing anxiety that I "must" leave Cancun in the morning. I decided to stop in *Ti Clara's*, a neighborhood family restaurant, for a take-out dinner to bring home. 'Yes' I thought to myself; 'To avoid an entire night of sadness I will eat.' And because it was to be my last meal until I was in flight and to avoid indigestion, I chewed slowly while I packed my luggage with only the essentials needed for L.A.; a few pieces of clothing, toiletries, the treasured books, and my heavy-weighted large professional black leather Portfolio containing photographs, resume, and papers of my international dance works. 'Hurry, hurry!', I repeated to myself a few times as I packed and took quicker bites to eat, knowing that, the less I packed and the faster I ate, the more time I would have to go out to "Club Cats" and simply just get stoned" and reggae-dance my blues-away!

The next morning at Air Mexico, Tia had arranged the flight booking to L.A. for me to leave at 10 A.M. "You need to go right away with your luggage, and see Casandra!" she said, handing me the ticket from her trembling hand. I could feel from her body and see in her face that her solemn sadness was going to be with her and last for a long time. "Thank you so much!" I said, feeling a relief from anxiety, but at the same time, overwhelmed with such heavy sadness. I said softly, "Please forgive me; I am leaving you, and everybody now only because I must," still without explaining the emergency. "You have made my visit here in Cancun, "a happy piece of *The Life* that I will never forget, my dear Tia." We stood there eyeing each other and I felt her hand clasp mine; "Please go now," she said, as her eyes began to fill with tears. "No, I am not going to cry; I can't!" She stated professionally; "Oh Ilanga, Perdoname (forgive me) I have cried enough!"

Our embrace was tight and long; and with her face buried deep into my shoulder, I could feel her wet eyes laying hard against the skin on my neck. She slowly pulled away from me, and began wiping her face with the end of my scarf dangling from my shoulders, and saying as brightly as she could; "And Carlos says "Adios!", he wanted very much to come see you here, but he must work, you know." "Ahh, my Carlos! A good man; and he deserves "all of you, and everything that you are," I said. "Thank you, forever dear Tia!" At that, we left each other without another word spoken, only our fingers wiggling small waves of "goodbye" to one another, letting us both know that it was time to quickly turn around, and walk our own way to wherever we were going.

The five-hour Air Mexico flight to L.A. was not as restful as I was hoping it to be. My desire after boarding, was to have an airplane breakfast and fall asleep quickly without being ridden with the thoughts of "all the friendly jewels" that I had left behind in Cancun. But too often, the flight turbulence and the Pilot's apologetic voice disturbed my sleep; and it was a rocking, bumpy, sleepless flight to L.A. Once arriving in Santa Monica, home, I hit the bed and it was not until early that evening that I had awakened from a coma-like sleep. Leaving my bedroom to go into the living room, there's a short narrow corridor you walk through; and I, still half-asleep and mentally "foggy" with uncertain and staggering footsteps, was swaying side-to-side, rubbing and bumping against the walls! "Yeah, he made it!" came a unanimous scream from a few of the family members sitting there in the living room riveted to the television's early evening news. Loud shouts of "Hurry, come quick, watch-this!" followed. The television anchorman was reporting: "This is a CNN update on the tropical storm that is causing disaster, havoc and turmoil, in the Caribbean Sea and its islands! It has now been upgraded to a Category 5, and named "Hurricane Gilbert";

threatening the Gulf of Mexico and the Yucatan Peninsula!" Three days later, on September 14th 1988, the vicious "Hurricane Gilbert" slammed into Cancun hard with its tropical wrath. The terrible Category 5 Hurricane disaster was horrific and caused a tremendous amount of damage and pain; and took away over three hundred beautiful human beings! Thereafter, all communications were "down" in Cancun and the affected areas that were targeted and destroyed by "Gilbert's" wrath! Any attempt to make contact with persons on the Yucatan Peninsula was futile. A few days later, I left my family friends and the "happy time" in Santa Monica to join my family and friends in Boston for another "happy time"! I left for Amsterdam five days later.

My dear ageless reader: "All of that tropical adventure and personal drama happened for me towards the end of my **7th Cycle** (43 to 49), the *Try Again* Cycle; The attempt to re-establish, succeed, and "move forward" onto the *Assessing* **8th Cycle** was my plan! But consequently, that didn't happen; by circumstance coincidence, or fate, Hurricane Gilbert had decided that for me and for the others who also had a plan to move forward! I had made the proposed attempt during the **7th Cycle** to succeed and move forward; indeed, I did try again, but it just didn't happen the way I thought it would. To this very day, my enchantment with Mexico remains; but I have never returned there since. And in my long absence throughout the many years that have passed, the remaining thoughts of Tia, Bernado, and all of my dear friends there somehow still linger with me. And, still dangling on my thin thread of hope is that they too are still alive and realize, recognize and acknowledge - as I do - this exact, precious moment of time and the "gift" of life. Somehow and somewhere, and in my mind, they are caught forever. in my web of loving friendship! Never again since, have I heard good news or bad-news of my dear friends there in Cancun! But anytime, and when I need to; I meditate, and I can envision their beautiful, brown faces, their honest smiles and their shining eyes revealing their love and all that they are to me! And my dear ageless reader; these insightful incidents are just a few spokes in the wheel of my 7th**Cycle**; and my "alternative thinking" has led me to believe once more that this also is "destiny" for me and for my friends in Cancun; and we were all in this together!" So, am I to think and believe that this is all circumstance or merely "coincidence" I certainly hope not!

———— CHAPTER SEVEN ————

Friends: Going beyond the bounds of friendship into the realm of Soulmates.

The mysterious country of Greece is like a brilliant white diamond with many facets to catch the eye. It has a magnetic power to attract with its natural beauty, its peoples, its music, its dance, and its culture; all seductive in their own way. It can entice and capture the *Soul* of a human being; hooking any man or woman who is vulnerable to a "new" kind of love. I believe its origin and nature is to seduce a visitor, "with the powers that be." Greece can mysteriously induce one with its indelible Mediterranean rapture; and thereafter, the visitor's desire to remain there becomes a taunting fixation. And if the visitor must leave; a return-visit is always a promise as she or he departs Athens by boat from the port of Piraeus, or by flight from Heraklion Airport, just outside of the city.

In 1975, at the threshold of entering my **6ᵗʰCycle** I had first decided, prepared, and began my inevitable "escape" from America on my quest for personal freedom, promising simply "to be and to find "more." But before that could happen, and for me to feel the assurance of confidence and positivity in my "Dare," I needed to undertake review and evaluate an important learned lesson in social education in order for me to move forward. I had to "unlearn" the lie that America is "everything" and undo the entanglement of its many false doctrines that we all get tangled-up in, caught, and eventually "strangled" by. Our real or imagined successes, relationships, (and for some, even our pets) cause us to become satisfied within our comfort zones and consequently, limit our self-potential and our needed expansion of knowledge. We hold truths that are being harbored in our silent and abstract illusions of Success, such as: the American flag of red white and blue is waving "liberty and justice" for us all. To "unearth" a rooted lie, change had to come for me and it was not to be "thought-about" it just had to be done!

Because of my previous years of world travel, I had acquired sufficient knowledge of "North, South, East and West" and had decided that it had to be Europe where I would establish a new home, create my work, and somehow "just become." I chose Paris, France, as my destination. Leaving my dance mentor, Halifu and the "Company" members and friends in Oakland California, was my first emotional adjustment to make. Halifu's new dance project *Everybody's Creative Dance Center* was in the works to be established. Oakland's dance community was excited to be a first in hosting this opportunity of Halifu's concept of dance exploration and I was as well; but had to leave. Ahead of me, in Boston, my work was to be six months of planning and preparing for my departure to Paris, and to liquidate *Image of the Nile*, an attractive gift shop of African Art that I had opened in Kennebunkport Maine which was being managed by my dear friend, Fred. Meanwhile, my time was also well-spent teaching African culture and dance to children within a newly constructed housing development in the community of Roxbury, called Academy Homes. Also, before leaving Boston, I had to take a few French language lessons so I could communicate in Paris, for instance at a Café, a Bakery, on the Metro, or wherever; and with enough confidence to say "Bonjour" to the French people with a smile on my face, rather than a frown of American-tourist ignorance! Throughout this period of anxious preparation, I would daily imagine myself living in Paris and becoming "whoever" or "whatever" I was to become. But that didn't happen! It was my well-thought-out plan, but it just didn't happen; interfered with again, by "coincidence," my romanticized plan of "April in Paris" just didn't happen!"

My city of entry into Europe was Amsterdam, The Netherlands. The allure and fascination of its canals, historical architecture, and magical "Toy Town" attractions enticed me enough to spend a few days there in this "Circus-like" environment, and had me easily thinking, "Why Not!" Within those few days of "checking-out" and "feeling-out" the quaint old city, walking the cobblestoned streets; I was selecting which Cafés, Coffee Houses and Music Clubs I should be frequenting during those few days to best meet dancers, actors, musicians, and artists of the community. I would then move on to my final destination...Paris!

Well, fortunately that didn't happen"! Whether by "coincidence, circumstance or fate," within those few days, wherever I went I was welcomed warmly. And because of my profession and previous world travels, it was comfortable, easy and natural for me to engage in and enjoyably socialize, meeting interesting people who were helpful with useful information and practical advice; especially for one like myself, seeking and ready to absorb good advice to take away with me to Paris. There were some whom I met who found me to be "interesting" and some found me to be a "novelty" but none of that mattered to me because I had also met those who had insight, intelligence, and vision, and who were soon to become friends. And because of "coincidence, circumstance or fate," my plan to live in Paris never happened, and I lived in Amsterdam for five years!

This unexpected decision to reside there began when the wheel of my alternative-thinking spun into its realms of "Why Not?" Amsterdam was very appealing! Socializing, networking and being surprised each day with helpful tips and offers to remain there were also appealing; and in time, a few days became a few months. And from the aspect of working there within my profession, it was colleagues and new friends that convinced me that I was a fortunate man and that no matter what I thought about my situation, all that was happening to me in Amsterdam was "conducive to my welfare" and that all was going extremely well! Therefore; my conclusive decision to stay, followed my daring thought of, "Why not!" Not living in Paris was not a disappointment because the city was only about three-hundred miles away!" (430 Kilometers); and because I was accessible to my dear friend Samantha's apartment there, I was able to frequent Paris and Belgium for my work schedule of teaching dance workshops and other theatrical projects that eventually came to be. Having a secure apartment and close friends were only two of the factors that kept me in Amsterdam for such a period of time; the other important factors were my successful works in dance, music, theater, and fashion. And as well; the disciplined drudgery of learning how to speak the difficult and guttural Dutch language.

Leaving America and taking with me my experience of the **6ᵗʰCycle** which fueled my determination *to Produce, to Apply, and to Succeed*; I was prepared. And also, I was feeling daily the exhilarating power of high achievement which was a great reward and a clear benefit of conscious efforts acquired during my **6ᵗʰCycle**! Consequently, my dear reader, it came to be that the main factor deciding my permanent stay in Amsterdam, was the young and old artists of that diverse community who were at first, colleagues, relating artistically and working jointly and collaboratively with me on various projects. And what happened was, a selected few became interested and involved with my dance-theater projects, and also, found an unusual "something" in me or within my work that they respected or admired, became attached to, and decided to become my "forever" friends.

Out of the many, a small handful of the younger ones, all within their 4th and 5th**Cycles**, recognized in one another the special qualities that they themselves possessed: *Personal Values, Trust, Honesty, Dare, Guts, Determination,* and above all, *Spirituality!* "A unique handful of beautiful Souls spilled from the hands of The Creator!" is how it unfolded and how I see it today! This self-recognition became realized by way of our serious work together, our serious play, and our personal, cultural and international differences; Germany, Peru, New Zealand, Suriname, Holland, and America! All different backgrounds but with the same initial goal; "To Become" whomever and whatever they decide to become! And because of our collective work, our related thoughts and genuine honesty, we became inseparable night and day. We didn't know then that we were creating a "lifelong dream" together! Within a year or two, this small handful of young artists who were working and playing side-by-side every day eventually mushroomed into a loving friendship and a supportive force; creating an environment for ourselves to endure the onslaught of obstacles that an immigrant faces every day in a foreign country when he or she wakes up from sleep every morning. Not only here in "Toy Town" does an immigrant wake up to this "nightmare"! The environment that we created to expedite the values of the 5th and 6th**Cycles** was impenetrable from any obstacle that confronted or challenged the powerful dynamics of real spirituality and consistent positive energy! These obstacles to positive energy could be an immigration matter, a housing problem or even an unfortunate personal confrontation. The everyday environment that we consciously created for ourselves was veiled and supported and protected by a "purposeful" collective energy consisting of highly creative work, positive attitudes and honest, loving friendship. This was a "spiritual" thing! And today, by "coincidence" this same progressive, diligent group of people who were once young and vibrant and full of dreams, are now older and have "become;" some married with children and grandchildren, and a few deciding to remain single, wisely comprehending what was best for them. But the ultimate "joy" for each one of us is that we still have managed to maintain the crucial contact and united front of the honest loving friendship that still exists now in 2020! This very unusual seed of collective and personal high-achievement was planted fifty years ago in Amsterdam, and it was not until about 15 years after we had organized that I had begun to evaluate and realize "Us" and what we had established and achieved collectively. I found it to be a comfort that this unique group of individuals, who came together and bonded so long ago, remained connected. And we must remember, my dear ageless reader that cell phones, emails and the social media of today did not exist then! A brief one-minute international telephone call had a considerable cost to pay; therefore, a handwritten post card or letter was our thread of communication, and to receive one was a surprise that always brought a smile. And although some of us needed to go our own separate ways to live our individual lives, we also knew that We "needed" to stay in touch! It was after the analysis and the evaluation of Us that the realization came to me that together we had found a sweet passion for one another. It was a lasting desire that can be found only in a pool of committed and honest Souls and it is fact that there is no end to this dream that we together have realized! The abundance of knowledge that we absorbed, shared, and have taken away with us because of this allegiance to one another, our spiritual values and everything we did together at the highest level possible, allowed us to highly value the happiness we still share today! That rare "seed" of loving friendship we planted so long ago in Amsterdam has now grown into a huge, blossoming "extended family tree"!

Here, I want to give you a brief insight into what I am hearing today; and these words that I hear are coming from a stream of wisdom that's being whispered in my ears from the aged inner-voice of my **12ᵗʰCycle** (78 to 84). And the "Word" is, that the evaluation process that I had undertaken, and its conclusive thought, is justifiable because of the deliberate and consistent *Action* that we undertook together at that time, and "consciously" continued to stay connected to one another throughout the remaining years. I believe it to be "fact" that this union of ageless souls is about "destiny" no doubt! The word "coincidence" lessens the value of our lifelong achievement. A word has power, it can send a message. The word "destiny" (that which is to happen in the future), conveys a message of undying strength and belief of its existence and possibility, to One who is spiritually-conscious, or even for One who is simply conscious of the "Creation" itself! And now that I am experiencing my **12ᵗʰCycle**, I have concluded that the dubious word "coincidence" is weak, "thin" and without fact! It has no legs to stand-on! After one year of organizing this union of inspiring and aspiring, intelligent young folk who understood me and my "Madness," I could feel that they wanted more of it; and also during this time, I was undergoing the official process of becoming a legal resident-immigrant of The Netherlands. Every day, I could feel the exciting energy of the city and my positive actions within my circle of friends, and the work I was doing, provoked me daily to do "more"!

Adjusting to the rhythm of the city and my new immigration status in the city of Amsterdam's vulnerable environment of "dare and do" I was being vigilant and cautious everywhere I went, scrutinizing everyone I met who wanted to be a friend. It had been a year now, and I was still without emotional closure on the death of my magnificent Mother, and I had not returned to Boston since; This was an everyday emotional hurdle to straddle! But nevertheless; It was a full-year of determination, focus, and **6ᵗʰCycle** "Action"! There was just "No-let-up"! In hindsight though; It was because of the disciplines of Dance, Hatha Yoga and Meditation that I had learned and acquired in the previous years, that helped me to maintain an accurate balance physically, mentally and spiritually; I had become more aware of my sensitivity to the environment and its sunless and soulless presence. For me, this was insightful and challenging. Day-in and day-out, working, playing, and meditating, with constant thoughts of the "reality" and the "truth" that I was seeing here in front of my eyes; but certainly never thought to include in the "big picture" of my life. After analyzing and evaluating my first year of challenges and accomplishments, and what I was being busy with there in Amsterdam; I could not help but think about the space and the place of "Where I was now" in this new process of "going forward." I knew that this was but a small step on my path to "where I wanted to be!" Being aware consciously, physically and spiritually, was my concern. Introspectively, I could see in the big picture that what I was experiencing that entire year was only a small slice of the whole truth that I yearned for in my quest of "being." And due to my insight and meditation on this small slice of *Truth* and *Being*, the past, present and the future, were being experienced and lived simultaneously! Every day, this remarkable thought of my life being in *Balance*- meshed blended and harmonized - became a trio in sync that I consciously became aware of. It grounded me, dismissed my fleeting thoughts of being elsewhere and enabled me to focus and work better! Even while teaching a dance class, "It" partnered with me. Steady *Balance* gracefully flowed and moved along with me in every dance step I took across the studio floor and I could feel our duet in motion. Even the pulsating drum rhythms joined in and we danced together, beautifully!

It was June, the dance season was coming to a close for the two-month summer vacation; an opportunity, to again "escape" from this reality and go elsewhere to find another slice of the "Truth." A two-month vacation in Boston with family and friends, or in Los Angeles, Jamaica, Cape Verde or Brazil, were my options. But this led me to thinking that those options would only be just another small-slice of the "Truth" I seek." I wanted and needed a "bigger slice." I began to seriously think: "Where does The Creator, God go for a holiday-vacation? Wherever that is on this planet, it must be the perfect place to be. He, or She, wouldn't go there if it were otherwise!" Within my *balance* and with my upcoming freedom from being "Professional" for two-months, I was compelled to allow these fanciful thoughts to stay with me; They also included images of the "Ornament" once again on display, wherever the Creator's "perfect place" happened to be!

One cloudy Amsterdam day, I was busy parking my bicycle in a rack on a narrow but busy canal street called "De Herengracht"

(The Men's canal). And after leaving the bicycle in its rack, I turned around and my eyes caught an attractive street poster with a startling image of The Acropolis, the picturesque white ancient temple that hosts the revered and beloved Greek Goddess Athena. The poster was border-edged with the "Greek-Key Symbol" (meaning, eternal life); and I mentally flashed-back instantly to images of a soft blue cotton bathrobe that I had attached to in my youth, also edged with this iconic key motif. Eventually, after years of love, wear and tear, I did have to emotionally and physically "detach" from it, with great reluctance! I had always thought it to be a hold-onto-forever treasure that I knew would have to be discarded "one day", but somehow couldn't! Its strange sentimental value had a tight grip on me, and forbade me to rid myself of such a treasure! For a couple years after abandoning the dreadful thought of its discard, I used it for a housecleaning rag because of its absorbent, soft cotton texture; but there too, its time came and it went into the trash.

The English words on the poster were the color of soft blue and one word in Greek shouted boldly, "HELLA! Come to Greece!" Instantly, flash-backs and images slammed into my mind with thoughts of London and my dancing partner "Thassos" the owner of the "Acropolis" Taverna in the Bayswater district. I began to recall his ambiguous words of why I must go "Home" to Greece one day, if I was to understand many things. Leaving the poster behind and walking away wasn't easy; I wanted to stay there and continue to be captured by this beautiful and seductive street poster! It felt good, to just stare at it; but the gut feeling was way beyond good. It was a mystery, a sudden yearning, even a beckoning, that overwhelmed me, but I forced myself to walk away. I did the errands that needed to be done, but did so with the runaway thoughts of that street-poster, beckoning me to a place where "just maybe" the Creator goes for a holiday-vacation! My old Amsterdam bicycle, unbalanced with weighted shopping bags on each handle-bar and the side-saddle bags packed with produce, wobbled me home to settle and think more of what I had just seen: *The Acropolis*!

The following day, arrangements were made for me to leave for Athens, Greece in two-weeks time, to travel south through western Europe by "Magic Bus" from Amsterdam to Athens. Magic Bus was a privately-operated tour led by three older "Hippies": A Dutch man, and two ex-patriots, an American and a German. It was a bus service for young hippies and hippies my age who preferred this option as opposed to flying and travelling with the traditional comforts and conveniences. This service offered only one route: Non-stop from Amsterdam to Athens and back! It was a low-cost fare for a two-day trip, offering a chance to sit back, relax and enjoy the landscape views, visit the needed restaurants, bathrooms etc., all while enjoying comfortable bus travel through Germany, Austria, Croatia (formally Yugoslavia), and through the very beautiful southern Balkan coast to Athens, Greece! My rambling thoughts of preparation went further. Certainly, two-weeks was enough time for me to pick up a Greek-Language book for tourists, maps of the country, its cities and the islands; and as well, a fresh new pair of tight-jeans and shorts to pack along with the "Ornamentals" of dress!" The two-weeks of preparation was filled with a schedule of finalizing the dance classes, exchanging "Goodbyes" with the students, the musicians, drummers and colleagues whom I wouldn't be seeing again until the following September.

On a typical cloudy gray and rainy Amsterdam Thursday morning, the Magic Bus loaded its twenty-five hippie passengers, their back-packs, guitars and an enormous amount of prepared foods and snacks; filling the interior of the bus-space with smells of "anything" edible! "It absolutely was a "magical" bus ride of wine, weed, and song! Never did we stop singing, dancing in the aisle, nor curb the attempt to eat! We even paraded with song, dance and guitars to a restroom visit every four or five hours, entertaining ourselves and whoever else was there at the rest stop of leisure and relief! No; this was definitely not your traditional bus-trip! Because of our enjoyment and the leisure of travel, it had taken us four days to arrive into Athens instead of the proposed two days! Finally arriving at a huge and wide city square that was artistically laid with marble, the bus drew up to an area where it could unload its passengers and baggage onto the ground. While unloading we heard the loud voices of screaming vendors, shouting their bargain prices at any one of hundreds of people strolling by, hurrying to work school or a taverna. "Platia Monastiraki" is the name of this city square," said Hendrick, our ever so compliant German bus driver. "The Greek word 'Platia' means Square, and 'Monastiraki' means 'Little Monastery', but as you can see, it's actually a big Flea Market!" he said with humor; "And this area, neighborhood, or 'Buurt' he said in Dutch, "is called 'Plaka'!" Being busy with the baggage and not looking at us who were waiting with patience, he then said nonchalantly, "Oh, and if you look up there!" he said, pointing his finger up to a high mountain hovering above our heads; "That's the Acropolis!" All eyes went to the mountain and were awed by the shimmering white marble temple capping the top and glistening with pride, with its monumental tribute to the Goddess Athena! After he had finished with the baggage and a few of the passengers had theirs and had dispersed to the designated Pension nearby, Hendriek quietly asked the question that "shocked, stunned and riveted" my body to a halt! "Is your name Arnold?" he asked. My eyes roamed his face while my mind asked "who is this?" My answer to him "Yes!" was meek and I was about to continue with a question to him, but he abruptly interrupted with one word in Dutch, "Godverdomme! (Damn!) I knew it," clasping both hands to his head. He was excited and spun himself around, saying, "On the bus, you singing and dancing; I knew it!", he said emphatically and with speed! "Look at me man; You don't remember me?" he asked. I replied quickly, "No! But to know me as "Arnold" you've got to be a "blast from the past" I quipped, and let my eyes steadily roam his face once again; "Now, how is it that you know me?" I asked him. Hendriek was eager to answer; "You sing with The G-Clefs, man! I was in Tokyo Japan way back in 1969, and you were singing at club "Mugen" in Akasaka! Godverdomme; that was seven-years ago! You look the same; you don't change, man!" He was waiting for me to say something but I couldn't, as I stood there absolutely "stunned"! Then his face brightened; "Don't you remember, being in the Typhoon during our climb to the top of "Mt. Fuji" with you and your brothers?" he asked. "Hendriek!" I gasped, and instantly recalling Tokyo Japan and every word he spoke. I slowly repeated, "Hendrick, the mountain goat? No!" I said in disbelief, and grabbed him for a needed hug. He was amongst the G-Clef's entourage on a two-day excursion to Mt. Fujiyama in Honshu Japan. Through the long, cold, rainy and windy wet night, with flashlights and gear, we had climbed high to the top above the clouds and felt a great achievement. The gentle Typhoon had ceased, we were hungry and exhausted, but we sat and waited for the reward after an intense climb: the big orange ball of the Sunrise!

After a hearty meal and a couple of hours of sleep, we headed down the sleek slopes of Mt. Fuji; and because Hendriek and I were the two most energetic and agile of the group, we both were running and sprinting the slopes as if we were two mountain goats on a spree of fun! This was the extent of our two-day bond of friendship; and this is why we had come to embrace each other tightly on this day, seven years later! Coincidence…?

This day was my arrival and entrance into Greece; a memorable day for all twenty-five passengers standing there with scattered baggage at our feet and our heads tilted-upwards experiencing our first moments in the land of *Mystery Knowledge, Romance Challenge and Dare*. Here in Greece, what is sacred remains so, and does not disappear with the passing of time and new ideas. The sacred is respected and allowed to be the symbol and the will of all mankind and never to be forgotten. Sacred is the day and the night and all that is "natural"! The logical people of Greece understand that this is a significant "key" to the chest of life's treasures, and have found a simple approach to living their daily Lives, which is unimaginable to anyone who has never left their comfortable confines, and/or the shores of the United States of America!

The Acropolis is a visual treat that captures and stirs the imagination. It sets all wheels of thought in motion, and physically rivets one to admire and honor its classic beauty! From whatever country one comes from and no matter what their religious beliefs are, once their eyes are set on The Acropolis, their many thoughts all funnel into one big question: "Why?" And oblivious to this seduction, the mind can wander and challenge the dramatic mystery and historical myths of Zeus and all the Gods and their spirituality." And an honest thought that one considers at this precious moment, is to "dare" the Gods! This supposedly answers the big question of "Why?" but suddenly the quickened thought evolves into a possible fear that threatens the Soul, and underscores the honest thought of "dare!"

Learning through the Ages, that when the mythical fact of the God's "super-human" powers and their infallible design of *Understanding, Love and* Respect and that of their "human plan" is challenged (should an ignorant human do so), wrath and everlasting consequences are to be expected or at least considered if one should *Dare!* I stood there motionless without the thought of challenge, but rather with a desire to explore the magnificence my eyes had fixed upon that was causing the beating pulse of my heart to throb harder. The vivid street poster that caught my eye in Amsterdam came to recall, and the thoughts of my old soft blue bathrobe with the Greek Key border and my dancing partner "Thassos" in London all came together for me in a rush of only one thought and one action to take: I must climb this mountain up to the Acropolis today; yes; at Sunset! This morning thought lingered and gathered momentum throughout the entire day.

Hendriek's last words to us few who remained to admire the Acropolis were final; "Zo, luister yongen!" ("Okay, Listen you guys!") I am now finished with you. Any questions?" he asked and paused and hearing no replies, said, "Good! Enjoy yourselves!" And Mr. Ilanga will be your guide now," he said and flashed a quick wink of an eye at me. Tired, rumpled, and smelling foul from our bathless travels, we began to disperse in various directions, saying "Goodbye, have a great-trip" and exchanged friendly hugs and kisses; sealing the fun-filled adventure and the new friendships established on the amazing "Magic Bus" with its bumpy ride from Amsterdam to Athens.

There were six of us who decided to stay grouped and we enjoyed our first Greek lunch together at a Taverna, and then at Sunset, vowed to climb the winding stone stairways "up, up, up" the big mountain to our destination, the Temple Acropolis. We gathered our baggage and walked to our designated "Youth Hostels" within the local area, to shower and change into fresh smelling clothes and meet again here in "Platia Monastiraki" in an hour! This We did hurriedly; due to hunger, desire, and with an anxiety of anticipation for authentic Greek food. The old marble-stoned neighborhood of "Plaka" has an array of Tavernas to select from, offering the best in Greek cuisine; We decided on one, resting just below the Acropolis because I didn't want it to disappear from the sight of my eyes.

His name, he said was "Yiorgos" (George). He was our young waiter, aged seventeen or eighteen, and he spoke English very well and was extremely polite, handsome, fearless, and confident. He cordially invited us to sit and gave us a few menus;… and because I had boasted so loudly that I had learned how to say in the Greek language, "Good morning, good evening, and goodnight" it was decided that I would be the one to take charge of deciphering the menu order and the various Greek foods listed. But; our slim and strikingly tall teenage waiter "Yiorgos" noticed that I was becoming frustrated and baffled with words and pronunciation and offered his help by explaining each item on the menu, its tastes, its content, and the method of cooking! His comprehension of the English language was impressive and his unique style, demeanor, and keen interaction with me personally, as the only "adult", astounded me! And as well, his natural charm and honest flattery that he deliberately showered upon the other five hungry hippies had me thinking, "Is this joker for real?" Or is this a **3ʳᵈCycle** "Wonder" that I am meant to "recognize" standing here in front of me beneath the Temple Acropolis and The Gods!" Yiorgos displayed easily, his natural abilities to serve and please. He was sharp and he was handsome, with light-tan colored curly hair shrouding his classic Greek face and framing his deep hazel green eyes. And although, each of the four girls within our group were college graduates, half-way into their **4ᵗʰCycle**, from twenty-two to twenty-five years of age; they went "high-school-silly" for the first hour that we were there! They quipped remarks, giggled, whispered and joked among themselves. One of the girls said to him in jest, "Excuse me, did you say your name was George, or "Adonis?" Then Julie and Christy fell into a spasm of quiet giggles! But he, catching on to her flirtatious quip, answered, "Yes, it's George but if you like, you may call me "Adonis." I know very well that I am "Yiorgos" (George), he said humbly, maturely and with such politeness, that I had to keep my eyes on him. "All of you are my guests, not my customers!" He said it as if he meant it; being very professional and hospitable. I began to admire how he approached each one of us with a flash of his genuine non-plastic smile, his pleasant attitude, and the handling of six excited "freshly scrubbed, starving hippies" who were loudly chattering, laughing, and commenting on whatever caught their eye walking-by, being driven on wheels, or even a feathered bird in flight overhead! The chair I purposely sat in faced opposite the Acropolis; This was my only "eye-catcher"! Yiorgos patiently took our menu order, and from then on he left us to do his work of servitude. He'd hurriedly dash back-and-forth from inside the Taverna's kitchen to our shady sidewalk table outdoors that sat in the hot afternoon sun!

He'd run swiftly, four to five times with both arms stretched full-length in front of him, balancing three to four small plates of food lined up in single rows along each arm and a plate in each hand! And each time he'd come running out of the Taverna's kitchen to us, the expression on his face would always be "serious" eyeing each item on each plate lined-up and balanced along both arms, checking to see what was missing, and if an item wasn't there where it should be, he would immediately turn around and quickly run back to the kitchen with his arms still lined with small plates. I had noticed that his swift returns from the kitchen were not only with small plates of food but also that he had a serious intent "to educate." He'd spread the small plates across our table separately to explain each food item and its content, and often, from what region of Greece these delicious foods derived!". Yiorgos' focus on whatever he was saying, whatever he was doing, and his intent, "Captured" my mind with a thought of, "Who is this quite amazing young man/boy, with this "natural ability, intelligence, and fine character"? It was noticeable that he had a self-confidence that could uphold any responsibility he undertook; and Indeed, I was impressed! Maybe, it was my facial expression that revealed my thinking; but intuitively, I knew that he had caught ahold of my thought! He finished serving his last plate and took a step back, scanning the table with squinting, serious eyes, checking the items on each of the many plates he had laid out for us. He gave himself a quick nod of the head and an audible whisper of the Greek word, "Endaxi" (Okay), and I could see that he felt satisfied with his work. My eyes followed his every move and every word; and before he left our table, he smiled beautifully and gave me a thumbs up, seeing that I too was satisfied with his efficiency, his lavish display of small plates, his professional service, his personality, his charm, his distinctive persona, and everything that my roving eyes were seeing in front of me; including the Acropolis! I returned a thumbs up to him, adding a smile of satisfaction and repeated what I had heard him say to himself just moments ago; "Endaxi!" "Oh, my friend!" he said; "you are already speaking Greek, bravo, bravo!" His words were encouraging enough for me to make another attempt; "How do you say and ask for, 'the wine of the House' in Greek" I asked him. "Krasi," he replied. "Oh, that's an easy-one!" I said, and followed that with my first chance to speak and shape a sentence in my primary Greek; "Kei parakalo; pare Krasi, kei polla!" (And please; would you bring wine and lots of it!) Yiorgos, wide eyed, surprised and pleased with my attempt, flashed me an instant wink! He hurried off and returned quickly with three quart-sized carafes of the light-tan color, barreled wine; "Retsina"! As he was placing them on the table in front of us, my eyes were glued to the carafes, recalling the hilarious thoughts of tasting Retsina in London with The G-Clefs and Thassos, the Taverna owner; and how the guys in the Band had gagged and spit out its horrible bitter taste! I kept these thoughts to myself in patient anticipation of the group's soon to be quick response to the resinous taste of Retsina. As he carefully poured the wine into our small clear transparent glasses, he elaborated with passion and pride, the facts of Retsina; how the villagers produce it, why it tastes as it does, from what village this particular barrel came from etc. He lifted his glass high in the air, signaling to us to do the same; "Styn-Yassas!" (Cheers, to all!) he said in a big man's voice! "Welcome to Hellada!" (Greece) and saying this with strength, power, and exuberant national pride! "You will enjoy my country, I know," I can see this in your style and on your faces!" he said and chuckled to himself. "It is a beautiful *Natural* country! Not like America or the countries in Europe, it is very different here in Greece my friends. The temples, the islands, the food, my people! I have never traveled out of Greece; but too much I hear from many tourists, that Greece is very special!" Lifting his glass higher, he said "Cheers!" We all raised our glasses high, proudly screaming out loud our first Greek word learned together, "Styn-Yassas!" The moment the Retsina wine touched their lips, all the sounds of Hell broke loose! All of the "aghhh's, eeek's coughs and spits" blasted out from their mouths all at once! For me it was another enjoyable moment of spitting, coughing and laughing, simply over a glass of delicious Retsina wine!" After his last small sip of Krasi, Yiorgos' eyes became serious once more and with concern, overlooking the group and saying; "My friends, Greece is beautiful, yes; but it can also be dangerous, so you must be very careful!" he said, probably imagining in his mind what this wild raunchy hippie group of six from Amsterdam could get into; individually, or as a group! I admired his words of caution to us, thanked him, and let him know that I appreciated his concern. "I must go inside now!", he said briskly; "I have much work to do! Yassas!" (meaning also "goodbye.") As he was leaving, he continued to say with a sense of sincerity that had me to believe its truth; "Very nice meeting all of you! And after you visit the islands and come back to Athens to return to your countries, come back here to the Taverna for your last Greek meal; it would be nice to see you all again!" he said, as he held both hands on his heart, "And now I must go inside to work, and you must go to enjoy Greece! Efharistos Polli!" (Thank you very much!) Yiorgos graciously nodded his head, then politely excused himself and quickly ran off to the kitchen!

Outside, it was a blazing hot sunny afternoon and the girls; Julie, Vicky, Mona and Christy, were tipsy, silly and full of retsina. Upon hearing the music of Mikis Theodorakis' "Zorba The Greek" being played on the Taverna's loud speaker, they started their own version of Greek dance on the sidewalk. Hearing once again the original music from the famous film starring American actor Anthony Quinn, I thought to get up myself and try a step or two of their version or mine; but instead I listened to the clamoring voice of Retsina speaking deep within me which said, "Don't even try it!" The girls were dancing and jumping about and Julie was flinging her arms and throwing her head back in a fling of ecstasy. When her eyes suddenly opened to the site of the Acropolis gleaming bright in the hot Sun, she moaned; "Ooh! Come on, let's go up there and dance!" All four frolicking dancers squealed "Yea, yea!" several times, vocally hitting exciting high notes of unanimous agreement! "No, no, not now, it's too hot up there in the Sun!" I said. "We'll go up in few hours for the Sunset, when it's cooler!" Christy, who was a glass more sober than the other three, said "Oh my God, he's right! We'll burn-up there! Let's go and do something else until Sunset!" she said wisely. Suddenly, Hans jumped up retsina tipsy, trying his best not to fall back into the chair or on the sidewalk! "Kompt!" he said. Hans, a slim vibrant wiry-limbed, happy, young Dutch boy who always enjoyed laughing, said again; "Kompt!" (Come!) He continued, mingling Dutch words with his limited English vocabulary: "Let us "Loppen" (Walk) down "Daar" (There), to the Flea Market, "Yongen!" ("Guys!") "Oh, yes, yes, yes!" the girls all screamed in one another's faces! "Kompt, Ilanga!" said Hans. "Oh no, not me," I said quickly, chewing my last bite of Feta cheese and pouring another glass of Retsina; "I'm sitting right here until Sunset!" and if you guys don't get back here in time and you don't see me here, I'll be up there"! "O.K.!" said Julie, bursting with high energy; "But watch us dance down the street!" she added, pointing her finger at me; "Because you are going to want us in your dance company! So, watch us, Ilanga!" She snatched Hans and the girls, and darted from the sidewalk into the street! "Yes, yes, I'll watch!" I yelled out; "And I'll have the contracts ready when you guys get back!" With their laughter, dance, and buoyant bodies fading away;...the five of them left me alone to watch the traffic and pedestrian crowded "Plaka" (area). In the distance, I noticed Hans gave up quickly trying to figure out the girls choreographed dance routine and did his own thing! I chuckled to myself and relaxed, listening to the sounds of the beautiful Greek music with the background of this authentic Greek street scene happening in the old "Plaka," an area of neoclassical beauty.

After a short while, Yiorgos approaches the table with another carafe of Retsina, and saying; "My father, sitting over there, sends this Krasi to you! He said, that he likes that your eyes stay on the Acropolis, and not the street!" Yiorgos went into a roar of heavy laughter! "My father has humor," he said, "He likes to joke!" Yiorgos' face got clouded with a frown and a slight eye-squint, saying, "But, he's a serious man and he is most of the time very serious!" I looked over and saw three, seemingly elderly men, sitting at a table a distance away from us. "Which one of those men is your father?" I asked him. "He is the big man wearing glasses," Yiorgos said. At the same time his father threw us a glance and I raised up both my arms, signaling him a grateful gesture. He returned a slow nod of his head, holding both hands to his heart. I looked at Yiorgos, who was watching me carefully and with interest. "He's a kind man, Yiorgos," I said; "I can feel and see, that he's a good man!" "Yes, he is!" was Yiorgo's quiet reply that ushered in a moment of silence between us. "I know your name is Yiorgos, meaning George," I said to him to him introducing myself. My name is Ilanga; which means "the Sun." I really have to thank you man, you know, for being such a great waiter and the way you served all that delicious food! It's amazing how you carry all those plates, and…" I stopped saying all that I wanted to say because I could see that his interest was not of flattery, but of something else. "Where are your friends, have they gone up to the Acropolis?" he asked, standing at the table opposite from where I was sitting. "Oh, no!", I said; "They've gone to the Flea Market! It's too hot right now, to go up there!". As I was about to explain to him our plan to walk up to the Acropolis at Sunset, I saw a middle-aged woman, petite and wearing a full-length white kitchen apron strapped tightly around her waist standing at the front door of the Taverna calling Yiorgos' name and intimately talking to the three gentlemen sitting nearby the door. "I'm sorry," he said; "I must go! That is my mother calling for me to come finish my work. She wants to go home now; it's Siesta time and she must go to rest. She's tired I believe; she has been here since early morning, cooking!" he said, seemingly concerned, and then added; "I will come back to you, if you are staying here, or, are you leaving now?" he asked, before he started to run off to his mother. "No, I am staying here I think; I like what I'm doing right now! But, tell me where the restroom is before you go!" "Yes; when you are ready, come in the Taverna and I will show you!" I felt confident enough to say in Greek, "Efaristos!" (Thank You!). His face lit as bright as a 100-watt bulb! "Bravo, Bravo, my friend! Your Greek is very good!" he said with a big, pleased smile, and then ran off quickly to his waiting mother at the door. I remained sitting at the table, sat back in my chair and fixed my eyes on the Acropolis, following my mind to the place "wherever" this beautiful and haunting Greek music that I was hearing, was leading me to! My wandering mind, just kept wandering; and I followed.

My ageless readers, I must say to those of you who have not yet been to Greece; You must go to experience the alluring and natural seduction and mystique of Greece! To be in Athens for the first time, leisurely strolling the old marble stone neighborhood of Plaka; and to find yourself sitting alone at a Taverna's sidewalk table resting beneath the temple Acropolis, is Paradise on earth! You too would be watching the Greeks in their display of innate gestures and observing the natural rhythm and motion of their daily life. You too would be sitting there taking notice of all things Greek, your eyes overlooking the tables cluttered with empty plates of recently consumed delicious Greek foods. You would see the remains of a few loose leaves of lettuce, bits of spiced herbs, small crumbs of feta-cheese and an olive or two, floating in a puddle of olive oil left on the small white plates, and the wine carafes, drained and empty of Retsina! You would be tempted by the Greek music and the atmosphere, the beauty of nature and the spectacular architectural treasures in the distance. All this would offer you great pleasure and satisfaction, but "unknowingly" my dear reader, you are being "seduced" by this natural scene and its rapture "happening" there before your feasting eyes! And what is happening and coming to you from "somewhere" is a "new" personal challenge; stirring and brewing within you that you've suddenly allowed, and it's about to surface and confront you "face-to-face," tempting you, luring you and daring you to "try me, experience me and this everlasting moment of your deepest pleasures, if you dare!" The secret voice whispers to you from "somewhere" and the challenge is that, "if what you *See Feel and Need* is all there in front of you, even if it's only for a presumptuous moment and not everlasting, embrace it, be fearless if you dare, and maybe for the first time ever, you will feel and "Comprehend" the triumph of Courage!

My obsession with world travel and the numerous questions and answers I have asked and received, have led me to believe that the country of Greece "purposely exists" for sensuous stimulation and to ignite "something" within human beings and all things alive; there, simply for one to experience that "something" if they dare! It is a precious moment for one to sit back, relax, sip a bit of "Krasi" with its bittersweet taste, and easily go with the flow of "new" thoughts that are just as tasty and bittersweet as life itself! And believe me; "if and when" you do accept this *Dare and Challenge*, it will be then, and only then that you will truly comprehend the undeniable fact that there is no greater exchange in "Loving" than this; there is no greater fusion of mutual oneness, than this! There is no other! This is Greece; this is its Purpose; and with its lasting, tenacious power, it captures but does not release neither Man nor Woman. The gift of "Loving" suddenly becomes understood and is accepted as you are so pleasingly captured. The veiled ambiguity of this country is laced with a feminine allure and a chiseled-sculpture of masculine power. Its rare natural beauty and its honest "Soul" beckons you to "try me if you dare!" And when one who has the need, hunger and thirst to quench a "temporary" desire or has an "eternal" yearning to mitigate the **EGO** willingly leaps into the fires of "Loving;" one becomes educated in what "Love" really is. The "Joy" that comes to one who can endure the rapture and mystique of this gift and its Nature and yields to its "offerings" will no longer harbor in anguish;

knowing that "something" will always be "there" for you, in your need! "There is no other, there will be no other; "This is Greece!"

Such stories of seduction and rapture are written, widely expressed and depicted in various forms of the Arts such as movies, music, dance, theater and books. But unlike any other country on this earth, it is Greece and its people that have created this uncanny mystique of how one is to live their long working day "enjoyably" and do so with a binding faith and respect within the laws of nature and all its living things! This country beckons and wields an irresistible force upon one who is a "naturalist, or for one who would like to be, or dare to be, a "lover"! The French, Italian and Spanish, also have their own tasty bites of "rapture and seduction" for world travelers to "taste" during a short vacation or for a longer period of time; And, they have the privilege and personal right, believing that the rapture they have experienced "there" on vacation, is "the best" and that "all desires" have been met! There is a measured truth to this; but my experiences have led me to me believe that those raptures are but capsules of "bottled time" and that this magnificent obsession, and the "Greek Rapture" is endless.

I continued my sit at the table, alone with the many scattered thoughts of Greece, its allure and *Purpose*; but the time that had passed felt like hours. My Mind wasn't thoroughly drunk or soaked with Retsina, only slightly dampened, when I realized that the thought of a restroom was more urgent than more wandering thoughts of Greece! I stood up from my chair to give my tired bus-ridden body a good long stretch before heading for the restroom inside the Taverna. Walking slowly towards the Taverna's door to seek Yiorgos, and zig-zagging in between unoccupied tables and chairs, the three elderly gentlemen in their chairs sitting nearby the

Taverna door had seen me at the table, and now took a serious look at what they saw approaching them. I noticed that their intimate conversation continued, but six-pair of eyes were upon me, staring with awe! I suddenly realized that their astonishment in what they were seeing and approaching them, was the "Ornament;" a startling sight, that maybe they had only seen in a photograph or movie! My flamboyant scarf, the flaming-red African motif Dashiki tunic draped across my body, the beads and bracelets dangling from my arms and neck, and my big full, round 1976 Afro-style hair didn't stop their conversation, nor their constant glare and stare! My intention was to casually walk by the gentlemen to thank the man wearing eye glasses, Yiorgos' father, who graciously sent to our table a carafe of Krasi! Before entering the Taverna, I stopped where they were sitting, excused myself, and interrupted their conversation saying, "Efaristos!" to the gentleman wearing the eyeglasses; "Thank you, for the Krasi!" I struggled for some words in English that he could possibly understand;… "You are a good man," I said, holding both hands to my heart, as I had seen in Yiorgos' gesture. "You have a big heart to do that!" He slowly nodded his head with a gesture of acceptance and thanks, but his eyes and the eyes of the other two gentleman never left the "Ornamental" sight that they were seeing standing in front of them! "Yes, yes, no problem!" he replied in English, but his eyes never met mine as they scanned every thread on my garments, every hanging bead, and every strand of hair on my head. The four of us "gawked" at one another in our "fishbowl-like" silence. "Ahh, my friend; You are here!" said Yiorgos who had rushed over. "The WC (Restroom), is just here!" I excused my "flustered" self from the three gentlemen, and followed him. "Wait!", I said, grabbing his arm to stop and met his eyes. I carefully said to him,

"Please Yiorgos! Will you go and explain to your father how grateful I am for the Krasi and that I can really feel his heart; and tell him that "I can see" that he is blessed with a wonderful Son! Please tell him that whenever you get the time!" Yiorgos' serious facial expression of concern arranged itself into a proud, broad smile of understanding. "Endaxi!" ("O.K.!") he said; "No problem; yes, I will say to him this, later!" His head gave a quick nod and a tilt to one side, and off he went running to return to his duties. I returned from the WC and back to my table, quietly passing the three gentlemen, giving them a slow head nod and a gesture of gratitude, holding both hands to my heart, and arriving at the table quickly. I hurried, and couldn't wait to arrange my chair to sit back, relax, and again have the temple Acropolis in sight, allowing this Taverna music so delicately haunting in my ears to capture and seduce me. And, I would allow it to continue to do what it was doing to me to take me again, to wherever it thinks I should go! The feeling that it was giving me then was just too good for it to be wrong.

Well into at least a half an hour of these pleasurable thoughts of my presence here in Athens Greece, sitting at a Taverna table here in Plaka, I began to contemplate my next day. My plan for the following morning was to leave Athens from the Port of Piraeus and board a Ferry boat to the far-South Island of Crete, not far from the coastal country of Libiya, northern Africa. I opened my traveler's map of the island to plan an itinerary and begin my four-week island adventure; alone, with dare, and freedom. With decisive thoughts, and my head and eyes buried deep into the map; I scoured the map to find an area which I have always been fascinated and in wonder of: the ancient Minoan Civilization! I knew this was the first sight in Crete to see; and also; another one of the vast island's principle tourist attractions that caught my interest, was the infamous Samaria Gorge, supposedly, one of the earth's most natural, pristine and alluring treks into nature's belly, hidden deep in the earth. This needed to be my second sight to visit, I immediately decided. "Ahh; I see you are going to Crete, my friend," said Yiorgos, who had been standing tall behind me overlooking the map. He boasted; "Many tourists say that it is the most beautiful of all the Greek islands!" but I don't know; I have not been there. You will have to see that for yourself; I would think!" he said, and sat opposite me at the table. I rested my elbows on the flat map widely spread in front of me, fisted both hands to rest my chin on and settled with the final thought of going to the Samaria Gorge. I began to ponder what I was listening to and said to "Yiorgos, "This music I hear now, It's too beautiful! What is it, who is it that we're listening to?" I asked, and continued without waiting for an answer; "How strange it is! I hear many stories of life inside this music, man! It's sweet and sad; and sometimes I hear the sounds of a strange happiness that I can't explain! This music, the stories, have been staying in my head and forcing me to listen since you've been gone! It takes my mind away Yiorgos, to many places here; and it gives me strange feelings of Greece! Nice feelings, but strange, you know?!" The conclusion of my statement ended in silence; No, he didn't know! He hadn't a clue as to what I was talking about. His face, puzzled with an expression of "Daah!" made me realize that what I was saying to this young teenage boy, went way over his head. I noticed his forehead frown with a wrinkle, then his instant and thoughtful reply was, "You hear life in this music?" he asked, squinting his eyes and desperately trying to understand "something" of what I was saying. "No, no! Forget what I just said!" I insisted; "Being a dancer, I sometimes hear and see different things in music, that's all!" With that being said, I could see that it relaxed his thoughts and any further questions about hearing and seeing life in music! And I too, relaxed from the reverberations of my adult rant and comments. "This is beautiful instrumental music," I continued to say; "Who is the Composer? I mean, would you know?" I asked him, and added, "I mean, can I buy this music, now, today, if I wanted to?" Yiorgos' pause was brief and with a sudden-thought he said, "Please. Wait!" He quickly got up from his chair and ran to his father and the other two gentlemen for answers to my onslaught of questions. He returned within a few minutes, pleased with all the answers. "This music you like, and hear in your Mind stories of *The Life*, is the music of "Starvros Xarchakos"! he said, empowered with the excitement of achieving his goal. He is a very famous Greek composer! He and my father come from Mani, a place far away; in the village where they were born!" he said proudly; "And yes, you can buy the cassette tape right here in Plaka, at the Monisteraki Flea-Market! There, at the corner, five-minutes away!" And then he said with a burst of fresh enthusiasm, "I will go and get it for you, if you like!" He ran off with the Greek Drachma currency that I had given him and within ten minutes, I noticed him in the distance walking back towards the Taverna, along with my friends on their return from the Flea Market. I could see that they were boisterous with laughter, their hand gestures and numerous conversations loudly happening all at once on the Plaka street- they being totally oblivious to the post "Siesta Time" of hurrying pedestrians, surrounding cars and bustling street traffic!

I welcomed them to the table, with my hands in applaud for their street dance departure and their triumphant return from their Flea Market hunt of Greek treasures! And amid the exchange of cross-conversations and noisy laughter, was Yiorgis saying; "Here! This is your cassette tape and drachma change! I must go inside now, but I will come back before you and your friends go up to the Acropolis; but; It should be soon that you go, because of the Sunset!" I thanked him as he ran off to the Taverna's kitchen, leaving me to hear the many hilarious stories told of the marketplace and who bought what and why.

"Siesta Time" in Greece was now over. The stray and abandoned cats and dogs lazily awakened to prowl the streets and Taverna kitchens for their evening meal as the loud voices of the eager vendors rose to a shouting blare. By this time of the day, the afternoon's hot blazing sun has softened and dimmed its glare and brightness, signaling to the foreign tourists, that "It's okay now, to come out of your hotel rooms, the Sun is harmless now!" A signal to "freshen up" with a splash of shave lotion on the face of a gentleman or a scent of lovely perfume lingering on a woman's neck is always a boost for socializing. "Hella!" ("Come!") "Come into the streets of Athens and play!", the signal announces. "Hella! it's cooler now, to shop the street vendors and stroll the streets of Plaka in search of Greek treasures and the perfect Taverna to feast, drink wine and spend the entire evening in Greek seduction!" A signal that rings clear throughout the city;.. And also, a signal that the Sun will be setting shortly to welcome the sparkling night lights of Athens and the dazzling "night-life" that follows their twinkle.

"Hey, guys; we must be going up now!" I said, getting up from my chair and collecting my table spread of personal items, and also to wave goodbye to Yiorgos' father and the two elderly gentlemen who slowly lifted their walking sticks to return their goodbye wave. Yiorgos' father beckoned Yiorgos from the kitchen and hurriedly he came out running to us for an individual goodbye embrace. "I will see you here again, in about four weeks, when I return from Crete!" I said to him after our friendly embrace. "Yes, my friend, and "Kalotaxidi!" ("Have a good trip!") he said; and stood there watching us walk away and up the ascending street and marble stoned paths and stairways that would lead us up to the Acropolis. The four girls were bunched together laughing and talking and walking a few steps ahead of Hans and I. We had not walked more than five-minutes, when Han's suddenly stopped his walk and yelled out loudly to the girls, "Hey, Meijes! (Girls), Stop! I forget the wine back 'daar' (there) at da Taverna! I must go back!" he said; and began to dart off, but stopped dead in his tracks, after hearing, "No! I got' em!", Julie screamed back at him; "I got the bag off the chair!" she yelled. Hans sighed with relief; and this abrupt pause in our climb allowed a moment for me to think fast and to scream back to her "Have we paper cups, also?" We all looked at each other in agreement that we hadn't! "Wait here!" I said; "I'll go back to our friend at the Taverna; maybe he has paper cups!" "Oh no!", Julie screamed; "Let's go! We can chug from the bottle!" This idea didn't sit well with me; "No, we can't do that!" I said quickly. "This is a sacred temple, you guys; we need to respect that! At least with paper cups we're more respectful," I said with a chuckle. "And besides, there will be people all around us; we won't be alone up there! Wait-here!" I screamed back at the girls, and told Hans; "Hold tight, I'll be right-back!"

Yiorgos, still outside of the Taverna, busy with his table duties, saw me running back and waited for my approach. "What has happened, my friend?" he asked with concern. I breathlessly explained the critical paper cup dilemma that occurred, and he could see clearly my fluster and anxiety! "No, we don't have paper cups, I am sorry; You will have to go to the market for that!", he said. His answer didn't satisfy me. "Well, can I borrow six small wine glasses and return them when I return from up there, after Sunset?" I asked, and respectfully added; "But please, first ask your father if that's okay!" His quick head nod and a whisper of the word "Endaxi!" ("O.K.!") left me standing there waiting with my eyes looking up to the sacred Temple Acropolis. "Here; and "Yes, It's okay!" Yiorgos said, when he returned with six glasses. "My father trusts you!" It was at the moment that he handed over to me the small glasses, when suddenly I felt my body become infused with a mild "electrical-charge" that was immediately followed by an unusual sensation of *Misplaced Time, Familiarity, Connection,* and *Knowing this family*! A 'Divine" sensation came over me that said I could trust this intuition and recognition; and that I was not to forget, ever! It was the same sensation I had when I was sitting alone at the table; and what I felt then, I felt again at this moment when Yirogos and I were exchanging the glasses and the skin on our hands touched. And I am sure that he also "felt something"!

"Hurry; You must go, your friends are waiting!" he said, as he flashed a pleased smile of pride for another accomplishment. "Yes, 'Efaristos!' and tonight, I will leave the glasses "there" in that plant pot with the small tree," and made a quick gesture towards the Taverna's door where the plant pot was located. "Endaxi!" he said. We embraced again and I sped off to join the others waiting for the paper cups that Julie "didn't" need!

Our climb up ended with our arrival at the top of the rocky ledged observation plateau just below the foothill and foundation of The Parthenon temple that is dedicated to and honors the beloved Goddess Athena. From this observation plateau you can view the city of Athens (and so much more if the Attica Basin isn't filled and polluted with a dirty orange-colored cloud that day). And if you lift your eyes to see higher, looming high above is The Acropolis.

There it stands in all its radiance; glowing a soft red color, poised, and waiting to be gently painted by the arriving colors of the setting Sun. This precious moment of the day will capture every seeing eye and thought of the Athenian people who are walking the streets in the faraway distance down below the rocky plateau. You cannot miss the target sight of the ancient "Agora Market Place" in its original location at the base of the mountain; laying low and outstretched in its own classic beauty, and laden with its own stories to tell. The ancient sites one sees below of "Agora" and the old area of "Plaka" cause one to think "differently" about "where things begin and where things end." That's if they ever do! And for me, these cyclical thoughts of evolve-to-revolve have a beginning that never really ends; possibly spinning itself and other wheels into a flurry of spins! "And I began to think that *Time* itself can only be told by the revolutions of the Sun and the Moon; and *Death* is an inevitable and foreseeable "something" that accompanies *The Life* of human beings and all living things, but also possibly has no end! The recycling of seeds, weeds, leaves, and also the uneaten foods on our plate leftover for the hungry were just some of the fascinating thoughts that still spin loops and make circles in my Mind this very day! On that particular day, should anyone on that plateau standing next to me had asked the question,

"What are you thinking?" and I had answered in my truth; they would have immediately walked away in disgust thinking, "a young Mind wasted and wandering and going nowhere!" But, on that day, nobody asked. The observation plateau views the city, its activity and an unmeasured distance of surrounding beauty. But when one lifts their eyes from the sights below to a higher level and view, they witness the scope and the breadth of life itself! They see the vast spectacular panorama of the Attica Basin spanning across the northeast horizon; and with a slight shift of the eyes, they will open wide with delight to see the city of Athens surrounding the sweet curvaceous slopes of gracious "Mt. Lycavittos" sweeping upwards to host a small chapel of Orthodox worship, "Aghios Yiorgos" (The church of Saint George). This religious relic of time, spiritually caps the peak of this glittery mountain of "entertainment" that proclaims its day and night tradition of tourists buying costly Greek treasures, enjoying their tiny bubble of international "sophisticated fancy fun and urban-flair" guaranteed!

The six of us sat high on a flat rock overlooking the golden-lit city of Athens and basking in the shades and colors of Sunset; each of us holding on tightly to our never-emptied small glasses that were being constantly filled with Retsina Krasi and carefully poured from the many bottles that Julie insisted on carrying in her climb up the steep Philapappos Hill to the Acropolis. Enjoying our rowdy behavior, our laughter, and the struggle of trying desperately to steer our many conversations to the focal point of "tomorrow morning;" the final decisions of "Who's going where, to what islands, and with whom?" is when it happened, twice! A very odd "Strangeness" was felt by all of us! It suddenly interrupted or "forced" our body movements to settle and relax; our fast talk and laughter just stopped instantly to silence; and a brief, soft wind carrying an eerie calm put a halt to our noise and muffled and blanketed our vocal joy with only a pure "Nothingness!" We were swallowed in a thin and airy silence that surrounded us, hovering lingering and haunting, for about fifteen seconds; and then just as quickly, left. The first happening of this "Strangeness" we all simply ignored; but when it came upon us the second-time, Vicky said, "Oh God, this feels so damn weird and strange when it gets quiet like this! "Yah, maan! Dit est vel t'gek!" ("Yea, man! This is really crazy!") said Hans, in flat-out Dutch, startled, his eyes filled with fear! He was compelled to say quickly, "Kippen-Fles, ik-hept, nieu! Kiek!" ("Look! I have goosebumps now!") He vigorously rubbed his long arms up and down trying to rid himself of the chilling goosebumps as the silence slowly faded into thin air, leaving us to wonder what had happened and causing our funny stories and laughter to subside. So we sat quietly together, talking softly, and watching the remaining colors of the Sunset blend into the flickering street lights; and the Taverna lights turning on to welcome the early evening.

"I wanna go!" said Vicky; "This is spooking me out! And anyway, I got things to get done tonight before we leave for Delphi in the morning!" she said, getting up from where she sat, crossed-legged and frightened. I could sense that her sweet gentle Soul was "ruffled" by such strangeness. Christy butted-in with agreement, slurring her words all over herself and at us; "Yea, Let's go! I'm pissed-off at my- self for still being here, dammit! God, help us, please; we're leaving at 6 o'clock in the damn morning!" she said in her "Jibberish." We all stood up, stretching our drunken bodies, preparing to depart and make closure on our new friendships; but I decided to stay a bit longer with myself, to make closure on the day and all of its sweetness, its intrigue, and its strangeness. Meanwhile; The circle hug of loving friendship caused the swell of new emotions now embedded deep within our Magic Bus memories, and silently "knowing" that we may never see each other again. The hurried movement, the loud rustling of paper shopping bags, empty bottles and absolute chaotic chatter alerted me to say, "Hey, guys, watch-out! Don't forget that we're on the brink of darkness here, and standing on the edge of a rock…be careful!" "Oh shit! That's right, Julie said; bracing herself from a "Retsina-stumble" and holding tightly on to Hans, apologizing and asking him in-between her stagger, "And, what time are you leaving for Santorini?" "The ferry boat leaves at 7 o'clock; but "Ik moet" ("I must") meet my friends there in Piraeus harbor at 5 o'clock!" A slight toe stub on a small rock made Hans forget his English and rattle off in Dutch, "Zo, Ik moet weg met een taxi van out hier naar daar, godvoordomma!" ("Damn! I have to go with a taxi from here to there!") Hans said in a shaky voice, guiding himself and wobbly Julie to the main path. Mona, the most quiet, sensitive and personal of the four girls, had the five empty wine glasses in her hands and placed them on a flat rock. "I will leave these here for you," she said; "And, thank you! You are so sweet!" Mona's hug was tighter than I had expected and filled with sincere genuine affection. I had to reveal to her our sameness; "And, thank "You" for being so sweet and so pensive and quiet, and always sitting over there "somewhere" in your own corner of the world!" I said, and holding her tighter than I thought that I would be! Christy and Vicky joined Mona and I in a close-knit group hug that sent them on their way to the path where Julie and Hans were waiting. From my high view on the plateau I could see them on the path below and I raised both arms high above my head, spreading them wide and slowly swaying my body side-to-side, visibly sending big waves of goodbyes to my departing friends. I watched and waved for quite a while until I could no longer see them on their descent, stumbling or stubbing their toes on the rocky stone steps leading downward to the old neighborhood of Plaka. Their voices died out and they were gone.

Alone in the darkness, waiting for the rise of the Moon, feeling deep within me a sense of sanctuary and the swirl of soft energy surrounding my body, I felt a quiet peace. This energy felt good; It felt protective; and I let its subtle tingle wash over me, throughout the nerves of my body, letting me know that it was "that close to me" and that, "Yes; I was fine here." I sat comfortably on the flat rock next to the five empty glasses that Mona had left there for me, and set my eyes to roam the vast distance and scan the dark horizon brightly sparkling with the twinkling lights of Athens. Sometimes I would hear soft voices drift over to my ears from other nighttime spectators and lovers who were walking the main path not far below my perch on the rock. Time eluded me, and the culmination of my thoughts of past present and future, family friends and places and things all fused together, blended into a couple of hours of "place, and being." I didn't realize that high above my head, a Moon had already risen during my thought-travels in a timeless vacuum of existences and experiences. By this time in my inquisitive young life, I had already learned the lessons of "The Fool on the Hill" from a song famously sung by the English group, the "Beatles." I smiled to myself; sang softly a few lyrics, smiled again, and decided that it was time to climb down from the rocky top of Philapappos Hill! I got up from the rock to stand tall; stretching my body and breathing deeply a few times, presenting a bodily gesture of "gratitude" to Athens, for this long moment of "universal understanding" that seemed to be accompanied by the love of all things dead and alive! So; a simple dance gesture of gratitude just spontaneously "happened" on top of the rock that night. It was dark, but I was at ease and it just felt like the natural thing to do.

I left the sacred site, my neck wrapped tightly in a new soft, blue cotton scarf that Hans and the girls had gotten for me at the Flea Market. The dangling beads and jangling bracelets catching and tangling between the fingers of my hands and the six empty wine glasses were not the problem; darkness was! Arriving at the main path was a relief. It was subtly lit with antiquated street lighting, but it was sufficient for us midnight strollers and devious night-voyeurs on their secret prowl, fiendishly lurking, roaming and hiding deep in the dark bushes. My concern was not of this, or of any harmful danger that could possibly come to me; but rather, of the past few hours up there on the rocky ledge being seduced by *Time and Thought.* As I usually do; I allowed my mind to spin in its own nature, and it had me thinking as I slowly walked, "It can't be me alone who goes through what I just went through up there on that rock"! My thoughts rambled on as I cautiously walked slowly down, allowing my mind to speak for itself; "I cannot believe that I am the only one who can sit there and "Not be There," feeling the "affinity for infinity," or, undergoing an unusual "Strangeness"! I am sure, that one cannot sit there without some type of "Experience"! Anyone who sits there must become that "Fool on the hill!" I carried these thoughts along with the wine glasses all the way back to the dark Taverna and placed them beneath the small tree in the planted pot, saying to myself, "Endaxi, Yiorgos!" and left them safely to "bond our Trust." And I need to say here that, a trust that was "coincidently" established well over forty-years ago, recognized by both of us and nurtured to this very day, still exists and maybe will exist "Forever"! One as inquisitive as I, and now into my **12ᵗʰCycle** need no longer ask "why?" or have doubt about our precious destined time here together on this earth! The absolute *Purpose* for he and I "To Be" in this union became clear to us both as our following years rolled into decades. The extended brotherhood, the work together, and our purposeful minds, helped to mushroom an Athens legacy that he and I and many others live with today, no matter where or in what country we are now living! This legacy, is explained in this memoir for them; so that they too no longer need to ask, "why?" and "how?" it all happened.

My short walk to the nearby Youth Hostel where I was lodging for the night, was a lonely walk with deep pensive thoughts and smiles, reflecting on the long and seeming day without end until I finally rang the late-night bell at the Hostel, alerting the night manager that someone had arrived. I entered, smiling and with a good feeling.

It took me less than an hour to pack essentials into the small sized military brown duffle bag I had purchased at the flea market in Amsterdam; and being packed and ready to go, I had a few remaining hours to sleep before for my 7 a.m. ferry departure from the harbor of Piraeus to the island of Crete. But to put myself to sleep and end the day right away, was not yet going to happen. There were still hours left for me to play; and I opened the wide map of Crete once again, to stare at it, and give my mind permission to once again "wonder and wander" wherever it wants to travel; there, on the island of Crete.

—————— CHAPTER EIGHT ——————

"I am Agnostine," he said quietly that night in the dark canyon.

The huge Ferry Boat from the port of Piraeus-Athens was crowded with hundreds of passengers; a seven to eight-hour restless sail to the port of Chania, the island of Crete's famous port of "welcome" and its proud 14th Century history. The early afternoon arrival to Chania allowed me the time to explore the old city, satisfy my hunger with tasty foods of Crete, find a local Pension/Hotel nearby the Bus depot, spend the night resting and organizing for my morning bus trip to the city of Heraklion, where the Minoan Palace at Knossos is located. I was exhausted from the early morning activity of a taxi rush to Piraeus, the boarding of the Ferry, its seven-hour calamity of people, voices, chaos and the one-hour of sleep from the night before. Certainly, this was not the night for an "Ornamental look" and the much talked about Chania night-life, its discotheques, cafes, and crowded streets of fun! That I would do upon my return. Therefore, with the map of Crete spread across the bed, a glass of Retsina, cigarettes, cheese, bread and fruits, I was content sitting there planning my next destination and point of interest, which was the "Samaria Gorge;" a national park in Greece located in the extensive Chania region southwest of the island. The gorge is a deep crevasse in the earth that runs about fifteen miles long from north to south, embedded with rocky terrains, small streams and pools of clean water. "A wondrous sight of natural beauty" is what I read of the gorge in small words that were printed on the map. A day hike and a wander through this majestic canyon was my interest; and with one finger charting my trek on the map and reading about the gorge's natural attractions of its wildlife, high-cliffs and waterfalls, I kept busy half the night, until I fell asleep trying not to feel anxious with the thought of the Samaria Gorge and the beauty that I would encounter there. The morning came quickly for me to reserve the room at the Pension for the coming night, knowing that I would be only one day in Heraklion, returning to Chania in the early evening to explore Chania's nightlife, and leave the following morning by bus to Omalos, the village from where I would begin my trek into the gorge.

I spent the entire day in the city of Heraklion with a few hours of a guided tour that led us tourists through the history and ruins of the Minoan civilization at The Palace of Knossos. As interesting and informative as it was, every now and then my thoughts would return to the night before, of sitting on the bed and reading words of the Samaria gorge and its alluring natural beauty. The thought was like a magnet that constantly pulled me away from being totally engrossed in the centuries old Minoan Civilization and its remarkable existence. Constant thoughts of the gorge kept interfering with my pleasure of learning more of the Minoans; I wanted to be at the gorge! These anxious thoughts kept beckoning me and I was yearning to be there, because "something" was there for me to see! The guided tour at the Palace ended with a city tour of Heraklion, and by mid-afternoon I was on another bus ride heading-back to Chania for an early evening dinner and a taste of the nightlife that was waiting for me there. I hadn't had any nightlife activity since I left Amsterdam; and I missed the nightly ritual of dancing wild at discotheques and being with friends until the early morning. To be dancing was my therapy, my emotional balance and my way to cope with the everyday; and whether it be in a dance studio or at a discotheque, it didn't matter, as long as I was dancing!

Once I arrived at the Pension/Hotel, it didn't take me long to shower, dress and put myself into the streets of Chania to feel the excitement that comes with "a night out" in any city or town that welcomes tourists and provides entertainment for them. After my first stop at a taverna where I stuffed myself with a delicious Greek dinner, my walk through the crowded streets ended at a small discotheque blaring the musical reggae sounds of Bob Marley and the Wailers; I needed to walk no further! I instantly knew that it is here where I would be dancing for the rest of the night. The young doorman noticing my interest and my body already in a subtle dance motion welcomed me inside saying, "Come in my friend, I can see this is where you belong!" My quick reply to him was, "Yea, I think so too!" as I made a dance move entering the narrow front door. Noisy with voices of loud laughter talk and an overcrowded dance floor, along with lengthy strings of colorful disco-lights blinking and flashing, I managed to amble my way to the bar and wedged myself into a space to order from the bartender my favorite drink, a Campari and tonic water; a bitter-sweet taste of Italy. Lifting the glass to my lips; the first taste was not a sip, but more of a mouthful, that would satisfy my thirst and quicken my readiness to get onto the dance floor and share my reggae-moves with the others! Those dancing were already in high-gear, sweating and prancing their dance steps to the pulsating rhythm and beats that provoked me to add another mouthful of Campari to my readiness! Standing at the bar, shoulder to shoulder next to others also gyrating subtle moves, and couples making the attempt to hold a private conversation was not my place to be; and with my glass now half empty I slowly squeezed my way through the crowd onto the dance floor and found a personal space to begin my dance. The moves were subtle and restrained at first, preparing my mind and body to get into the feel of the music and the vibe of reggae, when suddenly the DJ played a favorite for all lovers of reggae music; "Now That We Found Love" by a band group called *Third World*! An intoxicating and pulsating rhythm and beat that stimulates and provokes a dancer to move and rock their body incessantly into a healthy good sweat! Without restraint and within my personal dance space, I could feel my body "grooving" in its natural element of dance and freedom and whirling and twirling in an ecstasy of my own; when suddenly I felt the half empty glass of Campari being taken from my hand and realized that the crowd had opened a small space on the dance floor for me to "let myself go" to submit to "the moment" and humbly display every natural move that my body willed of itself to be in shape, form and design, and in rhythmic partnership with the soulful sounds of "Jah-Music" and its rooted nourishment. As my dance moves accelerated, likewise did the surrounding voices of those witnessing this trilogy of marriage between music, body and soul. My mind was dismissed and absent from this spontaneous explosion of movement, and I could hear "Bravo! Bravo!" in the distance mixed with whistles and cheers. A moment came, when I could feel the scarf draped around my neck sliding across my shoulders and being slowly pulled-off, and a soft hand with a gentle touch brushed across my sweaty face like a feather. Her name was "Nadia" and her skin was a dark, chocolate color, her eyes as black as coal, and her silky long hair as black as her snake-like slithery eyes. Nadia was from the country of Mozambique she told me later. Her beauty emanated from within, overpowering her physical appearance and delicate, long, thin body. With her fingers clutched to each end of the scarf, she swirled it and spun it 'round and 'round in eye-catching circles, and began swaying her hips and body very much like a snake; slowly gliding and zig-zagging its way through short blades of grass. Her dance was exotic and her moves towards me were as soft and smooth as her skin. Nadia's body understood music, rhythm, and how to play with it. Her long thin body knew its way to challenge every beat that it had to measure in time and within the space it had to move itself in, step by step and beat by beat to its target; me. Her eyes of black coal never left mine; A connection of instant solidarity swept us away and into a dance that we both felt and understood to be ours. Nadia circled me, winding the scarf around my waist and hers, pulling our bodies close, touching and teasing with expected sensuality. She too, became mindless, spontaneous, and free! The lively crowd cheered even more, with their feasting-eyes pleased with our mutual dance of seduction on the dance floor and began to engage themselves and clap their hands to the reggae beats, with shouts and whistles of encouragement. Within the rhythm of closeness and touch and our eyes locked on one another, we both shared a satisfied smile that ended our sacred union, and slowly we began to unwind ourselves from the binding scarf, setting us free to dance away from one another and into our own separate spaces. The vocals of "Third World" and their vibrant music began to diminish and fade as Nadia and I moved towards each other for a climatic embrace. It lasted long, as did the cheers from a satisfied crowd of reggae dancers and young lovers. "Come!" she said; "I owe you a drink! I took yours away from you! How else could we have danced!" "Ahh, it was you!" I said, and took her hand to lead us to the bar; "And, I owe you a drink also, for doing that; because I prefer dancing with you, rather than with a glass; even though, I did love and miss the Campari!" She laughed hard at that. Our move off the dance floor and through the crowd was easy; the shouting, happy people parted themselves, making a path for Nadia and I to saunter through easily on our way to the bar, where I saw that a Campari & tonic, and a Rum & coke were already waiting for us. With a nod of courtesy from the bartender, we took our drinks and carried them with us to the table where she was sitting prior to our dance. She held my hand, and I followed.

Nadia had come to the discotheque with her older brother, a younger sister, and two other friends, all from the country of Mozambique, together on a week's vacation in Greece. We talked, laughed, drank and enjoyed each other's company comfortably, as if we all had all been long-time friends seeing each other again after a long time. Food, snacks, drinks, and conversation all helped in our social joy and became an important part of the chemistry that kept us going through the long fun-filled night; never was there a let-up of laughter! The late hours after midnight were upon us when suddenly the DJ's turntable was spinning and blasting out one of my Bob Marley favorites; "Could You Be Love"! "Oh, come! Let's all dance together!" I said, grabbing hold of Nadia's sister's hand and heading for the dance floor, as the others happily followed. We danced hard together! We were wet, sweating and playing with the beats that often collided our bodies into one another, until there was no more of "Could You Be Love"!

Nadia's brother, my age and the group's chaperone, alerted them that it was late and time to leave. He turned towards me and opened his arms wide for a warm embrace. "We go to Mykonos in the morning," he said. "A very good night to remember, my friend, thank you!". I agreed; "Yes, it was! One we won't forget!" I said. Before releasing his arms from our embrace, he leaned his head close to my ear to whisper; "And I am happy that I am taking my sister away from you!" he said. "This is not her usual self!" He winked one eye and smiled. In my surprise at his words; "Yes, thank you for that!" I said, but I could feel my face pasted with an honest smile of embarrassment as we slowly released ourselves from our hug of mutual understanding. I turned to Nadia's baby-faced sister saying, "And you, young lady; thank you for the great dancing and our silly fun on the dance floor!" and added jokingly; "But you really should be in bed!" She looked at me carefully with her clean, bright eyes and cracked a cute innocent-like smile on her face, saying, "I know you think I'm a child; but I am twenty-four years old!" Nadia noticed my shocked facial expression and quickly interrupted its sting. "Yes! "Sao's" birthday was last week!.. This holiday trip to Greece is a family gift to her!" she said, trying to ease my embarrassment. "Oh! So, "Happy Birthday." Sao!" I said; "Forgive me!" Her smile opened wide and quickly became genuine. "Oh, it's o.k.!" she said; "Everyone thinks that I am fifteen. I used to be!" she added, as we all laughed and rose from our seats to prepare to leave. Walking the narrow aisle leading us to the exit door, Nadia and I were sharing big arm waves of goodbye to the courteous bartender and DJ, and leaving satisfied that we had a good time, hearing his music still thumping beats behind us.

We all left the discotheque together, but Nadia and I slowly walked behind the four others on our way to their nearby hotel, as I felt obliged in escorting them there; and as well, aware of our extraordinary night together, I felt that I needed to make personal closure with her before we parted from one another. "I hope that soon, before you leave Greece, we get the chance to dance together again, Nadia," I said. "I will be looking forward to that, and also, to talk and learn more of you, and maybe unravel your mystery!" She flashed her eyes at me and we both smiled at my comment. "Well, you know," I said to her with sincerity; "I know that there is so much more of you that I need to discover and keep with me, for lasting good memories of you!" I said, and adding; "our one beautiful dance together is only an introduction to "who we are" and "what's to become of us!" And, for sure, "another dance together would be our first step to finding that out!" I said bluntly. And with a quick thought, I then asked; "When you leave from the island of Mykonos, do you come back here to Chania, or to Athens before you all return to Mozambique? Nadia was quiet during the next few steps as we walked in silence and then she stopped with a touch on my arm. "No, Ilanga, we won't see each other again, this I know," she said, and paused without looking at me, casting her eyes out to the sea. Her words were articulate, and the sound of her voice softened, but continued on with a definite tone urging me to listen carefully. "We don't need to dance together again… we have met! We have satisfied each other greatly!" she said with poetry on her lips. "Must we be greedy and have it all? Why more when one is already satisfied? This is how I think; and I know and understand that our thinking on this is different," Nadia said with a sharp edge of honesty in her voice and flashing her piercing eyes of black coal. I was stunned by her words of wisdom and profound courage; and also, her clear statement of fact! Our parting embrace was tight, lasting, of friendship, and of a mutual understanding, that to "disconnect" from one another here and now would be a solution to the many future problems foreseen, for two independent young professionals of different cultures, geographically misplaced, and with separate dreams to dream and build upon. Her logic and young wisdom prevailed. The long scarf that we had danced with, I unwound from my neck and laid it lovingly across her shoulders, saying, "For you - to remember this night!" Her eyes stayed on me as she wrapped its length twice around her neck, saying, "Thank you! Yes, it will be remembered, always, I know," she said quietly, as if to herself only. She grabbed hold of my hand as our short walk continued without another word spoken. There was nothing more to be said between us, nor was there an address or telephone number exchanged; and we both let our thoughts drift away into the night air. In the foyer of their hotel where the others were waiting, we held a big group hug as Nadia's brother softly whispered a prayer of safe journeys and good health in their language of Portuguese. Our warm goodbyes were many, along with hand waves and big smiles as I made my way out of the wide glass door and onto the main street for my solo walk back to the Pension/Hotel. Now, there were only a few hours left of the dark night; and not too many of my belongings needed to be packed before leaving in the morning for the bus depot in Chania to catch a 6:00 a.m. bus leaving for the village of Omalos, and to the gorge of Samaria. After I had finished packing my brown duffle bag, with still a couple of hours left before leaving for the depot, I wanted to sit back and relax until then; but I knew well that to do this was not the best thing to do; that would only welcome sleep and a missed bus!" I decided that it would be best to leave immediately for the bus depot, find a nice, secluded corner and a lonely bench somewhere to relax and to think about the fading night, Nadia, and why all of that unforeseen experience of nature's unpredictable way of doing things unfolded the way it did. The depot was already crowded with travelers when I arrived there; there was no secluded corner or an unoccupied bench to rescue me from tiredness. The floor, and my head against the duffle bag sufficed until I boarded the bus, hurried to an available seat, "thanked God" and fell asleep.

The spectacular Samaria Gorge welcomed me with its magnificence and raw natural beauty as I arrived to its entrance to begin my fifteen-mile trek through its wonder. In the village of Omalos, I had purchased a liter jug of water, some fruits and raw vegetables for eating, and a small folding pocket knife for peeling and protection from any encountered danger. Even though it was early morning at the start of my hike and I had not even walked a mile, the sun was hot enough to have me dripping in sweat! Finding a large bush to camouflage, I changed quickly into shorts, a head scarf and left my torso bare, before my descent into the earth's deep crevasse. Traveling downward, the rocky cliffs on both sides of the canyon began to tower high above my head, preventing sunlight from reaching down here below, where the temperature was so much cooler than up there; and because of the extreme temperature change, I again had to change clothes back to jeans and a cotton t-shirt to cover my bare torso. The first couple of hours of my walk through the rocky terrain were rough and unstable; and often, I would have to cross and jump over small streams of running water, tripping and falling in with a big splash! I encountered fresh waters, scaling down from the mountains and traveling fast between small boulders of rock, creating long streams of miniature waterfalls that splashed downward into small basins of crystal-clear water into the small reservoirs and pools that were scattered here and there. I needed to stop and rest myself from the ordeal of my hike thus far; to eat, drink water and relax for a while before I continued onward.

The remaining hours didn't go according to plan; I had laid my head down, fallen asleep, and awakened long past the noon hours of the day. And I, not likened to wearing a wrist watch, assumed the time to be well after 4 p.m. The temperature was cooler and the canyon shadows began to cast themselves against the high walls of the cliffs stretching upwards on each side of me. To be here where I was, and still at least six hours away from my destination to the gorge's end, was not the original plan; and to be hiking in darkness was also not the plan! Deciding not to panic and to rid myself of anticipating anxiety, I decided to remain there with calm and do some meditation amid the crawling shadows. The darkness became black very soon, making the night long and seemingly endless. The only stars I could see twinkling in the sky were what little was visible within the narrow corridor of space between the canyon walls. I knew that the vast sky and its enormous span of twinkling stars were all up there, but I couldn't see them in full display and twinkling in their bright glory, widely spread across the sky"! This rare sight of stars parading between two walls of a narrow canyon became of interest to me, I had never seen a long-lined strip of stars like this, ever! The only sight of stars my eyes had ever seen were always shining across a wide, vast, dark sky. Like a child fascinated with a new toy, I became involved and let my eyes play with each star, carefully watching its super-slow movement on parade as it crossed the narrow slice of canyon space that was viewable. Counting each one of them was futile, even though I tried. I heard the sweet sounds of the night birds singing to one another; and also the noisy sounds of large flapping Bat wings. Both of these voices spoke clear, infinite sounds of wisdom into my ears and echoed loudly within the acoustical chamber of the sunken gorge of Samaria. How strange it was that "danger" was not in my plan; and whenever I did hear some unwanted crackling sounds in the bushes surrounding me or heard the hoofs of unseen goats leaping from rock to rock and thumping hard on the earth's floor, I did not anticipate harm or danger. I felt safe, and was relaxed and comfortable being with them here in their home that I had invited myself into! Somehow we "understood" each other and there was nothing to fear!"

The night air was not cold, but still chilly and the rocky ground that I was lying on was damp and hard. I was warm enough in a soft woolen sweater that I had pulled out of my duffle bag and put on for a bit of comfort and protection from the chill. Dwelling on the long, narrow strip of stars twinkling high above my head and listening to the sounds of the night creatures that lived here in the canyon were my only two focal points of thought, and the power of their presence was definite and hypnotic. The movement of the stars and the rhythms heard from the many night creatures of various species together created their own natural music and visuals and very soon became the eventual source of an unusual meditation. "The world that I lived in and the life that I lived outside of this canyon suddenly no longer existed; I had succumbed to the nature and origin of my being in this sunken gorge that made me feel the likes of "Home." Communal relativity swept over me, and kinship with the night creatures, the stars, the darkness, the waters and the rocky terrain was "all that I could be and feel" in this timeless moment of Omnipresence; and I liked it. I hadn't thought of sleeping, but that too came to me out of the darkness without me even knowing; until I awakened to the sounds of the early morning birds and crawling creatures. The night stars had disappeared; and were replaced by the approaching dim light of day that slowly crept into the narrow canyon space that loomed high above my head. A quick bite to eat and to continue my hike to its end was the plan for the day; but throughout the entire morning of my slow, trodden trek through a few miles of the gorge, the "new" fascination and experience of the night before accompanied me in every step; I was "hooked," I wanted "more"! To spend another night there in the gorge and to feel "home" again was a lingering thought as I walked, sipped on water, nibbled on fruit and continued thinking "why not!" Unexpectedly, I spent four days and three nights "living" in the Samaria Gorge; "This is where I had to be", until I felt certain that it was my time to leave from this secluded paradise of a divine Nature. The daylight hours of hiking at leisure, playing with a gushing waterfall all of one morning, and by not resisting its fresh cool beckoning, delayed my hours of hiking that one day. On the remaining three days during daylight hours, I occupied my time by reading, writing and doing meditation and yoga stretches on large, flat boulders when I could find them; and once I did, that boulder and its area of calm would be my camp site for the coming night of black darkness and the parade of stars. The daylight hours were joyful hours spent with passion and discipline because they mattered most; I was able to read, write and stretch my body in the Sunlight when it did pass over the crevasse. I rationed my food; eating the fruits and raw vegetables I had picked up in Omalos along with an abundance of wild berries I plucked and gathered along the way. It was only during the hours before noon that sometimes I would notice a small group of hiking tourists on their seven-hour trek to the gorge's end, and would soon find that they had arrived at their destination; a small coastal village called

"Aghia Roumeli," a tiny, but well-established village. The natives prided themselves on genuinely welcoming tired, hungry hikers and boasting proudly of their one small-sized flatbed barge that they called the "ferry boat"! It operated twice a day to take hikers to "Hora Sfaklion," a larger port nearby along the southern coast which had accessibility to the major city of Chania. I was never seen by the hiking tourists and their guides trekking their way to the village; I intentionally remained off the tourist-beaten path to be unseen by them or the hired Rangers that worked the gorge and often paroled their areas until sunset.

The nights of darkness were fully occupied with peaceful Meditations; and with the intent to focus on *Humility* and my *Gratitude to God, The Creator,* for the stars I see on parade way-up-there in the narrow corridor of tiny twinkling lights! I am grateful for my birth and for the extraordinary life that has been given to me to live every day; and for the gift of being where I am presently, tonight, and/or wherever I may be in any other "moment" of Time! And also, for my family and friends "who cradle me with love" constantly; for them, I have so much to be grateful for! Each night, there in a pit of darkness and wildlife and knowing not to light a candle or use a flashlight that can attract danger, I am fearless and feeling safe from a possible danger, and also without the thought of having to wield a pocket-knife; but rather "feeling" only the environmental protection of darkness, the night creatures, and a "nature of love" circling and surrounding me that I had never felt before!

Listening on my Walkman device to the new cassette tape of music that Yiorgos had purchased for me at the flea market, that of Greek composer "Stavros Xarchacos" it seemed to be the only music that I wanted to hear since entering the gorge! And whenever

I listened, be it hiking or lying on the hard rocks at night, I was mesmerized by this music. I would imagine visual images of an old Greek village and its habitants, and sometimes images of a "contemporary" Athens, the streets of New York, Amsterdam, Los Angeles, and other cities of the world that would "flash" quickly within the sights of my vast imagination! These images became the focus of my traveling thoughts inspired by this music that transcended me on a global journey, and constantly stirred within me deep emotion, and often, a sense of future "expectations"! It was not until five years later on a performance stage, that those images were finally "realized." It was on the third night of my four days in the gorge that I discovered my "purpose" for being there, doing what I was doing and "being" who I was being, which was simply being "Me"! Each night at a certain time, the light of the Moon would shine into the canyon for a brief time as it made its crossing over the narrow corridor of space high above my head. On this particular night and at this time of the Moon's crossing, a strange and unusual thing occurred. After about an hour or more of my stillness, I interrupted my posture of meditation to change my body position; a small pebble of stone resting beneath me was disturbing and had to be removed. Suddenly I caught sight of some movement in the distance, about 600 feet away; a white reflection in the moonlight that was slowly moving along on the unbeaten path towards me. I was startled by this and dared not make another move; only fixing my eyes on its dim glow and following its every move! It was slow and it was low to the ground as if it were gliding and skimming over the path! It moved into a shadow of darkness for a few seconds, and when it moved into the Moonlight again and as it got closer, I could see that it was a human figure; An elderly man using a walking stick and draped in white garb, as a village Shepherd would be! His walk was slow, tired and unthreatening, and his full head of curly hair was white, unruly and wild. I could see clearly now that he was coming toward me, and I could feel that he was harmless; and therefore, I quickly decided to pretend that I was asleep. I felt his presence close to me and I could hear his voice slightly sigh with relief from his walk as he sat down on a large rock near me. I had never heard silence so thick as I did at this moment! Even the noisy crickets, the night birds singing and the hard flapping sound of a hundred bat wings were silenced. The thick silence lingered and in my pretense to be asleep and unalarmed, I waited for "something"; but for what, I didn't know. I heard nothing move so I decided to stir myself and slowly open my eyes as if I were just awakening. I was surprised to find that he was sitting just about 5 feet away from me, with his head bent low as if he was in deep thought.

"Yassus, Kirie!" ("Hello, sir!"), I said to him respectfully; the two words in Greek that I had learned to say when greeting a gentleman. He raised his head, looked at me and paused a moment; "Yassou Peidthimou!" ("Hello, my child"), he quietly replied in Greek, and in a tone of voice as if he were my grandfather; "Sto Vlepo Mazimou, Pali. Ine Orea" (It is good that I see you and I together again"), he said, and held a long pause. The light of the moon was not bright enough for me to see his eyes, but I could sense a warm, soothing vibe of energy darting from them directly to me, penetrating, and meeting my eyes. "I did not want to disturb your pretense of sleep!" he said in perfect English; "I have patience." I sat up quickly from my reclined position, baffled at what he said, and that it was said in eloquent perfect English! He calmly noticed my surprise and continued; "My child, you can't remember me, I know. But in time you will; and also you will recall that you have heard my name. "I am Agnostine!" he said.

My first thought was, "Am I hallucinating?" and although I wasn't sleeping, I said to myself; "Wake up, man!" I was rattled and bewildered and quite conscious of how "awake and alive" I was! "You are awake," he said confirming that I was; and with a deliberate change of voice, saying; "And be conscious and "Know" that you are awake and fine! This is not a time of doubt," the old man said. "My child," he went on to say, but abruptly stopped, chuckled, and then added; "You are a grown man now; but I call you 'my child' because you are, Peidthimou. There has never been a time that you weren't!" I could feel that his piercing eyes never left mine during another brief pause before he continued on with his confusing words of, (I think) *Time and Prophecy*! "Ahhh!" he added, "This new understanding and your recall of me and other things will also come to you in time." His magnetic voice and its power reverberated throughout my entire body, calming anxiety and ridding my thoughts of hallucinations, sleeping and doubt. Never in my entire life had I ever been more conscious of a present moment and of this unusual stark and new "reality"!

"Akous!" (Listen!) he said, leaning towards me. "You must also remember in the coming time, that you came here to visit me; I did not come to visit you! This is your quest and desire, not mine," he said, and ending with a tone of care; "My desire has always been to assist you in your quests, Peidthimou, and you have finally traveled to me. But the time will come soon when you recall this day, and in your silence, you will understand the words I am speaking, and what makes me walk the path here to you tonight!", he said. Listening carefully to his words, I sat in silence; and although I too had words and thoughts to speak of, I was at a loss and did not know how to begin. In my confusion, I sputtered and stammered looking for the right words; but he "professorially" interrupted; "You are not here to speak, my child. You are here only to listen and take away with you what you hear! This is the "purpose" of your visit! The words that you want to speak are for you alone to hear; to find their value and to eventually disseminate to those in need of your words in the future. Cycles of events will occur, allowing all of what I am saying to unfold onto you as clearly as they happen in their own time; and it is up to **YOU** to capture the "cyclical threads" of endless beginnings that will occur," he said. Agnostine rested from his words, clearly tired. And I, though still listening carefully, understood nothing of what he had said, nor of what I was experiencing! Watching him resting in his long pause and he watching me in mine lasted until he decided to continue. "Akous!" ("listen!"), he said and leaning his body forward; "From this day to the next day and the days thereafter, begin to understand that it is usual to confuse between the two: the **EGO** and the **YOU**. Therefore; you must remember that that these two parts of you are two separate entities, and both are controlling factors with two separate goals; The goal and purpose of **EGO** is "to please you" with its desires and wants; and the goal of **YOU** is "not to please the **EGO**" but rather to confront it with your dire "needs" and is the entity that is the balancer and reflector of the person you are! The two are to be kept separate from the "physical" **YOU**, the you who absorbs the daily life - the you who does the thinking the dreaming the doing and the being - of whomever or whatever you think you are!" The battering of his words exhausted me; each word that he said came with a thought behind it! They began to all muddle together meaninglessly; although, within this whirl of confusion and fatigue,

I still knew that "each word meant everything in the world to me"! I also realized during this pause that I understood every everything Agnostine had said; but I "comprehended" nothing, nothing at all. I became weary of words and thought, and he noticed; He relaxed from being the insistent Professor in a class with one "tired" student, and tempered his tone and delivery mildly with more tact, but with the same intent. He continued; "You are tired of me, I know, but before I let you rest, I will end now with the important words that you must not forget, "Peidthimou," he said; "It is not your **EGO,** It is **YOU** who governs *You, the Ego,* and *the Mind*; And consequently, **YOU** are the *Controller,* the guiding *Spirit Essence* and *Nature* of your Being! And my child, once you have grasped the "cyclical concept" and the proceedings of this personally captured treasure, then you are to apply and follow-through with its *Purpose* if you desire. The understanding of your *Purpose* of being here in Samaria and in your travels to "elsewhere" will come to you in time, and will be recognized only by you, if **YOU** are listening today!" He said this sternly, and pulled back his bent old body to sit up straight. "And before I leave you," he continued, "You need to hear from me that I am grateful to you for your visit here to me; and that my words will enhance your comprehension of gratitude much more than the understanding that you now have of gratefulness. You must know that I am as grateful as you are, my child; and it is because of your consistent display of the profound gratitude, happiness, and love that you unselfishly share with others and all living things since you have been here in *The Life*; for this, I too, am profoundly grateful!" Placing his walking stick in front of himself to brace and support his old body to stand erect, I could again feel his eyes - still unseen - but emanating an energy with the power of his dutiful accomplishment and satisfaction.

333

"Yassou, Peidthimou!" ("Goodbye, my child!") he said, arranging his draped white garment from its rumple and then lifting his head to look high up between the canyon walls at the parade of stars. "Neh!" ("Yes!") he said and gave a quick nod of his head before taking his first steps to leave. "Kei, Kalo taxidi!" ("And, have a good journey!") were his last words as he slowly walked away from me, leaving me without questions or thoughts of who he was, from where he came or to where he was going. The "acceptance" of his presence and the words he had spoken ruled the moment with a sense of complete satisfaction and joy, and I needing nothing more. Watching him make his way down the path and admiring his lasted strength and courageous effort to make this visit, an immediate thought of "accomplishment" swept over me that I "somehow" understood, felt good and felt grateful, but with the enhancement of a "new gratitude" discreetly laced with the "comprehension" that he had spoken so deeply about. He heard me raise my voice to him, "Efaristos!" ("Thank you!"). He didn't look back; but only raised his walking stick high above his head and kept walking away. My eyes followed his white illumined-glow until it began to move swiftly down the unbeaten path and t became a glowing blur! The he just vanished and he was gone!" I lie down against the rocks that suddenly didn't feel as hard as they had the nights before; and comfortably rested my head on the cushioned, brown duffle bag. I smiled and somehow I knew that the feeling would last forever and my eyes slowly closed to the darkness and the parade of twinkling stars. But unfortunately, I missed another miracle. It happened even before I could witness the Moon's light fade.. into the morning and a new day!

I had to encounter the abandoned village of Samaria during my hike to the end of the gorge; haunted with negative activity, and yet, abandoned since 1941 during the German occupation and the horrific Battle of Crete. This site visit was very brief for me; a human massacre had taken place here and the vibe of evil death still lingered. Quickly, I stepped up my pace for the following fifteen-minute walk to "Agia Roumeli" where a ferry was waiting. This village is the last tourist site to be seen for gorge hikers on a day trip who have been trekking hard on rocks and boulders high and low for six or seven hours. Every hiker emerged with aching sore muscles, some disgruntled, some limping from an injury, and certainly all anticipating a delicious full meal! But the fifteen minutes of their walk to the ferry, I could see was an easy, joyful and "insightful" walk! Their happy faces were brightly lit with a radiance of high achievement, and their bouncing bodies were suddenly re-energized for their brisk walk to the ferry! This final accomplishment dismissed their woes and pain with laughter and jokes of who was aching the most and who was going to pass out first from exhaustion.

A vigorous day's hike in the sunken gorge of Samaria is made for one to "wander and wonder" and to make personal contact with themselves as they journey their way through the bowels of the earth and surprisingly discover at the journey's end, that it is "here" in the gorge; and arriving at Aghia Roumeli that one finds two significant realizations: "This is a place where God comes for vacation! And at the hike's end, it is "here" in the village that one experiences high achievement and the "purpose of the day!" Here, the hiker patiently waits for a Ferry to depart and is conscious of this moment in time; sitting comfortably with thoughts of the bittersweet hours of challenge and conquest that had just passed;

and begins a mental process of self-evaluation. Often, not even knowing why it happens, the process begins with four simple facts: The first being *Action,* which is the *Doing* of something and has the most importance. And the three essential facts that follow are: *Determination,* which is the *Will* and the constructing of habits of "doing." Next is *Accomplishment,* for one to aspire and to "feel" the most rewarding fact, which is that of *Achievement.* This internal exaltation of *Personal Achievement* is often physically displayed! Even though the hiker is tired and worn, the rewarding thought is to "celebrate one's self" with another "win" and enables the will to conjure up the explosive energy to jump-up and do so!

Laid back with these relishing thoughts, the *action* taken to *self-evaluate,* and the epiphany of an understanding of the "comprehension" of high-achievement, is an **EGO** pleaser and teaser. A hiker often forgets to be grateful. How important it is my dear reader, for **YOU** to intercede with the "Balance" needed at this time, for you to realize your dreams with the spirit of truth; and with a simple thought of *Gratitude.* Laid back, resting and waiting for the Ferry, one finds the *"Purpose"* of the day here! Each hiker personally carries away with them, "Somewhere" in their Soul, the fact that the natural gorge of Samaria has no mystery, no pretense, and no shields of imagery; it is a clear "in your face" *Physical Mental and Spiritual* "Happening"! A pre-existing yet "new reality" that simply unfolds itself here at the end of the gorge, at this special moment in time! But it is a new reality that also is lasting, and is to be added to the one that "you think is the only reality" that exists! The fact, my dear reader is; that it is not! What one introspectively experiences in the Samaria Gorge is the Reality of *Nature and her infinite purpose,* and is there for the *Dare*, to *Know, Challenge and Achieve.* And, I will say with strong belief, that it is not a "Coincidence" that a hiker is "Here"! I am certain of this; but they somehow will find that out for themselves later in *The Life* I'm sure.

CHAPTER NINE

**The eyes of a child see clearly who
you are and want to play. Challenge
that child and play honestly.**

After leaving Crete, the following twelve days were spent catching
Ferry boats and traveling and exploring three of Greece's many
islands; Aegina, Hydra, and Mykonos; each one having their own
character, attractions and special features of enticement for tourists
on an island-hopping venture. I had decided that those days on
the islands would be better spent in the simple, natural areas of
Greece, rather than in Athens, a city of congested traffic, humans,
and a severe problem of polluted air. The decision to be a tourist in
Athens would be on my next visit to Greece; this one had been for
The Acropolis and the Samaria Gorge. It was an early afternoon
when I arrived back in Athens for only one day before departing for
Amsterdam on the following day. My plan was to set my eyes on
The Acropolis once more, have my last Greek meal at the Taverna
in Plaka - purposely to say goodbye to Yiorgos and his father - and
to rest well and have a good night's sleep. My return trip back
to Amsterdam was already pre-scheduled and confirmed for my
departure in the morning on the Magic Bus.

When Yiorgos saw me walking up Dexipos Street approaching
the Taverna, he immediately stopped his duties of serving at table
and threw open his welcoming arms, flashing a happy broad smile.
And high above his head in the background, gleaming in white
brilliance on top of Philoppapos Hill was The Acropolis. My eyes

instantly framed this image of Greece in my mind and ever since, it's been an indelible image that I have never forgotten, even as I became older. And as a matter of fact, even after many passing years since it occurred, its impressive significance of time, place and person had a power of seduction. Its magnetic beckoning never left met; it became a part of me and an everyday thought. Eventually, it became an image of a "reality" happening within my mind that was existing there for me to explore. But It needed more clarity and so I decided to evaluate this indelible image of time, place and Yiorgos. The focal point that brought the needed clarity were the questions that I had to ask myself: What *transpired* and what *inspired* that "unforgettable" image? How did it happen, and Why? This was an evaluation that would be meaningless to many people, I'm sure; but shouldn't this be a natural thing to do, if one wants or needs to "know" and "comprehend" anything?

This wave of thought has me recalling the significant incident of meeting for the first time, my friend Janine at the café in Boston, who commented quite sharply; "Who in the Hell wants to evaluate themselves?" This thinking, I do understand; "Who in the Hell thinks about, or even cares to evaluate themselves"! And, to evaluate an old "unforgettable" image at that! Oh, how well, I understand.

But, the one who does care and does evaluate themselves, their surroundings and significant images as I do occasionally, will find the rewarding answers to those questions and will understand the reasons why this impressive image is indelible and unforgettable to me. To have "image" experiences such as this; memorable indelible and unforgotten, is not for me alone! Each one of us have one two or three, and maybe more, of these hidden tale-telling images that have happened in our lives and are possibly waiting to surface, be noticed again and recognized "clearly" for their worth and value; buried treasures that they have become. But now that time has passed, maybe these "forgotten" images need to be more consciously seen with a new perspective and re-evaluated! If the image was clear to you "then" in its moment, and is "unforgettable," then an evaluation will bring this image to its apex of clarity! The point here being, my dear reader, is: There is *a Meaning, a Reason, and a Purpose* for that image to still be with you; and maybe **YOU** should know "why"!

Yiorgos and I finally stepped into a clutch and strongly embraced as if we already had been friends for a half a century! He stepped back and looked at me with astonishment and surprise! "You are now black from the Sun, my God!" He continued with "Poh, Poh, Poh!" (A Greek expression that carries a sound of "amazement" whether good or bad). It begins with a hand raised, along with an open palm and a slow rotating hand gesture winding at the wrist, signifying that something seen or heard is unbelievable! It could be beautiful, ugly, or even disgusting. My reply to his hand gesture was verbal, dramatic and quick; "I did not know myself, that I could get so black! I hope it stays!" I said. We both laughed so hard! "Hella!.. Katsi!" ("Come! Sit down!") Yiorgos said, as he spun a chair out from the table and also knowing that I wanted the sight of The Acropolis in front of my eyes. "Hella!" ("Come!"), he said; "Sit! I will be back with you very soon! I must perform my duties, you know." he said and hurried off to his waiting customers. My eyes set on The Acropolis; and a flurry of new thoughts of gratitude and its magnificent beauty flooded my mind. I also noticed Yiorgos' father and mother sitting next to the Taverna's door; I lifted both my arms and gave a big wave of and decided to get up and go to greet them! Also, I wanted to thank him for the small wine glasses that he trusted me with on my first night in Athens with my friends to drink bottles of Retsina, and to sit high on the rocky ledge of The Acropolis. As I approached the both of them, I could see that their eyes were stuck on my "Ornamental" appearance as they whispered words to one another; and he, without saying a word but "making the same rotating hand gesture of disbelief" that his son had made to me just a few minutes earlier at our greeting. "Yassus, Kirie kei Kiria!" ("Hello, Sir and Madam!") I greeted them formally. And again; I hesitated, thought, and then stammered with my choice of the right words of thanks to say to him in English that he would understand. "I come back to thank you for the wine glasses you let me have that one night when I was here before!" I said; "I hope that you got them from that plant sitting over there! And, I thank you very much for that!" He also stammered with words in English, which surprised me. "Yes, I get them!" he said; "I know. You bring them back! Thank you; you are a good man!" Yiorgos' mother kept her eyes fixed on my colorful garments and kept a constant smile on her pleasant and calm face. I was shaking their hands, and asking their names. He said, "Me, I am *Petros* and she is *Chrissa*, Yiorgos' mother." With a sense of relief that he understood every word I said; I replied, "It is so good to meet you both; and, I am *Ilanga!*" Before I could continue to say anything further, Yiorgos came out from the kitchen to the Taverna door where I was standing and clutched in his hands, a small plate of appetizers and a carafe of Retsina; "Oh, you are here!" he said before he again hurried off. "I will bring this to the table for you and join you later!" While he was gone, I said to his parents, "You have a fine Son there, he is a special young man; and I am very happy to meet him and you both as well! And If ever I come back to Greece one day, I know that I will see you all again!" Petros, understanding

341

every word I said, smiled, and said, "Neh, Neh!" ("Yes, yes!") "You will come back to Greece, I know! Yiorgos very much likes you; I can see that he is your friend." "Hella!" ("Come!") When you come back, we are here for you!" he said, and pointing his finger upward to Philoppapos Hill, and saying jokingly; "And the Acropolis will still be here for you, also!" We both laughed, as Chrissa, not speaking a word of English simply smiled. Her eyes met mine finally, after releasing them from roving up and down and being stuck on my Ornamental attire. I Left both and returned to the table where the carafe of Retsina and the small plate of Mezedes (Appetizers) were waiting for me, I sat nibbling and listening to the Greek music being played on the Taverna's loudspeaker, and reminiscing with the many reflective thoughts of my past two weeks in Greece and the wonderful and strange memories that I would be taking back to Amsterdam with me. Comfortably sitting there, nibbling and sipping, I watched Yiorgos in his daily hustle, naturally pleasing and charming every customer that he catered to; an amazing waiter with astonishing skill.

He eventually returned to my table holding in his hands a plate of sliced bread and an impressive garden salad of greens, tomatoes, olives, feta cheese, green peppers, onions and special Greek seasoning, all saturated in a pool of pure natural olive oil. The sound of "Ahhh!" easily came oozing from my mouth; and with my tourist guide book of Greek phrases that I had studied with diligence while I was in Crete, I said with absolute confidence; "Horiatiki Salata!" ("A village style of salad!"). Oh, Yiorgos, "Efaristos Poli!" ("Thank you, very much!") and I continued with the attempt to form a long sentence. "Boro na ehkho, lehmonee? Mono leego; Parakalo!" ("May I have some lemon? Just a little; Please!") This single phrase I spoke rapidly, as if I were an authentic Greek; being that it was a phrase I often used daily at markets and Tavernas; "May I have some of "whatever" Please!" I had mastered this phrase simply by daily habitual use. "Poh, Poh, Poh!" Yiorgos said quite surprised; "You have learned to speak Greek, my friend! "Ti Aftos?" ("What is this?") You speak very good Greek now!" I plunged my fork deep into the salad, "Oh no, not really!" I said; "I only learned a few words for the tavernas and shopping!" and immediately stuffed my mouth with a fork full of salad. "Yes, I know!" he said; "But, you speak it correct, like a Greek!" I could feel his eyes staring at me with my head down stuffing my face with salad during his pause. I don't know what got into him; but he suddenly blasted me with about "five hundred Greek words" in one very long-winded sentence! They came at me fast, like speeding bullets! Then he abruptly stopped. I did as well, with both my cheeks bulging on each side of my face and a mouth stuffed with salad! Lifting my head and my eyes to his, I could see that what he had said was in jest; and he knowing, that I hadn't a clue of what he was saying! We both stared at each other; but my stare was of disbelief and eye-opening shock that he would even "think about" throwing all of that fast Greek at me! We held our stare with a short pause, both understanding his jest moment; and suddenly we burst into loud laughter with salad spitting from my mouth and flying across the table! "Poh, Poh, Poh, Ilanga!" he said, "Poh, Poh, Poh, Poh!" I found the rhythmic Greek language easy for my tongue to play with and for my ears to hear, and I had picked up a few words quickly in just a couple of weeks. It just seemed like a "piece of cake" for me to get into! Whereas in Amsterdam; I had been a year there already, struggling, spitting and throat scratching, learning the difficult Dutch language with its guttural hard sounds and sharply pointed words.

Yiorgos decided to sit down opposite me at the table after he had brought more plates of delicious foods for me to feast on. There were no words exchanged between us for quite a few minutes because my head was bent low into the plate most of the time! The only time that it wasn't was when I would lift it for my eyes to look over the table and see what taste was next to savor as my fork went from dish to dish, fixated with all that was in front of me. From time to time and in between my mouthfuls of food, I could see that his eyes never left me, they were intense and filled with thought and often, invasive. There were moments when I could feel their relentless probe upon me as if I were a human specimen of his deepest interest. "Tell me of Crete and your experience there," he stated calmly when he saw that I was finished with my last mouthful of food and about to stop eating for a while and take a breather. "Are you satisfied with your travel here to Athens and your experience in Crete?" he asked, and touting with pride, "There is so much more to Greece than that of course! And you will see more of it and "all of it" when you come again, I know! But, tell me how you feel about Greece today, now that you have come here for the first time!" he asked calmly without his eyes ever leaving me. But before I could reply, the strange sound of his voice was my concern. It was that of an adult, not one of a youthful 3ʳᵈCycle teenager's voice delighted in hearing a good travel story about to be told!" The pitch, the intent, and the volume had the sounds and fiber of an adult in conversation with me, and I was shocked and careful with my reply. "Yes," I said with hesitance; "I am happy that I came here; seeing the Acropolis, being in Crete meeting you and your parents; Yes, I am satisfied!" were my chosen words.

But they didn't satisfy the wants of Yiorgos; he was listening for more. He wanted to hear "something else" in my words, he wanted to hear detail. "Yes, I know that!" he said with intensity; "But, tell me of your new experience here, Ilanga! How you feel, and what your thinking is; you know, about, "Why?" you have come to Greece. And I think what is most important that I want to know, is: What will you do when you come again?" His hazel green eyes were deeply penetrating, almost making me feel uncomfortable with his stare. I did not answer. I picked up my small glass of Krasi for a mild, slow sip, when from the door of the Taverna, his mother's voice called out to him; "Yiorgos, Hella Etho!" ("Come here!") she yelled, and added words in Greek that I couldn't understand. "Oh, Signomi!" ("Excuse me!") he said;

"I must go there to the kitchen to help my mother! But I will come back to hear your new story!" he emphasized, and quickly got up from his chair to dart-off and make his usual brisk run past the tables and into the Taverna. I sat questioning and arguing with myself and thinking, he wants to hear of "my" experiences! How I feel, and what I am thinking?" No way, was this happening. He is just a child, was my instant thought; and he's going around here speaking and behaving like a thirty-year old man stuffed in the body of a young teenaged boy!" This thought of discussion I immediately dismissed; there was no way that he could comprehend my island "fairy tale" experiences, feelings and thinking simply because they were of adult understanding, and also, personal! And although his young Mind is of intelligence and has the desire to learn and know things; I felt that he still wasn't mature enough to hear and handle the delights of a "sensual dance" at a discotheque, nor of an inexplicable "spiritual encounter"! He just wasn't "there" yet! But I relished and admired his yearning to know and his "Dare" to ask. With my eyes on The Acropolis and my mentoring heart begging to The Gods for help in my dilemma of telling a young intelligent Mind the truth without revealing its total veracity and impact on me, I concluded with the thought and fact that he just wasn't ready yet to hear it all!

Yiorgos returned shortly with a small plate of sliced, ripened watermelon that he placed in front of me on the table and sat in the chair opposite me. "Here!" he said; "You must eat "Kapuzzi", Ilanga, because its natural fibre will help you to easily digest the food you ate!" He said this with a voice of "reason" and of "knowing" that, again brought my attention to his unique level of adult maturity. To rid myself of deeper thoughts on this, I said jokingly to him, (and adding a bit of theatrical drama with hands eyes and face!), "Yiorgos, my brother, you're a creep! Are you sure that you're Greek? How can you be doing this, man? The Gods don't like that you are sitting with your back to them you know! They prefer and demand "eye-to-eye" contact, you fool!" I quickly leaned in to him, right in his face; and with my eyes in a squint glaring and filled with scorn, I harshly whispered; "Stop it, Yiorgos, smarten up, man! Face the Gods!" If you're Greek, you should know better than that! You are so damn rude!" His eyes opened wide with astonishment, fear and delight happening all at one time in a fixed stare. His eyes were like two big round pools of hazel-green confusion! He paused a second or two, thinking of what I had said, its content, and how I said it, and then suddenly, a burst of husky laughter filled with the understanding of my jest and my delivery exploded from the mouth of this wise young man! We then, both howled with laughter of course; attracting attention from the few customers sitting at their tables as well as the folks walking by! It took a few minutes for us both to calm and settle ourselves; But every now and then and in between our long pause of unspoken words, I could hear Yiorgos murmuring quietly to himself, "Poh, Poh, Poh, Poh!" and each time I heard his murmur, my body just buckled over in laughter! He sat back in his chair with both his hands resting on his stomach, saying to himself, "To Stomakimou!" ("Oh, my stomach!") and "Ehkho Pono, ehdho!" ("I have pain, here!") as his hands slowly rubbed his stomach.

After our bridge of laughter, Yiorgos rested from that thought and said to me conclusively, "You play good comedy, Ilanga!" Then leaning forward towards me, his eyes and his face became serious once more and he said; "I like that you called me "your Brother;" I have only sisters, and, you say it like you mean it! How is that?" he asked with an appetite to hear more; "Why do you call me your brother, Ilanga? Tell me; Do you feel, that I am?" he asked with fervor and the desire to know. All of his words came at me at once like an unexpected curve-ball and I became convinced that here was an in-depth serious young man who latches on to every word he hears; and if there is one or two or three that he cannot digest comfortably, he demands an explanation! He was patiently waiting for this one.

"Well, first of all it's an expression that we black Americans use these days for the purpose of solidarity; and most importantly, the spiritual relationship that we have with one another," I said to him, trying not to include the racial and political connotations of "Black Power", "Black is Beautiful, and other slogans of racial proclamation, their derivation and powerful message of unity and their colloquial usage and development in the 1960's and 1970's. He wasn't totally aware of the past and current social movements of "Black Power" and the Civil Rights activity happening in America; nor of how and why the young black generation had established a brotherhood and made reference to one another by adopting this verbal expression; and how the term "My Brother" came to be.

I felt that to explain all of that history to him would be a lengthy and unnecessary conversation for us to engage in at this time, and therefore I approached his curve-ball with an angle that I knew would be conducive to an understanding. Looking into his eyes and leaning a bit forward, I said to him in an honest tone and with sincerity; "Yiorgos, I call you "My Brother" because you behave like a brother to me so naturally, and yet, you don't have one! I have five brothers! I know very well how brothers behave; and also, what their actions are and how they should be between one another." The lids of his eyes lowered and slightly squinted with a new thought; one that I could tell had never entered his mind before, until now. He was captured by my words; As I watched him digest each one, I also said to him: "You and I have met only once before now, and both times, you have behaved like a brother to me! You do so naturally whatever you can do for me; and we speak with honest words to one another! I cannot deny that I feel a closeness and a "bond" with you, somehow! All of my five brothers in Boston are older than I; but here in Greece, you are my younger one!" I paused, adding a bit of humor; "And also my brother, your father and mother like me! They wouldn't mind that I be your older brother, I think!" He laughed at that; "Neh, Alithia!" ("Yes, it's true!") Yes, they do like you!" he said and held a long thoughtful smile. And from his facial expression, I could see that the curve-ball Yiorgos threw at me was being curtailed by an understanding of his new thought, and I continued to say; "I think that what you have to remember always is, that this is my first time here in Greece! And like brothers would do, younger or older, you have been speaking to me of its beauty and its dangers, and teaching me things to keep me safe and "aware" of all things here, good and bad! So; it's natural and easy for me to call you "My Brother" because **YOU** make it easy!" I said convincingly, folding my arms in front of me on the table. His eyes were filled with deep thoughts as he gazed at me for a second or two, and then he slowly lowered his lids to focus on the attractive bracelet of colorful, dangling beads twisted around my wrist. As he thoughtfully played with the beads, I noticed how long and thick his sandy-colored eye lashes were! Without raising his eyes to look at me, he quietly spoke to himself and to me indirectly, without doubt, saying; "Neh, Neh; Katalaveno!" ("Yes, yes; I Understand!") The sound and tone of his voice was of satisfaction and that of an "adult" young man and his wisdom, "Comprehending" and affirming, that in fact, "He now had an older brother"! He smiled, as he pulled himself back in his chair to sit more comfortably. Yiorgos, felt his "Wisdom"! His relaxed body language, his eyes, and newly enlightened face, revealed this message to me. "So, my brother!" he said: "Tell me your story of Crete and of the gorge Samaria; did you like it? And Chania! Where else did you go? You said, that maybe you would go to other islands! Did you go?" he asked abruptly and leaned back in his chair on its rear two legs, folding his arms across his chest like a grown man, ready to listen! Quickly, I sat up in my chair to express my joy of Crete! "Oh man, Yiorgos, what a beautiful island! It felt "old" to me; You know historic, like it's been there forever! But from what I saw, I think that it has many stories to tell, I'm sure!" But, I am only just thinking that, because I didn't see the entire island! My travels there were only to the Chania province and Heraklion, to check out the Palace of Knossos; and after that, the amazing and incredible Samaria Gorge!" He was carefully listening, and I kept rambling on excitedly as my voice raised its pitch and tone; "I tell you honestly Yiorgos, I felt "freedom" once again! Man, it's been a long time since I could feel and be a bold man of the wild, soaking up its nature and feeling as if it were the first time experiencing the beautiful wonder of the earth and what it's like to wander and travel by foot, walking aimlessly like a nomad throughout the land!" He unlocked his arms, leaned forward in his chair and held his eyes on me to ask; "And, were you wearing clothes like this? My mother said, "Aftos Pedi; Vlepo Toh Dendro O Kristouyena!" which means that, "Seeing you, she saw a Christmas Tree!" he said, and followed it with a hearty laugh. "Of course I was dressed like this!" I said. His laughter ended with his quick admirable comment, "Poh, Poh, Poh!; Look at your skin! It is burnt black from the Sun! You are looking like an African Prince!" he said and we both burst into more laughter. Throwing up my hands and plunging my fingers deep into the wild thickness on my head, I said; "And look at my hair, man!" I said. "This big, wild afro-bush and this hooped earring in my ear, shocked every stray dog, raised fur on cats and stunned every inhabitant, young and old in every small village that I encountered, man!" My original idea of diverting his interest and attention from the "curve-ball" he threw at me, was working for me; and at this moment of my drama, it called for a huge burst of laughter and his several "Poh, Poh, Poh's!" until I was able to continue saying; "Yea, it was an experience I will never forget, my brother! I felt so very "normal" every day; sauntering into a carless, crowded village for an early morning breakfast! Oh man; except for one night, I made a spectacle of myself to a crowd at a taverna! But, I think that it was because of my abrupt, surprising and flamboyant entrance that instantly just made everyone and everything" stop, Yiorgos. Nothing moved for long seconds of time! I was the only one or thing in motion! Everything was still except for the taverna's music and "Ornamental" me!

Yiorgos had one hand to his chin and his eyes in squint, softly muttering his "Poh, Poh, Poh's!", and asked; "Do you think they were scared of you, Ilanga; you know, frightened maybe? Because those villagers who still live in the old style of Greece, have never seen anyone like you exploring their village! There are many tourists who do not go to these places, you know, because ferry boats, busses and cars cannot get them there! There are no roads; only big hills and many rivers to cross! Yes, maybe there could be one or two small trucks that travel on the road paths and service the different small villages on the island, but to see anyone like you in their village, or even in a picture, "Oki!" ("No!") he said bluntly. Yiorgos, in his insightful, young knowledge was describing accurately to me "all" of what I had seen and experienced in my small village travels on Crete; when suddenly he dropped his hands to his knees, slapping them hard, following with a burst of laughter and quietly muttering to himself, "Poh, Poh, Poh, Poh, Ilanga!" and then asked; "Tell me what you were thinking when you saw their frightened faces!

Weren't you also scared of them, and what they might have done to you?" My reply was quick, correcting his error of thought; "No, no, no, Yiorgos! I didn't say that they were frightened or scared; I said that they were "shocked" when they saw me! I don't think that they saw me as threatening or harmful at all! Their faces didn't show me fear; what I saw were merely questions in the many eyes that were "seeing me"! And although I dangled an earring, wore bracelets and beads hanging from my neck, I was bare chested; so, they could see that I was a male! But their eyes - intrigued with wonder and maybe delight - revealed their thoughts and many questions; "Who is he? Where did he come from? Why is he dressed like that, and Why is he here?!" These were the questions that I saw flashing fast across their simple minds and consequently became the village "buzz" of the next day! The outrageous encounter I had that night on my first village stop was so intense with such an uncertainty, that I said to myself, "Ilanga, please! Never again enter a village at night!" and I swear Yiorgos, thereafter, my village stops were early mornings or afternoons!" Never again. That one night stop "freaked me out" man; it just "blew me away" totally! But I also, freaked out "everyone else" there that was exposed to this unusual spectacle of the night!"

I paused after my emphatic statement to reach for the carafe of Retsina, but Yiorgos stopped my reach and began to pour it for me from the carafe. He was very relaxed, and absorbing every word that came from out of my mouth. He poured carefully, saying; "Yes; go on! why never again at night?" he asked, and he waited. Already feeling the "glow" of Retsina, I took a quick sip and said; "Oh man, Yiorgos, superstitious people believe that at night is when the demons come out"! It happened in the village of Loutro! The Sun had set, and the dark was following fast! I had been hiking all day and at this time, long after Sunset, I found myself standing on a high level of landscape looking at the twinkling lights of a small village below, and I hurried down quickly! Breathing heavily and nearly out of breath, my fast steps ended abruptly, as I found myself walking onto a huge flat concrete platform crowded with evening diners seated in this area designated for the taverna and its outdoor cliental. The noises of laughter, Greek music coming softly from a loudspeaker, loud talking voices and the clatter of dishes and glasses all blended together were festive sounds in fusion with those of the evening diners, who were happily enjoying themselves at the village's only Taverna. Sitting at the tables were mostly elders and their grandchildren, I suppose; and a few young parents. Those who sat at the tables that were placed periphery and closest to the edge of the platform's boundary and the woods, were the first diners who saw me approaching from the dark shadows and step onto the concrete floor. They were startled, Yiorgos, and I must say, for them sitting there on the periphery, yes, this was a moment of fear for sure; followed quickly by shock! They gasped loudly at what they were seeing coming towards them; their forks and knives dropping instantly from their hands; and the elders and young parents called their children from their play and held them tightly to their side as they watched my startling entrance from the dark woods onto the concrete platform where I stopped and sighed with relief that I had made it here. I stood there in my own shock and surprise and I suddenly became aware that I had disrupted something, because an immediate silence blanketed the noise that once filled the Taverna's space; and now, I heard only the Greek music and their mouths gasping for breath, and saw their eyes opened wide!"

"The rippled effect of my surprise arrival swept quickly throughout the whispering crowd of diners, and I knew then that I had to make a move, Yiorgos, I was so embarrassed, man! There was one small unoccupied table that I noticed in a far- off corner of the platform. I wanted to run to it; but instead I slowly walked and gave good evening greetings with a head nod as I passed the diners at each table. Oh man; that night was heavy for them, and for me, Yiorgos! So, I decided thereafter to make my entrance into a village during the morning hours only, and never at night! But you know what? Many days after that night, I had sad thoughts and I felt bad for the children whom I'd frightened, and those pure and simple diners there in Loutro! I'm sure that I caused a long, dark and scary and maybe sleepless night for the many folks that were there! But in the day light, it was different amongst the other villages that I encountered. My arrival and presence was always one of surprise and awe, but never with a threat or fear! I knew that it would be best for me to not roam and walk the narrow paths of interest and curiosity, but rather to sit in one place, try not to be noticed, and not to disturb the villager's daily routine. I had learned a new lesson of "obedience" when entering a village. I would spend my early morning hours there at a taverna, eating, reading, writing and listening to cassette music on my reliable Walkman, being obedient to my new rules and feeling comfortable. And sometimes, Yiorgos, basking in the tranquility of these hours beneath a shady canopy, 'a beautiful moment' would happen there. Like once; a child of about three-years old, while holding her mother's hand and walking past me, stopped abruptly! She stared at me for quite a few seconds, busy with one little finger digging at an itch inside her ear, her tiny lips squeezing tightly and twisting slowly the deeper she bored into her ear. But she kept her constant stare; she couldn't take her eyes off of me. She was calm, but also 'old and wise' and I could tell that she sparkled with many questions! The moment inspired me to play the role of 'Magician'! I stared at her and she stared back; our eyes in a deep conversation of play and talk and smiles as if we had been friends forever! Her Mom tugged on her other little hand and said "Hella, Hella!" ("Come, Come!"); "Pestou O Kiros, Yassas kei Pame Peidthimou!" ("Say to the gentleman, "Hello" and let's go my child!") she said, as she slightly tugged at her little girl's hand. Mother and daughter tugged at each other until finally the little girl exclaimed; "Oxi!" ("No!") with a childish whine and a stubborn refusal to budge from her place and her fantasy with me. Oh, she was such an "intense" little girl, Yiorgos! She was filled with self-confidence and innocence all at once; young but with the wisdom of the old. Her presence, her young/old wisdom and her glistening eyes all emanated an angelic purity of their own, and a desire to share with me. I stopped my stare to lift my head and gave her mom a quick 'trust-me' wink of an eye and immediately went back into our childplay of "stare and who are you'! Slowly, I lifted my hand and placed the tip of my index finger on the tip of my nose and said in a whisper, the word, 'Magic'! And then slowly with my long brown finger I transferred the Magic from my nose, by spiraling it through the air and onto the tip of her nose, as I hummed quietly the celestial yoga sound of "Om." I tell you man, this moment brought tears to my eyes, it really did! It was a spontaneous and natural experience that I am sure, I will never forget. Yea, it was that beautiful, Yiorgos," I said. And then leaning forward towards him, adding; "She was standing about two-feet away, directly in front of me! She and I were face-to-face in our stare when I began my finger move and her tiny brown eyes became larger as they watched my finger flying up in the air and spiraling down towards her, causing her big eyes to cross! And when my finger finally touched the tip of her nose, the immediate body-freeze and gentle gasp of breath overwhelmed her tiny little body and captured her in a delighted pause; just long enough for her wrenching face and ear-digging antics to stop. And when her mouth did close after her surprise and awe, I could see on her face that she could feel the "wonderful sensation of Magic" slowly creeping from the tip of her nose and upwards, filling her mind with a 'new wonder'! I watched closely, and with the touch of my finger still to her nose, I softly whispered, 'Hello!' I swear, Yiorgos, that I could hear the sound of my word echoing and banging against the walls of her tiny little mind! And I could see that her little rigid body finally became relaxed, as she kept her stare. And then suddenly, and so beautifully, her small, oval lips began to part and slowly take on the shape of a coming smile that took a few seconds to broaden, eventually erupting and soon bursting into a genuine, three-year old's long sustaining giggle that she held-onto and wouldn't let-go-of, until she finally said with her sweet tiny voice, "Yassus!" ("Hello!"). Her mom smiled at me, pulled on her little hand and led her away, but our targeted eye-to-eye stare continued as they walked! After every three or four steps taken, she'd turn her little head around to see if I was still there, as she kept staring. Mom would give another tug at her daughter's hand often, until they were finally out of my sight. The games of magic and stare were now over, and my new, little friend was happy! She was quite satisfied that her many questions of what and who I was were simply answered! It was just once that she raised her hand for her tiny little fingers to wave to me a last goodbye. This was a beautiful moment for me Yiorgos, and for her; because we both discovered that it was instant magic that made us see eye-to-eye and see deeply into one another's Soul to discover who we were; old friends? Maybe. Or perhaps just two infinite wanderers passing by one another again, "recognizing" the face, and suddenly stopping for a precious moment in time to once more say 'hello!'! It seemed to us both so natural that we stop and say hello and play a 'new game' together again; but this time in the village of Paleochora, Greece. Coincidence?"

My early morning hours at a village Taverna always had an unusual moment for me to notice, recognize its worth, and cherish "for as long as time itself." I find such personal value in these beautiful moments that happen instantly and somehow just "appear out of nowhere" simply to be noticed!

"You know, Yiorgas, just two days before I met my little three-year old friend and our 'nose magic,' I was at a Taverna in the village of Matala, sitting quietly writing out post cards. A group of five or six young boys ages 8 to 10 years old were running about playing with a Soccer ball not far away from me, when suddenly, I could feel the presence of eyes on me. He was about four-feet tall; hazel green eyes and locks of jet-black hair curled wildly on top of his little head. He said nothing and I said nothing, as our stare began; and I, needing to adjust the head scarf that wrapped my big afro-hair, untied its knot and dropped it over my shoulders. Oh man, Yiorgos, this child's eyes were bulging out from their sockets! Beneath the scarf of course, my hair was lying down and flattened! But suddenly when I untied the scarf and dropped it to my shoulders; my afro-style hair quickly sprung up and then mushroomed into a huge bush that instantly captured his imagination. They opened wide at the sight of the big bush, burnt red by the island's hot sun! His eyes wandered high up to my hair and then lower to meet my eyes, and then quickly and wide-eyed up to 'the bush' again! He did this a couple of times before suddenly darting away to his friends who were loudly yelling his name, "Yannis, Yannis!" Watching him run away, I chuckled and continued wrapping my big hair, adjusted the scarf, and involved myself again with writing. It wasn't too long after, Yiorgos, that once again I could feel the presence of eyes upon me; but this time, many eyes! I lifted my head, and was surprised to see standing in front of me about six-feet away, the group of young, rugged Soccer players dripping with sweat and nearly breathless, staring at me, and in wait of "something"! But what was strange and unusual to me, was that all of their little faces and eyes had the exact same expression as a child's **2ndCycle** of a brash *Dare!* I smiled and said, "Hello, you guys!" and said nothing more! Their eyes never left me, nor did their facial expression of 'mischievous dare' change, as their eyes went back and forth from me to one another. And then standing directly in front of me, the tallest and maybe the oldest of them all, pointed his finger at Yannis and bravely broke our silence with his primary school English that he spoke timidly and with little confidence. "He wants to"... (he then paused, in search of the correct word to use) "Touch, Neh! ("Yes!") Touch your hair!" he said confidently. I looked at Yannis and began to unwrap my head scarf, and meeting his eyes, I bluntly said to him gently and in question, "You do?" His ocean-green eyes opened wide again with the bright excitement of exploration and a small hint of fear as he watched me slowly reveal what was hiding under the scarf. My fingers purposely toiled and played with the ends of the scarf, and I felt I should embellish the drama with demonstrative gestures and theatrics before revealing the hidden secret. I then quickly "snatched" the scarf off my head and flung it in the air, singing loudly, "Da-Raaaah!"

"Oh, Yiorgos; that moment was brilliant and lit with surprise, shock and unforgettable little faces that beamed brightly with absolute astonishment! My 'big hair' was a sight that they had never seen before...and maybe never would see again! And therefore, they determined themselves to stay and take advantage of this brilliant moment of fun and dare. And Yiorgos, when my fingers sent the scarf flying high in the air, their eyes didn't even notice its flight!

Instantly 'the bush' sprung-up in its wildness! Each strand of hair, dry, long, and standing tall from its root to its burnt, brittle ends exploded wildly in freedom, as each child's eyes opened as wide and as round as their soccer ball! And the air around us swelled and hummed quietly with many new versions of a younger sound of, "Poh, Poh, Poh's"! I relaxed from the theatrics and motioned Yannis to come closer to me, "Hella! ("Come to me!") I said. His move towards me was hesitant, but fearless and stopping about a foot away, we met face-to-face. He then quickly turned his head away from me to face his friends, proudly showing them his bravery and courage, and as well, displaying his personal satisfaction of achievement that he had acted, responded-to, and trusted his own Intuition to dare and explore! This is a must-do of the **2ⁿᵈCycle**. I took ahold of his hand and felt its slight tremble. He turned and faced me quickly, and I saw clearly in his green eyes what they were seeing in my eyes; and that was, that he could "hear" what my eyes were saying to him, which was an intense, "I *Dare* you!" He remained in silence; but his quiet green eyes spoke the words, "I *Dare*"! I was lowering my head when I lifted his trembling hand and saw that his index finger was getting itself ready for a first touch. He stuck his one finger in the bush and yanked-it-out as fast as he could holding in a deep inhale of breath! His face lit up brightly and boldly, expressing his achievement. The grin on his face was as wide and broad as a "Cheshire Cat" smile! All of his friends gasped, squealed and shouted "Bravo, Yannis!" After his proud high jumps up and down happily with his bravery and success, he looked at me with more dare in his eyes! I challenged him with mine; knowing what his next move was going to be! He hesitated a couple of seconds; I lowered my head again, and suddenly he plunged his whole hand into the bush. I could feel all five fingers quickly wiggling, roaming and dancing in my hair! His small finger tips moved briskly against my skull, pouncing and digging deep until I felt another plunge! Now both of his hands were in the bush; all eight fingers and two thumbs scrambling and digging hard in search of a "new" feel and thoughts, that maybe would last forever! And with my head lowered between my knees, I could hear Yannis' voice above my head screaming loud with excitement and announcing to his spectating friends, "Hella, Hella!" ("Come, Come!") I could feel his fingers gradually come to a stop and his hands lift from out of my hair. While waiting for his next plunge, I heard the many voices above my head quietly whispering to one another in Greek and also the movement of small feet scrambling up to me. With my head still lowered, I opened my eyes to see little bare feet and toes standing next to me gathered in a bunch; the boys, all waiting for their turn "to make a plunge" with their hands in the big bush! And they did, Yiorgos, one after another!" I could feel rambling around in my hair many small hands and fingers touching something new and strange. They were fearless and simply feeling a new happiness! Like Yannis, they too, were enjoying the success and achievement of their collective *Dare* and *Act*. I felt joy come to me as I was sitting there, bent-over low without moving; and a sense of "knowing" came to me, that in this special moment of time, being with these children, I was an integral part of their joy, and that we were sharing this beautiful moment of time, place and new experience, together!"

"I was feeling good, man; and I was cherishing these thoughts as each hand reached-in; and each voice felt its own joy! Thinking these thoughts and being grateful for this, I felt the deep plunge and fast-fingering of the last hand. I waited; but there was no more. Lifting my head and seeing these seven little daredevils gathered there in front of me, I smiled with my heart, my lips and my eyes. All the faces of "dare" had suddenly changed and become bright, beaming faces, glowing and radiating genuine loving friendship, collective joy and admiration, for themselves and for Yannis! And because of what they had seen of Yannis' *Action, Challenge, Courage and Achievement*; they could now believe and trust in his "Dares." They were witness to Yannis' insightful performance and the attainment of his new and highest-achievement! This was consciously, a first-time personal accomplishment that often occurs during the **2ⁿᵈCycle**. Therefore; this was *Real, Big and Lasting*! And to think, Yiorgos, how fortunate I was to have witnessed with my own eyes, heart and soul, this special moment that had just happened for them! It was so much more exciting and thrilling than a goal won in a Soccer game!"

Yiorgos could feel me, he heard the passion in my voice, and he nodded his head slowly up and down with understanding. I sat back in my chair saying to him as a matter of fact; "These are what I call spontaneous, beautiful moments that just happened unexpectedly at my village stops!"

But, my dear reader; these moments can happen anywhere to anyone and at anytime! I think it's the fast pace of life that we are now living in that prevents more of these moments; and it's important that we learn to slowdown, stop for a moment and take notice of what's going on around us! We need to accept "what is" without objection, because what is, "Is." Include yourself in the scene that you are now a part of, analyze, filter and evaluate what you see!" And with that, you will recognize and feel the "core beauty" of the moment, its *Purpose*, and its harmless "sting" of another reality!

I could see that Yiorgos understood completely, the narratives of Yannis and of the little magic girl and that he now "comprehended" what a spontaneous and beautiful moment means to me; and I continued; "These moments are within our orbit every day to be realized, Yiorgos!" But we must stop what we are doing, absorb the moment for what it is and become a part of it, or else a spontaneous special moment will never happen!" He was listening and I could tell he heard "something." I concluded my village stories, saying; "And somehow, and for some strange reason, these stories and moments are special my brother, very special, because they last forever."

We both sat quietly in a long pause of thought. The afternoon had passed so quickly and the Sun was nearly about to set itself and shade the Acropolis. "I think I must leave you now Yiorgos!" I said, "I'm going to climb up there and bid "adieu" to the Gods, get back to the hotel and pack to leave for Amsterdam in the early morning!" Yiorgos said in haste; "Yes, yes, I know you must go," but wanting to hear more about "something," he quickly added, "But you didn't tell me about the gorge in Samaria! Tell me, did you like it? Was it very beautiful? I know it is, because of what I hear many tourists say; but, was it everything that you, "Ilanga" thought it would be? I remember you telling me that you wanted to go "where God goes for vacation!" I want to know; was it there?" he asked desperately; and his eyes never left mine. I answered him honestly, saying, "Yes!" But without the mention of "Agnostine" or of "Nadia" and our sensual dance at the discotheque in Chania! These two highlights of my Crete vacation, I felt that he didn't need to hear about; and I raised up from my chair as a signal to him that I was about to leave. His disappointment of not being able to hear a bit more of "something" was obvious to me. So, with an exuberant expression of delight to divert his disappointment, I said to him, "Oh Yiorgos, most definitely; the Samaria gorge is one of God's vacation "get-away" spots here on the planet; I am sure of that, my brother! All the true essence and beauty of Nature is there in one place, for any human to see and bear witness to their roots and origin!" I said, and followed that with; "Well, at least that's what I experienced anyway!"

My taking a step away from the table urged him to also make a move, and as he got up from his chair to meet me at my side of the table, I said to him quickly, and using my newly learned phrase of Greek; "Kei, Boro Toh Logareeizmo, Parakalo!" ("And, may I have the bill, please!"). Yiorgos' face lit up with excitement, and he grabbed both my shoulders with his hands; "Poh, Poh, Poh, Ilanga! You are speaking Greek like a "real" Greek, now!" he said; releasing his hands from the tight squeeze he had on my shoulders and taking a step back to look at me with amazement on his face. His quiet, repetitive and self-affirming "Poh, Poh, Poh's" were incessant! I continued proudly in Greek; "Efaristos Poli, Adelphosmou!, Kei, Toh Logaree.." ("Thank you very much, my brother! And, the bill.") Yiorgos interrupted my stammering words about the bill by saying, "Asta! Oxi! Dhen Parazzi! ("Stop it! No! That's okay!), and then he said in English, "I will take care of that!"

We held each other tight in a "goodbye squeeze," and hearing him say, "Yassou, Adelphosmou!" ("Goodbye, my brother!), made us both feel the union of the real friendship that we had established. "Give me your address," I said; "And I will write to you letters from Amsterdam! You go and do that, and I will go and say goodbye to your mother and father!" This was all done in haste as I said my last goodbye to the three of them, slipped his written address in my pocket and began my climb upwards to the Acropolis and into the

Sunset to bid "adieu!" to the Gods; to share with them an abundance of "soulful gratitude" for gifting me with this insightful journey and experience of their Greece. Little did I know then, that this was only an introduction to Greece and its people; and that I had planted a seed there for so much more to come.

A light drizzle of rain fell upon Athens in the early morning hours of the following day. Light and dark gray clouds loomed over the city as I watched from the window of the Magic Bus making its first mile out of Athens and its bustling chaotic traffic. Rain and cloudy gray skies followed me en route to the other "sunless city" where I was to begin a new season of dance works, plan new ideas with my friends and dance in discotheques nightly. These were my new plans and thoughts as I dreamily watched the rain's light drizzle, heading north on my way to Amsterdam, Holland, The Netherlands.

CHAPTER TEN

We trusted ourselves and "piggy-backed" on faith to attain great exhaltation.

It was not until three years later that I returned to Greece, in 1978, with my newly formed dance company "Kreos Dance Theater." My three years in Amsterdam were of serious work; teaching 15 to 20 dance classes a week to children and adults at the "Plenix Center," where I rented a separate dance studio space for professional classes, and made plans to organize an unusual company of creative dance students. During this interim of time, Yiorgos and I were sending letters to one another back and forth, cultivating our friendly "big brother" relationship via correspondence. He was excited at one point, hearing from me that I would be returning to Greece with the dance company for a month of intense work and study. By this time, I had developed my original technique and theory of afro-jazz dance and its application; which therapeutically incorporates the study and strict disciplines of "Hatha Yoga, rhythmic structures via the drum and dance, infused with the ideology of living *The Life* daily, in balance and in sync with your own personal rhythm". It was an unusual dance technique that was timely and apt for the dance scene in Amsterdam at the time, and it attracted dancers interested in "something new" or "something else." Something other than the usual genres of Classical, Jazz, and other contemporary dance forms. This unorthodox technique and my personal method of teaching - I must say - was difficult for some dancers; especially for those who had for years been technically trained in the Classical dance form. The Afro-Jazz form was particularly difficult for the professional dancers who were not able to "free their minds" from the more conventional techniques that included strict disciplines and grounded habits. Many would say, "I love your class, but it's hard for me to get into it and feel it and to move like that!" I understood their difficulty, likewise, I too had some difficulty in a classical dance class; but in the primary stage of my dance interest, I understood its importance for my development in dance technique and was attracted to its disciplines. On the other hand, I also understood that this form of the dance impaired and limited my desired expression in "natural" body movement, and that the afro-jazz technique that I had already been in study with for a year, "enhanced" the desire and the expression for me to get into it, feel it and move! Also, age is an important factor in classical dance. To be an "acceptable" well- trained dancer, one must begin training at least from the age of eight to ten years old. And another notable boundary to inclusion was the fact that one should be of the white race to be "acceptable" for performance on the classical dance stage. However, in the classes that I was teaching, it was not as difficult for the novice dancers, or for one who just "loves to dance"! They were able to connect more easily with their bodies to the "nature" of the dance, and its raw and primitive unorthodox technique! Afro-Jazz, like all dance genres and techniques, is an on-going study of disciplines; both physically and mentally! In addition this technique includes the element of "spirituality" as well. It does not discriminate against race or culture or body size; and therefore it easily made its way onto the Amsterdam dance scene in 1975.

I wanted to implement the technique with a specific group of novice dancers who were eager to learn the theory and its ideology, therefore, an intense dance workshop was needed. In the Spring of 1978, I made the announcement to students that I would be conducting a month-long Workshop of intense study for students who wanted to learn and were able to participate. I announced that it would not be held in a studio in Amsterdam, but in an outdoor environment "somewhere in Greece" that was conducive to the technique and its nature. I let it be known that the dancers would be "in residence" there, and they would be living and camping outdoors seven days a week' with a daily routine of classes and study that consisted of the disciplines of "Self-Realization, Hatha Yoga, and Dance. This included learning the technique and the beats and rhythms of the drum, or of many drums. Underscoring the Workshop, was the introspective learning of **YOU:** *self-worth, personal value, commitment, and potential.* It was imperative that each student over eighteen years of age clearly understood the *Commitment, Purpose, Self-Responsibility, and Dare,* that was required to engage themselves and endure this Workshop of diverse disciplines.

The majority of the twenty-six students were into their **4ᵗʰCycle** of *Challenges and Dare;* a few were already into their **5ᵗʰCycle** of *Determination and Action;* and I was in the midst of my *Active* **6ᵗʰCycle** of *Purpose.* My personal challenge and dare was to "educate" and to undertake the role of teaching "collective responsibility;" and the vehicle to do that was through Dance; including my past experiences with The G-Clefs and Family. It was a project in its first phase of development; and the possibility of this Workshop which was now in the process of being realized and becoming a "reality" slammed into my mind hard with an onslaught of all the factual logistics: transportation, management, and the operation of such a huge project! The hard reality of this proposed Workshop hit me full-on after the primary registration resulted in fourteen eager students, all prepared to leave Amsterdam for Athens Greece on July 1st, 1978, to engage in the one-month long Workshop and return to Amsterdam on August 1st. The July departure date was suitable for all except for one American student, "Samantha," who was a successful fashion model. She had to adjust a rigorous "Runway" performance schedule and had arranged that she would be joining us there upon our arrival. "Sam's" plush apartment in Paris was often unoccupied, so she had entrusted me with a key to her place. I was busy working there with projects for the *Caresse Theater* where I occasionally taught a dance workshop. Sometimes she would be in Paris two or three days and we would cook and she would invite a few of her friends or modeling colleagues to join us! We'd be there together, talking, eating and laughing for hours! Her laughter was like a witch's unending cackle, which was infectious and was also her "signature."

Two of the most eager of the students: one, about to end the **4thCycle** and the other thresholding the **5thCycle,** were both energetic, naïve "American Apple Pie" youths, bubbling with the passion for life and all living things! Their zeal and zest for freedom and an adventurous lifestyle stemmed from their active involvement within the country's raging "Flower Power Generation" of "Peace and Love," a climactic social movement that destabilized, shattered and dismantled the American social and political agenda during the 1960's and early 1970's! And to distract the American people from this dire upheaval of social unrest; the "tool" of all day prime-time television was used; a tool that saturated minds with the horrifying images of the Vietnam War; the impactful political Hearings of, Anita Hill and Clarence Thomas, Oliver North's "gun-deals," the transition of ruling power in Iran and the sensational "Watergate" drama were only some of the intended public distractions perpetrated by the Government and the new era of "Sensational Media" that became their weapon against "Peace and Love"! A new and stark "television reality" emerged and these effective optics and poignant distractions eventually "crushed" the idealistic stems and petals of the fast-blooming and attractive "Flower Power Movement" and of the "Hip" and "Beat" generation in America.

Her name was Shawn and his, Terezzo (Terry) both, middle-class Americans with healthy, fresh, white skin and who were in a position, physically mentally and spiritually, to commit and assist in the detailed organizing and management of this now "enormous" Project. A young couple who appeared to me to be "inseparable," they were comfortably traveling Europe together for an extended period of time, back packing and enjoying their "hippie" style version of freedom. They too, became allured to the city's many attractions, its world-music sounds, its lifestyle and new friendships. They decided to remain in Amsterdam for the Summer months, check out the fun city and take dance classes! Fortunately, by coincidence or however, this is how we met!

They desperately wanted to take charge, help organize and spearhead this workshop and do whatever they possibly could to make it happen. It seemed that their need for the Workshop was greater than mine! So, I had given them both the authority to organize and delegate to other students the required duties and responsibilities; and I was to arrange with "Magic Bus" the round-trip bus rental, its costs, the departure/return schedule, and work on the Workshop's location, travel itinerary and planned program of studies. One day, within a week's time after the registration and at the end of one of our exhaustive dance classes, Terry came to me with the surprising news that he and Shawn had just that day purchased an old, operable 22 cubic-foot sized truck! He excitedly told me "It was once used on a farm to transport chickens! The space inside is fantastic! Yea, ok, right now it's a mess, huh Shawn? It has little wooden cages inside where the chickens slept, and yea, there's chicken shit all over the place, but man, it's cool; that's not a problem!" Shawn agreed to all of what he was saying, and if she had the same excitement that he had, she didn't reveal it to me! Her calm demeanor was unusual as she was changing from dance wear to street wear. She was usually the mouthpiece of conversation, but she was wordless this time with subtle eye glances at Terry, shifting them quickly to someplace else whenever she saw his excitement accelerate, about to explode, and his mouth about to open with a "magical" explanation to his story. She listened, he continued; "Shawn and I were driving north of Amsterdam and saw it on an old farm road with a For Sale sign on it, parked in a yard of an old farm house. So we stopped and checked it out, you know; aww…and the little old Dutch guy was so cute and happy, huh Shawn?" he asked without waiting for a reply. "But he was cool and told us in what condition the truck was in and why he was selling it and everything! Really nice guy; huh Shawn? And Ilanga, just like magic the guy sold it to us!" Terry said, and followed that with a high-toned ambiguous giggle, and continued; "Shawn and I gave it a test drive, and…" I interrupted him; "Hold up Terry; is this about us driving this truck to Greece and back to Amsterdam?" I asked abruptly.

Speechless, Shawn was wrapping her neck with a scarf but her Irish blue eyes held mine. "Does this mean that I am going to pay for an old farm truck full of chicken shit, that 'might' work getting us there! Totally unsafe for all of us, Terry!" I said; I had to strongly emphasized the fact, that; "It might get us to Greece, but it "might not" get us back!" Terry was astonished; surprised that I could say such a thing! He butted in; saying, "It works fine, man!" and then saying quickly with his enthusiastic **5ᵗʰCycle** "Determination;" "We'll clean it up! No problem man; I will check out the mechanics and see if it'll make it to Greece and back! And also, in the back of the truck, I will build a few sleeping racks inside the big cargo space so that some of the dancers can sleep at interval times!"

Terry was excited telling me of this "great deal" without a "risk" of safety; and that he was confident, that the "old chicken coop on wheels" would make it! Shawn; by this time, was standing next to him with her face beaming bright and waiting for my approval and a "green-light" to go and begin the big clean up! She had listened carefully to every word that had crossed between us and she eyed both of our faces, and from the "I'll think about it" expression on my face, she could see a possible consideration of an approval from me. I could see that she was anxious with her thoughts of traveling throughout Europe in "Hippie-style freedom," no conventional bus rules to follow. We could stop when and wherever we wanted to stop, have singing hootenannies in the truck and just be "free"! One of the thoughts that she pointed out and vocalized (knowing that it would be of interest to me) and with a hope that my ears heard every word; "And in Greece! Oh my God; Imagine us having our own mode of transportation to follow the travel itinerary that you've already planned for the Workshop!" Shawn's voice raised a pitch higher to plug in the "thrift" factor and saying with urgency, "And man, this truck cost us 'nothing' compared to what Magic Bus is going to 'rip us off' for, damn!" She made her point, not even blinking a

371

blue eye, and stopped. They both were just standing there waiting for the Director's approval; and I stood there, astonished that they had purchased a truck specifically for this Workshop to happen, first of all; and my immediate second thought was of the truth, insight, and belief that these two young, intelligent "Flower Power Petals," (survivors of the defunct powerful social movement) actually believed in me and the "work" I was doing! My appreciation for this gesture swelled as I reflected on the old "Flower Power Movement" and the work that these two wanted to meld with my new work. Here was commonality.

I was humbled, and more than impressed with their interest in the Workshop, their genuine enthusiasm, and the work they were doing to get it to happen precisely as I did; but my underlying thought and concern was for the student's safety as we traveled on the "old chicken-coop on wheels" limping along and "putt-putting" its way across the international Borders of Europe. This was not my idea of a "safe trip," and I could not give Shawn and Terry a direct answer immediately. "Let's get dressed and go to a Café on the Leidserplein, have a Cappuccino, roll a "Doobie", and talk about it," I said. ("Doobie" was a word used for a rolled joint; derived from the Band, *The Doobie Bros.*) The three of us agreed to that, got dressed, jumped on our bicycles and headed for the Leidserplein to a Café to sit and discuss the issues of safe travel and international border-crossing regulations for such a vehicle and its passengers; and its costs, expense of fuel and emergency maintenance if needed. Aside from the truck issues, and enjoying our café drinks and the usual fragrant aroma of marijuana that floats daily within the air and space of the Leidserplein, we sat and also thoroughly discussed the legal issues of travel documents, because the dance company consisted of students from five different countries: America, Germany, Holland, New Zealand, and the Caribbean Island of French-colonial, Guadalupe. Passports and official papers are required by each student/passenger to have on person, traveling through the five western European countries of Germany, France, Italy, Switzerland, Austria; and then going south to the Yugoslavian coast to Croatia-Bosnia, and into Greece. Our conversation on these issues lasted for hours at the Café, and Terry, being the handyman and mechanic that he was, convinced me of his skills, and we three agreed to use the big "old chicken coop" for our travels. There sitting on the Leidserplein, I dismissed every other option of our travel to Greece, gave thought to the duties needed for pre-departure, and then rested with a strong intuition of "trust" that our plans of travel, safety, and official documentation, was "all in my hands," and that I would go, and "feed the children." I gave Shawn the "green light" to clean up the truck and for Terry to pull out his tool box and pursue the mechanical work needed to be done; and also, told him to not forget to build his sleeping racks! The last Cappuccino sealed our agreement.

A week before our departure to Greece, fifteen students had registered for the Workshop, including a three-year old boy child by the name of "Pacheco." His mother "Rano," a single parent, and an exotic and wonderful dancer from Suriname; would not be able to go unless she could bring her son! This was even more of a concern for me, of course! But, Rano "needed" to come; I saw the soulful need in her face "Just dripping with her passion for dance; and I could sense that to share this experience with her son, was her "purpose" to fulfill during this period of their life together. She needed to go to Greece! Tears came to her eyes and fell hard while she was telling me of her dilemma; they were seeing the reluctance of approval on

373

my face, and her mind was reading my thoughts… "A three-year old child!" in need of extra-care, vigilance, protection, guidance, and oversight of course were my immediate thoughts!

"I have to think about this Rano," I said to her; "And I also think it's best that I discuss this with the other students. I don't want Pacheco to be a distraction to the Workshop, the students, nor to you in the many ways that he can be;" I was saying to her regretfully. Although he was at every dance class, never disturbing, and pre-occupied with his own play in a corner of the studio. Rano prepared and arranged his play to never interfere or distract the dancing students throughout the ongoing two-hour class; and if, or when he did, we all loved it!

Pacheco was a well-behaved, obedient, respectful, and unusually mature three-year old boy. Sometimes during a portion of a class when I would refrain from instructing to observe students, I would sit with Pacheco in his play corner for some minutes, and he and I together loved watching his mother's waist-long silky black hair fly wild in the air whenever she danced and leaped across the studio floor! His eyes were always dancing with his Mom.

I gave considerable thought to Rano's request; and the pros and cons were thoroughly discussed among the students at the following dance class. To my surprise, it was unanimous that every student welcomed Pacheco, and shared with Rano and I, that they would assist her in every way possible and with daily all-day oversight of her three-year old son. We never did get to do any dancing at that class; It was held for finalizing the trip that we would be departing for in a week's time. Shawn's efficient organizational skills had the procedures and delegates in place, Terry overhauled, serviced, and built six sleeping racks in the now spotlessly clean

22 foot "chicken-coop," and I, laden with plans for the Workshop, collected all the official documents needed from the students and Pacheco; and still, because of the excitement and anxiety, much chaos ensued among us. Consequently; the appropriate name of the dance company became "Kreos Dance Theater" ("Creative-Chaos" spelled with a "K" because it had a sound and a resemblance to the Greek language!). I also was inclined to have a professional photographer among us for the official documentation of the Workshop. "Mano" was an intelligent vibrant and energetic young man from Lima, Peru, South America, and already into his **5th Cycle**. Tall, lanky and slim, with smooth, brown skin, handsome with a rugged swagger and style. He sported thick and slick jet-black hair that often fell loose and prevented one from seeing his deep and serious eyes, revealing that this honorable Peruvian was "unyielding to any nonsense whatsoever"! Mano was always direct and to the point on any issue, and was aware and super conscious of global politics, his environment, his personal values, and quite protective of his spirituality that he too felt was the force and source guiding him safely through the precarious streets of Amsterdam and the other attractive, dicey cities of Europe.

He and I had met three years earlier when my friend Benjamin opened his new dance studio, "Benjamin's Jazz Dance Center" where I was teaching, creating afro-jazz choreographies and doing administrative work. Benjamin was a talented choreographer and he and I had developed a close friendship and partnership in our work together. We both had separate styles and goals within jazz dance: My style was "Afro-Jazz" and my goal was to develop a technique; Benjamin had a Classical dance background and his hope was to bring authentic "American Jazz Dance" with all of its aspects and "flair" to Dutch Amsterdam; and his goal was to proudly establish and root this style there at his new studio. Our united goal was for the center to become the magnet and mecca of Jazz Dance for all European dancers. Benjamin was teaching the "Luigi Jazz" technique and I was teaching the "Afro-Jazz" technique. We decided to introduce the "Lester Horton" technique. In Holland, this was just incomprehensible, and the Dutch always referred to both techniques as "Jazz Ballet"! But neither Benjamin nor I agreed or approved of that definition of the work we did; and so, we were adamant about making that distinction to our dancing Dutch colleagues. Mano, the photographer, worked closely with us there at the studio and also joined me to photograph the other creative projects that I had worked on throughout those years; solo-dance performances, Workshops in Belgium. Also I did a stint as a very reluctant Artistic Director for the *Caresse Theatre* which was a plush elegant showplace of the erotics; where I was busy directing, organizing and choreographing actors and dancers working in the theater's performing company. Mano had a keen eye for candid photography and he loved to photograph dancers. His work covered a full spectrum of eye-catching images; for he had worked as a photographer for an advertising company as well as being a novice photo journalist; (as did Samantha, the fashion model who arrived mid-week). Mano joined us later in Greece at the Workshop one week after our arrival there.

On the first day of August, the dance Workshop to be held in Greece was well on its way. Myself, Pacheco, and fourteen students, anxious eager and happy, left the cloudy gray city of Amsterdam in its own drizzle of early morning rain; but we were sheltered in a small space of darkness and "packed-in-tight" within the big old gray chicken coop on wheels. At last, we were heading for the Sun!

Driving into and throughout the various landscapes that obviously differentiated the countries of western Europe was an eyeful and a geographical lesson in itself for Terry the driver, Shawn and I. We were comfortably sitting together in the broad front seat of the truck and enjoying the beautiful sights. We had windows to see everything we wanted and needed to see. The big gray truck was loaded with twenty passengers and their baggage; Pacheco and the twelve dancers (two males, ten females), along with three Percussionists, their drums, and an extra passenger, Rita (a girlfriend of one of the drummers), and Glenito, Glenn-2, and Danny, the three Percussionists. They were all enclosed in the back of the truck with the tailgate doors shut tight, windowless, and comfortably situated and packed in the black darkness. The first thousand miles of our journey we drove the old rehabilitated gray truck slowly and moved with precarious caution as we traveled along on Europe's fast-traveling Autobahn (Highways). We three in the front seat, hearing a "knuckle-knock" on the metal panel behind us almost hourly to signal to us the need to use the restroom. Just about every hundred miles or so, one of us drivers would slow down to make a necessary "piss-stop," and we could hear the bursting loud voices of relief coming from the crowded back space of the truck. And once we stopped, one of us three would get out of the truck, run to its rear and swing open the huge tailgate doors to the sudden outpouring of frantic bodies dramatically leaping off the tailgate; their springboard to fresh air, freedom, and sunlight! Like quick lightning darting here and there, some would run-off swiftly heading in different directions for privacy; while others would remain nearby the big gray truck, exercising and slowly stretching their aching cramped bodies in the bright sunlight, inhaling and exhaling the natural clean air. Often at some "piss-stops," and feeling "relieved," some of us would frolic and dance together in the open air to the beats of a drum that one of the drummers would haul out of the truck. Each one of us gasped over the panoramic view of the impressive natural beauty before our eyes, appreciating and being grateful for this blissful moment outside of the truck. One such "piss-stop" stop was our arrival at the absolute "take-your-breath-away" sight of the majestic Swiss Alps! White capped and sweeping along for miles, poking high up into a powder blue sky, they were a riveting sight; a hypnotic and compelling example of nature's reign and glory! The awe in front of our eyes and the adoration of its pure magnificence captured us there for hours, celebrating this wonder.

Terry Shawn and I, were the three drivers manipulating roads and highways and charting out our journey as we traveled along the way. One of us would sleep, while the other two kept each other awake with talk, food and often laughter. It was in this confined cabin that we three got to know one another and became friends. After a couple of days of our honest talk and laughter, we "understood" that the chemistry between us was a positive energy, and that together we could do great things with it! We were sure of this, and agreed to discuss our new ideas and many possibilities once we returned to Amsterdam if they decided to remain there after the month of August. Night driving was without beautiful sights to see, less frequent "piss-stops" and a quiet cargo in the rear of the truck; punctuated by the occasional burst of hard laughter. After a few long midnight conversations of personal stories revealing our adventurous young lives, our dares, challenges and the deliberate paths that we had taken purposely to "get here, where we are now," our lifelong friendship began. Often during these late-night discussions, we exchanged words and thoughts that were meaningful to us; and soon discovered that "family" and "friendship" was our common bond of personal values. And that being was comprised of two separate delicate threads; each one having its own strengths - strong, reliable, and supportive - and they become one, and were "purposely" woven into the fabric of our life.

One night, an in depth talk of "Reincarnation" and its possibilities of existence triggered our colorful imaginations to extend further into the intriguing realms of the unknown that sparked the question: If, Reincarnation did exist could it be the connecting factor of our being together at this moment in time during this particular cycle of a Reincarnation? And, not being scholars of such ideology, we left those vague thoughts and discussion in limbo, and silently agreed that our meeting together in Amsterdam, was not of coincidence, but personal choice.

It had taken an unforgettable journey of six days for the big gray truck to arrive in Athens! This was inevitable because of the many piss-stops; some that would last for an hour or more! Often, one of us drivers would pull over to the side of the road at a day's end, stop abruptly and fling-open the tailgate doors, allowing the fleeing dancers to view a gorgeous Sunset, practice long moments of meditation, and stretch their aching bodies! At every stop, a remarkable thing would happen that would always stir a sweet joy within me. I couldn't help but notice and deeply appreciate, the respectful gesture from the anxious group waiting to flee, how they patiently let the three Percussionist jump off the tailgate first; and with brotherly, gentle care, assisted Pacheco and his Mother; allowing them both to disembark the tailgate first, before the frantic leaps began! This to me, was such a beautiful sight for my eyes to see and my Soul to feel, many times a day.

One memorable Sunset stop that delayed our travel for about six hours happened in the rambling mountains that edge the beautiful coastline of Yugoslavia (Croatia). At this point in the already five-day journey and at this border stop, we had decided to celebrate our onset into Greece! We needed to eat and dance before Sunset! All five drums and percussive instruments were pulled out of the big gray truck to be beaten upon, played and danced to! Bread cheeses and fruits that we had timely purchased at a stop earlier that day, were spread on a blanket for us to pick-at and eat, in between a spontaneous dance and the rhythmic beats sounding from many drums. Suddenly; one of the dancers gyrating her "well-knowing" hips in our dance circle, stopped. "I just saw three children! Kids! Over there in those trees!" she said, startled! Immediately the dancing stopped, and the sound of the drums gradually lowered without being directed to, as the drummers instinctively felt a strange vibe and responded, continuing to play in low-toned subtle rhythms. Even those who weren't in the dance circle joined us with questions of "What happened?" as we all fixed our eyes on the movement in the trees. And although all of our eyes were glued to that spot, we saw no movement; no animals nor children; only trees and large wild bushes. We watched closely and waited. The drum rhythms continued quietly, hampering the dance that was no longer happening. The mood was different now; we felt a suspenseful and locked-in mystery of "maybe" we are not alone in this hidden wilderness. We intensely watched the "over-there" point of focus, waited, and saw only motionless trees and bushes. Nothing moved!

The sunlight was fading now, leaving us only a little daylight left to finish picking at the spread of foods and do a quick clean-up. Glenito and I were in conversation when he abruptly stopped talking, squinted his eyes and said, "Ilanga, look over there maan; I think we got company!" Two adult men and three children were standing and watching us from a distance. The other dancers also took immediate notice; we were startled! All the chewing giggles and chatting ended quickly, resolving to whispers of question and astonishment. I instantly took charge of the situation. "Don't be scared or alarmed guys! There are children there so this is not a threat," I said, to create calm and to ease the overwhelming tension that corralled us all closer to one another. I deliberately went on to say; "And stop looking! Just continue eating or doing what you were doing! Just act normal, as if they weren't even there!" Shawn, Terry, and I, proceeded to walk over to the strangers, and find out what it was they wanted from us. "No, Ilanga! Don't go there!" said "Winky", a handsome and talented Amsterdam dancer of Indonesian/Dutch descent. He nervously continued; "They look dangerous! No, you guys, don't go!" Winky, bare chested and modestly showing his slim muscular dancer's body and light-brown skin kept his fingers fidgeting with the sarong-wrapped scarf that draped his torso. His moves were nervous and agitated two of the dancers who were standing next to him. "Please! That fidgeting must stop!" said Austin with a strict tone of direct discipline that she intoned with her thick New Zealand accent. Sabina, who was clinging to Austin and supporting her school teacher-like words, was a cat-like gorgeous feline from Germany who was sensitive and daring. She also was trying to escape from the social "traps" and pressures of her country's strict and rigid conventional thought and tradition! The same ones that made us all feel like "misfits" living in our individual countries of birth, and leaving, simply to discover ourselves and who we actually were. Sabina did not like to speak her native language as she felt that It labeled her, and to hear it and speak it annoyed her. She spoke fluent English and Dutch, and spoke German only when it was absolutely necessary. Both she and Austin did their best to calm Winky's nerves and thoughts of danger. "Now calm down Winky!" Austin said, with her prissiness. "This unsettled behavior and these outbursts do not help matters any, I say; and somebody needs to go out there and confront those gentlemen, and it's certainly neither you nor I!" Sabina clutched Winky's hand, saying, "It's okay man! Terry, Ilanga and Shawn need to go to them; we're here to back them up if we see anything crazy start to happen; so, cool it!" Austin butted in again; "Yes, collect yourself, man! I am sure that those three will handle this matter in the best interests of us all, including those two gentlemen and children in the distance," she said with certainty.

While in Amsterdam and teaching this class of twenty-two students and planning this Workshop; I noticed and embraced the diverse cultures within the group. I soon became aware of the natural and clear communication that they had established amongst themselves, and with me; and also, the positive vibe of extraordinary harmony that harbored within this group of 4th and 5th **Cycle** intelligent young students. They were having two classes a week (requesting more than two) thirsty and in need of experiencing "something else". They not only wanted to learn the technique and dance steps of afro-jazz dance, but they also wanted to reach its source, and the reasons why they were attracted to study this unusual dance form for a year, rather than another form. I also became aware of the fact - and was reminded from such observations - that it was me who inspired this new experience, and it was me who quenched that thirst! A fact, that I had forgotten, until now. I was suddenly alerted to another fact that was there right in front of my eyes, that this was a special class of students who were giving me the only opportunity (presently in Amsterdam) to act by choice and to take up my personal challenge to be responsible to oneself and to one's "purpose." The purpose was to educate and to organize a "collective unit" of positive energy for its own "purpose," and this became the mission statement the afro-jazz dance "Workshop!" This was a **6ᵗʰCycle** opportunity for me to serve others with my purpose, to improve upon the qualities of myself, and to simply create a better me and to satisfy my on-going quest for higher achievement! Therefore, this was a once in a lifetime opportunity dangling before my eyes like the "golden ring" on a Merry-Go-Round," and I had only one chance, so I snatched-it!

Austin's remarks of certainty, that Shawn, Terry and I would handle the situation, with the two strangers behind the trees were steps paced without fear, and with a sincere determination of friendship. One of the two men spoke very little English; although enough to pleasantly greet us warmly, keep his smile, and convince Terry, Shawn and I to follow him. Together we all walked a short distance through the thicket of woods and arrived to a cleared space from trees and brush that startled the three of us! Little did we know that we had parked the big gray truck near the campsite of a band of wandering Gypsy families! The cleared space of trees and brush was bustling with clucking chickens roaming about, children, dogs, campfires being set, and families living their lives! It was a surreal sight that my eyes had only seen before in movies or in colorful photos in a National Geographic magazine! Likewise, for Terry and Shawn, the three of us were riveted by this new and amazing scene that relieved us of any pre-supposed danger or fear. We were greeted and welcomed with genuine warmth, and a few women and children came over to us with smiles on their faces that also revealed their sudden astonishment of seeing for the "first time ever" in their lives, "white American hippies and a black man"! It was still early evening and not yet dark; but campfires were now being lit and sending streams of smoke billowing high into the sky, as women were gathering food to prepare and cook for their evening meal. Children were playing and scattering-about the campsite teasing barking dogs in their play, already forgetting that they had just given their smiles to the three funny-looking strangers a few moments ago. The one man who spoke his few words of English (and never in a complete sentence) had momentarily left us but returned to say, "Tonight; You, friends, and boy baby, come... Eat!" His invitation for us to join the campsite with them for their evening meal surprised the three of us. We thanked him and accepted his invitation; but as we were standing and talking next to his pick-up truck, my eyes latched onto three rifles resting on the floor along with two guitars in the front seat. "Oh, you make music?" I surprised him by asking. "Yes, yes, yes!" he quickly answered; "You come, I play! I give you music!" he said with enthusiasm. Shawn, Terry and I slowly eyed each other to confirm our mutual delight of sharing the same blessed thought: guitars, music, drums, dancers, and Sunset! It was clear to the three of us, that "this was really happening"! Our faces were beaming brightly with flashing thoughts of a spectacular night to come! "Yes!" we told him and his friends; "We will be back!"

When we returned to the big gray truck, the dancers were anxiously awaiting us, not knowing where we had gone, and they immediately surrounded the three of us with many questions all at the same time. "What happened? Who were those men? Where did you guys go?" they asked. I could see that each face and pair of eyes were burdened with worry. They hadn't moved from the blanket spread with food nor the gathered huddle they were into since the three of us left. "Monk," a male student from Guadalupe, with a long, thin, black body and saucer-like eyes, expressed dramatically with his worried voice and thick French accent; "Oooh, Ilanga; za dainjuur I see, when za men take you away! Oh Ilanga, my mind, it goes krazee, mon! I am tsinking maybee ze kill you!" he said anxiously holding his head with both hands. "No, no, Monk!" I replied, enjoying his drama; "There was no danger! They are Gypsy people and they...Monk, abruptly interrupted, standing tall, and still with his head between both hands opened wide his big, round eyes and squealed out loudly, "Jeepseees!" Whaat and no dainjuur?! Oooh-la-la! Tzaht is news to me, mon!" he said to the entire group. He then cocked his head to one side and held a statuesque pose of grandeur that caused instant, loud laughter among all of us. "Tres bon! C'est la vie," he said, still holding his grand pose. Already into our fourth day of the journey, we all were used to Monk's humor, wit and drama by now. He was wise and he was deliberate! He knew that his spontaneous antics and visual "acts" of drama could always ease and calm any simmering tension that he sensed had arisen within the group that would be soon surfacing to boil in the hotpot of emotions that often were simmering on the back-burner. Monk was brilliant at making sure that nothing would ever boil over! So this was just another one of his wonderful acts that caused our laughter to be big and loud; and causing body gestures that scattered us around, instantly breaking up the gathered huddle and dispersing the looming ill vibe of danger. This was Monk's "purpose" for the day, and he knew it.

The five-minute walk to the Gypsy's campsite was full of jokes and laughter due to another of Monk's humorous quips. Before leaving the big gray truck, as we were gathering our bread and cheeses to take with us, Glenn quietly said to Terry and I that he and Rita would stay behind and not go with us to the campsite, because somebody should stay and watch the truck. "These are clever Gypsies," he said. "We all could be over there having a good time and meanwhile over here, the truck is being stolen, or we could be robbed of everything we have here! So, I think somebody should stay; and Rita's not feeling too good anyway, so we'll stay here with the truck!" he said. Terry and I, agreed with him; "Good thinking!" Terry said, and added with sudden concern; "You're right, man! Because we don't know what can happen here while we are there, "jamm'n and boogie'n"! I mean; I think these are good people and everything, but this area has many Gypsies roaming all over the place! So, if nobody's here, and should that happen, we really can't blame these guys! It could be that somebody else is watching us right now, maybe even followed us, and still watching our every move! "Yea, Glenn, good thinking!" Terry said. We agreed that it was the best thing to do, just as Glenito and Danny approached us with their Conga drums strapped on their backs, ready to go. We explained to both of them our discussion and they too agreed. I capped our conversation with, "Yea, Glenn; Thank you man! Although, I don't believe that scenario is going to happen to us tonight, there's always a possibility that it can! Maybe Glenn, you're here for that! You know;

I mean, like taking upon this responsibility of protecting our stuff, and even thinking about it. I didn't and nobody else did! So, this is your gut-feeling that you're responding to; it's personal, and I think it's great that in this decision you have included all of us, by taking upon this responsibility and 'acting on it' and, I thank you for that, man, honestly!" Hearing myself and the rambling of words starting to rev me up to high gear and on the way to a lecture, I continued; "And you know what? I believe that you have made this 'choice' with discernment as one of the Workshop's personal disciplines! You know what I mean, man!" I said, as a matter of fact. Glenn's blank stare had me turning my head around to see three faces and eyes also staring, and three jaws slightly dropped, and all with the same honest facial expression of bewilderment that read, "What the hell is he talking about?" I continued; "And also Glenn, there is the possibility that "five or ten guys could come and approach you and Rita. Then what, 'Mister Gladiator.' Who knows what they would do! Are you prepared for that scenario also? I admire your bravery and courage; but this too is a possibility that you have to think about; So be careful Glenn, and be prepared!" He acknowledged the warning as the three of us left him to join the others, still huddled together and waiting to depart. Proudly, and noting the opportune moment to use my new Greek phrase that I learned earlier that day:

"Hella, Pedthia, Pame!" ("Come on guys, let's go!") I said, "The Gypsies are waiting!"

The walk there was with the anticipation of food, fun and dance, which did happen for a good two-hours or so; but also within those five-minutes of walking and group chatter, we stopped once to howl with laughter, because of Monk's antics. He, Sabina and Winky were talking and walking-in-dance about ten yards ahead of the group when Monk turned his head around to see us behind them and suddenly stopped their walk. The three stood in place there waiting for us to arrive to them. Monk's warrior-like lanky body, as strong as it was, always appeared to be even more powerful whenever he stood tall and erect! With both hands fisted and set tight on his hips, his shout to us was boisterous!.. "And now;.. Tell-me! Where eez tzaaht brown skin lover boy and tzaaht lazyee white gurl who does notheeng all day but 'be in love'?" he asked, and with drama, slapped his hand to his forehead, pretending that he forgot Glenn's name, and saying, "Oh, Oui! ("Yes!"), Glenn, aan tzaaht gurl Reeta?" he added in due respect. Danny and Glenito, who were in lead and in front of the group as we arrived to the three, were taking the onslaught of Monk's theatrical humor. Danny, always with dark sunglasses that usually sat on the tip of his nose, peered over the rims and explained to the three Glenn's decision. Monk cupped one hand to his ear to listen, and responded quickly. He reared back his lanky body and squinted his big saucer eyes, as his face easily twisted into an expression of disbelief and doubt! "I seé, so, tzaaht Reeta gurl, aan tzaaht boy eez alone een tzaaht truck, yes?" he asked sternly. Shawn Terry and I at the rear of the group, eyed one another with a connected mutual thought; "Monk! Oh-oh, here we go-again!" and prepared ourselves for another outstanding performance! One of the dancers, "Anita" shouted; "Oh, stop it Monk! Your shit iz gett'n heavy now, maan! Don't staat dat bool-shit, maan!" She, also from Surinam, was a soulful singer and a strong resilient dancer whose body was voluptuous and energetic; and her voice in song, was as powerful as the selective words that she would speak to get her point across to someone. "No, Aneeta, no!" quipped Monk; "Dees eez not Boolshit, my bew-tee-ful seester, dees eez realite my dear!"

His comedic remark threw us all into a fit of laughter, including Anita! However, the comedy that Monk was demonstrating with flamboyant, elegant flair in the style of "grandness" only "ignited" the spark of Anita's wit! She turned to three of the dancers standing next to her, "Sandra and Hella", who were also Surinamese, and "Anemieke," an elegant, wispy fairy-like Dutch girl who was also within their quartet. All were listening to Anita's brash words; "Dit yongen es te gek!" ("This boy is crazy!") and then she shouted out boldly to Monk, "Hey, meester beeg joker maan! Shut your foolish mouth! Turn around your ugly black face from me, and take us to the Gypsies, maan!" An explosion of laughter burst into a mix of body clutter and fumbling footsteps and stumbles! The effective repercussion of Anita's blasting remark to Monk continued all the way to the Gypsy's campsite, where we were welcomed and greeted with fiery Gypsy music and many hands clapping to the rhythms being strummed on two guitars. It was in a matter of seconds, that the sounding beats of Glenito and Danny's drums slowly introduced themselves and blended with the rhythms and melodies being strummed by the Gypsy's on the strings of their guitars that soon evolved into movements of melodious sounds, resonating, and reaching for its own new sudden passion. The dancing began with Anita and Monk, in a duet of what they called "Afro-Flamenco." How beautiful it was! Their interpretation of natural, primitive body movement, earthy and raw with abstract shapes that soon turned to eye-to-eye contact and a direct "I dare you" stare; both daring one another to spontaneously leap or thrust themselves into a sensual moment of a touch. But instead; both held strong their powerful stance of passion, softened the glare of lust in their eyes, and with a smoothness, fused the posture images and statuesque body-lines that pronounce and define the power and dignity of Flamenco dance. They both were superb students in the afro-jazz dance class, and knowing well what their bodies were capable of doing within the natural and primitive dance form and structures. Their original and natural interpretation and execution of their "Afro-Flamenco" duet dance was scorched with passion and deliberate challenge. Primal body movements were danced with vibrant intimacy, and suddenly took on the postures of self-pride and dignity! They were dancing Flamenco, as raw and as natural as the Gypsies would dance it themselves!"

What I was witnessing before my eyes, is the exact intent that I had imagined when I was creating the Workshop, its concept and design, being that; "The students must "Explore" the nature of their external environment, themselves, and their daily interaction with one another! I had summarized that the positive outcome of the month's committed, diligent, and insightful-work, would be that they had learned the elements needed to process the study of *Self-Evaluation* for themselves. The purpose of the Workshop was to help students to become more engaged and concerned with "Self" and of the development of a "new" and disciplined conscious habit of *being Aware, being Alert, and Acting* when it is time to do so! The disciplines involved are acute and necessary; and are to be practiced daily to create and develop a pattern of self-control, to enable one to circumvent and divert the possible "triggers" of an emotional issue or of circumstantial events that could hamper one's initiative in achieving their "purpose" to move forward in their lives. And as well; the student learns the discipline to selectively "dare" and to purposely select a dare that opts for self-challenge, personal high-achievement an adventure, or even a harmless satisfying pleasure!

One must learn to Dare selectively with a purpose and no fear; and with the absolute passion and determination "to-do!" Consequently; to "not dare is to not Live!" This subjects one to stagnate in their "boxed-in" thoughts of fear and failure, and never climbing out of that box to take that daring-Step to-go-forward! But; one must "dare wisely" to live *The Life* and be able to select from its options of many adventurous dares! I emphasize that because in not daring wisely, it becomes clear that you haven't yet outgrown your 4th**Cycle**, and there's a lot of work yet for **YOU** to do in your study of "Self-Evaluation!" One must "reflect" on the selective Dares that we had taken in our 2nd and 3rd**Cycles**, and actually feel that same sensation to achieve and conquer! Upon these reflections, one must consider and acknowledge that we were children then and we were innocent! In our ignorance, "we were protected" and with any "wrong dare" that we took we would be comforted, scolded or rescued by Mom, Dad, or whoever else cared for us. This new selective dare option that one may attempt during the 5th**Cycle** is different, and it comes with "self-responsibility;" which is absent in a child's dare. Now that we have grown and understand its importance and value, we will be inclined to act responsibly and this is when that old-time "childish fear" dissipates by the very act of our taking up the challenge.

Monk and Anita's dance fascinated me; it had all the elements of *Dare, Challenge,* and the *Act of Doing.* Their sudden "Action" was not a performance, but rather a spontaneous urge or impulse to display their desire to "simply dance!" Both of them, prompted by "environment" and the haunting musical sounds that teased their ears, tempting and beckoning them to demonstrate the *Acts* of *Challenge* and *Dare.* We all were fascinated watching Anita and Monk; they captured our eyes moving over their bodies and it was like seeing them dance together for the first time - which was not the case - as on numerous occasions they had danced together. But somehow, this time their dance was different; it was "Afro-Flamenco," an original form of their own.

While I was watching, I thought of the Workshop's concept and design; thinking and reflecting back on the orientation class given to the students in the month of June. Also, I thought of the maintenance on the big gray truck; a three-year old child, and the courageous plan to begin August 1st! I was in grateful prayer, that "all of this had come together and was actually happening!" Sitting there in my contented reverie and joy watching the dance duet; I also began thinking and recalling the past five-days, and of three noticeable incidents that had occurred pertaining to the planned Workshop's concept that were already taking effect. They were: The group's (especially the drummers) honorable gesture and on-going consciousness of respect given to Pacheco and his Mom to let them disembark first at every needed stop. Glenn's subtle and maybe, unconscious choice to take responsibility to stay behind and protect the truck and our valuables while the rest of the group went to the Gypsy camp. And finally, Monk and Anita, working together as a duet, demonstrating personal challenges and dare! Unknowingly, they were inspiring me at that moment to suggest to them a "Workshop Project" to do jointly. I would ask them to create a duet-choreography based upon the original theme that they had created tonight!" The inspired suggestion was made; and yes, they did just that! My eyes remained fixed on their Afro-Flamenco dance of *Challenge and Dare. Challenge, Responsibility,* and *Respect* - which are key components of the dance Workshop - got me thinking, and I believed, that the planned Workshop's effects were already happening, and we hadn't even started a class yet! I could feel a smile beginning and my humble thoughts were of modest pride and satisfaction at what my eyes were seeing unfold right in front of me. And it was soon within that precious moment that a whisper of confirmation quietly laid upon me, confirming that "Yes, I was doing my job well, to the best of my ability, and serving my "purpose"!

The Workshop's curriculum and agenda for seven-days a week was one of rigid physical and mental disciplines and was as follows:

Daily Schedule

6:00 a.m. - 2 hour class of Meditation and Hatha Yoga.
8:00 a.m. - 3 hour Afro-Jazz dance class.
11:00 a.m. - 2 hour Lunch Break

Students take note: On Mondays and Fridays, we will be "fasting from foods" from Sunrise to Sunset.

1:00 p.m. - 2-hour period of "Silence" for reading and introspection.
3:00 p.m. - 4-hour recreational break of choice.
7:00 p.m. - 30-minute session of Hatha Yoga.
7:30 to 9:00 p.m. - Workshop Projects: Created and Worked-on.

Periods of a half-hour and one-hour will be allotted to those requesting specific rehearsal days and time needed to work on the project of their choice, within the elements and concept of the Workshop.

After their dance, Anita again joined Anemieke, Sabina and Austin; and Monk sat himself on a large rock next to Winky, Sandra, Hella, Rano and Pacheco, and shortly after his sit, saying that "he was exhausted, and was leaving to go back to the truck"! Raising his lanky body from the rock to stand tall and once again become the focal point of our attention before his grand exit. "Oui!" ("Yes!) I need to tzink aan clear good my head now! I am tired, mon!"; He then added with a raised voice and signifying Glenn; "Aan also mon, I am going to tzcheck-up on tzhaat dirtee naasty boy aan gurl tzhaat eez in tzhaat truck doo-een 'nice tzings' mon!.. "Oooh La La!" My dear boyz aan gurls, I know!. A good life is with a little 'hanky panky', Oui?" he said jokingly and flashed a quick wink to Anita. He masked his nose and mouth with his neck scarf and fluttered his big saucer-like eyes saying, "Oh, you know Ilanga; Meester Naivite, he tzinks tzaat boy aan gurl is deescussing ze Arts and God!" he said with his "flair" and statuesque-pose, simply to making us all laugh again! He and Winky left together, holding one another's hand as if they were lovers going on a stroll into the dark; maybe they were, I never asked them I guess, because I didn't need to know! And as well, it is so common to see two males walking the streets holding hands or with an arm slung around the shoulder of another! Not because they are lovers, but because they are dear friends. This sign of friendship is a cultural value, and is seen in various countries such as Europe, Africa, South America, Asia, and around the globe; but it is not a usual sight to see in America, outside of the Gay communities. Winky said, "Ciao!" from a short distance as they were walking away. Monk turned his head around to us saying "Au-Revoir," and letting go of Winky's hand to saunter gracefully alone, and with obvious self-adoration, Winky followed him.

The eleven of us that remained at the campsite continued dancing, eating and enjoying our new Gypsy friends for the next couple of hours, completely ignoring the language barrier until it was time to leave. When we arrived at the big grey truck, it was still there and quiet. The two couples were separately huddled together in their own peace and pretending to be asleep; but from inside the back of the truck with its large tailgate doors wide-open. It was impossible to not hear our many voices or faintly see our group approaching in the darkness. We didn't even pretend to be quiet and we woke them from their pretend sleep with chatter, laughter and noise to tell them about our adventures.

At Sunrise the next morning, we departed for the border of Greece and arrived into the noisy bustling city of Athens by mid-afternoon. The big gray truck we parked in the square of Monistaraki Platia and I quickly ran to the Taverna nearby to find Yiorgos! I wanted to let him know that we had arrived and that I would be returning to the Taverna within twenty-minutes, with a group of fifteen starving dancers, musicians, and a child! I wanted him to meet the members of Kreos Dance Theater. I had mentioned him often to Terry and Shawn during our front-seat conversations, and I wanted them to meet him! I had not seen Yiorgos for three years and I had grown older and he had grown taller. He was no longer the slim, young boy waiter! His body was now larger, and as strong and as confident as his deep sounding, manly voice. His two years of military duty had done that to him; and now, in his 4ᵗʰ**Cycle** he had shed his gentle teenage boyish-look, and his appearance was that of a strong, healthy, intelligent young man of twenty-eight years old approaching his 5ᵗʰ**Cycle**. Our embrace was long; and I could "feel" within our tight squeeze, that he had also missed me! It was a feeling that our absence from one another never existed, and as if we had never been separated, "ever"! And therefore, we held our embrace even longer. He whispered a couple of times within our tight fold, "Ti Kanis, Adelphosmou, Ti Kanis?" ("How are you, my Brother; How are you?") He could see and feel that I was fine, I did not have to answer him. I just took a step-back and looked at him, saying, "So, Yiorgos, We're only here in Athens for a couple of hours! We only have time to eat and for you to meet everybody, and then, where we are going in Greece, I don't know yet, so, I am hoping that you can help me with that! You had said on the phone a few weeks ago, and after our conversation, 'that you would try your best'! Do you remember that?" It was during our correspondence and the last telephone call to him that I had mentioned the pending Workshop and the quiet, isolated environ- ment it would need for it operate as planned for a month's time. And also that it would need a beach location, a beautiful nature setting and not too far away from a small city or town that would be accessible to our needs of health care and provisions and supplies for camping and outdoor living. I had mentioned to him that we would need candles, matches, flashlights, fine, thin netting to sleep under, mosquito spray, sunscreen, and anything else needed to survive outdoors day and night!" He, recalling the last phone call, said "Yes; I think that I have a place for you on the Peloponnese Coast of Greece! We will talk about it when you return here with everybody to eat!" In jest; my quick comment to him was, "And not too much food Yiorgos! Don't forget, we're dancers! And anyway; we've only got a couple of hours to eat before we leave to wherever it is we're going!" His laugh was small, but tagged with a cynical remark of disbelief in my words, "Oh, come on Ilanga! You dancers eat very much food, and fast! I have seen this my friend, and I know this!" he said. I just looked at him, laughed hard, and then quickly ran off to Monistaraki Platia.

All the dancers, musicians and Pacheco were ready to go when I arrived at the big gray truck. We immediately headed back to the Taverna and I introduced them all to Yiorgos, who stood there astonished, fascinated and amazed at what he saw standing there greeting him respectfully with excitement and with hunger. "Poh, Poh, Poh, Poh!", I heard him murmur to himself, and many times thereafter, as he ran back and forth to the kitchen, serving our table, and we all reveled in our gluttony while feasting on the delicious foods of Greece. Before I took my seat, I went inside the Taverna's kitchen to greet, hug and share myself with Yiorgos' Mom and Dad; spending a few minutes with them, talking small-talk, and meanwhile watching Yiorgos swiftly pass by me with three small plates lined-up along one arm, and the fourth plate grasped by the fingers of his hand, while carrying two other small plates in his opposite hand! This he repeated as he ran back-and-forth from the kitchen to the table outside, performing his show-like skills and moving with swift and methodic motion. My absence from the group was less than ten-minutes, and I returned to sit and speak with Yiorgos about the travel itinerary to the Peloponnese Coast, as soon as he had finished serving.

He, Terry, Shawn and I, sat at a smaller table adjacent to the long table that was seating our loud and talkative, noisy laughing group who were feverishly chewing on their Greek salads, the Mousaka, tzatziki, and lamb. The four of us heard repeatedly from their fully stuffed mouths, muffled sounds of satisfaction from any bite of food taken from the many plates of food laid on the table in front of them! "We are here in Athens, and down here, is Kalamata!" Yiorgos said to Shawn, Terry and I, and pointing his finger to a place on the map of Greece spread in front of us on the table. "Here, in this area of the coast, I believe is where you want to be Ilanga; because many regions are isolated. What you guys must do is travel from this nice beach town of Kalamata, where many Greek tourists go," he said, and pointing on the map its location; "Keep driving north along the coastal road, because I am sure that you don't want to stay in Kalamata, once you guys have seen it for what it is! Keep traveling up this way," he said, using his pointed finger to trace the route; "See here, along this main road you will pass many villages and towns like Kaparissia, and Pyrgos, up towards the city of Olympia. I am sure that you will find something you like up here in this region." Yiorgos said this without doubt, knowing well the specifics of my needs.

The enjoyable feast at the long table had come to an end. The big smiles, the happy chatter and burps of satisfaction signaled to Shawn, Terry and I, that it was time to leave Athens and begin our drive to Kalamata, and then head north on the peninsula of the Peloponnese region of Greece. The formal and respectful Greek word "Yassus!" ("Goodbye!") was said many times to Yiorgos as he was standing amidst the large group of eaters that he was exchanging small chatter with, and accepting the long string of complimentary words about his foods and service.

"I will call you and let you know where and when we are settled," I said to him, as his eyes were scanning the beautiful bunch of dancers and musicians, and admiring Pacheco. "Poh, Poh, Poh, Ilanga, he said, and added "Kreos Dance Theater, look at them!" I did, and scanned the group with my eyes and had to say what I saw; "Yes, they are beautiful and funky, aren't they!" I stated this as a matter of fact and continued my scan, assuming that he knew this

American/ English word! "Funky?" he questioned, with a twisted expression on his face; "What is that?" I hesitated with my reply, and thinking I had made a mistake using that word, became a bit pissed-off at myself for saying it, knowing only too well that his ears were perceptive and always listening carefully to every single word, its sound, and definition! For Yiorgos, there is a "long story" to be said for every new word that he hears; and this was not the time for a "Story"! "Oh Yiorgos…funky… I'll just say right now without a long story, that it is a word of slang usage, and that it means (I hesitated), "a mixture of good and bad things, beautiful and ugly, and often stripped of the glamour our eyes are used to seeing! And seeing a funky-thing, an image, or maybe even hearing a sound, can all be of "funk"! That's all I can say right now because of our limited-time; but, I'll just add that being funky, is living and being a mixture of this pure, raw and natural expression of good and bad, Yiorgos! This is what you see standing there in front of us," I said and continued with, "And we have to go, now! So, if you want to hear more about the slang-words "funk" and "funky", you'll have to wait until we return here to Athens, before going back to Amsterdam! But, knowing you, always thirsty for a clear definition; you're going to run home later, open your thick American-English dictionary, and be very disappointed, my brother! You won't like what you see, because, my definition and its definition is as different as night and day!" I said, and in my hurry to leave. Yiorgos said, "Yes, yes, I will do that" as we embraced each other. He then hugged Terry and Shawn with a tight squeeze of genuine friendship. She stepped back, still holding his arms and eyeing him with her Irish-blue eyes, saying, "I am so happy to meet you, honestly! Driving down here in the truck, Ilanga spoke so much about you, and told us to expect to meet a unique young man! And, yes, he was right dammit! You're a very special guy, I'll say!" Shawn exposed her natural humor by dramatically adding, "And, We'll back here to see *you* in a few weeks, because we really haven't finished eating yet!" Her comical remark brought us much laughter and big goodbyes from all. Yiorgos watched the tribe of "funky people" leaving him behind as we walked and danced away. He was standing there; and from our short distance, I could see him shaking his head side to side. And I am sure that without a doubt, he was repeating to himself many times, "Poh, Poh, Poh, that Ilanga!" Poh, Poh, Poh, Poh!" It was if I could hear his sound floating and winding through the air, and finding me beneath the Acropolis, saying "Yasou!" ("Goodbye!") to an old friend. The "funky" tribe made one last quick stop at the Flea Market for Greek trinkets and cultural scarves before arriving at Monistaraki Platia and the big gray truck.

We drove along through the Peloponnese on the coastal road north from Kalamata, passing small inland villages and catching the breathtaking views of the Ionian Sea whenever we'd arrive at a coastal seashore scouting for a workshop space. Terry, the driver and "Scoutmaster" would stop the big gray truck for a needed piss-stop, the tailgate doors would swing open and the back space would empty the funky tribe. The drummers first, Pacheco and Mom, and then the un-showered stinky dancers would follow, emerging with leaps and bounds from the tailgate to the pavement, with their bodies hot and sweaty and all breathing heavy, as if they had just finished an exhilarating dance class!

Terry, our driving Scoutmaster slowly drove into a small town called, "Kiaffa"; A small depot stop for railway trains that serviced the Peloponnese Peninsula and stopped here twice a day to service the small community of residents who worked or served the depot in some way. Not far away from the depot-station was a large, Orthodox Greek religious structure. This was a well-known Hot Springs facility that attracted mostly elderly Greek tourists who arrived at the depot specifically for this attraction. It was operated and managed by the church Clergy of that building, offering Hot Springs health care to the young and elderly in need of such treatment. A busy, carless community with only a few shops catered to the sparse foot traffic, and the town only "bustled" with activity when a trained pulled into the depot, arriving at 10:00 a.m. on its route to the city of Olympia, and on its 8:00 p.m. return trip to Athens.

Kiaffa, is where we decided the workshop would be held. It was an ideal location with a beach shoreline that met an area of woods, thinned with small trees and brush; an isolated area suitable for pitching tents, camping and sleeping; and also, for individual privacy when needed. But the most important feature Kiaffa offered for the Workshop was a large clearing surrounded by huge trees of Pine that trimmed and surrounded this space of flat land very suitable for the yoga and dance classes to be held. Shawn, Terry and I were astonished and shocked at this spectacular sight before our eyes! "Oh, this is perfect, Ilanga! What a 'dynamite' space!" Terry said. He quickly left Shawn and I and darted away to dance in the wide-open space of the clearing with his arms raised high above his head and opened wide in gratitude to the beautiful Nature spot that surrounded him! He leaped and danced in circles. Shawn and I, in agreement with Terry's joy, hugged each other and said to one another repetitively; "This is it! This is it!" The three of us were overjoyed with our find and were excited to get back to the group and to share the good news of our discovery. It wasn't long before we unpacked the big gray truck, established a central campsite for group cooking, campfire talks, and the settling of individual camping spaces for privacy. The closest small town nearby was "Pyrgos" where we would go and do our "needed" weekend Saturday night "Disco-Dancing"! We had discovered a small cubicle of a discotheque there, after our second weekend in Kiaffa. The DJ's music on his cassette-loop was that of the American "Top 40-Hits" and that suited us fine. So, we danced! It was a necessary "outlet" for all of us to break away from the tedious daily academic routine and to "blow-out-steam" from any harbored frustrations, grievances or group tension that might have occurred throughout the week. We would leave the small cubicle, drenched in sweat, happy on high energy, and always feeling relieved of "Something"! The twenty-minute ride back to Kiaffa in the big gray truck, was always filled with genuine, harmonious laughter, jokes, and memorable stories of the hard dancing night in Pyrgos.

The largest city nearby, was "Olympia." One night, during our last week of the Workshop; Kreos Dance Theater was invited to Olympia to do an outdoor evening performance among hundreds of spectators! The performance was brilliant and perfectly displayed the outcome and results of the dancer's and the musician's month of hard work! They executed beautifully and combined the sparkling elements and expressions of *Body, Mind, and Spirit*, and naturally shared their new knowledge and goal of "High Achievement" to an audience eager to learn something new and different.

This is the essence and "purpose" of the *Afro-Jazz Dance Workshop*. Although some of the students had personal projects that included journal writing, poetry, photography, and such; the performance in Olympia was to be one of dance, action and energy."

I had instructed that each student was to deliver their personal project within the aspect of visual performance to work harder, and try to transform their project into a "visual realization" to the best of their ability. That night, every member of the Company could "feel and believe" their individuality and their unique artistic value! And, as an energized and positive "collective-unit" and through their personal and group efforts, they had attained a very high achievement. This feeling and realization is an inspiration to reach even-higher; and this is when one experiences and ultimately "comprehends" "exaltation"!

We were invited there to the city of Olympia by the Mayor, who had come to Kiaffa for the Hot Springs, and had heard about the "unusual" activity happening there in the community with a group of foreign artists "dancing on the beach" every day for the past three weeks! He decided to investigate what was going on down by the seashore in Kiaffa (not that he had heard anything negative about the foreigners, he was just, "curious"). He and the head of Clergy from the Hot Spring's facility came down to our campsite one morning during the time of our dance class to witness the unusual activity and was quite surprised at what they were seeing: Order, discipline, respect, education, harmony, music, joy, dance, and Pacheco, who caught their eye with his participation in the dance and his three-year old knowledge, attempts, and interpretation of afro-jazz! And to my surprise, the two gentlemen who spoke English very well were quite impressed by what they had seen that morning, and also by the Workshop's routine and daily schedule that I had shown to them after the class.

"You must come to Olympia!" said the Mayor; "You must come and perform your dance and theater in the big square of the city!

The children and the people of Olympia will enjoy to see this! Please come Saturday night!" I will tell the people!" The black-robed Clergyman then said, "Yes! And you must bring your dancers here, to the Hot Springs to bathe and relax! It will be good for their bodies! I invite you all to come; and bring the little boy, he too can see the Greek Hot Springs!" I accepted the invitation to both of these offers. Shawn, Terry and I watched them leave, all waving goodbye. We were happily excited, and the three of us began a quick run to tell the others. "A performance and hot springs too!" said Shawn, "You can't beat that, dammit!" She always used that word "Dammit" in a delightful, positive way.

Terry, Shawn and I had assessed and decided that the month-long Workshop had been a great success. We discussed all this in the front seat of the big, gray truck that had served us well, without fail, throughout the month and was now rumbling its way through the Peloponnese region on the coastal road heading South to the beach resort town of Kalamata. After leaving Kiaffa, we returned to Athens to the Taverna and gave Yiorgos all the details of the Workshop's specifics, its location, the Hot Springs, the performance in Olympia and the hilarious, fun stories we had about our time there. We stayed at the Taverna talking, laughing and eating; long enough to relax from the truck's bumpy ride of our early morning travel, and time enough to fill our hungry stomachs with delicious foods before we had to depart for our three-day journey to Amsterdam.

Thinking of another departure from Yiorgos was stirring slight emotion (but not as much as I had anticipated); and profound thoughts of a return to Greece for the third time, one day soon in *The Life.* I strongly felt that there was still "something else" there for me to discover and to do. I entertained these thoughts as I sat in the truck's front seat, saying not a word to Terry and Shawn. My eyes were watching from the window at Yiorgos standing there in Monistaraki Platia, once again waving his goodbye from beneath the Acropolis.

CHAPTER ELEVEN

New Yorkers had given birth to Pride Week. Let's go...why not?!

During the month of July in 1980, I had arrived at the age of forty (appearing to be only about thirty); and by choice; unmarried, partner-less, companion-less, and child-less. The reason was simply because there was no cause to; I had zero interest, need or desire for this and saw no purpose in engaging myself in such complexing "traps." The absence of love was not the issue; I had abundant love from family and friends. There was only one significant romantic relationship that had almost "trapped" me during the first years of my 4th Cycle. The tradition of marriage never happened, and yet, still today, we have maintained a "loving friendship" and bond that continues to be a joy to me. Also, by this time in my adventurous and curious life, I "felt" and "knew" that I was stable and balanced, emotionally, physically and spiritually; and was experiencing an "alignment" within myself, and maybe with the Universe itself! I was satisfied with the decisions I had made, with my personal self, my professional career, and where I had taken myself thus far in *The Life*; I had evaluated that it was not because of my Ego's greed that I wanted "more," but because of the knowledge that I had gained that there is *More* and also there is a *Something-Else* and a *Someplace-else* to aspire to! If one has the truth and knowledge of their personal worth and value, then they have *Self-Discovered*." One must self-evaluate themselves and their purpose for being. He or she must become self-secure, positive, confident assertive, and diplomatic, leaving no "burning bridges" behind! And in time when this person "becomes who they are meant to be," they will be discovered by someone else.

I had been in Amsterdam five-years now, and well into my **6ᵗʰCycle** at this point of measure, or footsteps on the path of life's journey to become "who I am" and "what I am." And now that I was approaching my **7ᵗʰCycle** (43 to 49 years of age), all of that was being considered, evaluated, and analyzed. And I was still as yet "undefined," "unlabeled," and "unanswerable." I had learned the Dutch language, the country and its flat, watery landscape, its people and the ambiguous channels of their thoughts. The goals and the "purpose" of being in Amsterdam had been achieved, and the originality of my afro-jazz dance technique had become more established within myself and its application. My "determination" was for the continuance of dance classes, and the Workshop in Kiaffa-Greece had solidified that for me.

The "apex" of the **6ᵗʰCycle** - and as well, it being the apex of this one lifetime or the apex of a Cycle of "another" divine Incarnation - is to "assess"! By this time of living **The Life** daily, with all of its ups and downs, failures and successes, there comes the inevitable moment of "thought" that suddenly comes to play in the mind of one during their **7ᵗʰ** and **8ᵗʰCycles**, and that is; "I've been around for quite a while, now; I'm still here but for how long?" These are some of the insightful thoughts and recall of the efforts and all of the achievements accrued during the past **5ᵗʰ** and **6ᵗʰCycles**. How fortunate we are to still be here, and again, to have the given opportunity to evaluate these two **Cycles** of dire importance. The first opportunity is to thoroughly evaluate the significant "happenings" that occurred personally and also externally during the **5ᵗʰCycle**. And the second, is to simply analyze what is happening now in the present period of the **6ᵗʰCycle**", regarding the self-imposed conditions, or those of circumstance; Including and evaluating "family members (whom are most important to you), the significant relationship, (if there is one), friendships, associates, environment, and productivity".

Fortunately, the **7ᵗʰCycle** is the "try-again Cycle". A dream was being worked-on, and for whatever reasons, it didn't manifest into the expected realization! All the eggs of effort, passion time and dedication "went into one basket" and it just didn't happen! It is during this try-again cycle that it is most likely to be the last opportunity and attempt to *Establish, Succeed, and Realize* the dream that was deferred, or an opportunity to dream another dream.

My mother always said: "Don't cry over spilled milk!" when a dream attempt was made and for whatever reasons it just didn't happen. She'd wisely use this old cliché along with the remedy she prescribed which was to just "get over it"! The acceptance of this fate is crucial, because the **8ᵗʰCycle** (50 to 56), "dovetails" with the 7ᵗʰ during the similarities of "finality" and the "last" attempt to capture that dream and succeed! Consequently; these two Cycles are "Jointed" and could be the most critical fourteen years of your lifespan to be scrutinized! And why is that? Because you already have accumulated a half-century of experiences, both good, bad, and whatever. The *Mind, Body, and Spirit* have been tirelessly "working-on-the-dream" and now, suddenly, a new "something else" is beginning to happen and it just mushroomed out of nowhere! This new something else is health care. The issue of health care starts to become a major priority around this age and from this point on going forward in *The Life*, a constant focus of attention is warranted.

"Health care" is a popular word used these days and is synonymous with aging; a wonderful life process and opportunity for the living human being to understand and comprehend. Aging should be accepted and embraced! Embrace it now my young people; because if you don't, the wrenching thought of your endless deterioration from this point on going forward will destroy you and cause you unnecessary anxiety and stress, and eventually, health care becomes even more of a requirement. "Aging" is an inborn energy and force of nature that measures a living existence, and has an eventual "visible" outcome. Its undeniable process begins on the day you are born and lays dormant and disguised by youth; and a "year-at-a-time" birthday party acknowledges and joyously celebrates that you are a year-older! The essential ongoing activities that shape and constitute the life to be lived, such as family, school, personal interests, career, relationships, become the primary focus of our days; meanwhile, the aging process within the physical body continues. Quite a bit of life has been lived before you arrive at your 7th and 8thCycles. This time of surprise is when the dormant energy of aging is sparked to finally come into the light! The day comes when suddenly you will recognize its long-processed outcome in the mirror! Suddenly you will see that there's a newly indented facial-line here, and a new line there! A new mark, spot, mole, or crack, appears somewhere on your body where none was before! "What is that?" is always the first question asked! Thereafter; you cease to ask that question, because the facial-line, the mark, the spot, the mole and/or the crack, has not gone away! It has not vanished from sight! It has remained there, to be seen daily; an indelible mark, blatantly obvious on your body until the day you die! Once more, an "acceptance" must be embraced. To some of us, this is a "shocking realization," and a "mind-blower" that the bloom of youth has left us, maturity has flourished, and now, it is the time to become and physically show that you are a bit older than you were yesterday! And yet, to some others, they see or envision aging differently. The image they see in the mirror on that revealing day is of course just as shocking, but fortunately it is buffered by their "intelligence" to assess this "new-thing" on the body; and very quickly, they arrive at an "acceptance of the aging process" and begin to "radiate from within." This new, undiscovered beauty and the personal values that come along with this "new gift" is called: "The Coming of Age"! At the conclusion of the **6thCycle** one must be prepared and ready for this life changing "face-to-face" realization that appears before us in the mirror during the "awakening" years of the **7th** and **8thCycles**.

After five years of my consistent, productive work, sincere friendships made, and the cultural and personal development that I was experiencing in Amsterdam, I could feel "Intuitively" my time there had come to an end, (even though I could still envision my continued success there). But I also knew that to remain there was not the thing for me to do. The process of *Self-Evaluation* began to take its natural motion in my daily thoughts; and within two to three months of time, continuing with the hard work of meditation and discernment, "I began to feel and understand, the turning point" of the **7thCycle** beginning to disrupt and interfere with any new plan or projected project that I had an interest to get into and work with, except for one! I had decided to adhere to the turning-point and concluded with the thought that this project was the one that would liberate me from the environment, compensate me with financial gain so that I would be comfortably able to proceed forward with my dance-works-in-progress.

It was on a very cold Winter's day in Amsterdam at Benjamin's Jazz Dance Center's "Koffie Bar," bustling with Cappuccinos and hot drinks and it was time for my 4:00 p.m. afro-jazz class to begin. "Let's go guys; Drink up! Class time!" I said, and went into the dance studio to give Glenito and Glenn instructions for the class plan, light a candle, and prepare myself for the half-hour Yoga session that began the two-hour class. After the session of Hatha Yoga and brief Meditation, the percussive sound of the drums would heighten and set a rhythmic-groove, and this would begin the dance section of the class. A wide-paneled glass window framed one side of the studio walls which faced the interior of the administrative office and was an area for spectators to view an on-going class. Just about the last half hour before the class ended, an elegant, handsome couple and Benjamin were standing at the window observing my class and they caught my eye as I was walking past the window to instruct the drummers that I needed to hear a rhythm change. The dance exercise required a slow-tempo, pulsating beat for a dance movement that gestured and suggested an "offering." The students offered up themselves completely in their dance to "whomever" or "whatever" they cared to make an offering to. They were brilliant in this exercise, and they danced hard in this section of the rhythm change that signaled the dancers to escalate their movement and passion to celebrate themselves and their offering. The student's respectful applause ended the class; and they left, leaving the drummers and I to compliment one another's work with cries of "Bravo!" I became aware of the percussionist, Punt's arrival. "Welcome my brotha! I didn't know that you were here; but I did hear "something special" in the rhythms," I said, embracing him warmly. I liked Punt; his presence and talent always added something special. Again, my eyes randomly noticed Benjamin and the couple still standing there at the window observing the class that just ended. Benjamin gestured to me with his hand to come out! "This is my friend Karel, and his wife; and they'd like to speak with you! "Goedenavond Meneer!" ("Good Evening, Sir!"), the gentleman said eloquently, extending his hand for a formal handshake. "Your dancing is very nice!" he said in well-spoken English. "It is very special, I can see it is a unique style! Benjamin told me that it's not 'Jazz-Ballet' and now I can see that! This is African, and what Benjamin teaches, I know is 'Jazz'! It's like a mix, a 'cocktail' you know what I mean?" And the metaphor he used of a "cocktail" like that of a "dance-fusion" I liked very much. It hinted to me that he was observant, has a mind capable of expansion that was able to grasp something "new"! He was the type of man who discovers an interest, thinks about it and from whence it came, sees its worth or value, and then crystalizes it for himself so he can satisfactorily understand it for what it actually is! I had met only a few Dutchmen of this caliber during my time in The Netherlands. "Yes!" I said, "I know what you mean!"

"Let's go into the office; we can talk there!" Benjamin said; as I followed the three of them to his large office. Karel and his wife were both dressed in glamorous full-length fur coats; and she with a hand-muff and fur hat to match, that crowned her head of long blonde hair. Her facial beauty was striking; it had to be noticed. Her eyes were warm brown and clever, and they would sparkle whenever she smiled. Her skin was silky white and smooth; like that of a European porcelain doll. He was tall, broad-shouldered and hatless with dark brown hair; handsome and impeccably well-groomed. They were both highly polished and represented perfectly an international fashion statement of classic high-end elegance and grace.

"Karel and I have been friends since high-school!" Benjamin said abruptly as we had seated ourselves for a discussion; "And I wanted him to meet you. He has an interesting project that he discussed with me earlier this week; but I haven't the time, the skills, or the interest to do it," he said with reluctance and continued; "So, I told him to come by the studio to watch your class and see the work you do, talk with you, and you know, maybe you would like to work the project!" Benjamin paused, making an eye gesture to Karel for him to take over. Karel quickly did after a pause, and then to me; "Yes, yes," he said, speaking English mixed with a Dutch word when the correct word in English wasn't available to him. "I am opening a new elegant theater op (on) the Leidserplein this coming Fall!" (The Leidserplein is an infamous city square/plaza in Amsterdam with numerous outdoor terraced cafes, bars, restaurants and the all-day-and-night congregation of hundreds of people at a crossroads junction of Trams (cabled Trolleys Cars). It was the city's traditional, established location for "busy and un-busy" people to meet, greet, drink and eat, and to observe, converse and/or to gossip about "who is there and who is not."

"My wife and I see you daar op (there at) the Leidserplein many times having coffee with friends, but I don't know then, daat you were working with my friend Benjamin! "Daat, is Te gek!" ("That is strange!"), he said, meaning that it was uncanny. "Daat is echt niet te geloven!" ("That is really unbelievable!") Karel said to himself, more than he was saying to the three of us sitting there. "A small world we live in, "Echt vaar! ("The truth is!"), he said convinced, and then continued further with his thoughts, saying; "I am looking for a Choreographer. And I don't want a German, French or Dutch Choreographer, unless it was Benjamin; because he is like "Americaans!" you know?" Karel turned his look to Benjamin and said blatantly, "You are Dutch, but you dance like Americaans-style, you know!" We all got a good laugh out of his dance-like body gestures and insightful humor as he turned to me again and continued talking. "Maar!" ("But!") "But, look what Benjamin has here, maan. He is too busy to do anything else but this! So, I understand why he cannot work with me. A pity, that is; it is good when friends can work together; it makes the business strong, maan!"

I could see that Karel had taken a liking to me, relaxed himself, and had more to say. "But, now I come here and see you, and I like your dance-style also," he said and kept staring at me. "Benjamin tells me daat you are Americaans, but you don't look Americaans; You are looking like... Egypt, or Morocaans! But I see now that we talk and I see your style; Yah-Vel! (Yes!), you are Americaans!" He was very cordial, and there was an honesty he exuded that I recognized quickly, and he always looked me straight in the eye as he spoke! This constant eye to eye contact was as if it were a magnetic force bonding us together in trust somehow and it had sealed a mutual understanding of honesty.

"Kompt, nieu!" ("Come, now!"), he said; "We will go to eat dinner, and we can talk more at the restaurant!" His wife, who had not much to say, agreed with a tilt of her head and her beautiful smile. "Oh no, not me!" quipped Benjamin; "I got a class at 7:00, and much work to do after that!" I accepted the invitation, and added; "Tell me where the restaurant is and I can join you there in an hour. I can't leave immediately now because I have things to do before I leave here tonight!" Karel interrupted me;... "Oh, no maan! The restaurant is very far away at the beach, in Zandvoort. We will come back here for you in one hour! "Daat is echt hein problem voor onze, maan!" ("Really! That is not a problem for us, man!"), he said. We agreed to that arrangement with a strong hand shake and all smiles, and they bid a friendly farewell to Benjamin. I, still wrapped in a scarf and dressed in dance-gear and leading the glamorous couple from the office to the main exit-door of the studio, humored myself with thoughts of being "The Royal Court Jester followed by the full-length fur-coated King and Queen, in promenade to somewhere magical!" Passing through the studio's "Koffie-Bar" that they admired greatly, I heard them say "Bravo!" to Benjamin for the chic and creative ambiance that he had created there. A few dancers waiting for the 7:00 p.m. class to start were gathered, chatting and laughing together along with the photographer "Mano" who waved a big hello to me as we passed them before the three of us arrived to the main door.

"O.k.; Tot straaks!" ("See you later!") Karel said, as I watched them both hurry in the cold to their luxurious black Citroen sedan parked in front of the studio. "Yes, later!" I hollered to them and shut the door quickly against the cold wind that lashed at me. I returned to Benjamin who was sitting in his office waiting for my return. "Nice guy!" I said to him. "But, he could be a little crazy, maybe; I mean, who goes to a beach on a winter day like this, Benjamin? It's freezing cold out there!" I complained. "Yea, that's Karel," Benjamin said with his head buried in paperwork. "I don't know if he's crazy or not, but that's Karel! He likes you, I can tell," he said without looking up at me. "He will take you to a very expensive fancy restaurant in Zandzoort, talk your ear off, and maybe, also buy you a long fur coat to stand with him by the shoreline to watch the sea," he said as a joke and laughed hard at what he had just said! However, my thoughts were of total confusion, scrambled thoughts and once again, hearing ambiguous Dutch-thought! It always seemed to my ears; that hearing the words and thoughts of a Dutchmen speaking to me were an endless sound. And within my mind, that one thought, somehow extended itself and multiplied into many. "What are you saying, man? What does 'all that' mean?" I asked demandingly. "Does that mean I'm going to be warm? Does it mean that he's generous? Or, are you insinuating and saying that if I 'walk the gay-plank' that by midnight I may get an after-dinner fur coat or something?" Benjamin fell back in his chair with loud laughter and fists banging his desk. I stood there in front of him becoming annoyed with his unwarranted laughter. "Stop it, man! What's so funny and what the hell are you talking about?" I said, leaning forward on the desk and resting on my knuckles. He noted my escalating annoyance and gradually ceased laughing to say; "No no no, don't go getting upset, Ilanga, I'm making a joke!" Benjamin said, and convincing me that he was, continued; "He's a great guy, really! An unusual man of taste; and he has always been that way since high school! You know, handsome, always well dressed and proud of himself. He was always going somewhere with older guys and girls and being busy doing other things than what the rest of us were doing, like getting together for sports and fun things! Sometimes he'd be doing 'shady' things I guess, sometimes not! I really don't know," Benjamin said, without any judgement of his friend Karel, and getting up from his chair to go to a nearby file cabinet, he continued, "He's made a fortune in the sex business! And I must say, he did it in his unusual way. Not with his handsome looks, his charm, or vibrant personality as a Playboy or Pimp; but, with his brain!" Benjamin pulled his face up from the files quickly and turned to me saying sharply; "He's very smart Ilanga! You're very smart, but also naïve in many ways! He is keen, clever and sharp, with admirable character, and a 'winner' as you can see! I am not warning you of anything; and I'm not saying that Karel is anything like as they would say in New York, a polished 'Sleaze Ball'! This, he is absolutely not! I am only informing you, and advising you that if you do anything with him, do not be careful of him, but of yourself, please. You both are honest and dedicated to the work that each of you do; but your differences are, that he is Dutch, and you are American; and, a Black American at that!" he said firmly, with a quiet tone of respect and returned to his chair. "Well, you have traveled," he added; "You know as well as I, how we dancers and artists can sometimes be used as a 'novelty' and don't even know it, until it's too late!" He started to arrange the paper work scattered on his desk as I thought of the many words he had spoken and our pause was long. My thinking funneled into one conclusive thought; that Benjamin said it all 'in a nut shell' and that Karel was an interesting person with a magnetic personality. "Well, all that I can say Benjamin, is that your friend is an interesting man! He has a good energy that I like; and he's just loaded with ideas, infectious enthusiasm and charm! And maybe this new plush, elegant theater that he wants to open in the Fall is his new 'adventure in the theater business' to make more millions," I said. "Well, at dinner I'll hear what he has to offer about the choreography project and what ever else I need to know. But hey, Benjamin! Right now, we're too busy here to be even thinking about involving myself into anything else! Anyway, a good fancy dinner tonight at a Summer beach-resort on a very cold Winter day, and also to be 'gifted in a long fur coat to keep me warm for the rest of my life', is not bad for tonight's menu, don't you think!" I stated jokingly; "I'll tell you all about it tomorrow; "Ciao!" I said, making my exit from his office. Benjamin raised up from his chair to holler at me, "Wait!" he said in jest; "you know Ilanga, first of all it's not Winter, it's April; cold, but it's still April! And second, I am reminding you that "Almasi" comes in from New York next week! He said that he finished his piece of choreography and wants to set it and begin rehearsing with the dancers as soon as he arrives! We've got a lot of work to pull together in just five-weeks before the concert in May! I just brought 'that' up for you to be thinking about tonight when you're talking with Karel, that's all!" He didn't need to remind me of Almasi's arrival; but the 'We've got a lot of work to do' part of his statement had me chuckling! "Benjamin!" I said, up in-his-face, with a bit of sarcastic humor;

"Well, Almasi's Modern piece is finished, and my Afro-piece is finished; so, we're both cool! Both pieces are ready to be set and rehearsed, but you said yesterday that your piece is not finished. Zo, Meneer! ("So, Sir!) you have a lot of work to do before Almasi comes; in fact, so much more than he and I, if you don't mind my saying so!" Benjamin got my message and laughed guiltily, saying in Dutch, "Godvoordammer!" ("God, dammit!") I know!" He looked flustered and stared at me with a look of finality, and then returned my sarcasm ambiguously in Dutch; "Daag, Ilanga, Smaakelich Eten!" ("Goodbye Ilanga, and have a good dinner!") "Ciao, Meneer!" ("Goodbye, Sir!") I replied as I was leaving his office to go into mine, tossing back and forth our play ball of sarcasm; "And Professor, have a 'wonderful' class!" I hollered out to him, strutting-away like a hurried Peacock and flinging my dangling scarf over one shoulder! He instantly threw the ball back to me, loudly saying, "Careful, Isadora; don't strangle yourself with that thing; or choke yourself at dinner!" His quip was in reference to beloved American dancer, Isadora Duncan, who in 1927, was tragically strangled to death by her own silk scarf! He couldn't see me laughing as I entered my office holding my head high in grand dignity and imagining myself as Monk, my dance student; lamenting the loss, saying "C'est la vie!"

The hour or so of travel to the beach in the small town of Zandvoort was a plush and quiet luxurious Citroen car ride. I sat comfortably in the rear seat listening to selective jazz music playing in a low volume from the car's radio. I was relaxed and thinking what Benjamin had said about it not being Winter! and also thinking of my own constant complaints of Amsterdam's cold, always; even in the Summer as far as I was concerned! Relaxed and in quiet thought, the sudden recall of the "Reading" I had in 1968 with "Jack Miller" - my Roxbury neighborhood's "Spiritual Reader" - quickly flashed in my mind, and he saying then; "I see you in a place far-away somewhere, and you're always cold, man!" That memorable reading had occurred ten years prior by coincidence. I arranged myself more comfortably, sat back and began to analyze and evaluate past incidents that had occurred since then; specifically, the one with Jeanne piercing my right ear, and I deciding to insert a gold-hooped earring in my ear to constantly remind me that "everything" goes in **Cycles!** And also the one of "Thassos" the Taverna owner in London; saying to me, "You must go home to Greece, to understand what I am saying, my old friend!" and I had just met him for the first time that day! Jack Miller spoke the truth; I was "always cold" in Amsterdam and my work had "many children" surrounding me on a daily basis! And also in 1968, Thassos spoke the truth; but his truth didn't unfold to me until fifteen years later! And Benjamin's "Karel really is a nice guy" and "it was the month of April, not Winter!" was prophetic. And even Jeanne's truth as well when she had finished piercing my ear! She sat down in a chair, sat back and looked at the hole plugged with jellied white thread and said admiringly, "Oh God, Ilanga, that's beautiful! And you know what?" she stated as if she were seeing a gold hoop earring there instead of a thread; "And, that's going to be forever!" she said and smiled proudly.

I believe the sudden recall of these unusual experiences are significant to me; and that they are some of the elements of energy that inspire creative ideas for me to think more about **Cycles,** its intrigue, and its "7-year itch" of changes! I deeply internalized these thoughts while listening to the good, mellow music that was emanating from inside the Citroen and I was lured into a time zone of years past.

Eventually, hearing Karel's voice above the sounds of great music in my ears; I realized that he was "consistent" with his talk! From the moment that I got into the car, Karel never stopped talking!" His wife never said a word, and we both were "bombarded" with only "his" words of "his" new theater to open in the Fall; and boasting of the extreme change and impact it would have on Amsterdam's sex-business!" Karel never stopped; his mouth kept sputtering words rapidly as if it were "motorized." "My theater is not the same like others in Amsterdam," he said; "My theater is going to be "Modern and Chic, maan; a new style with high-value entertainment that the international tourist industry is sure to welcome and appreciate!" he boasted proudly; "And my friend, I want to have only beautiful shows in my theater! You know; Like in Paris, Monte Carlo, and Las Vegas, maan!" he said, quickly darting his eyes back-and-forth from the road to the rear-view mirror; "Can you make shows like daat?" he asked, and held his stare in the mirror. Our eyes met; "Well, yes; If you can afford shows like that!" I answered him bluntly! And to assure him, I purposely continued; "And my work is to make the

Producer and the Director happy seeing a packed-house all season, and happy to be making money!" And, if they are making money from my work and from my choreography, then I am too! That's my job! That's the kind of work I do in the theater business for the Producer, Director, and the Audience, making people happy and making money!".

Karel kept his drive steady. There was silence in the front seat as his eyes kept shifting fast from the mirror to the road. I listened to a few bars of music before I said calmly, "As you know quite well Karel, money is power the world over; and for a man or a woman with lots and lots of money, 'life is but a dream'! And I think that, maybe for those who are wealthy and greedy it can also be, or can become, a 'Nightmare'!" His eyes stayed focused in the mirror more than on the road at this time, and I, making an attempt to explain what I had said, kept him swerving the car left and right in its lane. I continued; "The nightmare for those of financial wealth and greed, is that the "power" they have has distorted the 'One World' reality that we live in by creating 'two'! One for themselves and one for those without 'power'!" I said; "And I think, within that weird world of theirs, they create 'another'! "One that is personal, more privileged, and controllable, which their operate and manipulate within their own world, or 'kingdom' that they have now created! And so often (and knowingly) limiting their circle of friends, being 'ultra-selective of where to be seen, and when;' selfishly destroying the values of the family within, purposely, because of a non-agreeable member's opposite opinion; and dismissing him or her 'forever' from this self-created nightmare"! I continued on with my rant, half wondering why I had started on this path at all, but determined now to finish what I had started; "Some, never awaken from this sleep of greed,

Karel; a sleep of *Personal Gain, More Power and Self-Destruction.*"
I could hear myself chattering away, as "motorized" as he had been
earlier, and decided to say no more. I saw his eyes in the mirror
watching me, and deciding that I had finished, fixed his eyes on the
road. But; after a long pause, I decided I wasn't quite finished and so
I continued; "The truth is, Karel, life is but a dream for all of us; the
rich and the poor; but I think that the wealthy dreamer has a moral
responsibility to help the dreams of other dreamers to be realized!
And of course, there are some wealthy people who are aware of their
financial power but are spiritually conscious in their everyday lives
as well; and these special people are different; they are benevolent
with their wealth and position! The "One World" reality that I live
in, these benefactors also live in, because they see the other dreamers.
They see, they listen and they act! They are the builders of dreams;
their own and others. Thank God, for these rare wonderful people
who care, feel, and respond to a cry for recognition from a serious
young artist or entrepreneur who is determined to succeed! And then
we have the other type of wealthy one: "The 'King or Queen' who
lives this living nightmare all day long is not a happy person! If you
know of one, you will recognize and see clearly that the ignorance or
deliberateness is revealed in their cold eyes and there is no honesty
in their smile or laughter! And the only sound you will hear barking
in your ear is the echo of an inflated Ego that has grown and
developed through the years and has 'conquered' and 'taken charge'!
Listen to the demons biting and nibbling on the unhappy Soul of
your friend, associate or leader, and you can clearly hear that he or
she is in denial that there is personal suffering happening every day
within themselves because of this malady of 'conscious greed' that
permeates and feeds their Ego and knows no shame." Karel held his

stare in the rear-view mirror for a couple of seconds to say agreeably, "Yah, Vel!" ("For sure!") he said and paused in thought, and then added; "There is a balance, or a very fine line to walk between your purpose and the greed, maan! You must be careful!" Before his eyes in the mirror could shift from me to the road, I said; "No, Karel, *you* must be careful, not me! I am not the wealthy man, *you* are!" His sudden burst of laughter and apologetic facial expression came to me as a surprise, when he said, "No, no, maan, I don't mean that you are a rich man and for you to be careful! I speak to myself, Karel, when I say 'be careful!' His burst of insightful honest laughter was loud and awakened his wife Carla, who had nodded-off to sleep at some point during the ride. "Ahh, bent we nog niet daar?" ("Aren't we there yet"?), she asked in her sleepy voice. And Karel, still self-analyzing his insightful thoughts of 'walking on the thin-line' of his wealth, and holding balance between greed and purpose, answered her; "Yah-Vel! Op de hoek heir, nast de kerk!" ("Yes! Here around the corner next to the church!"), he said softly, as if he himself had asked the question that she asked. He drove carefully, and slowly pulled into the restaurant's parking lot directly in front of a uniformed Valet who was standing there waiting to park his car. "So, Karel, what is the name of your theater?" I asked. He didn't answer until he shifted his car into park and looked in the rear-view mirror where our eyes met again. He answered with a gentle smile on his face; *The Caresse Theater*! His smile lingered and his eyes were watching mine to see and capture my immediate response to the images and sounds I was imagining, when he said the words, *The Caresse Theater*. I didn't respond or reply; but he wanted to say "something" as the three of us were stepping out of the car and he handed over his car keys to the valet. As we began our walk towards the fancy restaurant with

Carla leading our way; he placed his arm around my shoulders to encourage my reply. "Heil moi naam voor een theater erotieks; Vel?" ("A beautiful name for an erotic theater; Yes?") he stated and asked as we were walking side-by-side. Not giving him a look, I only said, "Yes, yes, it is!" This was my honest reply as we entered the ornate foyer of the fancy Indonesian Cuisine restaurant. Assisted by a petite, wispy young Hostess, Carla and Karel gracefully shed their elegant fur coats, and I disrobed my black peasant- style Mexican Poncho; a woolen relic I had recently purchased for three-dollars at the heavily congested "Waterlooplein", a large flea-market area in the heart of Amsterdam. It was a mecca of worldly objects, furniture, clothing, wares, and wonderful "things" old and new; all to be cheaply purchased or bartered-for, seven days a week!

The dinner table was lavishly spread with tasty and exotic foods from Indonesia, and laid with porcelain dinner plates edged in gold, and ornate Silverware that was shining next to the delicate crystal glassware. Each glass sparkled and dazzled with reflections of light that flickered and bounced from the dancing flames that were burning on the tip of six candles that were standing tall and stately in the grand, elaborate silver candelabra that centered the dinner table. The Maitre D offered frequent tastings of wines and food, and the service by six classic Indonesian males was attentive and proper. They quickly ran back-and-forth with hot dishes, condiments, and a smattering of small bowls filled with various tasting sauces: hot, mild, sweet and bitter. One waiter announced thirty small bowls of sauces for us to select from and tease our palates, and each sauce had a very distinctive taste and a *dare* to try.

"So; what is it that you want me to do in your erotic theater, *The Caresse*?" I asked Karel and Carla as we began to finger and fork our feast of appetizers. "Well; The name that Karel likes, "Caresse" says it all," Carla said; "And the work that you would do has to be about that name, you know; to hold close to you, warmly embrace, and with a good feeling of love! That's what I think," she said, surprising me. It was the first time since we had met earlier at the dance studio, that she had actually engaged in a conversation! She continued; "I like what you said in the car, about how you work in the theater business and make the audience and the Producers happy! That's the kind of quality we want in our theater, heh Karel?" He agreed, dipping a snail into a small bowl of sauce; "Yah-vel, Natuurleik!" ("Yes, of course!"). It was the first time that she had established herself as a partner in the business. She wasn't just a quiet, dumb blonde, or a special girlfriend just "tagging-along;" She was his wife and they were a happily married couple. They had been dating for years before they married two years past. Chewing his last bite of snail and quickly wiping his lips with a silky, red napkin, Karel said: "I want you to choreograph the dances and the shows in my theater; and also to teach the artists who are working there for me how to be professional and love their work! We don't have that style now in Amsterdam!" Not knowing anything at all about the adult sex business there, I asked, "I don't know what you mean by 'style'? And why do you want them to learn to love the work they are doing? They're making good money, they feed their families, spend and buy the things they need and want, just as you and I do! What do you want to change in that, and why?" He replied easily, revealing to me his true nature. "They need to learn how to respect themselves and appreciate what they do, and "show the art of what they do" to a nice respectful audience; and we don't have that kind of theater here! I want to bring that Americaan's style of working here to Amsterdam!.. "Weetje vel?" ("You know what I mean?") Karel said, and after pausing in thought he continued; "Yah Vel!" ("Absolutely!") We have artists who love their work, respect themselves and appreciate their "Cadeau" ("Gift") of beauty from God, but there is no place elegant for them to work! They have to work in strip bars and old houses that have been changed into private show places where they can perform; these are not theaters, maan, they are just whore houses. How can these artists show the quality of themselves and their work?" He was advocating just as I would for the dancers of my own company. "Their work is a profession like any other business, maan! They want quality choreography for their shows, to be professional and be respected like anybody else in any other business; this is "Normaal!" ("Normal!"). So, they leave here and work in Germany Paris, Monte Carlo, America. And also, because the other artists make it difficult for them to work here also, maan!" he said and then with a tone of disgust; "These Amsterdam artists in the sex business here are all drug addicts, maan! They only work for the Heroin. They have no respect for themselves or their work! The work they do can be beautiful, maan, but 'they make it look dirty'! They have no class!" he said; "I don't want these kind of people in my theater because you can't work with them! "Neh; Ik kan niet, noit!" ("No; I can't, never!") he said with profound dignity and adding the question; "Can you work with these artists?" he asked; as if it were a plea! I listened carefully to Karel's words, his advocacy and his "purpose," as he continued; "The shows you will make for my theater will have class and a new style, I know. I saw it tonight in your dance class! You have a classy, sexy style, maan! You know what I mean?" Carla quickly interrupted him with a tone of scold in her voice; "Karel, Benjamin told us not to say that word to him!"

she said, and kept her eyes on him. It appeared to me that they had already had a discussion of the word "Sexy." Shocked at himself for the blunder; he raised his voice saying loudly, "Godvoordommer! Ik voorgeten et vel!" ("God-dammit! I did forget!") He quickly turned to Carla and asked; "Wat zekje daat woort is, Carla?" ("What did you say that word was, Carla?") She eyed him and slowly lowered her eyes. "Sensual!" she said articulately. He quickly turned to me with a look of apology. "Yah-vel! ("Yes!") 'Sensual'! Your dancing is not 'Sexy' it is Sensual, maan!" he said, and continued to explain himself; "Yes it's true, Benjamin said you wouldn't like that word, and Carla said to me; 'Don't tell him that he dances sexy, because that's what the other dancers do in the sex business here! They dance sexy to make money and are able to sell themselves!' And she said that 'she thinks that you won't like that word for your style of dancing.' "Is that true?" he asked with a childlike innocence. I could see on his face that the distinction between the two words "sensual" and "sexy" had him puzzled. "Well," I said; "It is true for her, because her mind and her eyes see the difference between dancing sexy and dancing sensually; but, is it true for me? That I can't answer because I don't think of my dancing as being sexy or sensual. I only think of it as being 'spiritual' I guess, and I just dance! Now; how anyone interprets in their mind, what they are seeing with their eyes, and needs to label, judge or compare is their choice; I just dance!" I said. And wanting to make clear my position and convictions, and as well, the fact that she comprehended the English language so much more than he did, my words to her were direct; "And I will tell you Carla now, before we go any further in this conversation: you will never see me dancing on your erotic or sexy stage, believe me! So I hope that's not what you are thinking, because I have nothing to show or sell of myself! And hopefully, that is very clear to you both!" I said firmly, and lifted my glass to sip some wine as their eyes met mine. Instantly, we locked them into a mutual agreement.

Carla, holding her crystal wine glass with both hands and smiling at me with her eyes that never hid her quiet thoughts, held her stare peering over the rim of her glass. They were quietly telling me "I admire you, and that, Karel is a good man; and I like that you can see and feel that!" is what her eyes were saying to mine. Her smile was intelligent and understanding; His were as well, shifting back and forth eyeing both Carla and I, until his subtle smiled turned into a grin and a chuckle of personal defense to his thought of me dancing on his stage! "Neh, neh! Daat ik denk et vel niet!" ("No, no! That's not what I was thinking!") he said and looked at the scold still held on Carla's face and quickly said, "Yah Vel!" (Well, yes!"), I was thinking that when I saw him dancing," he said apologetically like a child whose wrist just got slapped slightly for telling a small lie"! He chuckled admittingly and then turned to me again. "I said that to Carla; Because it would be nice to see you dancing, maan," he said with a low-tone of disappointment and added, "Maar; (But;) Okay! What you now tell me, I understand and respect you for that; and I say, "Bravo!" You are a maan of truth; I think, now that we talk!" Karel paused briefly, finally resolved; his highs and lows of excitement gone, and said; "Okay! You make only the choreography for the dancers and the show; your sensual-style will be there; and that's what is very important in theater; the Choreographer's style, maan!" He said this with his knowledge of theater-going the world over. He was satisfied with his final thought and Carla was as well; but for myself, there were still specifics to be discussed. I was still unsettled and concerned with my thoughts of his position, his possessive Ego, his uncontrollable passion, and how he would wield his overwhelming power; all of which are the elements of greed and destruction, and could eventually destroy anything he touched. I refused to have him control me. "And your Director?" I asked him bluntly; "What does he or she say about all this? You know, about the artists that you want he or she to work with? The show's themes, the direction of the shows, the direction of the theater, and all of that! And what have you two already discussed?" By the looks on their faces, my question clearly had them baffled.

Karel was hesitant to answer, so I decided to immediately get to the point and my bottom line. "What does your Director think about you? Also, the idea of working with you…I mean I don't really know you Karel," I said to him, slowly setting my glass of wine down on the table. "I am now meeting you for the first time; and I think it's a great meeting, but I will tell you what I am thinking, about you and the possible difficulties of us working together. And furthermore, I think the difficulty may also apply to the Director, or anyone else who is working with you!" Karel was listening while he reached for a cigarette without taking his squinted eyes away from mine; and Carla's smile of disappointment lasted until the glass of white wine finally touched her lips. I don't know what came over me at that moment, but suddenly I felt that what I was saying wasn't enough for them; there was still more to be said. And because of this powerful urge to continue speaking, I knew that I had to be cautious. Not only did I have to carefully choose my words to Karel; but also, to somehow disperse the surrounding bubble of gloom that I had created among us. I suddenly realized that my sincere words to them had "missed the point" and were not taken as "information," but were taken as "discouragement." The words that so easily spewed from my mouth were from my professional perspective and experiences with music and theater Producers. My honest intention was not to discourage or disappoint, but to "educate!"

My assumption of Karel's resilience to a personal attack however, I did trust and this provoked me to continue; "You know what my biggest concern is Karel?" I said; "I sense you to be a head-strong Producer whose **EGO** is bigger than the show! And who has his own vision and ideas of how a show should look, who should be on stage, dressed in what costume, and what the music of the show should be! This is a 'control freak' man, and it's not good!" He didn't like what he was hearing, but resisted his urge to speak. And since I was 'on a roll' I continued; "I think, that you are a Producer who is demanding with the specifics and with your personal ideas of how things must be; and who will interfere with the show's direction, casting, rehearsals, and everything and everyone involved! This madness causes production conflict, Karel, and creates pre-opening turmoil with the show; and that's if the show even gets to open! That's why I am asking you, what your Director thinks. It's important that I know this, so that I will know what to decide and what my next step will be! And I have to tell you, Karel; you can't be the one who determines that man!" He was a bit stunned at my assessment of him as I expected him to be; but I needed and wanted to be certain that they both understood completely, my thoughts and view of the issues that I was being confronted with. Stunned and surprised at my blatancy, he summoned up his voice to say; "I don't have a Director! That's you, maan! You make the show! You direct everything; the music the artists, me, and everything! He looked at Carla for a supportive word or look but she only smiled at him from behind her glass of wine. I responded to him by saying sarcastically and in a joking manner; "So, what does that mean? Do I make all the costumes too, Karel? Do I operate the Spotlight and maybe sell tickets at the box office too! Do I come in the mornings and clean the theater and the restrooms, or do I choose to come in the afternoons?" And since you have just given me 'your permission' not to perform on stage, does that mean that I will be able to be a theater usher also? He got the sting of my words and the humor; and his facial expression began to change from a threatening shock to a child's innocent-smile whose hand had just got slapped again for naughty behavior. Carla flashed her eyes at him and said, echoing her experiences with his sometimes-naughty behavior; "Ah-huh! You have finally met your match!" she said pointedly, and turned to me quickly asking, "Isn't that how you say that in English?" "Yea!", I said; "You said it perfectly! "Vaat zekje, Carla? Nog een keer!" ("What did you say, Carla? Say it again!") he asked her. She repeated her wise comment, but with more emphasis and confidence, knowing that she was perfectly right in her delivery of words. Karel's face brightened, and his child-like smile burst into laughter as he shifted his eyes quickly back and forth to Carla and I. Poking his index finger at us, he said accusingly with a twist of humor, "Conspirators!" You and you are out to get me for something; I don't know why! But I know that you two have something against "the Boss"! he said; and sat back in his chair "Boss-like," folding both arms across his chest. Carla calmly sipped on her glass of wine with grace and elegance, waiting for the "crossfire" to begin between he and I. I too, sat back in my chair and folded my arms as he did. "Whoa!" I said, with the intent for my words to penetrate. "No games! I don't do games, my friend!" That sudden statement emerged from quick flashing thoughts of the trick Bernado and Mamasita played on me in Cancun Mexico, the Movie

431

"Who's Afraid of Virginia Wolf," and of the games that couples and people play with one another, and on others.

"Yes, I know we're joking now," I continued to say; "But you need to check out what you and your dangerous paranoia just said - though jokingly I know - saying that Carla and I are conspiring against you, and that you are my 'Boss.' Don't you believe that Karel!" I said without a hint of a joke; "I have no boss! I am my own boss! I haven't told you yet that I will even work with you; and should that ever happen, you still wouldn't be my 'Boss'!" We would be only working together as partners to get a job done, and that's it! There would be no boss telling me how to behave or how to do my work; especially if they know nothing about it!"

My verbal thrashing created a lasting silence at our table and I felt that I had said enough. I could see in his eyes the scope of his intelligence, his understanding and respect, some admiration and a signal to stop; I had hit my target. Karel's eyes never left mine, nor did Carla's ever leave his! She silently applauded him; she knew the character of her man. Her eyes also, were softened with a stare to him of understanding, respect, and admiration. There were no more words to say to one another; The three of us relaxed and settled ourselves quietly in a harmony of mutual understanding. Karel beckoned to a waiter and softly spoke with him, as Carla and I sipped on our wine and eyed each other. She smiled beautifully, and flashed me a quick wink of an eye. I responded with a comical flutter of eyelashes from both eyes, and a wide smile. The waiter returned to our table; pushing a small, polished brass beverage cart topped with a bottle of champagne in a fine crystal ice bucket. "Ahh, dank u vel, meneer!" ("Thank you, sir!") Karel said to the waiter. He looked at Carla and I, and flashed a youthful grin across his face, saying, "Ik zul een joint maaker!" ("I'm going to roll a joint!") The waiter's work was done and with a loud pop-of-the-cork, he left us in giggles and laughter that had all the sounds of celebration. We were celebrating something, but "what?" Well into our celebration, it wasn't long before I returned to the purpose of our meeting together and began to speak; "So, Karel, in your elegant and beautiful theater of Erotica, exactly what is it that you want me to do?" His eyes narrowed a bit to focus on the 'vision' that he was seeing and to find the correct words in English to express what that vision was. "I see your work is to make beautiful shows, Ilanga; with quality and a touch of class, and..." he paused. He was searching for words, being careful, and continued; "And I see your choreography "sweet", maan! I see it in a "Melange" ("Mix"), with the raw and natural feelings of sex that human people have, you know! "Not porno, or the dirty sex business that we have here in Amsterdam!" he said, softening his voice, eyes and bearing to quietly say; "There must be a way to tell a beautiful story here in Amsterdam about sex, and it not being about porno or making it dirty! You know what I mean, maan? Or the dancing! It should be "hot" with feeling, energy, emotion and dancing a beautiful story; not being sexy, but..." he stammered with his words before saying "sensual." He looked at Carla with a winning smile and then again quickly turning to me, he asked with genuine sincerity; "Can you make that? "That I can!" I confidently replied, "Yes, I can do that; but why should I do that?" I asked bluntly. Karel was surprised and astonished by my direct question; and he burst into laughter and said with a greedy gleam in his eyes; "Money maan, for money!" He then leaned towards me and lowered his voice to say with knowing; "Benjamin has told me of your work and how you like to travel the world! That takes money, maan! I have friends who are artists like you; we talk, so, I know!" Then he rested from his words and holding on to a lingering thought as he gestured to Carla to light up a cigarette for him, said; "I think that you are the same as my friends," he said, while taking the cigarette smoothly from Carla's fingers and giving her an appreciative nod with his head. He became more relaxed and continued; "Like my friends, you are an artist that likes and needs to create better and bigger things to make your life happy, yes?" I quietly nodded a "yes" and kept my eyes on his. He raised his voice again; "Well, come on maan, that takes money, yes?, he asked and said with a constant stare. "You must create to be happy! I pay you money to create, and be happy! Where is there a problem?" And then he said with a tone of frustration; "You make the problem with your 'principles' and your Americaan's way of thinking about sex. They are still stuck in the old days, in the old style! They make it dirty; it's not dirty maan; it's natural!" The young people here in Europe are free of that now, maan; This is a new time, new minds, new thinking and a 'new world' today! You, Carla and me, we are old people now living in a new world of technology and new thinking; and if we want to continue living here, we must change our thinking and think like the young people! They are free, they are happy! And the smart ones are 'more happy' because they understand that it takes money to be free, happy and to make good work for themselves. They are smart maan; they only know that life can be good or bad, and that money controls either situation. Hell, maan; they are not thinking about principal, old traditions and old thought! They are free of that; at our age, we are not! But, I tell you; we must try to think and live young, because if not, we will become old fast and die young, maan! You know what I mean?" His question, was left unanswered. He pulled back in his chair, re-lit the joint that extinguished itself, passed it on to Carla and relaxed himself. His eyes revealed to me that he had more to say, so I let him; Carla passed the joint to me, so I smoked and I listened. "Don't be stupid, maan!" he said, pouring champagne into Carla's glass and then into mine. "Take this work, make money! It is the only way that you can make good work for yourself. You are smart, and you know what I mean, I know!" After filling his glass to the brim and taking a small sip to catch the spill-over, he smiled at me; his erratic demeanor simmered to a low and his eyes suddenly warm and his voice mellow. "You are a good maan, and you have a good heart, I can see that! Maybe too good; he said, followed with a small laugh to himself and continued; "But, you can be a good person and still work in this business! Yes, sometimes the business can change a person, because the sex business is strong with evil or bad things that can make a weak-minded person change! But you are not weak, maan! You are strong in your mind and in your heart and, you know how to work with people, Benjamin told me! You are good for the business," he said firmly, looking at Carla for agreement which she gave with a slow nod of her head, lowering her eyelids slowly, confirming it.

Our long pause of a thick silence allowed my thoughts to digest all of what Karel had said; I came to the conclusion that I agreed with his words of wisdom and advice and to consider the opportunity. The "present time,' my age, my nomadic lifestyle, my immediate future and the makings of the work I do were all taken into consideration during our extended silence. They began a whispered intimate conversation, leaving me to be alone and to continue with the thoughts of my American background, of social and religious dogmas that he spoke of; and his significant message that was also caught in the web of my thoughts. Because of my interest to hear more of this possible "new" challenge of *Dare and Responsibility*, I interrupted our silence asking Karel; "Besides making beautiful shows, is there more of your 'vision' that I should know about, think about, and according to you, *Be* about? I asked in sarcastic jest and with a smile. His reply was instant and genuine. His words flowed so easily from his mouth and so natural in their flow, that it shocked me! In the delight of his visual imagination, he wandered with an aim and began to speak: "The theater will have an intimate Champagne Bar where the audience goes after they have seen the show. They meet the artists there after their performance, to talk and you know, drink champagne," he said with nonchalance and adding; "It's a good thing, when you share with someone what you feel in your heart, he said from within his own nature, and continued; "I want the audience to meet and talk with the artists you know! Artists are strange and interesting people, maan! They like to talk about their work and themselves; and it is interesting, what they say about their strange lives! I want to share this rare experience with an audience who is interested in beautiful stories that are 'real', maan!" he emphasized the 'real' aspect and began to go into "high-gear" again; "I don't like 'Whore Bars'! You know, the kind of bars where men pick up women! That's old-style," he said with disgust and then continued his flow. "So, in the Champagne Bar I want you to choreograph beautiful 'Strip Shows' with the dancers, both girls and boys! And, in the main theater, choreograph the 'Live Shows,' making them beautiful with nice music and a story, or stories; I don't know, that is for you to decide! The stage is yours to make the dream that you see! Your fantasy! You know what I mean?"

I was stunned, that he proposed this to me! I had never seen a "live show" in Amsterdam, simply because I had no interest! In America and elsewhere in the world, to see a "live show" is to see an on-stage show with persons or animals in performance action. An "Amsterdam Live Show" meant something else in The Netherlands! "I know that you don't mean the "Amsterdam-like Live-Shows" is what you want me to choreograph in your theater," I questioned him. "No, no!", he said strongly in defense of his moral values; "That is porno, cheap and dirty, maan! Those people on stage are not artists; they just "fuck" for the money to buy Heroin! There is no story, no beautiful costumes! Only an empty stage with two, three, sometimes four, all addicts, all fucking together!" he said, and fuming with disgust. "No; the shows that you make will be "Heilemaal" ("Altogether") different!" Karel again shifted his attitude by taking a slow puff on the joint and keeping his eyes on me before passing it to Carla. His eyes could see that mine were questioning, and that what he was withholding, is what I wanted to hear! His last puff on the joint withdrew his honesty. He relaxed and became more comfortable with his body language and his delivery of words; "Yah, vel, natuurleik!" ("Yes, of course, naturally!") our artists will fuck; but not like dogs and animals!" he said strongly and in fact; "Yes, they must make a sex-show; but in some way, you must make a show with "real love" inside the story," he emphasized with a tone of passion. "This is theater, this is erotic-art, maan! This is what I want you to make; you are an 'Artist', you can make this!". He paused, and noticing my interest and relaxed demeanor, he could see that a possible acceptance of his offer was circling in my thoughts. Again, he flashed a childlike smile of innocence and the incessant question; "Can you make this for me?" he asked once again. "Yes!"

I answered; "I have told you already Karel, that "Yes, I can do that for you;" and you also answered my question of why I should do it for myself and what the problem is - if I have one! And, I thank you for that advice; but I cannot give you a confirmed answer tonight. This, I have to think about and give you an answer in a few days because this is heavy, man! Not that it's so much for my mind to think about, handle wisely, and decide; that's easy! Remember; You said that I was a smart man, I said to him in jest; also thinking of how and what I was going to say next. "I will tell you both honestly," I said insightfully; "If my *Mind* decides to do it, I know well that my body is capable of following through with that decision; but, it is my *Soul* that I'm concerned about! I have to take the time to hear what *it* has to say about all of this!" I said; and concluded my thought with; "I must take the time to listen!"

The three of us sat in a silence that allowed me to think more of this "soulful" thought: that for many years now, I had been trying with great effort to establish a rapport and an alignment of balance with my *Mind, Body, and Soul*! And in eventual time and with effort, I had discovered or "realized" that these three "Entities" (My reference); each have a voice of their own, and I listen carefully to each one! "Psychotic"? Possibly! And to misguide or disrupt this established harmony that I had found within myself, was a concern. I must live every day with these three separate "Entities" that live, and are very much alive within me to govern and control! I must "keep watch" because each is able to go their own separate way; and therefore; none can ever be ignored. Our long silence ended when Carla turned to Karel, and with her sparkling eyes opened wide, said to him;.. "Nog een keer, Karel;.. Wiltje een ondere joint maaker? Ausjeblieft!" ("Once more, Karel; will you make another joint, please!") She then turned to me and smiled, saying; "That is our fuel! The first one was to blast-off and this one is to continue our flight!" Her eyes twinkled and her face lit up with a big, beautiful smile; and she said, "I like where we're going!" I discovered somewhat later in our relationship; that for us, laughing together was as easy as talking together! I could always feel an honesty between us three, whenever we met thereafter.

My decision to work with Karel was decided within a few days of deep and serious thought. Working in a business such as this! Where would it take me? How much of myself do I have to give or sacrifice for a greater return? And above all; to explore sex; to be every day immersing my mind into this pool of unknown dangers, delights and distraction was not at all an attractive thought; and to be deliberately channeling my creative energy in this direction and daily dwelling on ideas of "creative sex" was another absurd thought for me to be pondering. And for what? Money? My lure and attraction to Karel's offer was the *Challenge and the Dare* that always sparked me to make a "new" move and take *Action* on an idea! My overwhelming concern was that for me, this was to be a "new business" about an "old something" that I absolutely know nothing about! And why is that? Simply because for me, sex was never a main interest! As a child raised as a Roman Catholic, sex was taboo and not to be thought of! And as a **3rdCycle** teenager, this was a *Challenge and a Dare* for "fun" only; never to be taken seriously! My sex drive was never normal in comparison to my male friends in high school whose hormones "bounced and dribbled like basketballs" all day and night, with an excessive drive to score! And the male friends that I had worked with and traveled with during the early years of "The G-Clef's" - our performances and road

439

tours, living the entertainer's lifestyle in the glamorous spotlight and sexy lifestyle of "Show Business" - had thrived on such opportune encounters! Their sex drive was not just to score, but rather, to feed the **EGO** with greed on a daily basis! Needless to say, there is no daily "hunt" for females in attendance because for many of these men in show business, their next target is sitting right there in the audience, front row! So, my "drive" was usually in low gear, and its pace would rev-up to high gear only when a great desire or need for someone came into play with another one in need who also had the desire to play with me! And certainly; whenever an unusual sexual occasion did arise, what "splendor", what a joy! What an explosion of "oneness" it was, for two wrapped up in one another's desire and need, experiencing new feelings with every new touch and slight body movement; and both being "most-alive" in that moment of the day or night, and maybe even that week, month, or for years! For how long a time that these two meet is not the point; it's knowing, that each time that they do, there is a coming together as if it were for the first time, ever!

At the table, and after our intense conversation, the one more joint that Carla requested Karel to make, set us in a mood of relaxation. They engaged themselves in an isolated conversation as I quietly pondered with one thought and one unanswered question: How do I interpret and incorporate my sexual-experiences, fantasies and ideology into a non-Amsterdam-like Live Show?! This became a question answered only onsite, at mock-rehearsals; and it would be only at the time of performance, when I would be sitting alone in the last row of the theater observing the "creative sensuality" I had created and attempting to evaluate my input.

It was a few days after we had enjoyed our fancy dinner at the Indonesian Restaurant in Zandvoort, that my decision was made. I was to become "Artistic Director and Choreographer" of Amsterdam's new erotic theater, *Caresse*! Why not? All the components of my nature and character were crystalized. The *Dare, Adventure, Curiosity, Creativity, Intuition, and the ever-present desire for Something Else* all came into play! And let's not forget The *Money*; the newly designed global *Power* that can materialize a dream, or create a nightmare depending on the choice of the "Dreamer."

Within the following few weeks, during frequent meetings with Karel and Carla, we shaped and planned their dream. They agreed to the artistic and practical concept I proposed; which was to organize and establish a small company of eight to ten intelligent and "capable" performing artists. They would be auditioned; then advised, trained, and conditioned to be the nuclear Company; and we would outsource glamorous, beautiful females as solo feature attractions that Karel referred to as "Bombshells" to highlight a specific theme of a show. And most important was that the company of artists were be treated with respect and dignity; and they, to respond likewise. I had to instill the professional rule for the artists, which is: "That they must learn to feel pride in their work, and to produce the quality of performance that the Producer and the Audience expect!" I had also proposed that Auditions be held in June. There would be eight weeks of scheduled rehearsals during July and August and the Company would debut in September, with one outsourced featured attraction: An international "Queen of Burlesque." The proposal included the immediate acquiring of operational stage properties, a technician of lighting, sound, and visuals, and a resource for diverse music; "my key to creativity!"

These essentials "appeared" within a couple of weeks. Raul, became my tech-engineer, and John, my music resource. Thereafter; The stage properties, special lighting effects, and costumes, were acquired by Karel due to his knowledge his contacts and wealth. Frequent trips to Paris, and traveling in a plush Citroen auto were weekly with Carla and Karel during those two months of July and August. It was Summer vacation, the dance center was closed, and time was allowed for me to "diligently" work! Karel's personal and reliable contacts in Paris were always on target and provided sufficient stage properties for us to open a show with style and quality. He would have lunches and dinners with friends there who preferred a "chat", rather than a telephone call. Keep in mind, dear reader, this was in 1977; online contact and cell phones did not exist! This was a time of eye-to-eye contact; and a hand-shake was all it took to make a deal!" Karel had negotiated with the management of an exclusive Parisian night club at that time called the "Crazy Horse Saloon." The deal would allow us to purchase costumes, props, and special lighting, for the theater's grand opening; and as well, for the shows we were planning to stage for the future. season. Whenever we needed specific scenery for certain themes, or a special tailor for a specific costume, Karel would have a go-to contact. I was learning that Karel was quite a diverse, amazing man; dynamic, with charm, strong character, sociability, street-knowledge, connections; and he always found a way to achieve.

I limited my discussions and conversations of my involvement in the "old business" and of my "new job" to only a few close friends; Benjamin was one. He was always a great advisor on important matters. And also, I had discussed it with the authentic Dutch couple, Lynn and Dick, in whose home I had lived for three months before deciding to stay in Amsterdam and acquire my own one-bedroom apartment in the center of the city, nestled on a quiet narrow street called, the "Fagelstraat." It was not necessary to discuss my "New Job" with anyone, outside of my circle of friends. Even Benjamin was concerned greatly about my new job position with his friend, because he knew of Karel's seductive charm, and the possibility of my entanglement with the project could interfere with the abundance of work yet to be done for the dance company's debut Spring performance. I assured him to not worry, and that my dance classes and the performance was my work priority. He felt comfortable hearing those sacred words from me, and the tone of loyalty that he was hoping for was there.

Our newly acquired teacher dancer choreographer and friend, "Almasi" had arrived in April from New York. It was a joy for us to see him and have him with us; sharing his exuberant dance Spirit and refreshing high-energy of the New York dancer! He, Benjamin, and I, worked vigorous, long hours with the company dancers and the newly choreographed pieces which were being worked on for performances to be held in the city of "Den Haag" in the month of May. After the dance company's acclaimed success, I began my "new work" with Karel and Carla. Our frequent and productive trips to Paris during July and August had come to an end; there was now, "work to do"!

September came quickly. The *Caresse Theater* had its elaborate "Grand Opening," featuring the "Queen of Burlesque," and *Benjamin's Jazz Dance Center* opened for the Fall and Winter school semesters. I resumed my teaching of classes and administrative duties along with orientating Almasi to the school's culture, the city of Amsterdam, and Benjamin. The three of us were fascinated with one another's abilities and approach to our individual responsibilities and each one of us was exploring and discovering who each was as a person, what kind of character, and who was apt to do what in the work that we were all sharing. The working chemistry between us was organic and natural; it flowed evenly and smooth and made things work harmoniously. It was as if it were purposely formulated and designed for us to be together for a period of time in this life to incorporate our skills, and to be governed by the same Purpose! Our distinct differences set us apart in visual appearance, body-language, character, speech, and personality; but the bold colorful threads of *Dance, New York, Intelligence, Respect, and Laughter"* had woven us tightly together to do our work in harmony, and to never forget that: "We are dancers", and above all, "we are educators"! We had to exemplify that, and let it be known, because dancers are not usually recognized as such. We are generally considered as "just dancers"!

By the time the festive holidays of December had arrived, the Proposal to Karel had been successfully implemented and its positive outcome and results were presented in artistic, erotic performances on stage nightly. The production team of Karel, the Producer, Dick, the Stage Manager, Raul, the tech/engineer, and John, the music director, brought the show to life for the Winter-Spring Theatre season. Karel's passion for his fantasy, his social position within the circles of the Dutch elite, his business colleagues, and his significant "Amsterdam notoriety" allowed him to share his pride by inviting his personal friends from the arts and politics, and CEO's from Dutch tourism to the city's new *Caresse Theater*, for the shows and champagne events. Mano the photographer and his camera were always by my side, and he soon became part of the working team.

Karel was a "happy man;" and, consequently; "I got paid to be a happy man!"

At Spring's end, the close of the theater season and the close of the dance school sessions had finally arrived. I knew that it was time to go to Boston - I hadn't been there now for a year - and I had given my family only partial information about the "new" work I was doing throughout the year, through letter correspondence and a couple of limited telephone calls to my sister Karen. And whenever she would ask details of my "new" work, my answer would always be vague, evasive and hurried! "Oh, it's fine!" I would say; and "Yes, I'm fine!" adding quickly, "How's everybody, and the kids?" to divert from her question. But she, wanting details, would ask again; and my answer would always be, "Oh, my new work?" "Oh, I'll tell you all about that later! I know, I always tell you that; but it's a long story! The next call, not now!" I would say; "Gotta-go! Bye!" Therefore; my return to Boston was overdue. There was a long story to tell and a lot to be talked about back home.

At the end of the last class of the semester, while sitting at the studio's Café-Bar together with Glenito, Glenn, Austin, Mano, Benjamin and Almasi, I said to them after the first sip of my Cappuccino; "I'm going to Boston next week, for a couple of weeks! And then I'll be coming back here for a week to pack bags, and then I'll be going to Morocco, for, I don't know for how long yet! I won't know that until I get there!" Almasi butted-in quickly, with the raised voice and timbre of a New York dancer; "Oh no, you needn't!" he said; as if I were so privileged to be leaving Amsterdam. "I'm going to New York next week too!" he continued saying; "We have-got-to-hook-up there, child!", Almasi said excitedly with his New York drama and flair! Austin also chimed-in with her next-week plan of leaving for her country of New Zealand!... She decided then and there, to depart for New Zealand from New York. The following week, Almasi, Austin and I, boarded our flight to Boston and stayed a few days at my family's home. I explained to my sister "what I could," of my "New Work" in Amsterdam; and the three of us then left for New York, and became "New Yorkers".

——— CHAPTER TWELVE ———

"Information is not knowledge," he said, and left.

The remaining three years in Amsterdam were all of what I expected them to be, a time of relentless diligence; It seems there was never an end to each day in the seven-day week. Accomplishments were well-met and my ultimate "purpose" of developing the Afro-Jazz Dance technique was achieved; its foundation solidly laid, "What more would I be there for?" My "dance dream" of technique development had been fulfilled, and the dreams of others had been as well! Benjamin's Jazz Dance Center, Benjamin, Almasi, and I flourished in its established success; and Benjamin was now on his way to branding the style of American Jazz Dance in the small country of Holland, (The Netherlands). And nightly, the stage of the *Caresse Theater* hosting erotic fantasies, was brilliantly lit with lighting from Paris and with imaginative "live-shows" that titillated the loins of men and women from around the world who arrived on tour buses to be seduced by a "live" fantasy, a short story, a theme or a selective piece of music. And post-performance, the Champagne Bar experience welcomed enticing conversations.

The performing company of artists excelled in their efforts with quality performances, began to learn the value of their work, and discovered a dignity within themselves that they fervently aspired to. And Karel, the wealthy dreamer who would never think of himself as being wealthy, was satisfied to see "His Dream" materialize before his eyes. Carla, his supportive wife, was more than proud of her man;

she had told me this in secret. "I wouldn't tell him that!" she said; "His **EGO** wouldn't know what to do with it!" Her eyes and smile showed her love for him.

The Show that I had conceived and helped build was expedited with professional care; signed sealed and delivered! During those three wonderful years of "delivering the goods," of *Personal Challenge,* and the accumulation of "Power".

Money I had matured. My naivete had disappeared and left me with the wisdom to differentiate myself from the norm, accept it, and continue on; to "simply be outstanding in my difference," because, "it made a difference"! I had learned the "precise" definitions and differences of sex, sexy, sensuality, gay, homosexual, straight, transgender, and all the "labels" that define "who we are by gender," and how we are to behave within that definition! Fortunately, I had learned, that I did not fit any of those labels. I had discovered that the only label for me, was "Misfit" and that did not bother me at all! I had already decided that the only label I could accept to tag myself with was "Me"! On certain nights I would stand in front of the theater and watch the tour buses park, unloading its passengers of men and women with curious minds; all parading in line, in their need to know more about their secret behaviors, stimulate their sexual fantasies, and imagine that "it is they themselves on that stage" identifying with, and exercising the sexual freedom that they desire and long for, after being "tagged, labeled and stamped" for a lifetime. They would never know such freedom unless they "peeled off" their label for a length of time, and became the innate primal animals that they are! This is an adventure that only the seekers who are weak and in need of challenge may attempt; or for those who are very strong, and will "Dare" to take! And for those who could care less and were oblivious to this "real" life, every day mental habit of thought; they would never discover the true joy of really knowing themselves.

After five years of my strict and disciplined work ethic which I had worked hard to establish in Amsterdam, my "Purpose" for being there was successfully achieved. I had developed a cultural dance technique that educates, inspires, and "opens many doors" to Self-Awareness and the Natural Rhythms of daily life and habits that a student learns about him or herself, and of the global community that he or she lives. So, basically…"Mission Accomplished!" But also, during this period of contemplation, I could feel that my residence there was soon to become a past experience, and the trail I was to leave behind would only manifest in memories and old-time stories, for myself my colleagues and my "forever friends" who had "collectively" made this all happen.

In 1980, my move from Amsterdam to Athens Greece was permanent. The first year of being there was like that of a move into any other city where I intended to make residence, which is: Orientation to locations and places of interest to me and my work. And also, to become recognized within the community of artists and to find a studio where I could teach dance and apply my work! The only difference that distinguished this move to Athens from the other cities of making residence, is that my dear friend Yiorgos was here. He became my "mountain" of support and strength to achieve "any" dream that I thought was possible to be realized there. The male name "Yiorgos" ("George") is popular in Greece; but he was "Mountain Yiorgos" as far as I was concerned.

The dance classes that I was eventually teaching were being held at a site that caught my eyes during the orientation period, after my arrival there. It was a blistering hot, sunny day of aimful wandering through an interesting and quiet area of Athens called, "Pangrati." A white stucco building in the traditional, classical Greek style sat high on a rocky ledge on the corner of Domboli and Archimidous, two small streets that intimately crossed one another. Raising my eyes to this beautiful building sitting high up on the ledge, gleaming white from the bright sun, and so delicately graced with hanging Bougainvillea Vines and flowers and plants, I was enticed into climbing the few steps upward into the pebbled courtyard. "How interesting," I thought; and so it was here, at *The Athens Center* in Pangrati, where Afro-Jazz Dance was born in Greece.

As in western Europe, Greece and the Mediterranean area were also familiar with jazz music and American jazz dance; but my experience in western Europe and their bastardly use of the term "Jazz Ballet" taught me lessons in diplomacy. I learned that it would be best to avoid the unknown and confusing word "Afro", and to creatively introduce it within the class structure itself. "Yes, this is the technique that I teach; but here in Athens, let's just call it 'Jazz Dance'!" I said to John Zervos and Rosemary Donnelly; the Founders and Directors of their dream, *The Athens Center for Cultural Arts.* During our first year at the center, we successfully worked together and established a professional relationship that eventually blossomed into a "forever" friendship; and this was the catapult year that magnified my "purpose" and the beginning of my next four incredible years in Greece. The three of us developed the "new" dance department within the center's other various cultural activities of theater and literary arts. The courses of study were seasonally offered to Greek nationals, foreign residents of the city, and students engaging in Summer Study Programs of ancient Greek culture and the arts, as well as courses in Greek, German and French language. Within that first year, the dance classes multiplied from one class a week to eight classes. Two students who were members of my company in Amsterdam, *Kreos Dance Theater* and DJ-John, my music resource man from the *Caresse Theater*, had decided to leave Amsterdam. They felt the need to join with me and become involved in the work that I was doing at the Athens Center. John, Sabina, and Austin, also became residents of Athens. The four of us were strong in our work together, and then, there was Yiorgos, now, well into his **4ᵗʰCycle**. We were a team of five dynamic individuals that electrified Athens with an energy the Athenians had never seen or felt before! When we'd walk the streets together, the diversity of the group itself turned-heads: An Englishman, a German, a New Zealander, a black American, and a Greek! The noisy chatter that hummed and buzzed loudly from the voices of walking tourists and the crowded outdoor café tables placed and lined in rows, was always in a constant buzz as we'd stroll by; but the voices always lowered to whispers as we five in our conversations and nonchalance, walked our way through the bustle, confusion, and the chaos of "Platia Syntagm" (Constitution Square).

By September, the beginning of the second school year, the dance classes at the Athens Center were attractive enough to Greek and foreign students from all over the world who were then residing in Athens. Some of them were beginners in dance and some were dancers who were advanced in Classical or Modern dance.

The large conference room that John and Rosemary converted into a mirrored dance studio on the scheduled days of dance class, was now filled with a multi-cultural group of talented young dancers; some who were not technically talented but were "inspired" to dance anyway! This enigmatic collection of cultures and worldly understanding, enabled me to comfortably induce and apply the "Afro-Jazz" technique. Some students suddenly discovered that they had "hips to move, shake, and roll"! And there were others who knew they had hips, and knew exactly "how to move them"! The formula for me to "produce" was all there, "dancing" in front of my eyes; and it sparked within me the idea to organize the best of both groups - beginners and advanced - and to present them on stage in performance five months later, in January of the new year. There was only one person in the city of Athens who could listen, understand and *comprehend* this new idea, and who would advise me well in every aspect of the vision that my eyes could clearly see, presented "live" onstage. He was at the Taverna. "There is a stage performance that I am envisioning in my mind that I want to present here in Greece," I said to Yiorgos one day at the beginning of October; but seeing that the Taverna was extremely busy with hungry customers, this was not the time for a "long story"! Pulling him away momentarily from his "fast-runs" back and forth to the kitchen; I said briefly that an important discussion and his advice were needed. Within seconds, he and I planned a meeting together at a time when he would be free from work, his studies, and social life. It was a period when we both had little free time to spend with one another, and by now, he was "hungry" for a good long story; and I was hungry to hear his repeated "Poh, Poh, Poh's"! Our scheduled meeting happened a couple of days later during the morning hours just before noon when it was most quiet at the Taverna. We sat to begin our conversation at a table placed in a far corner of the outdoor terrace. "You are anxious to speak with me, Ilanga; I saw that on your face when you were here two days ago;" said Yiorgos, quite concerned that I had a serious problem to discuss with him. He leaned forward across the table to ask, "What is it that I can do for you, Ilanga? You need help with something serious, I see it in your eyes!" I didn't hesitate to answer and began enthusiastically asking him my single question; "What I want to do Yiorgos, is to present a theatrical show here in Athens that tells a story of Reincarnation; its possibility, and how I interpret it to exist! What I need to know from you is, how do you think this idea would be received in the Minds of a Greek audience?" I could see a new look on Yiorgos' face, an expression that I had never seen before now. He was dumbfounded and asked me; "Is this serious? Am I missing something here?" I interfered with his puzzlement by interjecting more pieces for him to deal-with; "I know; it sounds weird doesn't it? But the strangest thing is, I don't yet know what I'm talking about...but I see it!" Yiorgos sat still, slowly lowering his eyes to a squint and leveled an intense stare at me. He leaned forward and said; "Yes, yes, go on," urging me to continue so that he could possibly solve his puzzle of bewilderment. I did; with continuity and a flow of rambling thoughts that I was hoping would help him to unravel his confused thinking. I approached him in a narrative tone of voice because I knew of his love of a long story, and said to him with the intent that he would listen carefully; "I think that I can do this Yiorgos, by writing reoccurring scenes of the main character going through the process of evolution step by step from each death to each incarnation; and the purpose of each incarnation is to advance in *Love* and the *passion for life*! I paused, collecting my thoughts and questioning myself, as to why I had just said that; and then I remembered; "It seems to me Yiorgos, that we as human beings have forgotten why we are born, and why we live every day, which I believe, is to include as much *Love* in our lives as we can! I believe we are born to do this," I said convinced and with certainty. "Living my life in America and in Europe, and all around the world, what I have observed during my travels is frightening, Yiorgos! I experienced, seen, and witnessed a dreadful wave of deliberate ignorance, hate, evil, and a surmountable force of greed, seeping its way into the minds of humans and our global culture, my brother! And this wave of greed that's fast becoming a "norm" within our societies, will, I think, soon peak and drown the *Love* that we know of and are born to share, and this new wave of "personal greed" and "deliberate misunderstandings" will eventually become the global trend and the "norm"! I know it may sound crazy; but, it's what I see, Yiorgos!" And those of us who are without greed and its "power" and who are filled with the nature of *Love* must learn more about it and must actually find its root and reason, its definition and its *Purpose*! And they will have to learn to exercise it more in word, thought and deed, to survive in the "belly of the beast," I said to him pointedly and with a hint of warning to his generation.

His stare became more intense, as my words started to hit home. "But; do you understand what I'm saying, Yiorgos?" I asked him needlessly; because I could see in his piercing, hazel green eyes that he did! Without an answer, his eyes left mine to scan my neck beads; and then they roved their way to the copper bracelets that clutched tightly on both of my wrists. And then his eyes arrived at the gold hoop earring in my right earlobe. He reached his hand out and fingered it, which is not an unusual thing for him to do with my beads and bracelets or anything dangling, whenever he's in thought or has a serious question to ask (or if he's hungry for a long story). For a few seconds he played with my earring, until he murmured softly to himself; "Yes, this is nice, this is nice!" I don't think that I ever did remind him that "everything goes in cycles," and I could see that he was beginning to drift away in his wandering thoughts, but I didn't let him. Taking his hand away from my ear, I said brusquely; "And leave my earring alone!" He quickly responded to refocus on our lost conversation; "Neh, Neh!" ("Yes, Yes!"), I am listening Ilanga, go on, go on." And just for the fun of it and the need for a break, I said; "Yiorgos! I am not saying another word in this conversation unless you run to the kitchen fast and get back here with a Cappuccino as fast as you can; and if that's not possible, the story's over!" He was stunned at the curve ball I threw at him and said; "Sigura, Sigura!" ("Sure, Sure!") flinging his chair back for the quick run. His hurried return was in just a few short minutes; and not a drop of Cappuccino was spilled over the rim of the cup! "Parakalo!" ("If you please!") also; ("Thank you!") he said serving, and placing the cup on the table in front of me, he quickly arranged his chair and sat, saying the one word, "Etsi" which translates to "There! It's done! Accomplished!" Yiorgos relaxed and immediately, leaned forward, and anxiously said; "Neh (Yes), Ilanga! Go on!" as if he hadn't ever left his chair for a run to the kitchen. "Parakalo!" I said thanking him for my coffee and taking a slow sip before filling his ears with more of my thoughts on a production based on reincarnation and innate love as the underlying themes. This was certainly not a "Broadway Blockbuster" of a show, but I rambled on anyway; "I think that I also want to include a scene of 'obsession' and its rabbit hole of self-destruction, if you know what I mean! It is a "trap," Yiorgos, with winding and endless paths of mental torment, anguish, and suffering! This 'obsession' is not love; and its possessive nature has weakened many strong men and women who got caught in this trap of overwhelming emotion! And man, if

I can capture that in a scene, it would add a dynamic to the colors of passion that I see; and I think that need to be seen, Yiorgos! But also, I am thinking I would like to do that scene in a filmed segment of the show; so the show would be a multi-media presentation, with theater, dance, music, and film! The dance scenarios I see, are of four prominent Cultures; Greek, American, Latin, and Love!" His eyes went into a tight squint, and I continued; "Yes; because I believe that *Love* is the one culture that embraces all cultures! And Yiorgos, I see the dance being danced authentically, and with the real passion of each of those four cultures!" Exasperated by my own words and thoughts, I concluded by adding without defeat; "How this is all going to happen, I don't know! And, the crazy thing is, I see it all happening in January! Somehow a theater in Athens will host this show! But more than anything else Yiorgos, from all of what you just heard, what I want to know from you is, "Will the Greek audience appreciate and actually 'like' a show such as this? I'm asking that, because my past two visits here have led me to believe that they would surely understand and relate to the show's concept. But would they appreciate that I, as a foreigner, should interpret my idea of how I first got to Greece and why I'm back here again now, firmly believing it to be because of the reincarnation process?!" His eyes held their tight squint and his lips shaped his words in silence, "Poh, Poh, Poh, Poh;" but in his words I heard a whisper of astonishment. He was listening carefully, and I continued; "From what I've seen and experienced during my past visits here, Greece is as mystical spiritual and mysterious as I am; and, 'as silent in its purpose' as I am! And Yiorgos, I don't feel like a "misfit" here. I have found that when I am here in Greece, I am comfortable with myself and with my thoughts of who and whatever I am! And also, I will tell you honestly that I feel akin to you my brother and also with nature, the people and the Acropolis as well! Truthfully, I don't think that I could do a show like this in any other country but Greece! I see Greece as a vehicle of 'truth' and I think the Greeks know this as well!" He became still, with a laser-like stare that penetrated my soul until I interrupted our awkward silence by asking, "Well, what do you think about this idea for a show? But more than that, I want to know, how do you think the Greek audience will take it - you know, in a good way or a bad way?" He didn't answer. "Actually, I think they can handle it;" I said and rested my case.

What was interesting to me was that even without total comprehension, he was quietly astonished and amazed at his own "understanding" of all he was hearing, internally digesting, and visually seeing in his mind! This was clear by his facial expression, but his mood was tranquil. "You are Greek, Ilanga!" he said pointedly, as if he had come to a sudden realization! "And, you know that too!" he added, murmuring a long sustaining, "Poh, Poh, Poh, Poh"! His intention for me to listen was clear, and he leaned forward on the edge of his chair and continued to speak of his conclusive thoughts. "I see now, that you are Greek Ilanga, and the Greeks will see that too! And whatever you do here, the Greeks will like, and they will help you to make anything you like, Ilanga! You can see that from your dance classes! Whatever you do here, they will come to you Ilanga, because you are like a magnet here in Athens, you know that!" Yiorgos said convincingly and without a pause. "Tell me what you want me to do! I want to help you with the show and anything else that I can do. Tell me, Ilanga; you must tell me!" His words were unspoken but I heard in my mind from his young wisdom that within his nature, his generosity extended only to the deserving; and it seemed that he definitely "comprehended" everything clearly.

We concluded our meeting with a small carafe of Retsina and discussed an initial plan of what our first steps would be for a January production in Athens entitled "Somewhere." In the following three months, the diligent team consisting of Sabina, Austin, John, Yiorgos, and I were on a daily mission to achieve a good day's work. We followed every lead that Yiorgos gave us from his research of possible locations, technical equipment, music sources for John, fabric shops for Sabina and Austin's skillful costume making, along with the assistant Chrissa, who was Yiorgos' mother! Wherever he told us to go, we'd go; and whatever he said to do, we did!" There wasn't a street in Athens that didn't see our scurrying footsteps in search of our needs! He delegated our every day to be a morning, noon and night obligation to succeed. Although Yiorgos was in his 4th**Cycle**, he was enacting the *Determination, Energy and Action* of the 5th**Cycle**. He was relentless in his every day achievements.

One day in early November, John Zervos surprised me with the news that he had arranged a meeting with the theater Manager at the *Hellenic-American Union*, an organization that catered to the arts of Greek and American cultures. The building was located at the foot of Mount Lykavittos, nearby the sophisticated "Platia Kolonaki" ("Kolonaki Square"). Yiorgos, John the DJ and I, anxiously arrived at the meeting to observe the theater and its stage and technical facilities that were available to us; and to discuss with the Manager the concept of the show, the possible dates available in January, and the logistics of the production. I agreed to the contractual conditions that were presented to us by Michalis, the Manager, and confirmed the date for the opening of the show. "What is the name of the show?", he asked; "I need to write it in our events calendar which goes into print next week, so your timing is good!" An unusual feeling of warmth came over me when I gave him the title of the show: *The Human Contract*! He didn't look up to me from his paperwork as he began writing the title. "That's appropriate!" he said to himself, "It works with the concept;" and then raised his eyes to me saying with final satisfaction, "Orea!" ("Beautiful!"). "It's only three words, along with your brief bio, it all fits perfectly in the only available print space in the calendar! And, those three words '*The Human Contract*' say all that needs to be said; from what you have explained the concept to be! So, I think that's it; we're set;" he said, rested his pen and looked at the three of us who were in disbelief that we were already at this point and that it had all happened so fast! John, Yiorgos and I left Michalis and the Hellenic-American Union joyfully "babbling" to one another and "walking on air" as we headed our way to Platia Kolonaki to celebrate a day's work done successfully in two-hours! Sitting at the café table and toasting to one another with our small glasses of "Ouz" and licking the sweet licorice taste from our lips, we were fully excited to bring this good news to Austin, Chrissa and Sabina, who were ready and prepared to take action.

John acquired the specific music and recorded the sound-effects that I needed and the costumes were being designed, sewn, and fitted for eighteen dancers, models and actors. At that time, I was also engaged with the fashion industry in Greece and had choreographed exclusive fashion shows for Greek and French designers. Therefore, I had access to young, beautiful models and actors who knew how to "work" a fashion Runway, as well, a few having the talent to dance. Yiorgos and John acquired film and equipment for the scene of

"Obsession" that needed to be filmed for a segment of the show's first Act. Vigorous Rehearsals began and dance classes were on-going, as the Christmas Holidays arrived. My next production duty was to design and do a layout of the Program that the audience would be holding in their hands for that that evening's performance.

The Hellenic-American Union

Presents

Kreos Dance theater

The Human Contract
(A Modern Musical in Two Acts)

Written, Directed, and Choreographed by: **Ilanga**

Program: Friday, January 25ᵗʰ 1980 at 8:00 pm.

Audience: Upon arrival, please note; The murmuring sound you hear pre-curtain opening, is the introduction to the upcoming visuals to be seen on screen. It is not a technical or electrical distortion.

Act 1

Scene 1. The Parental Conception: The Dressing and the Teaching and the arrival of the Human Contract into Greece.

Scene 2. The Greek Incarnation:

    a.) The Joy of Physical Entity and Awareness.
    b.) The First Lessons of Life and Love.

c.) The Meditation and Self-Realization.

d.) The Union with Death, "to move-on."

Scene 3. The Funeral and Second Conception.

Scene 4. The French Incarnation: The Incarnation of Isabella.
"Obsession:" The Liberation of Isabella.

Scene 5. Ego's Triangle: (The Male and Female in Ego's play).
(Sabina Von der Decken, Margaret Austin, Ilanga.)

a.) The Misunderstanding of Opposites.

b.) Finding the Balance.

c.) The Union, Harmony, and Fusion of Gender.

d.) Death: Its Joy and Pain.

—Intermission—

Act ll

The Final Scene: The Present Incarnation.

a.) The Human Contract arrives into The Life, today!

b.) The "Street Life"…(Full Cast)

c.) The New Beginning…(Full Cast)

d.) The Greatest Love…(Full Cast)

Finale:

After the celebrated Holidays, the following four weeks were in a complete spin, a whirlwind and a cyclone of conclusive thoughts of the upcoming production and thinking of "how all of this began" from its beginning and the spark of an "Idea" through its interval-times of research, organizing, rehearsals; and above all, its costs! And finally, being here in the final thought and moment of its pending end; which happened in one week, Friday night January 25ᵗʰ! During these intense four weeks of thought and "action" I was "wrapped-up and numb" in the rapture and love of the work I do! No thought of the production was untouched by my congested mind; there was no space left in there for anything else to be thought about!" I was "obsessed" and "trapped" running down the "rabbit hole," a path of "angst," but with an eventual end!

The one night, two-Act performance of *The Human Contract* was a successful event that evening. It was triumphant for the performing artists, the Team, the Hellenic-American Union, and the Athenian theater goers! The performance registered with the audience; They "took something home" with them, besides a paper Program and a burp from a drink at Intermission! The acclaimed "Word" of *The Human Contract* spread throughout the city of its unique performance, style, and of "Afro-Jazz Dance." For weeks after, I suffered from being recognized on the streets of Athens, in tavernas, discotheques, and even the places I would usually frequent, alone or with my crew. It became uncomfortable for me at times being constantly noticed; and if my whining and complaining of this occurred too often, I was told blatantly that "I was famous now"! This new wave of public notoriety and attention was disturbing my personal affairs and resonated within me once again in my life. It was an annoying recall of the deep emotions and struggle that I had with this issue years before, being a successful, famous "G-Clef" doo-wop singer in America! My lessons and study of humility became a priority; and finding a balance with that knowledge in mind ultimately saved me from distorting the "glamorous fame and glory" of my career in "Show Biz." Fame was an honest glorification solely perpetrated by an inflated **EGO** and for me, this was a path to self-destruction. Once again, I had to find the balance between humility and glorification if I were to remain working in the business of entertainment.

I am a loner by nature; where there is silence, I go to it, and where there is unduly and undistinguishable clamor and confusion, I run from it! The dressing rooms of the theaters hosting doo-wop shows were filled with noise and activity; and when emptied of the "noisemakers", as I dressed for the upcoming show, the dressing room became my solitude and chamber of study. My priority to find a balance and a way to handle this dilemma succeeded, because I had learned more of how to be humble and survive all of the glory and fame. I had to assure myself that I could handle this here in Greece as well; because if not, my departure from Athens at the end of the dance season would be certain, and it would once again be time to go "somewhere else" where I would be unknown.

With the *Courage* and thoughtful *Dares* of the **4ᵗʰCycle**, the *Action* and *Determination* that I had acquired and continued to follow through with in the **5ᵗʰ** and **6ᵗʰCycles** provided me with the *Confidence* and *Drive* to "never give up"! These are the elements of personal *Choice* and of a human quality that allowed me to *Produce* abundantly in the **7ᵗʰCycle**. The achievement, the success, and the young intelligent and vibrant team that collectively produced "The Human Contract" laid the solid foundation of my future success, and enabled me to establish myself in Athens Greece as Director, Choreographer, Dancer, Singer, and Actor, for the following four years.

"I see you walking through the park here in Kolonaki Square every Wednesday!" said the stage director "Yannis Diamondopoulos." "I see you always walking fast to somewhere; but if you got a few minutes now, I'd like to speak with you, here at the café!" Every Wednesday afternoon I taught a private dance class at a sports gymnasium there in the square; and after class, I would "supposedly" be dressed in a style where I would be incognito. I would dart out the door and do some fast walking through the park, avoiding the square and the afternoon cocktail sippers, cappuccino drinkers, and the hungry eyes in search of someone or something to chatter about. But Yannis had recognized me! "Sure," I said; "I have a few minutes to chat before meeting with some friends later!" Usually, my reply to an invite like this would be to bypass it by saying "thank you, but maybe another time; right-now, I'm off to an appointment!" But I sensed that this was not the usual "invite." I did not know this man, but he knew a lot about me, and therefore our two-hour conversation was about his work as a director of stage dramas and of his new dream of staging an unusual play about human behavior titled, *Prosopa Physika de Allotoka* (*The Faces of Strange People*). It was difficult for him to explain its complex message.

It was based on a play written by Italian playwright, Giuseppe Patroni Griffi, which had been translated into Greek. Promoted and advertised as an "adult only" theater play grabbed theater goer's attention, (the tag "adult only" was because of verbal dialogue, nothing more). But still it was a bit risqué for Athens at the time. The intense drama, intrigue, and feisty action takes place in one room of a small-town Brothel in Greece on a New Year's Eve! The four Protagonists; the Madam of the brothel, an intelligent, witty and sassy Transvestite, a writer and author of books, and a young naïve male college student, come together in one room to celebrate; "Not New Year's Eve", but "themselves." The night becomes a "Hell" of battling Egos and personalities trying to attain the understanding of one another and the strange life that each one of them had chosen and must live while being identified as "misfits" within a society of norms!

Yannis wanted to fulfill his dream by having me as one of the actors whose role is that of "a black American writer of historical events, a social activist and an ex-revolutionary" who had just arrived to Greece that day, to begin writing his new novel of Epitaphs of the black American soldiers killed in Greece during the second World War. "You will be the first black American actor who plays on the legitimate stage of Greek theater!" Yannis said. "Yes, the first! And you don't have to speak Greek, only English!" he stated with humor, and with a smile on his face that revealed his relief that having to speak Greek could be a possible reason for me to reject his offering. Respectfully, he congratulated me for the success of *The Human Contract*; "a profound piece of work!" he commented; "Your imagination of life is vivid. And I like what you did with Love, and how you expanded it into more than what we know of it!" he said, and adding the "take-away" of what he had seen onstage. "You understand that life must be lived with reason and passion, to know death and its reason. Very interesting!" Our intended brief meeting extended into a couple of hours discussing his new play, the "if, why and how" conditions of my participation in it, and the future meetings needed to further discuss my involvement. At the final meeting we sealed an agreement for a twelve-week show run in Athens, and its labor would begin immediately for the theater season's opening in April. Therefore, the Spring and Summer of 1981 was a busy time of rehearsals. Studying the Greek language within the context of the script with Yannis and with the three brilliant actors allowed me to increase my comprehension of the concept and the roles that each of us were to be playing. Simultaneously; the dance classes mushroomed to twelve a week at the Athens Center, and a few private performances that had already been scheduled for me to perform accompanied by two or three dancers, also had to be worked on and rehearsed! I was spending sixteen to eighteen hours a day away from my apartment, running across the city or jumping in Taxis to get from one rehearsal to another; traveling the streets, getting a quick bite to eat and being a part of the Athens chaos! This challenged me daily to find a "silence" to run to, somewhere, anywhere! I could not even go within myself to find it and silence came to me only in my depths of sleep.

Yannis' dream became fully realized in the Fall theater-season of 1981 at the *Athina Theater* on Patission Street, in the theater district. The show became the most successful of the season, the four Protagonists became "Stars" and I became famous again and learned to "handle it" with the balance that I was aiming for. I had figured out finally that, "this is part of the job"! No longer was "fame" an issue; "I handled it!" With Yannis' dream realized, he was happy man; another grateful "Dreamer" who had gratitude for his production team and the four protagonists and he let that be known to us throughout the season. Meanwhile; the dance classes at the Athens Center were ongoing and becoming more interesting with the amount of diversity and talent. I discussed with Rosemary and John, that the talent and abilities that existed in these classes needed to be seen by the public, and that what I was seeing was inspiring me to do something about it! "Well, let's do something about it!"

John said; He was always eager for new exciting projects that would boost the Center's notoriety. Rosemary was efficient and ready to administrate and said agreeably, "Yes, let's do something!" She asked; "What do you think that is, Ilanga?" Her question sparked another "new" idea that became realized and was shown to the public later that year: *Ilanga's Jazz Dance Theater.*

This company of performing artists were the professionals who I extracted both from the production of The Human Contract and the dance classes specifically to organize a nucleus of members and prepare them with set choreographies and themes of the four cultures; Greek, American, Latin, and Love. And adding to this nucleus - depending on the performance venues of clubs, discotheques, art galleries, and private affairs - I would feature as guests, "other notable artists" who also were in their prime, and famous in Greece.

During this period, the political climate in Greece was in upheaval. The ruling Democrat Party was being out witted by "Pasok" the Socialist Party, and became the rule of the country. The people's everyday life of routine habits and thinking had to change, adjust, and chaotically try to find a new plateau of levelness going forward; and to prepare itself for the coming force of the new European Common Market, the currency changes, and the adaptation to social change. And Greece; about to be stripped of its desired "national pride" was becoming a threat to its own people and foreign residents who had been living there for years and finding it to be Home. Should this happen, how would Pasok heal the lasting wound of a country who had lost its national pride? Could it find a way to move forward? As a foreign resident, I watched violent demonstrations being vocalized and carried out in the streets of Athens almost on a daily basis; along with the banks and post offices sporadically opening and closing their doors at the whim of the global market rates being announced that day! The extreme "bittersweet" changes that were happening in the country had a devastating effecting on its people and the foreign residents who called Greece home.

And, Austin, who had nomadic inclines like myself, also had the awareness that there is always "something else" and "something more." She was a poet who had decided to become a poet at the Workshop in Kiaffa. "To become a poet and a writer of books" was her passion and personal project. To "dance" was her love and inspiration "to become"! Her stance on residency came into question, and she made an announcement one day to Yiorgos, Sabina and I, saying with an eloquent delivery; "Austin is just absolutely fed up with this Greek nonsense! I don't know, and nobody knows what's going on here, but, "something else" needs to be done!" she said with an attitude of certainty, dismissiveness and *Dare*. She soon decided to leave Greece for Paris and became a "Star" in the infamous *Follies Bergere* stage extravaganzas, dancing nightly with fishnet stockings and glamorous costumes adorning her sleek body and her head crowned with feathers and plumes! She was "unrecognizable" under thick make-up, big false-eyelashes and her eyes rimmed with sparkling rhinestones! Along with the required procedures of the *Follies* auditions; her audition included two assets that she possessed that enabled her to become a "Star." And those two assets being: her execution and delivery of a dance choreography that I had done for her, inspired by the masterful Charlie Chaplin, and the second asset being her beautiful, eye-catching legs! Within the onstage line-up of thirty (or more) gorgeous females costumed in colorful feathers and plumes, all looking identical, the eye of the audience was sure to go to Austin's legs! It was as if they had a spotlight of their own! In Paris, she became a "Star" and authored her first book *Footsteps in Stardust*. Thereafter and through the years, she wrote two other books with tales of her passions, adventurous *Dares* and experiences, entitled, *An Amsterdam Affair* and *Dancing Naked*. But it must be remembered that Austin's innate "poet spirit" remained the "vehicle" of her "purpose." This is the apex of "high-achievement" my dear reader. One can only say, "Bravo!"

With the Baltic countries in a wave of social change and calamity, and the political chaos and eruption happening in Western Europe's confusing dialogue of the new Common Market, Mano the photographer, sensed the changes about to come to the environment, to his career, and to his recent "new" family. Mano decided to leave Amsterdam, join the Crew in Athens, and within a short period of time became an International Photo Journalist documenting the major changes sweeping throughout Europe and the Middle East. Shortly after arriving in Athens, he became the city's most sought after camera man! I'm not too sure if he knew as I did, that the *Afro Jazz Dance Workshop* in Kiaffa is where his "purpose" was found! Maybe unknown to him at that time, was that his personal project, the art of "Documentation" was to be the lesson learned. I don't know if he knew that actually, because I never asked him; but nevertheless, he too reached the apex of "high-achievement." Another "happy man"!

As archaic Greece was going through the turmoil of changes to become a "new" Greece; *Ilanga's Jazz Dance Theater* was being organized and preparing for its upcoming debut. Within the dance class, there was one exceptional student who in time became my Greek "Sister"! She, along with my Greek "Brother" Yiorgos, and

John and Rosemary; were the dynamic energy-fueled group of energy that launched the new and lucrative "Jazz Dance Theater" project. Anne's interest in the project and its "purpose" was evident in her desire to support the project in any way that she was able to. Her observance of the work that was also going on "behind the scenes" attracted her, aside from her interest in the dance. And with the "Spirit of Dance" within her, she very soon joined the project's dynamic production Team. She, a young **4ᵗʰCycle** beginning dance student; had been inspired to take classes at the *Athens Center* since they began three years prior, and therefore, her indoctrination to this Afro-Jazz technique was well-internalized and understood. Anne's preference in music to dance to was American heavy metal rock and London's raging "Punk" music that she was introduced to on her frequent trips there. This music of explosive energy, sound, and its dynamics was the only music that inspired Anne to dance! That is, until she heard the music of Afro-Jazz and discovered that it made her body move "differently." She did not care to hear or like the idea that she had to adhere to conventional dance class structure and technique, and her body resented and rigidly resisted such rules; it had its own knowledge of how to absorb rhythms, react with expression and pointed delivery. But Anne's "new passion" to dance Afro-Jazz came to her when the doctrine that she had learned, understood and was exercising "connected" with her Spirit of the Dance! "Because, I *feel* it!" she said while thumping on her heart with her fist, during our intense conversations; "It's inside here, I want it to be free, Ilanga, but it can't come out," she said that day. I listened and felt her anguish. Her frustration prompted me to remind her of the class meditations, once again relaying the message within the Yoga aspect of the teaching. Her challenge frustration and struggle was her "blockage" to receive the message, and I suggested that she succumb to the Afro-Jazz technique of rhythm and body control and relax and absorb its nature; and that she had to adhere to the American Jazz-technique as well"! "Maybe you should think about this from now on; from the beginning of the class to the end, and see where that focus takes you," I said to her on that day of our conversation. Anne excelled! She eventually heard the message and in due time, the harbored dance that she felt within finally "came out" and danced with her! She discovered that there was a satisfying harmony being experienced between her *Body*, what she knew in her *Mind* of the dance, her *Spirit*, its *Essence* and its *Purpose*; and now, her dance was "free" to be seen and appreciated. The mental blockage that had prevented her from succumbing to the afro-technique was removed by focused meditation; and her confidence and ability to do "more" was proved to me in every class thereafter.

Anne, became my Greek sister, as Yiorgos, is my Greek brother. They were my other dear friends along with my family and relatives.

Ilanga's Jazz Dance Theater made its debut at the Athens Hilton Hotel, May 11, 1982. The collaboration of Hilton Hotels, the Athens and New York Chambers of Commerce and TWA Airlines, were doing a global promotion to launch "The Big Apple's" new advertising slogan, "I Love NY." The Athens Hilton contacted me, saying, "The black American Jazz dancer from Boston is who we need to initiate the campaign; for its "Authenticity" is what I was told. They were quite explicit in wanting the show to be so "Apple Pie," tasty with "P-Zazz", and delicious enough to satisfy the eager audience of Athens who had an appetite for New York! The debut "sparkled" brilliantly! The spotlights that swept across the stage captured the vibrance and the smiles and flashing eyes of every dancer! It was exciting and unusual being there, "seeing and feeling" the Athens Hilton Hotel vibrating with American Jazz Dance, music, style, energy, rhythm and "love for Manhattan"! The phenomenal success of this presentation introduced me to the emerging new channels of the promotional advertising that was now happening in the "new Greece". Choreographies were being worked-on for television commercials, and photo-shoots took place to showcase private dancers and singers who were desperate for a polished presentation of their show! Meetings with Modeling agencies who represented specific designers would call me for a chat and cocktails; and suddenly I found myself choreographing high-end Fashion Shows for Greek and French designers who asked for "theater" on their Runways to express "more" of their creation and design! There were times during this hustle and bustle when I myself felt like a "commercial" that was selling "Me and my talents" for a Drachmae, a Franc or a Dollar!

The next overwhelming success for the Jazz-Dance Company was the *Hawaiian Tropic Global Tour* sponsored by the international suntan oil company launched in 1983. This was a two-month promotional tour of clubs, discotheques, and island hopping to luxurious hotels for on-the-beach performances. I had organized a ten-member Dance Company of all black dancers: three males, six females and one gorgeous white female dancer; Sabina. Almasi, who had no Summer classes to teach at *Benjamin's Jazz Dance Center*, flew into Athens from Amsterdam to join the Company. His strong muscular body and beauty was that of a "black diamond" and powerful enough in brilliance to match that of Sabina's "white diamond" beauty. Within the concept and narrative of the tropical show, she was the target of attraction and he was the island's handsome Prince." The scenario was about island natives who were "terrified and surprised" at the sight of a tourist with such white beauty, doing "something" they had never seen before! A "Goddess" had arrived at their beach, and their eyes watched carefully as she narcissistically applied "Hawaiian Tropic Tanning Oil" gracefully and with self-love beneath the hot sun to become "even more beautiful for the handsome Prince! Thereafter; her days of a sunny vacation became joyful, jubilant and "well-tanned" in tropical song and dance! Sabina's pale white German skin could never really tan, which was my salvation, because the beauty and "the target" was always there for the show to go on! She simply showered-it off after each performance; and her skin, never showed a hint of brown!"

Hot September came after the Summer months of *Hawaiian Tropic* fun and hard work, not only in performance, but the management of the dancers and their conflicting Egos was a job in itself! Monitoring and supervising, guiding and being "Inspector Clouseau" watching and following their wandering "social moves" after the show, daily! Once the full stage "on the beach" performances concluded at sunset; the dancer's "freedom" was theirs to roam the island or cities of the scheduled mainland performances. Often, my mind would flash to my "back-in the-day" Cycles of doo-wop singing with "The G-Clefs," and spying on their after- the-show social moves. Managing the work, monitoring, supervising and guiding, was a similar task with the dancers during the Hawaiian Tropic tour. On most mornings there would be early rehearsals or a departure to somewhere else for the next day's performance. I always had to be sure of a nightly head count in both these cases! A mandatory 1:00 a.m. curfew was set with financial penalties because this group of "dazzling performing artists" who all needed supervision and a good night's sleep, were the targets of every male on the island! A tempting cluster of seven beautiful young ladies and two gay males satisfying the fantasies of every island man, and being offered "yachts, villas, and olive groves" in a heart beat! Anything was offered, "for one night only"!

Also, that September; I reduced the number of classes I was teaching at the *Athens Center* and chartered a new direction for myself and the selective dance works that I had chosen to accomplish in the coming new year. Almasi, who was now approaching his 7ᵗʰ**Cycle**, decided not to return to the gray, cold city of Amsterdam. He said he felt the "turning point" in his life; a "new Cycle" and a "new something!" He remained in Athens to explore and discover what that "something" was. With his learned knowledge of *Dare, Challenge, Action and Determination* - accrued from his previous three Cycles - he found that new something. He was now at his plateau of "productivity," the 7ᵗʰ**Cycle**! This realization was discussed thoroughly. He evaluated himself, he understood; and he felt his new *Power and Inspiration*. And with his newfound "comprehension" of the Cycle he was now into, Almasi found what that "something" was and that he was now able and ready to "Produce"! He had found his "purpose" through his exotic dance and paintings! He also joined the Team of *Ilanga's Jazz Dance Theater* along with Anne, John, Yiorgos, Sabina, and Mano whenever we needed his camera-eye.

Also, that busy hot September; my Greek sister Anne and I partnered to open a private dance studio on Imitou Street, in the area of Pangrati. She had already smartly operated a *Massage Therapy Salon for Healing*, in the city's suburb area of "Aghia Paraskevis." Her dynamic energy to take "action" on the "spark" of an idea was always quick and as fast as her spontaneous dance movements! The only thing that I had to do was "strike the match"! Anne was a phenomenal woman of many talents, who also became a "forever" friend through our "five decades" and many **Cycles** together. She felt that it was part of her purpose to help design my Dream.

I will always believe Anne and Yiorgis to be a significant "Gift from the Gods" to Ilanga, and my return to Greece to be one of "purpose," not of "fantasy"! The truth and fact is; there would have been no production of *The Human Contract* nor the absolute realization of *Ilangas's Jazz Dance Theater* without these two "soulmates" of mine. They made possible the dream we three are living today. They were, and still are, the "instruments of my music" and "the steps of my dance" in Greece! How fortunate I am to have known or have had the "intuition" to follow their young **4ᵗʰCycle** wisdom of *Challenge and Action*! And I did so with faith and learned humility, with my "fantasized" realities and my "unusual" understanding of Greece, its culture, language and people! And also, with my sincere appreciation and my honest love! Seduced by honest love.

My last theater performance in Athens Greece, in 1999-2000, occurred during my **9ᵗʰCycle** (57-63), at the "XYTHPIO" Theater located on Ireados Street, in the newly designed theater district of Gazi. The title of the play was advertised in three languages for the international theater audience to recognize. It was called *THE TIGHTROPE WALKER, O ΣΚΟΙΝΟΒΑΤΗΣ and LE FUNAMBULE;* Written by French author, playwright and essayist "Jean Genet" and directed by "Sotiris Hadzakis". It featured two Protagonists: Greek actress "Roubini Vasilakopoulou" and myself, "Ilanga" and also Sudan percussionist/singer, "Amin Allagaba". I portray a dedicated artist/dancer and circus performing acrobat on the high-wire, who manages to sacrifice his life and his purpose to make his statement of "gratitude." The extreme passion for his art had overtaken him, so he decides to plunge to his death. His voice is never heard until the end of the final Act, and it is his articulate "body language" that speaks of his *Soul*; He is "The Tightrope Walker" and "She" portrays his alter-ego who speaks his mind and his words through the rhythms of the intrinsic percussions of Amin, that sound out the heartbeats, the strengths, the weaknesses and the power of the acrobat. And "She" - also being the Master of Ceremonies of the Circus - forcefully delivers the poignant message. At one point during her monologue, she tells the audience to "Listen carefully; the death I am talking about doesn't follow the fall but happens before you reach the wire!" During one of our final rehearsals, "Sotiris", the director said to me, "God! I see you so "dead" up there Ilanga, but, your body is speaking almost every word that Roubini is speaking! It is beautiful to hear and see them working together and making it so "real"! You are "dead" up there, and yet so "alive"! "Threla Ine, Toxero!" ("Sounds crazy, I know!") he said with a lingering thought. "But, it's strange," he continued saying; "Now, I am thinking that the audience "needs" to hear your physical voice, for the human value!" He said this calmly, rolling his cupped hands into one another and lowering his head for a brief thought. For those of us who worked with him, we knew of his soft and gentle character and Sotiris was a wise and an intelligent, humble man of silence.

Whenever the "noise" of life blared too loudly in my Mind and filled my ears with its clatter, he is the one that I would run to when I was in need of the silence and inner peace that he would so generously share with me; or with anyone in need of that quality he quietly possessed. And with his artistic skill, insight and approach to me, his next thought followèd with his words; "I don't want the audience to hear your voice speak words, but I want them to hear your "sound or song" of the life You have lived! I have heard your singing voice here at Café-Bar, and that is also your sound! Maybe you know of an old negro spiritual song that you can sing after your fall off the wire? he asked. My thoughtful pause lasted long enough for me think of myself "back in the day" when I was a Civil Rights social-activist and public demonstrator, singing the songs of freedom. And also I had a quick thought of my friends in Boston, the *Band of Angels* group of special lifelong friends who as teenagers in the 1950's organized ourselves as a youth social club (which we were referred to as a "gang" in those old days! The club was one of friendship and benevolence, and we had given ourselves that moniker from one line of a song sung by the dying slaves of early 20th century America. It was an old song sung by the dying slaves during the slavery times in America. "Swing Low Sweet Chariot" is the only song that comes to my mind, Sotiris," I said after my thoughtful pause; "And maybe from its verses I can sing only the last!" I began to sing the last two lines of the verse's end, with the baritone voice of a dying old negro slave:

"Swing low, sweet chariot, comin' fo to carry me home, A band of Angels comin' afta me, comin' fo to carry me home!"

"Bravo!" Sotiris said; "That's it!" "Orea, Afta!" ("Beautiful; That's it!"). The lighting faded to black as I lie on the stage floor, gratefully humming to my death.

The play was a typical Jean Genet mind-bending masterpiece, and "back by popular demand," the show did a six-month run of success, six nights a week, until the nightly Circus finally came to an end. And upon its triumphant conclusion, the celebrations were high with drinks song, live music, dance, and crowds every night in the theater's attached Café-Bar. The "highest Peak" of celebration for me was being totally surprised one night by two of my lifelong friends from Boston who flew into Athens just to see "The Tightrope Walker" in live performance. It was not until after the show that their two faces appeared to me at my dressing room door! Still costumed, my body dripping in sweat and "spattered" with sparkling glitter, I opened the door from a hard knock, and experienced a moment of shock, surprise and joy all lumped-together in one long tearful embrace! I had not a clue that "Marla and Carolyn" were in Athens that evening; and during the following week we never stopped celebrating our fabulous lives of sparkle, our "forever" friendship and their introduction to Yiorgos and Anne! What a precious moment this was, being in Athens Greece, together! Fate, or Coincidence? The final curtain of *The Tightrope Walker* dropped for its last time on the actors, the dancers, Roubini, Amin, our genius director Sotiris and the fantastic tech-crew that always kept me sailing smooth and safely on the high-flying trapeze.

At that time, my **10thCycle** (64 to 70) was fast approaching. The new "what to do now Senior Cycle" of assessed achievements, introspective thoughts, and leisure was upon me. For some of the active and outgoing, happy, coupled seniors, Grandchildren had now come into their lives and had become the new "bundles of joy" to make and realize a dream for their new future! And to be sure, happy coupled "Granny and Gramps" will be cautious in settling "limited" baby-sitting arrangements with Mom and Dad! They are too busy catching up with lost togetherness; and would say "We'll see," when faced with the prospect of the weekend baby-sit proposed by Mom and Dad. And for some other seniors who are widowed, single, happy and childless such as I, we have our cherished Nieces and Nephews and other people's children in our lives to help make and realize dreams. This is our newfound desire to share, teach, guide and become the model Aunt, Uncle or Foster Parent to a child in need of someone else to help them *Become* and aspire to their greatest potential. And the plan that we "young" seniors of the **10ᵗʰCycle** have already charted years before for our long-anticipated retirement, unfolds in this Cycle and becomes a "crossroads" of the two paths that one has already traveled of "direction and purpose." During the passage of time, these two paths have crossed and eventually combined, and now it has become one path. However, this path of travel has an unknown destination: To Where, for What, and for "Whom?" The *ability, energy, and discrimination* of the active Senior, Single or loving Grandparent, is the "sustenance" and is the source "responsible" for the senior who has chosen wisely the path they've been traveling on! And it is their well-deserved right to continue to exercise and share their practical skills and insightful wisdom to whoever they meet on their way to this formidable intersection. For a quick moment I stopped and I glanced left and right at the deterrent paths of "retirement and leisure" and their already known "destination to nowhere." Without a doubt and quietly, I kept stepping forward, in the direction of my continued dream of just being "Me" and with my "purpose" to "educate" staying very close to me. "Retire!" "To Do What?" and for "Whom?" just seemed to be a "no brainer" for me! "There was still work to be done! There was still an abundance of energy in reserve, within my body and mind to expel and to do whatever it is next, that I am destined to be doing!

The *Challenge, Dare, Determination, Disciplines,* and *the Purpose to Educate*, have all been in *Action* and have been well-established and in "balance" since the onset of my **6ᵗʰCycle**, at the age of thirty-six young years! My very brief thoughts of retirement ended quickly, knowing that this collective energy of dynamic and diverse elements and their combined force, would one day instantly "explode" within me, and leave me lifeless if I "capped" tightly my remaining days with a leisured life of retirement! My mind, cycling through the many **Cycles** and achievements past and present was quite refreshed, and I welcomed these thoughts. They just spun and swirled in the "wonder" of what was to come! And the already planned thoughts of; "What is it I am to Produce?" in this upcoming Cycle; and also; "What new seeds are to be planted and sowed with love and deep affection?" were profoundly considered and were just circling around in my mind soothingly, and in a steady, calm pace. I was settled with my honest acceptance of leaving Greece.

My return to Boston to work, make residence once more, and to be with my family and friends in The United States of America came shortly after my performance of *The Tightrope Walker*. And being here since, in this "new" old Boston, and living through my **11ᵗʰCycle** (71 to 77) I have found that it is the Cycle to not forget that getting older can be just as much "fun" as it has been in the past years of cycling. I pray, that I can just continue to always "remember" that! It is *the Imagination, the Will, the Attitude, and the Purpose*, that open the many portals to "Fun"; but to get "old", is not fun! To be thinking that "I am old now" can become a daily negative habit. "This is a mental exercise to avoid!" I am older now; wiser, and almost "complete" with *The Life* as we know it to be!" These are the thoughts that should be exercised today, and discrimination is essential. "I am not too old to do that; it is because I am 'wise' that I choose not to do that."

Many seniors who arrive at this **Cycle** "forget" that there is still fun left in the game of life, and some get lost in their "should be forgotten past" of displeasures and unattained goals and wishes! They soon become overwhelmed and tainted with attitudes of bitterness, disappointment and disgruntled thoughts of non-achievement in specific goals, desires, and/or personal expectations! And also, the tormenting obsession of not letting go of someone or something that just "didn't happen!"

And apparently, it didn't happen because it wasn't destined to happen! This very important fact is what they didn't get in any lesson of "detachment" that they might have had; and then "letting go" becomes a burden. Some of these now aging "young" people who during an earlier period in their lives have experienced the **2nd Cycle** (8 to 14); the Cycle of *Exploration, Fun, Wonder, Challenge and Dare*, are now "Seniors" who must be careful to avoid the trap of leisure and retirement that beckons in this Cycle if they want to continue being active, having fun, having a "purpose" and continuing to move forward! And should there be a "blockage" for this awareness or realization, they need now to recall that important **2nd Cycle** and to "eliminate" the *Challenge and Dare* aspect. Their only "take-away" from that Cycle should be *"Exploration, Wonder and Fun,"* as it was with all the previous Cycles to this one. Extracting only the "take-aways" and realizing the fact that, "I've been-there-and-done-that-now for over a half a century," is a wise thought! "Wisdom" is the only gold to look forward to in these golden years of aches, pains, doctors, more love, more time to play, grandchildren, great and grand nieces and nephews, hearing the sad news of the peers that have passed on, time to go fishing, time for gardening and more time for very close friends. It is the time to evaluate everything that happened over a lifetime of living.

It is such a pity that those seniors who have had this life experience as we all do, now deny themselves, in this **10thCycle,** the remembrance of those past years of everyday wonder! They have "forgotten" and are content to now live life in another "dimension" of their long existence here. This has become their comfort-zone and safety-net of self-confrontation, and now they refuse to recognize the moment or are maybe not able to. It is sad that they are not tapping into the remembrance of that fresh energy of surprise and excitement that accompanies the "wonder" within the **2ndCycle**! They have become numb to making a move forward and are aimlessly "stuck" living in the **10th** and **11thCycles;** and whatever *fun, love, joy and excitement* that was had in any of the past Cycles has become forgotten; or maybe because of a significant disappointment, has caused them to become bitter! No longer do they care to taste the sweetness of life; and sadly, this stagnant moment of time very soon yields to becoming the "cranky, bitchy, old lady or man" who believes and says that "nothing is funny or interesting" and prefers isolation and solitude to live-out their remaining days, mentally depressed and refusing to cry out for help. This is what constitutes "living", for a tired "old" senior who thinks and believes that "I have seen it all!" The new surprises are many within the **10th** and **11thCycles.** The encroachment of new aches and pain "piggy-back" the early morning rise from bedtime. Mumbles of, "Oh! I must change my mattress!" are heard daily across the land, and the usual "first run" to the bathroom has now become a "step by step stagger" at the start of a new day. Vanity is no longer an objective when facing the bathroom mirror.

The objective has now become the discovery of new blemishes and wrinkles that first appeared in the **10th Cycle** and have bored deeper into the skin; and worst of all appear to be permanent! There comes another day or night when suddenly it is noticed that your skin appears to be dead, dry, bumpy and flakey, and now demands a lot of moisturizer just to look like it is still "alive"! And as a daily routine, that too becomes permanent! The fixation with the mirror increases and the daily intrigue becomes almost habitual. There will come the unpleasant day or evening, when flashing a pasted-on smile at the mirror, one will see that the lips now have slight creases imbedded, but that is acceptable because the authentic smile is still there. And what is left of any original teeth from birth, have either tarnished or look worn-down and no longer compare to the custom fit, polished, partial dentures or implants that were perfectly placed there in earlier years. Then there is the once taut chin line that has drooped into sagging jowls. The twenty minutes of time that was once spent in the bathroom is being extended to forty-five minutes of trying to "arrange" whatever beauty there is left to the eyes of the beholder! The woman's primping and touches of makeup are applied with the skill of a surgeon, and the man's shave or grooming of a moustache and beard are handled with more caution and slower strokes, due to elbow, wrist or shoulder joint pain. Nevertheless; he manages his razor to twist and turn for an outcome of absolute satisfaction for a close shave. All are arranging their beauty as they see fit; "vanity for Me only!" becomes the objective as they realize no one else will care.

With nothing much left to "figure out" about life, the aches, pains and mirror discoveries remain in play. Still, the pending fears of "ill health" mount in the **11th Cycle** more so than they did in the **10th**! The medical appointments seem to be more frequent, and seeing peers and friends who still exist "here" are now living their lives "differently"! Some are patiently sitting in wheelchairs waiting to be fed breakfast, lunch and dinner; others walking with a cane, a walker, or toting an air-tank with thin, transparent cables clipped to their nostrils, so they can breathe more comfortably. "Good feet, good teeth, and following your heart beat" become our major concern in this "different" Cycle of awareness and self-evaluation! Our health, our environment, family, and the smaller circle of intimate friends, are now the focus of our thoughts. These four essential values consume our days and our nights now. And any received invitations of social events being held, soon become an effort to attend; and therefore, discrimination comes into play. And should you decide to attend, selection is influenced by your "required" presence only! To go anywhere, has to have a "purpose" otherwise, "Don't ask!" And any "social events, stadium concerts, etc; I just think: "Been-there and done-that and no, thank you!"

I find that the **11ᵗʰCycle** provides a living soul a "long story" to tell, if one cares or dares to tell it! And within that, there are many smaller stories to tell "how" that long story came to be. A trail of significant incidents that may have occurred, places been, and people met, could very well lead directly to the *Purpose* of why the story is even being told! Its content could be advisable and of value to anyone younger in age who is living *The Life* and "trying to figure it all out"!

Left behind in this long trail of small stories of your *challenges, dares,* friends, loves, fun and laughter, is the way they are now all looked at from the perspective of a vague understanding and acceptance of the Spanish cliché, "Que Sera Sera!"

("What will be, will be!"), and the significant small stories of *Your Dream* and its *Purpose* including all the big actions taken - achieved and also unachieved. These stories must be relayed with disciplined determination and love, to one who cares to listen! I say this simply because a "word from you, can change a life" my dear reader! Who knows how infectious and effective the words are that I am writing here could be for one who is an "alternative thinker, doer, and believer"? One word or many, could be of help to a *Soul* trying to "figure it all out"! The Cycles that have been lived, and the accumulated knowledge of "how they have been lived" is to be applied and shared with those in need who have yet to figure it out. This **Cycle** is the "11th Hour" of your life being lived; the remaining three or four **Cycles** thereafter, "may or may not occur" here on this planet, but may occur "elsewhere." Therefore, when the "midnight hour" strikes for you; it could be comforting to make closure with your final thoughts, knowing that your work, your words and your big *Dream* has come to an end, by simply considering the long trail of energy and force of its *Purpose* generously being left behind to be traveled or evaluated by those in need of your valuable knowledge of *The Life*.

This **11thCycle** of my life today and the cumulative Cycles of the past with their experiences therein, have me believing and living alternative realities, scrutinizing the various paths all of which may take me to "somewhere," every day, all day, and into my 11th hour! And also, "intuitively" charting and analyzing the movements of my professional career; *where, what, and when*, were questions and thoughts that did not hamper my moves. I allowed and trusted that my intuition would guide me! This is not the route a professional would usually take; "Why would he or she take such a risk in their career development and expect achievements to be made?" I was able to challenge that risk because of my professional confidence, and an intuitive "trust" that always seemed to be the "light" that guided me to become an "alternative thinker, doer and believer!" During my 4ᵗʰCycle (22 to 28), it was my innate intuition that inspired my thoughts to analyze "time" as we understand it to be, or as it could be. I chronically charted my experiences whether they had been "fantasy, coincidence or destiny," and deliberately framed both of these factual realities of *Time and Experiences* within a period of every seven years, and began to "evaluate." Why I had chosen every seven years to evaluate is because, "Why not?" I was born in the month of July, my parents bore seven remarkable children, and during my earlier years of metaphysical, philosophical and spiritual studies I had read in reliable Scriptures and essays that the number "7" has a lot to do with a lot of things and was known to be a sacred or magic number in many cultures. Its significance to me mattered greatly! Intuitively, I knew that to begin serious *Self-Evaluation* with a process and a measure was the right thing to do! Within a brief period of time, I had discovered and come to believe that "all of what was happening" in my life -personally and professionally - during this Cycle had occurred "by coincidence" and that "destiny" was unreachable, untouchable and too far away. My conclusive decision to live my life shadowed by coincidence was vague; but living with a destiny guided by the *Trust of Intuition*, was of certainty and without doubt! It was at about this time that I began the process of evaluating the past experiences that I had thought to be "strange or coincidental" that had occurred throughout my past Cycles; "The recall of birth (or a vision during a few days of infancy), a childhood adventure that instilled the first desire to unwisely *Dare*, and thereafter, learning to *Dare* wisely. And becoming an eleven-year-old Godfather to baby Pamela, who today is as bonded with me as *Forever* could ever be. The exciting bicycle trips to Walden Pond during my **2ⁿᵈCycle** of exploration (8 to 14 years of age); and the "coincidental?" meeting of Mary Sherwood, a fellow Walden Pond lover during my **6ᵗʰCycle** (36 to 42). I can recall the experiences of being a member of the infamous doo-wop singers the *G-Clefs* and evaluating the "Eight Cycles" of being together in professional harmony and a fortunate spotlight of fame and entertainment that has dimmed in time; but still has not "blacked-out!" The G-Clefs are now legendary; seen and heard on "YouTube" and are mentioned often in the articles written about music's historical culture and are also included in the design of the American Music scene today. Was it a "coincidence" or not? Recalling how the "Dance" caught up to me on that day in 1971 at the age of thirty-one while walking on the campus of Harvard University in Cambridge, Massachusetts, and the portal of Dance was opened up to me by Halifu Osumare, the great dance teacher, and how it remained open wide to me for the following seven Cycles thereafter, including today! I cannot deny, doubt or ignore the fact that the G-Clef's trail of events and the meeting of Halifu, was one of "destiny!" And when I abruptly departed from Cancun Mexico, simply because of a "whimsical premonition" that came to me two days before "Hurricane Gilbert" arrived and destroyed the Yucatan Peninsula; I left behind dear friends that were sadly, never to be seen again; yet I believe that it was my *Destiny* to leave. And in 1977 at the onset of my **6ᵗʰCycle**; The fortunate meeting of Karel, the Amsterdam business man and friend, suddenly happened! And today "five-Cycles" later, we are bonded still. Then there was the "inexplicable" meeting of "Glenito Hahn" via drum rhythms being heard in my sleep on a bumpy bus ride into Amsterdam in search of a jazz club called the *Bim Huis*.

Glenito was a novice percussionist who quickly became a Master of the drum, making it speak volumes of rhythmic messages and beats for one to hear if one is also listening to his *Soul*. "High achievement" was his aim and he attained this by also becoming the prime "source, staple and foundation" of the Afro-Jazz Dance technique that we successfully achieved together. That inexplicable meeting was not arranged by me or Glenito, nor by "coincidence"! Our friendship flourished for well over two decades of working together with honesty, love and brotherly companionship, until he became ill in 2004, passed on, and left this earth for "someplace else" to do "something else"! I am so grateful for him, his loving *Spirit* and his time with me; his powerful energy still within me; another "forever" bond.

The recollection of these incidents, past experiences and the evaluation of each one had me also thinking of the one that I believe to be the most significant stepping stone on my path to "someplace else," "something else" and "whatever else", occurred in April of 1968. Most of the American populace were grief stricken, outraged and in anger when the assassination of Dr. Martin Luther King Jr. shocked the nation! Fortunately, not "coincidently" the G-Clefs were doing an extensive tour of performances throughout the United Kingdom. This is when the "destined" meeting with "Thassos" occurred; the Taverna owner in London who I danced with, and who insisted that "I must go home to Greece" to understand his stories! It was "intuition" that forced me to "listen" with "trust" and to continue to hear thereafter his prophetic words. And also the prophecy of Jack Miller, the Spiritual Reader from my old neighborhood of Roxbury, who along with Thassos hinted to me with words of wisdom that "Greece beckons!"

It was eight years later in 1976 that I finally made my first entrance into Greece. I honestly introduced myself and willingly became seduced by this mysterious and mystical land, its people, and its classic antiquity; but it was not until years later that I found it to be "Home". And at that time in 1976, the first meeting with "Yiorgos" that had happened "coincidently?" at a Taverna in its mysterious way; and his sending me off to the island of Crete and down into the Samaria Gorge, neither he nor I "knowing" that it would bring me closer to home, to him, and to a *Self-Realization* that "Reincarnation" does possibly exist! This was an intense Cycle of production, progress, and success, aided by the talents of Yiorgos, Anne, John and Rosemary of The Athens Centre, and the company members of "Kreos Dance Theater" and *Ilanga's Jazz Dance Theater*. There were also many more colleagues and friends who understood, enjoyed, and supported the work we were doing collectively. Consequently, a new "extended" Greek family was born in Athens then which remains for all of us to be a part of now, today. And we are still bathing in our loving friendship that also will be "forever," as forever can be.

Sometimes, as strange as it sounds, when I am home alone here in my Roxbury apartment near Boston, writing dancing or being "with and in the moment," I still hear whispers of *Wisdom* from the quiet voice of "Agnostine" echoing from the earth's deep gorge of Samaria Crete, saying his final words to me; "Be sure to understand, that the "information" I have given you is not knowledge; this information is simply a way to 'acquire knowledge' for your happiness, here!" And for that I am eternally grateful.

Ilanga, Spring 2021

Printed in the United States
by Baker & Taylor Publisher Services